VARIETIES OF WORK EXPERIENCE

VARIETIES OF WORK EXPERIENCE

The Social Control of
Occupational Groups and Roles

A Text with Adapted Original Studies

by PHYLLIS L. STEWART
and MURIEL G. CANTOR

A HALSTED PRESS BOOK

Schenkman Publishing Company, Inc.

JOHN WILEY AND SONS

New York : London : Sydney : Toronto

Copyright © 1974

Schenkman Publishing Company, Inc., Cambridge, Mass. 02138

Distributed Solely by Halsted Press, a Division of John Wiley and Sons, Inc.

Library of Congress Cataloguing in Publication Data

Stewart, Phyllis L., comp.
    Varieties of work experience.

    "A Halsted Press book."

    Bibliography: p.

    1. Occupations — Addresses, essays, lectures.

    2. Social control — Addresses, essays, lectures.
I. Cantor, Muriel G., joint comp. II. Title.
HF5382.S74   301.15   74-6158

ISBN 0-470-82477-8
ISBN 0-470-82478-6 (pbk.)

To Melville Dalton
in gratitude for his encouragement

CONTENTS

CHAPTER FOUR: THE CLIENT

Preface

Two themes are developed in this book. First, occupational autonomy is examined by distinguishing between occupational group and role levels. Second, sources of control that regulate group and role autonomy are: society and culture, organization, degree of organization in an occupation and client control. These two themes are explored in many diverse occupations in the form of original empirical and theoretical papers. Our chief debt is to these contributing authors.

Many others helped in different ways. The following professors in the department of sociology at the University of California at Los Angeles provided the seminar environment for the genesis of these ideas: Richard Morris, Raymond Murphy and Charles Wright. Drs. John Brewer, Melville Dalton and George A. Miller gave generously of their time critically reading several drafts of the manuscript.

Finally, to those who helped with typing, editing, indexing and general support we express our thanks.

P.L.S.

M.G.C.

Introduction

This collection of original empirical studies and theoretical essays on work and occupations is unique in several ways. Each author has centered his attention on the basic idea of the impact of the social structure on the development of occupational norms and relationships. This book derived from an awareness of the paucity of systematic comparative studies of craftsmen, artists, professionals, and other occupational roles. By systematic comparison we refer, for example, to evaluation of commonalities and differences between less skilled work roles and highly skilled work roles in terms of some common sociological problem.

The basic effort here is to bring together a variety of descriptive contemporary studies representing a broad spectrum of occupations and to determine what factors or processes of social control are common to these occupations. *Four levels of social control are examined—cultural and societal, organizational, occupational, and client control.* From these four levels, social control can influence occupational groups and occupational roles; conflict may be generated in combination or separately. We are presenting our cases on the basis of the primary source of control investigated by the contributors.

It is important to determine the impact of the social context on the occupation in regulating, modifying, or controlling role relationships. Therefore the primary interest here is not why cab drivers accept their trade but rather what kinds of cultural, societal forces, etc. modify the chosen work role. Organizational control in the form of restrictive security conditions in a jail setting does modify the discretion allowed teachers in their work role. Furthermore, occupational group control in baseball is so extensive that activities in and out of the work role are carefully monitored with little autonomy granted the baseball player. Finally, client evaluation of the librarian in their encounter may modify the role relationship. Those who have taught and studied work and occupations know the difficulty in finding recent case studies which provide evidence of the points made in texts. Also, the case studies provide life to what should be but often is not an exciting area of study. One reason students study sociology is to find out what people do in the real world. Here are examples to show them.

Since the present edition (1965) of the Dictionary of Occupational Titles (United States Department of Labor) lists more than twenty-five thousand titles, a comparison of individual occupations is obviously an impossible task. However, the patterns of adaptability to the social context as these emerge across diverse occupations can be comparatively analyzed. Furthermore, the comparative study of diverse occupations at this level will, in the long run, contribute more to the general level of theoretical knowledge than studying occupations by classifying them on a basis of status or function.

For example, the distribution of status associated with occupations requires a minute specification of tasks. Moreover, not all industries or occupations are included in the Dictionary of Occupational Titles. Congressman, governor, and housewife are occupations that are apparently difficult for the Department of Labor to research in its present organizational form. The following description was obtained from an informal conversation with a member of the Department of Labor who is responsible for this process. The general process for designating a task to an occupational title by the Department of Labor involves assignment of an industry to one of eight occupational analysis field centers for study. This includes evaluation and description of jobs before a title is given by the field center. The title is then reviewed at the Washington office to avoid duplication. However, there are several problems with the designation of a task to an occupation. Similar tasks may be given dissimilar titles in different regions of the country and by different industries. The Department of Labor recently estimated the number of occupational titles in 1971 to be approximately thirty-five thousand; yet a breakdown reveals that fifteen thousand are different tasks, seven thousand are undefined related titles, and thirteen thousand are alternate titles (information obtained from informal conversations with Department of Labor personnel). This discussion on occupational titles demonstrates the difficulty of classifying occupations in a meaningful way. However, as Lee Taylor (1968) states, this classification is a technical device and of little use to individuals aspiring to occupations.

Occupations differ in 1) the type of work undertaken, 2) the degree of skill required, 3) ideology, 4) recruitment, 5) status and other areas. Despite these variations, occupations can be compared on the basis of how the social structure, formal and informal, influences the development and survival of the occupation. The occupations in this book are related on one analytical framework: the impact of the social context on occupational roles. The social milieu does influence work role relationships and norms of each occupational group; it is significant to delineate the kinds and degree of social control on occupational roles. That is, development of occupational norms does not stop at the boundaries of the occupation but carries over to the social milieu.

There are several ways these occupational studies could be categorized. Studies of occupational structure usually have been classified according to their rank on a hierarchical scale (See the Overview for examples of some status classifications.) A few scholars have tried to order occupations according to function (situs) as well as status (Morris and Murphy, 1959 and Krause, 1971). Neither functional or status categories are satisfactory in this attempt to analyze the impact of the social structure on role differentiation. Some of the studies reflect an interactionist and exchange approach, others a structural-functional approach. The former approach leads to an examination of the adaptive processes of occupational roles as interaction occurs in the social context of the work setting. The structural functional approach also involves adaptive processes whereby occupational groups are modified and regulated to some degree by the larger social structure and cultural mores. (See Percy S. Cohen [1968] for a detailed comparison of several theoretical approaches used to study social phenomena generally. He compares and explains structural functionalism, exchange theory and social interactionism). Since all occupational roles involve interaction within the social structure and must cope with the same problems in the work world, this analysis hopes to bridge the gaps between varying perspectives.

The similarities and differences between the occupations presented in this book are focused on how the levels of control affect the autonomy of occupational groups and occupational roles. Autonomy (that is, whatever discretion is left to the role members after other sources of control have operated) is the chosen factor since this is ideologically and theoretically relevant in a changing social world. It is also politically and economically important as several of these papers show. In addition, job satisfaction, status and alienation seem to be related to the perceived control members have over the work role.

Occupational autonomy can be conceptualized as a feature attached to occupational groups and secondly to occupational roles. The structural functional approach examines how occupational groups are regulated, modified or controlled by the social structure in which occupations are performed. The interactionist perspective is concerned primarily with role activities in the work setting, and thus the role autonomy of the occupational group. Since these two perspectives will be bridged, autonomy will be compared on both levels. The idea of job satisfaction for example, is seen by most sociologists as a structural effect rather than a personality effect. Studies of job satisfaction compare various strata often emphasizing alienation among blue collar workers. (See Sheppard & Herrick, 1972.) Donald McKinley (1964) argues that men at lower socioeconomic levels are oppressed by job frustrations. These manifest themselves in direct expression of hostility on the job and with efforts to compensate by rewards from non-occupational activities. In summarizing his data, Melvin L. Kohn (1969) states that this is plausible and consistent with available findings. He points out that job satisfaction seems to be associated with the acceptance of the status quo and job dissatisfaction with a more questioning stance. Robert Blauner (1964), too, finds a relationship between satisfaction and social class. While job satisfaction may be related to autonomy and alienation, our concern with these areas is very limited.

RATIONALE-METHODOLOGY

The studies in this book, with two exceptions, are individual efforts. That is, they have been conceptualized, designed, and carried out by researchers without the aid of supporting research structures. For students interested in field work and possible graduate study, these cases should spark ideas for discovery, replication and verification. While no substitute for a research methods text, this book will provide the undergraduate with examples of how an individual can do research with little or no help from others. Usually students begin to acquire knowledge of the assumptions, strengths, and weaknesses of various methodological perspectives and techniques in the abstract. When the challenge arises of actually creating a researchable objective, often students wish to read detailed descriptions of how other researchers began the process of investigation. Some of the studies in this book illustrate various stages of the research process. For example, participant observation is used in several of the studies. For her study of aspiring actresses, Peters elected to live with them, study in an acting class, work as an actress and attempt to engage an agent. In the course of these activities, she could observe systematically and record notes. Henslin, in his participant observation study of cab drivers, used a hidden tape recorder as he interacted with other cabbies before and after work. While Peters did inform the staff of her study, none of the cabbies was aware of being a subject. The problems of determining when to participate, when to observe, what to observe so that data are reliable, valid and whether or not to inform research subjects are discussed in our studies.

Studies were commissioned on the basis of data which were collected within the past five or so years and which could address one common sociological concern. Several problems arose when we initially decided to write this book. First of all, we limited our studies to contemporary research rather than reprinting the more classic studies. Why? The sociology of occupations in the last decade has changed considerably since the classic studies were published. For example, today there is considerable emphasis upon the influence of the formal organizational context and the persistent theme of conflict between occupational and organizational norms and constraints. How various occupational groups adapt to the organizational environment is an ongoing issue in the sociology of occupations. Thus the variable of occupational autonomy is emerging as a central area of inquiry in occupations and organizations. In addition, a revived interest in symbolic interaction theory and participant observation techniques in the last few years have contributed to the changing field of study. While we are not stating that the new emphasis is progress, these studies do reflect changes in the field of occupational sociology since the classics were written.

Since these studies were completed as individual efforts and data were collected without the intention of use in a collective analysis, the selection of studies became a difficult one. Attempts to locate ongoing occupational studies were quite extensive. We began by reviewing the appropriate literature and then using the American Sociological Association directory of persons listing occupations and organizations as specialty areas. From this combination we wrote to over one hundred professional sociologists. A review of our table of contents will show that we had limited success in finding in-depth studies of the less skilled workers although several are included. Many of the studies represent occupations which require highly developed skills and talents: the scientific, professional and creative occupations. This may reflect a differential response on solicitation or a trend in interest toward the arts and professions. Our limited success in finding contemporary studies of less skilled occupations does raise interesting questions for students to ponder. If this book were to be rewritten in ten years, what occupational issues would be included? For example, the emerging phenomena of second and third careers for many workers of all skill levels would probably be conspicuous. This condition may reflect the search for greater autonomy by various workers, especially since so many occupations are performed in complex, large-scale organizations. Another explanation for changing career patterns can be found in government programs such as Operation Switch. This is an experiment with re-educating Ph.D. scientists (at present, an excess category of workers) to become medical doctors. A further area of study might be the impact of the counter culture in defining career relevance. This may be related to autonomy and the ideologically motivated worker. The student would find all of these areas interesting and challenging to study.

Overview

Social Context of Occupations

In this discussion, it is our purpose to review how sociologists have studied work and occupations in the past as well as to present a new framework. Our review of how occupations have been defined includes common sense, economic and sociological conceptions. The most common definitions of work are concerned with the labor force and earning a living. David N. Solomon (1968:5) says work is a generic term for the activity leading to the production of goods and or services, that is, for economic activity in any society. Nels Anderson (1964:1) sees work as economic activity for a purpose, while leisure activity usually is an end in itself. Essentially all the definitions have in common some economic component; the problem with using a solely economic definition, however, is that it does not approximate social reality and everyday meaning. For example, David Riesman (1950), using a definition which has an economic base, has noted that time spent in work is difficult to distinguish from time spent in non-work activities. This may be true of those who earn their living at intellectual or artistic pursuits. It is not our purpose to try to distinguish work from leisure. It appears that the philosophical and conceptual problems of trying to define work are complicated in everyday life, and economic definitions are limiting. For our purposes we are defining work as an activity performed by members within occupational roles. As will be seen in our definition of occupations, we have not limited ourselves totally to economic activities.

Occupations may or may not have a market value depending on time and place. Richard H. Hall's (1969:5) definition is close to our concept of an occupation. He says that an occupation is the social role performed by adult members of society that directly or indirectly yields social and financial consequences, though not necessarily rewards. Hall's definition has the advantage over others of not tying people and groups too closely with remuneration and can include starving artists, housewives, and philanthropic millionaires. Yet in the everyday world, everyone knows that occupations also have the eventual if not immediate promise of economic rewards.

However, an occupation, as Hall and others have pointed out, is more than a way of doing work to earn money. Several writers (Dubin, 1958; Saltz, 1944; and others) note that work helps people define their social class in relationship to others. For example, Jack Roach, Llewelyn Gross and Orville Gursslin (1969: 127) state that occupation is the most frequently used socioeconomic index. In fact, to many sociologists, occupation is a major determinant of social class position. Much of occupational sociology is concerned with the problem of how to classify occupations in a way that will reflect the prestige and status of the occupation for the incumbents of the role. (See Goode, 1960a for a detailed consideration of role. In this context occupational role is patterned behavior associated with an occupational group. It includes the privileges attached to a social position in a work place.)

Furthermore, an occupation is not merely a set of activities or tasks as the Dictionary of Occupational Titles (DOT) would lead one to believe. Rather, occupations are socially organized sets of activities (Hughes, 1958) and social roles which are usually achieved through some training or apprenticeship. Because an occupation is a social role, incumbents of that role are treated in specific ways by others and behave in certain ways as well. Certain activities, other than role performance and role expectations, become part of the way people behave outside the work situation. In many cases a person's occupation gives meaning and direction to his life. Achieving an occupational role means that one achieves a definite status. Occupational status then becomes important, if not the most important status, a person can have. Income, life-style, life-chances for one's children, and honor are tied closely with occupational identity. *In sum, we view an occupation as a social role which may or may not guarantee a financial reward.* (For a review of how roles have been classified, see Michael Banton, 1965). Thus an occupation is more than a set of tasks or activities. It is intimately associated with all aspects of a person's life.

APPROACHES TO THE STUDY OF WORK AND OCCUPATIONS

How occupational roles are affected by the structural arrangements of the work environment or the larger social organization has been a major area of inquiry by sociologists since the nineteenth century. Karl Marx, for example, attributed alienation to capitalism and industrialization. Writing on alienated labor, he presents a series of hypotheses and questions based on the major proposition that the product of labor under the factory system is alienation where the worker is separated from the means of production. The work in a factory, on a production line, is external to the person, that is, it is not part of his nature:

> . . . and that, consequently, he does not fulfill himself in his work but denies himself, has a feeling of misery rather than well being, does not develop freely his mental and physical energies but is physically exhausted at home only during his leisure time, whereas at work he is homeless (Bottomore, 1963: 125).

Marx's theory is based on the effect of structural changes and what happened to man when the economy and the means of production changed.

Max Weber agreed with Marx that the position of the worker, the worker's feelings, his productivity, and his power over his environment are tied to the organization of society. Weber concludes the effects of the structure are more complicated than those presented by Marx. Weber (1964: 251) notes that the occupational structure of a group may vary according to: (1) the degree in which well-marked and stable occupations have developed at all; (2) the mode and degree of occupational specification or specialization of individual economic units; and (3) the extent and kind of continuity or change in occupational status. One general effect of industrialization which concerned Weber was the tendency of organizations to become more bureaucratic under industrialization regardless of the political or economic system. Weber's theory of organization is not of as much interest here as what he said about people who work in a "rational-legal" authority structure which was the model of the recurring "bureaucratic" organization. Weber saw this mode of interaction as limiting the freedom of workers and filling the world with little cogs and little men.

Emile Durkheim (1964) was also concerned with the relationship of modes of organization and the social structure with the performance and well-being of those in the work force. The basic dilemma that concerned Durkheim was how men can at once be more dependent on society and at the same time be more autonomous as the division of labor becomes more complex. Social life under these conditions becomes more intense to the extent that interactions among the units of a society become more frequent and dynamic. Individuals, for Durkheim, are far more a product of "common life" than its determinant. While there is necessity for more interaction in a complex, industrial society and therefore more interdependence (organic solidarity) there is also more individualism and therefore more autonomy. To quote Durkheim:

> . . . The individual is not sufficient unto himself, it is from society that he receives everything necessary to him, as it is for society that he works. Thus is formed a very strong sentiment of the state of dependence in which he finds himself. . . . Yet as regulated as a function may be, there is a large place always left for personal initiative. . . . It is we who choose our professions, and even certain of our domestic functions. Of course, once our resolution has ceased to be internal and has been externally translated by social consequences, we are tied down. Duties are imposed upon us that we have not expressly desired. It is however, through a voluntary act that this has taken place (Durkheim, 1964: 228–229).

All three of the theorists mentioned (especially Marx and Weber) and the questions they have raised have generated a good deal of research and controversy. Their concern with the structure and social organization has often been turned around in the sense that personality characteristics have been more important while the structure is taken as given. The problem of alienation of workers has generated a body of literature predominantly about industrial workers and intellectuals (see Melvin Seeman, 1959; Robert Blauner, 1964; and Joachim Israel, 1971 for an examination and extension of Marx's ideas). Much discussion has been speculative but a number of people have tried to separate empirically the components of alienation and its relationship to work. The work of artists, intellectuals and those working for mass communication industries has essentially looked at the problems of alienation and frustration from the point of view presented by C. Wright Mills in *White Collar* (1951: 142–160). Mills has suggested that such people have become "tools of the system" who have their autonomy and freedom limited because of their employee status in the work situation. Findings from empirical research show the situation is far more complex. Robert Faulkner, (1971: 178) found that along with feelings of discontent, musicians have balancing elements of intense pride in their skill and confidence in their abilities. In general, he concluded, they adapt. Blauner (1964) in his study of industrial workers draws somewhat similar conclusions.

Because of the importance of occupational roles and positions in industrial societies, it is not surprising that occupations and work have been the focus of much sociological inquiry. Interest in occupations has focused on stratification of work roles and the division of labor. A study of Western history points out the importance of occupations as a means of stratifying people. In feudal societies before the industrial era, occupations provided people with the prestige and rewards of their society. In medieval cities one's occupation and one's status could not be disassociated. With the rise of capitalism and the factory system, occupational status has become only one status—an important one—among several.

Occupation as a means of stratification has become an important and complex problem area of inquiry. Empirically a case can be made that no other single characteristic is as important a prediction of an individual's life chances as his father's occupation and occupational status. On the other hand, one's position in society is no longer entirely tied to that of one's parents and especially not tied to the father's occupational group as was the case in medieval cities (see Form, 1968: 246). The complex division of labor, the growth of technology, the separation of kinship status from the political structure along with the possibility of geographic mobility have provided a few in industrial societies the chance for upward mobility on the status ladder. While this is limited, the chances for mobility for both social groups (women, blacks, etc.) and individuals are theoretically and actually possible.

The two related problems of mobility and occupational status as the major determinants of a person's place or rank in a social system have led scholars to ask how positions in a changing technological society are filled. The structural-funtionalists (in particular, Davis and Moore, 1945) take the position that society must distribute its members into positions which will maintain the system and induce them to perform in the positions. Some jobs are more agreeable than others; some require more skill and training; and some are functionally more important in maintaining the social order. Rewards must be built into the system in order to insure that difficult, unpleasant, necessary roles are filled. These rewards are not only financial but can be intrinsic as well in that they contribute to a person's enjoyment and to his self-respect. In other words, scarcity determines the importance of an occupational role and the rewards which go with that position. While the structural-functional view of how positions in a society are filled and distributed has led to considerable discussion and criticism, there has been little empirical work to justify either those who agree or disagree. Nonetheless, Davis and Moore and others (see Parsons, 1968) see occupational roles within the social context and the allocation of occupations as a social function. Its determinants are seen in the whole context of society. The criticism of the Davis and Moore thesis has not been directed to this point. Melvin Tumin, (1953) the most verbal of the many critics, sees power as the major determinant of role ascription rather than societal need or functional necessity.

This leads directly to the issue which concerns many of the authors included in this volume—the problem of freedom and autonomy in work. Freedom to choose one's work is obviously related to the problem posed by Davis and Moore. They stress the importance of ability (talents) as a functional prerequisite for the individual's recruitment in order to be able to fill the roles necessary to maintain a technological society. However, empirical studies show that occupational choice at the individual level is very complex. The controversy on how people select jobs ranges from theories of purely economic dominance to psychological dominance. Studies have to be evaluated carefully on this subject because of conceptual problems.

There have been a number of studies on aspirations and job expectations, for instance. These two ideas are conceptually different and the results from such studies show that occupational expectations tend to reflect more accurately the occupational structure of an area and a time than do aspirations. Here, too, structural factors become important. Occupational choosing is closely linked with experience in an educational system, family background, etc. Studies also show that occupational choice depends on the occupations familiar to individuals (see Taylor, 1968: 189–220). This, too, is a structural problem as well as a problem in socio-communications. Other problems include fitting the most "talented" or capable persons into roles and occupations needed by society. Our purpose is not, however, to try to prove or substantiate either the critics or the followers of the functional position. Rather, we are more interested in the problem of freedom and autonomy to perform the tasks required by an occupational role once the role is chosen or assigned. Work autonomy is politically, ideologically, economically and theoretically important in a society experiencing changing forms of social organization. This is suggested in Gilb (1966) who provides examples of how occupations have worked for autonomy through control by licensure and other professional standards. These ideas will be integrated and extended in the last chapter.

RECENT LITERATURE ON OCCUPATIONS

In the very recent past there have been several books on the sociology of occupations which cover the range of occupations and the various types of work available. These are: Slocum (1966), Taylor (1968), Hall (1969), Krause (1971), Pavalko (1971), and Zald (1971). The tables of contents of three of these (Taylor, Hall and Krause) can give the reader some idea of how the field has been defined since no book covers the entire field. Essentially they cover broadly such topics as occupational socialization, choice, identification, mobility, and the work setting. All these divide the labor force according to a classification which combines structure with function. Hall, like Theodore Caplow (1954) on the sociology of work, shows that occupations provide the link between the individual and the larger society. His purpose is to describe and analyze the various types of occupations as they exist in the social system. He presents a dynamic structural approach viewing change and conflict as part of the relationship between occupations and the social system. Types of occupations are categorized according to a modification of the classification scheme of the Bureau of the Census (first used by Caplow, 1954: 23). The following classification is a combination of hierarchical stratification according to rewards (incomes) primarily, and Alba Edward's ideas of prestige plus a functional component (1943).

1. Professionals
2. Managers, proprietors, and officials
3. Clerks and kindred workers
4. Skilled workers and foremen
5. Semi-skilled workers
6. Unskilled workers (including farm and nonfarm workers) (Hall, 1969: 68).

This classification has several weaknesses as well as some strengths. The categories are too broad, and specific occupations are often difficult to place in the framework. The actual census code (see Robinson, Athanasiou, and Head, 1969 for the code and variations of it) used to categorize occupations is more specific. Problems arise when these codes are summarized. Hall (1969: 265) like Caplow (1954: 43–47) points out that the scale in no way can let us assume that there are equal intervals between the categories. Furthermore, the assumption built into the classification is that white collar work is in some way superior to manual labor, that self-employment is superior to employment by others and that larger organizations carry more prestige than smaller ones.

Elliot Krause's (1971) approach is essentially different from the works mentioned above. Krause not only asks different questions but also divides and classifies occupations differently from the professional-occupational continuum presented by Pavalko and from the division of labor approach taken by Hall and Taylor. His basic question is: What changes have there been in the historical role of major occupational and professional groups (Krause, 1971: 1)? He is interested not only in new roles as they develop because of technology and need, but also in the relationship of occupational groups to the society as a whole in various periods of time. A second question he examines is the relationship of an individual to his occupation. This is very close to the question we are asking in this book. Following the lead of Everett Hughes (1958), this book tries to relate the individual to the institutions of the society by showing that the relationship is, as Krause states the problem, "a two-way street" (1971: 3). In each case, we must ask if the individual is taking a major part in creating his own occupation or whether the occupation or profession is bearing down on him to the point where he is made over in the image of the occupation. Also Krause's work is broader than ours in that he is interested in the role of the occupation as a mediating force between the individual and the wider society. He has tried to combine the structural-functional, conflict and interactionist approaches to describe the development of occupational consciousness.

No literature review on occupations is complete without mentioning the emphasis sociologists have placed on the "professions." The selections in this book are additional evidence (see Grusky and Miller, 1970) that professional occupations are the object of much investigation. There are several possible reasons for this. One of the most obvious is, as Talcott Parsons notes, the institutional structure of the professional world has crystallized and the university-academy has come to be its center (Parsons, 1968: 536). A second reason is that work has become more specialized, requiring knowledge and expertise for performance. This has resulted in a number of people asking if the whole labor force is becoming professionalized (see Nelson Foote, 1953; Harold Wilensky, 1964; Howard Vollmer and Donald Mills, 1966). Related to the above is an interest in trying to distinguish the professional role from the non-professional role (see Ernest Greenwood, 1957; Bernard Barber, 1963, and Wilbert Moore, 1970). A third reason for the interest in professions and professionalization is that occupational groups, in order to be self-regulating, have consciously tried to emulate the more traditional professions by working towards professional status.

Finally, and this may be the most important reason, we agree along with Elliot Krause (1971: 79) that the major professions are functionally powerful. Their key place in the division of labor is reflected in political power, rewards, and prestige. While many occupational groups which may be classified as non-professional may also enjoy power, prestige, and material rewards (high level business executives, for example), the professional occupations are responsible for the health of a society, for its laws and its protection (Krause: 1971: 79).

The above points are presented as possible explanations as to why sociologists are concerned with professionalism and professional roles. Yet, it still remains unclear how sociologists define a profession as distinguished from a non-profession. Most of the authors cited are using the term "profession" as an ideal type (see Vollmer & Mills, 1966: 1–2). Much of the literature asks two questions: 1) what is the process whereby an occupation becomes a profession; and 2) why is a specific occupation a profession. These questions can be answered only if there is consensus on what constitutes a profession; on this there is little agreement (see Greenwood, 1957; Barber, 1963; Moore 1970 for different definitions). Moore's (1970: 15, 16) definition includes:

1. The professional practices a full-time occupation which comprises his principal source of income.
2. Commitment to a calling.
3. A formal organization for members of the occupational group.
4. Useful knowledge and skills based on training or education of exceptional duration and perhaps of exceptional difficulty.
5. A service orientation to clients.
6. Autonomy, restrained by responsibility and training.

Moore's definition differs from Bernard Barber's (1963: 672), who says a profession has the following characteristics:

1. Exclusive specialized knowledge.
2. Community orientation.
3. Self-regulation by a code of ethics

Sociologists usually agree that all occupational groups have some characteristics of the central professions (law, medicine and traditionally the ministry—Vollmer and Mills, 1966: 2). Both Ernest Greenwood and Wilbert Moore state that it is the combination of characteristics rather than their absence or presence that distinguish a profession from an occupation. A basic difference between the definitions cited is that Barber stresses the presence of a code of ethics while Moore places autonomy as the highest value (also see Sussman, 1965: 181–189; Goode, 1960b).

Moore considers autonomy to be the most important distinguishing criterion between a profession and a non-profession. Moore states that a professional has autonomy when he proceeds by his own judgement and authority which is backed up by skills and training. Moore is aware that non-professional occupations may enjoy autonomy as he defines it. He states (Moore, 1970: 16) that the autonomy of the professional is not qualitatively distinct from that of other specialized and useful occupations, but rather builds upon the professionals having passed previous selection points. Thus the model or ideal type definition presented by Moore depends on more than the criterion of autonomy.

Others trying to distinguish an occupation from a profession place a higher value on commitment to the standards and values the occupational group has developed for its members (Goode, 1957; Parsons, 1968; Note: this is one of Moore's points as well). However, occupational group automomy and commitment to occupational standards or values (social control by the occupation itself rather than outside control) probably represent the major areas of study of professional occupations and roles. Professionals and semi-professionals (nurses, teachers, social workers, engineers, librarians) who must practice their skills in organizations have been the object of much study. The standards of behavior set by the organization can conflict or differ from learned occupational standards. Conflicts may or may not arise between groups who claim specialized knowledge but differ in standards and objectives from the employing organization.

Thus, the literature on the professions stresses the interrelated ideas of autonomy and commitment. The medical practitioner and medical practice have provided the basic model for various definitions of profession. Yet as Oswald Hall (1948: 327) noted, specialized medicine is no longer an independent profession, a free-lance occupation. It has become interdependent rather than independent, and it is carried on within the framework of an elaborate social machinery rather than within a freely competitive milieu. Hall is writing about physicians in private practice, but obviously this theory could also apply to those physicians working in organizations. Both the free practitioner (lawyers, dentists, physicians) and the salaried professional (academians, engineers, scientists) all experience social control which limits autonomy regardless of their commitment to occupational standards. Vollmer and Mills (1966: 2) point out that characteristics commonly attributed to traditional professions can be found in occupations not commonly considered professions, while several traditional professions no longer fit the pure professional model. They argue rather than simply defining a profession, it would be more useful to analyze occupational institutions in terms of a concept of professionalization. They make an assumption that many, it not all occupations can be placed on a continuum between ideal-type categories, professions and non-professions. By this heuristic device, professionalization is a process that may affect any occupation to a greater or lesser degree. This would be a productive method for categorizing certain occupational groups if there were agreement on the definition of a profession. However, even if agreement could be reached, the method lacks complexity for differentiating many occupations at the non-professional end of the continuum. Moreover, it is inadequate for handling artistic occupations, crafts, and those groups Everett Hughes calls "learned societies."

We see little useful purpose in trying to analyze work and the adaptative process either by using the occupational-professional continuum or by establishing still another definition of a profession. Several of the authors in this book use profession-occupation distinction or designate the occupational group in their articles as professionals (attorneys, engineers, accountants). Some might argue whether all are professionals. Because this book shows the commonalities and differences of various work roles in adapting to the changing social milieu, the professional model is not appropriate.

OUR FRAMEWORK

For the most part, these diverse occupations will be compared in terms of autonomy. The sociological literature is filled with definitions of autonomy and discussions of how autonomy is sought, acquired and maintained by specific occupational groups. (See Goode, 1960b; Kornhauser, 1962; Vollmer and Mills, 1966; Moore, 1970; Freidson, 1970; many others could be cited but are referred to in these works.) *We are defining autonomy as whatever discretion is held by occupational groups and roles after other sources of control have operated.* Work autonomy is politically, ideologically, economically and theoretically significant in a society moving toward changing forms of social organization.

We are interested in examining how social controls operate to modify or regulate the degree of automony experienced by individuals in their work activities. By social control we mean the structures, both formal and informal, which condition and limit the actions of groups and roles. We see control as an interactive process between the structure and the occupational role. The subtleties and nuances of the process are not limited to the formal structures such as tables of organization, the law or even to formalized societal arrangements, such as caste systems. Informal controls may develop in work groups or control may come from societal and cultural norms. *In addition to these forms of control in the work setting, occupational group and role autonomy may be regulated by any or all of the following structural levels: societal and cultural, organizational, occupational and client.* Organizational control of occupations has been a main area of inquiry for many social scientists. They have focused on the clash between the goals of the organization and the interests of the professional and intellectual. Wilensky (1956), Merton (1957b), Gouldner (1957–1958), Caplow and McGee (1958), Kornhauser (1962), Blau and Scott (1962), and Stewart (1968), are a few who have considered the problems of the professional, the scientist, and the intellectual who have to satisfy clients, the organization and the public of the organization. In the case of scientists, for instance, it is suggested that the internalized goals of the discipline are in direct conflict with the objects of the work organization. Stewart (1968) concluded that the key consideration in the area of goal difference was more than conflict or approval, but also whether professionals perceived opportunity to meet professional goals in the employing organization. We are interested in how such professionals, semi-professionals, craftgroups, and the like adapt and conform to conflicting expectations.

Most sociologists generally accept the proposition that no occupational group or role can be free from societal influences, that is, control. How occupational groups adapt to the social milieu in which they perform is both timely and historically relevant. Adaptation is seen as a process which can generate conformity to the prevailing controls, both informal and formal. Autonomy may be granted to an occupational group for many reasons. Those occupational groups which provide a service to a client based on specialized knowledge or expertise obtained through extensive training and socialization are epitomized by the traditional professions of law and medicine. Autonomy for those occupations usually includes such group freedoms as recruitment of members into the occupation, determination of and protection of standards of excellence for the occupational groups, and evaluation of occupational role performance primarily by colleagues.

There are other occupational groups that do have autonomy, though it may be limited. Teachers, nurses, librarians and social workers have autonomy to exercise professional judgment in their role relationships with clients. However, recruitment into the ranks and the development of requirements for entry are subject to considerable control outside the occupational group.

Another group of occupations has autonomy as a function of expertise based on extensive training and yet is not necessarily involved with direct service to a client. Many of these are dependent upon large organizations for support and opportunity for occupational role performance. Occupations such as scientists, professors, some engineers, and some of the traditional professions have moved away from the sole-practitioner arrangement to dependence upon large organizations.

In each of these types—and this is not an exhaustive list—there are problems of trying to fit diverse occupations that differ on only one property. There are other occupational groups that also have autonomy.

The extreme example is the housewife, but other examples include craftsmen and artists. Our concern is not to develop a model of occupations but examine under what conditions social controls in the work setting modify occupational group and role autonomy.

Few studies examining autonomy move beyond asking what it is and what occupations hold it or are losing it. A more appropriate question seems to be how much the autonomy of an occupation can be reduced without modifying standards of excellence. Physicians carrying out role tasks in large organizations may still provide competent service to clients even though some limitations are imposed on decision-making in exchange for resources and an opportunity to carry out the occupational role. The answer to such a question cannot be provided at this time since few researchers have directly addressed this concern. However, most of our studies are examining occupations that are viable and have been somewhat successful in maintaining occupational identity, autonomy, and survival.

In addition to societal and cultural norms, the organizational milieu and the organization of the occupation itself, client control is particularly important in a participatory society. Besides reducing and enhancing autonomy, clients do reflect societal and cultural norms. In some states today, laws demand that psychiatrists evaluate and predict the probable effect of an unwanted child on the mother. Many psychiatrists argue that they cannot make this prediction in brief consultation with a patient; some are convinced that a patient must make her own decision. Schisms have developed in which certain doctors are labeled abortion psychiatrists by their colleagues. There is some feeling that a profession (professional) should not respond to a market situation, and that society (through legislation) should not have power over a psychiatrist to regulate or change standards of performance.

Throughout the literature there is evidence that the client for the services of an occupation either *should* have or *does* have some influence both on the product produced and the way individuals perform in their occupational roles. Client-control is considered more by those interested in professionals and the arts than by those who study industrial workers. However, we believe that this is one of several types of control operating on all groups in the labor force. Many use service orientation to a client as a distinguishing feature of a profession. In addition, direct interaction with the client has often been defined as a characteristic of true professions as contrasted to other occupations. Obviously, the communicator and artist have to be communicating to some audience, however small, in order to continue their artistic production. The number of clients, their social class, and the frequency with which they use the services or buy the product are only a few of the clients' ways of influencing occupational roles.

Wilbert Moore (1970) sees the client as the employer for those in private independent practice, e.g., physicians and lawyers. Freidson (1960) shows clearly that the reputation and the professional success or failure of the independent practitioner rests with his potential or actual clients. Freidson contrasts this client control which operates through a lay referral system with colleague control which operates through professional referrals. Freidson writes that the lay referral system operates to impose clients' standards rather than professional standards on the physician. These clients' standards may be representative of the larger society or of a minority sub-cultural group since there is differential access, differential use, and a variety of beliefs about medical care. (See Moore, 1970: 90 for a discussion of the clients' control over the lawyer.)

The artist or creator of either popular culture or high culture and his relationship to the audience has also been explored. Those working in this area have conceptualized the "client" to approximate the bureaucratized mode where a service ethic is absent. Several investigators (see Breed, 1955; Gans, 1957; and Cantor, 1971) of the mass media define the audience as those to whom the communicator is directing the message. These can be one's peers, the employing organization or the actual audience. We acknowledge the importance of those termed as secondary audiences by Raymond Bauer (1958); but we are defining the ultimate receiver of the communication as the client (audience) because those other reference groups can be considered in the societal, organizational and occupational forms of control.

Thus, the conditions under which all occupational groups work are in some way controlled by the client as well as by the societal, organizational, and occupational norms and structures which interact to define work and occupational roles in a changing society. *In summary, we are presenting the cases according to the kinds of social control most influential in determining the way specific occupational groups and roles maintain or obtain autonomy.* The kinds of social control emphasized in this book are social and cultural norms, organizational arrangements, occupational and client control. For all occupations we see these levels interacting but one or another level has been emphasized in the various papers we are presenting.

1

CULTURE AND SOCIETY

Introduction

Cultural and Societal Context

The papers placed in this section are primarily about norms and values which are reflected in the whole society; norms and values which may be changing and which affect the occupational roles being discussed.

Law as a profession is organized, as Cynthia Epstein notes, so that women are underrepresented in proportion to their numbers in the labor force. Because women are systematically structured out of law (as well as medicine, academia, etc. at the higher levels), the organization of the occupation itself reflects the cultural values concerning the woman's place. The internal organization of law as an occupation reflects the larger society in that few women will attain the same prestige, rights and duties as their male counterparts. The idea of universalistic standards which are supposed to apply to occupational members obviously do not apply to these women professionals. Nor do universalistic standards apply to all males who enter law as a profession. Informal structures develop in all occupations which systematically reward certain qualified people more than others equally qualified; the social control system of the profession itself operates to undermine a variety of groups and individuals. Epstein is focusing on women. However, she is presenting a societal problem which can be generalized to other occupational groups. How the societal values work both on women and men to help them define their own roles and how such values are reflected in a variety of occupations and their organization should be explored further by students. Epstein's paper provides clues for this further investigation.

Whereas women are systematically structured out of law, medicine,

23

the ministry and academia, and other occupational groups, housewifery by definition and in actuality could not exist in its present form without women. Jessie Bernard is presenting two models in Western thought which have been reflected in policy. She argues that our thinking is handicapped by the incompatible assumptions, values and goals of the two models—economic versus societal, pre-industrial versus industrial. In the actual operation of housewife role with its low prestige, its isolation, and lack of tangible rewards, the satisfaction for women may be negligible. Yet the institutions of society still provide intangible rewards. The role of the housewife is seen as "normal" and appropriate for women. On the other hand, the housewife role, though autonomous, is by itself low in prestige and has no economic rewards except through the husband's status and position. Jessie Bernard is suggesting that social norms can be changed and the role of housewife can and should be brought into the economic world. By her definition, housewifery at this time is not an occupation. By our definition, the housewife role is an occupation because it is a social role with economic ramifications and, for many housewives, it occupies most of their time. This is not a disagreement because all agree that the labor performed as housewife is not rewarded by the same standards as other similar occupations. The dilemma facing the housewife may be reflected in her role performance. More important is the larger problem of whether the functional differentiation of work roles by sex is indeed disappearing and whether such differentiation should disappear.

Not all the "women's occupations" were put in this section (nurses, librarians, ballet dancers are in the section on *Occupational Control*). However, the way actresses are defined in a particular culture is an area in which societal control can be made more explicit. The problems of a struggling actress provide a prototype of how certain values about age, sex and occupational identity control women in relationship to their work. Women see acting as one of the few occupations where the rewards are equal to those received by men. Popular belief is that it requires little training or skill to be successful. Any female can call herself an actress. Anne Peters states that whether or not a young woman earns her living as an actress, adopting the title "actress" offers more occupational dignity than the title secretary or clerk. Women striving for success believe the image they present is more important than skills in order to gain the desired goal of stardom. A case can be made that the actress's role is defined by those in charge of production. However, the myths that surround film-acting in particular are partially responsible for the way aspiring actresses work toward success, in the image they try to present, and in their actual job-seeking methods.

Clarence Tygart's paper on the clergy is one of the most important papers for our focus. Changes in the clergy role are directly related to changes in both social structure and the importance of religious ideas in a particular culture. Once the only profession, its decline to an occupation of less importance is directly attributable to social changes in Western history, to the separation of Church and State, to the decentralization of authority and laity control, and to the scientific ethic taking precedence over the religious ethic. Loss of public acceptance of the clergy as an exclusive profession has affected the degree to which society permits it to be self-regulating.

This study provides a basis for evaluating the process whereby a profession experiences encroachment from changing values and ideas. Also, how it loses autonomy and adapts to this by division within the profession provides considerable sociological insight on the deprofessionalization of occupations.

The occupation of cab-driving holds little prestige in American society. In fact, Henslin in his study of cab drivers reports how the capitalistic system with its primary emphasis on profit exploits the role of cab driver. The societal value of profit at any cost is exemplified in patron's treatment of cab drivers, management abuse and cab drivers' attempts to cheat each other. Autonomy in this occupation is quite limited but can be found at the role level where innovators can find ways to beat the system. This may result in striking at the group level or taking on extra jobs at the role level on company time. Henslin's paper presents only one view of this occupation. However, the enlargement of his perspective to include rewards of the occupation would probably still confirm the limited autonomy, prestige, and income of this occupation.

Cynthia F. Epstein

Ambiguity as Social Control: Consequences for the Integration of Women in Professional Elites*

Social and legal attention has been focussed on the underrepresentation of Blacks, Puerto-Ricans, Mexican-Americans and other disadvantaged groups of Americans in law, medicine, science and other elite professions. Lately this concern has been extended to the underrepresentation of women as well.

The exclusion process in the professions is more than a simple matter of quotas on new recruits. The professional community embodies a social control system, a system of rewards and punishments that sifts recruits on their entrance to careers and their way to the top. The present analysis asserts that the social control system undermines the motivation and participation of persons who possess statuses viewed as negative by the gatekeepers of the professions;[1] our inquiry focuses on the control system as it especially affects women.[2]

Membership in an elite profession is synonymous with "success" in

---

* Note: A preliminary statement of this paper was reported in "Women Lawyers and Their Profession: Inconsistency of Social Controls and Their Consequences for Professional Performance," presented at the annual meeting of the American Sociological Association, San Francisco, California, September 4, 1969. The research reported was supported by grants from the Manpower Administration, U.S. Department of Labor, The National Institutes of Health, and the Research Foundation of the City University. The author is indebted to the fruitful suggestions and discussions of Howard Epstein, Fred Goldner, William J. Goode, Harriet Zuckerman, and anonymous referees in considering many of the issues involved in this analysis.

American society. Few women are found in the professions, and the larger society, which has not especially noted their absence until recently, does not believe that women aim for occupational success or it is fitting that they do so. Even when women do attain professional success, they are usually judged by a set of standards very different from those applied to men.[3]

Success in the professions is more than a matter of membership or even commitment, and talent. The "real" world of the professional— the arena in which he or she will battle for recognition and success— begins with legal, medical or academic training but does not end there. In the "community" (Goode, 1957) of profession into which the graduates enter, women find themselves unwelcome and unable to perform to their full ability or even to learn the norms for performance.

Of course, all such systems do reward talent and hard work for many of their members. In addition, since not all who enter are equally endowed, many men and women will achieve no more than a modest success. It has been suggested that women do not do well in certain professions because they lack talent for specific types of work, or perhaps because they cannot or do not work hard.[4] But some evidence suggests that the women in some professions are at least equal to their male colleagues in potential at the *early* stages of their careers.

L. R. Harmon (1965) and Jonathan Cole (1971) have assembled data indicating that women graduate students and professionals in the social and physical sciences have, on the average, higher I.Q.'s than their male peers.[5] In my study of women lawyers (Epstein, 1968), close to one-third of a randomly picked sample had been law review *editors* while in law school (until recently, only those students ranking in the top ten percent of their class were invited to join law review staffs). Further, women who have carried out preliminary, unpublished investigations for feminist groups report that college administrators have admitted privately that higher grade averages have been required for women's admissions. And over the years many law schools have imposed quotas on women entrants, thereby assuring that women students were more rigorously selected than the men.

These data suggest at least that up to the time of beginning their professional work, women are not conspicuously deficient. What happens afterwards?

SOCIAL CONTROL IN THE PROFESSIONS

Analysis of the problems women face is instructive in identifying the "holding operations" of the society's stratification system; the mechanisms which insure women's poor representation in professional elites are generally the self-maintaining mechanisms of the stratification system. This analysis suggests that these mechanisms facilitate passage into the elite for those who are preferred and hinder or exclude those regarded as inappropriate.

For the preferred, those with desired status-sets, the path to success is made clear. The status-sequence from recruit to full member is outlined and the person who deviates is rerouted with further information about how to perform on course. The messages are direct, instructive and motivating. For the recruit who is defined as inappropriate and is regarded as outside the system and incapable of becoming part of it, the messages are less clear, often ambiguous and contradictory.

No doctor becomes a brilliant diagnostician simply by going to school nor can a lawyer become a persuasive courtroom advocate by taking courses. There are no objective tests for competence at high levels. Here, the status-judges of the profession and to some extent one's clients bestow the crown of competence. The lawyer does not really learn law until he has had the experience of handling real cases and courtroom situations.[6] He learns to some extent by trial and error, but better, he learns from the tutoring of an older partner who sees it his duty to guide the neophyte through the maze.

In medicine, law, and the academic world (and this is true for business as well), competence is created by exposing the new professional to the tasks, giving him the opportunity to learn the tricks and avoid the pitfalls. He is given access to persons who can help him and information about the important people in the system. The accepted newcomer learns by observing and performing because he is put in a position where he can observe and *must* perform. His important colleagues will watch how he does and give him feedback vital for his improvement as a professional.

Those who teach the young professional, and those who lead the profession usually agree that the "appropriate" candidates are competent and will later become more competent in important ways beyond their talents and formal training, and that the "inappropriate" candidates cannot become competent. It is believed that those with the "wrong" statuses cannot be part of the subtle, informal collegial system, will be unable to catch the messages, will be ill-prepared in the necessary etiquette of professional behavior and rules of reciprocity, and will be incapable of proper behavior toward a hierarchy that may not be clearly labeled (see Epstein, 1970a). Cleverness is not sufficient, nor is a medical or law degree, even from a "proper" school. Because failure is presumed, few will act as sponsor to prepare the unwanted professional for a successful career.

The person with the "wrong" sex status or racial status may succeed, idiosyncratically, as a "deviant," and without the systematic set of rewards and punishments by which the professionals within the system acquire standards and professional taste and learn to identify with the occupational status so that it becomes a defining part of the self. The latter enlists the person in the elite social control system by socializing him to monitor his own behavior, his professional commitment and aspirations, by reference to the norms of the profession (Goode, 1957).

The general socialization process and the control system which further socializes professionals within their profession give them a different orientation toward work than people in lower level occupations. Typically professionals rank high on scales of work satisfaction (Richard Hall, 1969: 48) and job commitment, and they have high aspirations and personal involvement in their work (Gross, 1958: 78). This is predictable not only because their material rewards are great[7] and their work is interesting[8] but because they are also subject to a social control system which reinforces this commitment (Goode, 1957: 194).

Furthermore, the social control system of the professions usually interacts with the social control systems of the larger society in a harmonious way. Performance to high professional standards is highly regarded and respected and often the professional is asked to serve on public committees and to aid in decisions affecting the larger society. Similarly, poor performance by a member of the professional community typically means that the larger community will also regard the person as a failure and not worthy of respect though he may be a decent person and community member. Indeed, the community often will grant the dedicated professional exemption from community responsibilities in the belief that he is serving the community better by performing his occupational role.[9]

The standards of professionalization are usually left by the community to the professions to decide. Thus, the measure of the individual's worth, criteria of performance and recruitment selection all are set internally. The profession's elite are the norm-setters and the gatekeepers of the profession (Oswald Hall, 1946). Their standards and their evaluations determine who rises and who falls.

Until recently, the selection mechanisms of the professional elites have remained largely unquestioned even though they have not been devoted to judging the functionally specific capacities of recruits. The professions have usually limited their selection to recruits of like kind, insisting that they come equipped not only with the techniques of craft but the preferred statuses of class, ethnicity, race and sex.[10]

Discriminatory professional recruitment has not been considered unjust by the outside community, but rather part of the natural order of things. Furthermore, because of their high place in the outside community, elites in the professions and other decision-making spheres have been able to maintain control and counter challenges to their legitimacy. There is no doubt that the acceptance of this system by the outside society, including those who are excluded, comes not only from lack of power, or resignation. It comes from acceptance of the idea that those who are rewarded *are* worthy; that some are "suited" to enter these spheres and others are not, and that *what is, is right*. Certainly women as a group have typically believed in their own inadequacy to compete for high positions in the society, becoming conspirators in their own exclusion.

The mechanisms of exclusion affecting women are similar to those affecting *all* disadvantaged groups. But women do constitute a special situation. My interviews with women lawyers and other professionals were filled with experiences of differential treatment stemming from the fact that they were women as well as lawyers. Remarkably, the victims showed little sense of outrage. They were often aware that the definitions of justice for women professionals varied substantially from the definitions applied to men, both within the professional community and outside of it.[11] As a group, for lawyers of their age, ability and experience, they voluntarily chose to work at levels beneath their capabilities and expressed lack of commitment to the profession by taking part-time jobs. A few women who had strong aspirations early in their careers radically reduced them. Although men do this as well, it is clear that the overwhelming majority of men in similar positions (for example, with three or four years' investment in career) push hard to get ahead. The paucity of striving was evident in the cases of the women studied, but what was more striking was their belief that reducing aspiration was entirely appropriate and that they did it without regret.

TYPES OF REWARD-PUNISHMENT AMBIGUITY

The manipulation of rewards and punishments in the professions and in the larger society create ambiguities for women which often cripple their professional attainments.

A positive relationship between work, approval and advancement is construed by society as "justice;" conversely, a lack of reward for excellence is seen as "injustice." [12] But the clarity of this equation does not appear to extend to women with regard to reward for work. It is clear that women who go into law practice can have a "successful" career. Of course, as for men, measures of success are relative.

Income is an indicator of success that can be measured with accuracy. The women lawyers I interviewed in 1965–66 reported fairly high earnings—a median of $13,500 per year—and forty percent of the respondents reported earning $16,000 or more per year.[13] The incomes reported by respondents who worked full time—two-thirds of the full sample—averaged nearly $20,000 per year.

Precise information is unavailable on the incomes of male New York attorneys, but discussions with law practitioners indicate that the incomes reported by these women lawyers, though lower than their male colleagues, are reasonably close to what the males' earnings would be if they were in the same types of practices—the "female specializations" of matrimonial and real estate law and probate work.

Partnership is another indicator of reward, but it is more difficult to appraise because the prestige conferred by it is measured by the size of the firm, the specialty to which the partnership is attached, and how many years it has taken the lawyer to become a partner. Several of the women in my early sample were members of partnerships with varying degrees of prestige. Of the nine women I interviewed who were partners, one was a semi-retired partner in a large firm (one of a grand total of three women partners in Wall Street firms at the time) and four were partners in medium-sized firms, all of good reputation. Four others were partners in smaller firms, three of them in partnerships with husbands. By the standards of the profession all of these women must be considered successes, even if they had not attained the pinnacle of the profession. Griffen (1958) has assembled some national statistics, unfortunately a bit old now, which indicate that on the average when women attain partnerships they do not tend to be partnerships of the highest quality.[14] Historically women were assigned low-ranking specialties and therefore tended to get low-ranking partnerships.

High-ranking jobs were attained by several of the women in the sample: one was a municipal court judge, several were private practitioners with large practices, one was a city commissioner. But though these women were successful, they did not believe they were as successful *as the men who constituted their reference group,* nor as measured by their own standards of accomplishment. The judge, for example, felt she could have gotten an appointment to a more prestigious court had she been a man.

The rewards of women professionals may also be more closely linked to their female status than to their status as professionals.

These situations are not uncommon in other elite systems in which women are rewarded in terms of their female status rather than their occupational status or roles. Bright women graduate students are often satisfied with gifts of approval and attention from professors for whom they work and are content with the vicarious pleasure of contributing ideas as an ancillary partner.

Like wives who act as research assistants for their husbands (without benefit of title) they are seldom given co-authorship or even footnotes acknowledging specific contributions. Like the wives, they are given florid acknowledgements in prefaces. But professional reputations are built on publication and citation; not on dedications.

Because women are typically considered to be outside the exchange system, the rewards for their efforts may not correspond to normative exchange rates. Furthermore, if they accept love instead of money where money is appropriate, they are conspirators in driving their own price down or in accepting alternative definitions of the worth and kind of performance they are rendering, and the goals they are seeking. Instead of becoming a true disciple, entitled to the senior person's sponsorship for launching her career, the woman is defined as being outside the system. I suspect that women's talents in professional activity often go unnoticed because of this phenomenon. On the other hand, their work is still utilized and "waste" is reduced. Women's talent is probably tapped in this way more than the talent of any other group of "outsiders." The others' prices may be too high in that, unlike women, they would insist on being brought into the system.

Despite the ambiguities of the reward system, women, like their male colleagues, are "punished" by the profession for violating its norms. The women in my sample who worked part-time and had discontinuous career lines made less money on average than their male colleagues and were not awarded high-ranking jobs. Since they did not aim high and exhibited little assertiveness, they were not given career-line jobs or assigned clients who could assure them positions of power. Their histories illustrate that there are certain absolute professional standards which, if not met, result in negative consequences.

The ambivalence-producing mechanisms which reduce women's representation at the top of the elite structures are shown clearly in the cases of women who are *not rewarded for good professional performances* and *women who are punished for good professional performance*. The latter is the result of role-conflict stemming from expectations that fulfillment of professional role obligations will entail violation of role obligations attached to the woman's sex and family statuses.[15]

Many of the women lawyers interviewed felt they were under-rewarded for good professional performance. Many had the experience of seeing men in their firms rising to partnership while they were frozen at associate rank despite demonstrably equivalent competence. Even women who could be considered successful by male career standards often feel relatively deprived; that is, they believe they should be regarded as *great!*

Part of the problem stems from women's lack of power in the bargaining process. Power is itself a reward, but a degree of power must somehow be attained to bargain successfully for more. No powerful client will permit an important case to be handled by an associate, and many associates achieve partnership for this reason, but women do not often have powerful clients who will press the firm to make them partners. One lawyer interviewed who had long waited for partnership pointed out that if she had brought a substantial number of clients to the firm she could not have been refused partnership because she could have threatened to leave and take them with her.

The women attorneys I interviewed felt unanimously that they had to "be better" than male lawyers. But being better only gave them the opportunity to be where they were; it was needed to cancel the disadvantage of their negative-sex-status, and they did not feel it necessarily gave them entree to career advancement. Some felt that since more effort did not win them promotion, there was little sense in commitment to hard work and they refused extra or overtime assignments.

The case of the woman who succeeds in her profession but is punished for supposed violation of her female role obligations—a violation which is presumed if she is a success—is equally destructive. Here the woman is the object of sanctions, both from alters in the professional sphere who believe that success detracts from a woman's femininity, and from alters in her family who feel that her success makes their relationships insecure or uncomfortable.

Although men acquire added ranking in *all* spheres when they are rated a success in their work, at times the woman seems to be subject to a zero-sum evaluation in which the greater her occupational accomplishment, the more likely she is to be rated lower in her performance of female roles. This evaluation usually is not based on whether or not she can take care of both her clients and family, but is due to cultural *assumptions* that she is neglecting her family.[16]

The successful woman lawyer continually meets expressions of ambivalence in the evaluation of her role performance. Respondents reported being told that they were taking work away from less successful male lawyers. One was told she "thought like a man" by her colleagues, who offered it as a compliment but implied that she was less of a woman for it. Two successful women who did trial work claimed that opposing attorneys complained they often won by female "wiles"; but other respondents were told by male lawyers that women attorneys who do not use wiles are "masculine." Here women are subjected to the "damned if you do, damned if you don't" syndrome experienced by other people with negatively evaluated statuses (Merton, 1957b: 426).

To some extent women have the same experiences as men who are being phased out of the running for important jobs. The messages, for example, are disguised as protective "concerns." One respondent reported that an employer denied her promotion because "it would be too demanding of her energy"; another because she would be hurt by hostility in a truly male domain. Some women saw through such explanations and experienced them as sanctions, but many accepted them at face value. This was especially so when it was a husband-partner who was "protecting" her from her profession.

The sanctions attached to violation of female-role performance are often relevant where women are experiencing professional success. The women who made high professional incomes rarely seemed to view these as a desired symbol of success or an unmitigated reward. There was evidence that some respondents would view a sharp gain in income as an intolerable burden on their relationships with their husbands. Few men view a rise in their incomes as a burden or destructive to their other roles.

These professional women's "sense of reward" was related primarily to their husbands' incomes. They reported a sense of accomplishment from their earnings, but it was true that those reporting the highest incomes generally were married to wealthy men and conceded their personal earnings had ceased to matter. For women, financial reward may not have the consequence of motivating them for future performance in the same way it does for men. Significantly, as many high-income respondents dropped out of practice as stayed in.

The case of the woman who does not comply with professional norms but is rewarded anyway is sociologically interesting because it runs counter to common sense and arouses the cultural distaste reserved for those who "get something for nothing." This involves two sets of phenomena: too much acclaim for routine performance; and acclaim for little or no performance. In the latter case, the woman typically violates professional norms by her lack of commitment, working only occasionally or dropping out altogether at the peak of her career; yet she continues to enjoy prestige in her family and community, although probably not in her profession. She is honored for *having been* a lawyer, although a man who leaves the profession and does not work is generally labeled a has-been and failure.

Women, especially married women, settle for lower incomes because having any income gives them a feeling of accomplishment and making too much might cause trouble. Even single women in my lawyers sample who were concerned about providing for themselves did not have high economic aspirations.

For women lawyers especially, membership in a high-ranking male occupation is itself an indicator of great success to the world outside the profession. The women in the study who had a network of friends who were not lawyers felt little impulse to rise within the profession; they had attained sufficient rank by just entering law. The woman's network, whether or not her friends were working women, was always important to her evaluation of her career.

The ambivalence of expectations and rewards faced by women professionals arises from the following conflict:

1. Normative prescriptions for attainment of occupational success require that the professional demonstrate commitment, talent and hard work.

2. But normative prescriptions weigh against women's occupational success because the female role requires a lack of assertiveness and a non-competitive work role vis-a-vis men and is assumed to require a fundamental commitment to home and family.

3. There are also normative prescriptions that women are incapable of conforming to professional norms, with the consequence that different standards are applied to their performance.

4. Women professionals are subject to a contradictory reward structure which may confer rewards not commensurate with the levels of their performance or contributions to the profession. Further, success may brand them as failures in the larger society, or, concomitantly, failure in a profession may result in rewards from the larger society.

Although the control systems of the elite professions violate the rule of universalism with respect to women, this violation does not undermine the professions' general normative structure. Within the professions, by undermining the motivation of women to engage their talents at the highest levels, this control process maintains the cohesion of the collegial group, makes for ease of social intercourse in the male legal community, and reduces competition.

NOTES

[1] As in my other analyses of women's place in the professions, the discussion of the dynamics of status-set interaction draws on the conceptualizations of Robert K. Merton which have not as yet reached print, but which have reached audiences through "oral publication" (again, his concept) over the past decade in lectures at Columbia University.

[2] The analysis presented here developed from earlier inquiries (1965–1966) into the place of women in the professions (Epstein, 1968, 1970b). The insights and theory presented derived from intensive personal interviews with sixty-five lawyers who practice in New York City and environs chosen from the Martindale-Hubbell Law Directory. Although this discussion leans on their accounts, later studies added interviews with women doctors, social scientists, physical scientists, architects, journalists and administrators. Their career profiles and experiences have given further evidence that the patterns suggested by earlier interviews were indeed institutionalized in other elite professional spheres.

[3] Harriet Zuckerman has brought to my attention one example of the different and lower standards used in evaluating eminence of women as compared with men in American society. Because Americans of achievement listed in Who's Who, a directory of prominent people in the United States, tend to be almost entirely men, a separate volume, Who's Who of American Women, was introduced in 1958. In establishing criteria for inclusion the editors noted in their preface to that first edition that they were "scaling down" the Who's Who standards because (as they said in their letter to potential listees) for women, "national or international prominence . . . is not a requisite." (See Preface to Who's Who of American Women, First Edition, 1958–1959, and most recent form letter dated 1968.)

[4] Nor are they equally endowed with personal "connections." Connections can be important, especially in steering the neophyte professional to a promising first job, though presumably they are less important in achievement-oriented fields. It is true, however, that under certain circumstances and in certain sub-fields of the professions, the well-connected lesser talent has opportunities and rewards denied the greater talent.

[5] Cole found that women Ph.D.s, as a group, had higher measured intelligence than men at every level and in every field of science even when controlling for specialization and quality of doctorate department.

[6] At this point I feel I must at least note the constraints of language in using the generic "he" for "the person." Although "he or she" would certainly be more appropriate as a substitute, it is awkward. I will restrict my energies currently toward an identification of processes which result in the cultural identification of "professional" with a male-gender pronoun, and leave it to the linguists to come up with a neuter-gender pronoun resonant with language style.

[7] Only groups such as the owners and managers of large businesses consistently attain higher incomes than successful professionals. United States Bureau of the Census, Statistical Abstract of the United States: (1960: 325).

[8] See Richard H. Hall (1969: 70–137), for an analytic review of the literature in the field of professions.

[9] Thus the conditions for creation of role strain are ameliorated by activation of a number of social mechanisms reducing it for the professional person —by insulating him and providing him with a hierarchy of priorities (Goode, 1960a; Merton, 1957a).

[10] Abel (1963) and Kucera (1963) reported the results of a survey done by the *Harvard Law Record* of 430 private law firms, of all sizes, and throughout the country, which indicated extreme resistence to hiring women, members of minority groups and those candidates with rural backgrounds or fathers in blue-collar occupations. Jews, Negroes and women were most consistently rated negatively. Of all the "deviant" statuses reviewed, the female drew the most negative rating (4.9 on a scale of from zero to plus 10 for those least likely to be hired). *Only poor scholarship drew greater opprobrium than being female.*

[11] Homans (1961: 325) poses this "role" of distributive justice as: "a man's reward in exchange with others should be proportional to his investments."

[12] If, according to Homans, justice is an equation between investment and reward, and women are believed to make less of an investment (background characteristics such as sex, race and ethnicity are included with hard work as "investments"), then they should not expect as much reward as a man who has "put in" a *higher* investment (i.e., by being male). Homans (1961: 236–237) further suggests that being Negro or a woman is an *unchanging* value, unlike "experience" (another investment), which increases with time. If one takes the legal profession as the context in which the appraisal of justice is being made, the woman is not unfairly treated, since it is true that, on balance, women are believed to have a lesser investment in the structure than do men. If "society" is taken as the structure, the balance scale is not as clearly weighted. If women in law (as a group) are taken as structure, then a different system of weights and values surely emerges. We do not agree with Homans that we are using an "olympian" view of justice when we appraise as "injustice" the situation in which women get a lesser reward for hard work than men. Goffman's perception of the situation seems to hold more truth: that "in America at present, *separate* systems of honor seem to be on the decline," and that even those with so-called "abnormal" characteristics have come to believe *they* "deserve a fair chance and a fair break." (Goffman, 1963: 7). See George C. Homans' (1961: 232–264) discussion of the "principle of distributive justice" and its application for behavior.

[13] The data reported here on women lawyers may be found in detail in my Ph.D. dissertation (Epstein, 1968) and appears in *Women Lawyers* (Epstein, 1972).

[14] Her information is from *The Bar Register*, 1957, which rates three thousand firms as preeminent in the profession on the basis of investigations and recommendations from local bar members and groups. Thirty-two of the three thousand firms listed women as partners. The thirty-two firms reported thirty-five women among their 262 partners.

[15] This has as source and consequence two types of sociological ambivalence. The first, specified by Robert K. Merton and Elinor Barber (1963), comes from the conflicting demands of different statuses ordinarily involving different people (e.g., demands of the senior partner *vs.* demands of the woman attorney's husband). The second is a type in which ambivalence arises from conflicting expectations of role partners in a role-set attached to one status because of visibility of the role incumbent's other statuses.

[16] An example of differential expectations directed to men and women in political elites in Germany is reported by Harriet Holter (1970: 113). In an assessment of attitudes about women active in political life, those holding political office were considered unfeminine and were believed to neglect their families by a majority of people. No such view was held of the men in political life.

Anne K. Peters

Aspiring Hollywood Actresses: A Sociological Perspective

The title of this paper may evoke images of starry-eyed young ladies gazing with envy at the theatre marquees on Hollywood Boulevard. The images are not incorrect, but these are incomplete. One of the purposes of this study and of any sociological study of a particular occupation is to demonstrate the complexities of that occupation. Without an intense probing of the subject under scrutiny, what is to be understood will remain superficially appreciated and in no further need of explanation. The world of the Hollywood actress is publicized in ways which allow people to feel very familiar with this occupation. An aim of the present study is to illuminate certain features of acting and of show business (the entire area of social life concerned with the commercial performing arts) so that they can be compared to features of other occupations studied by sociologists. The relationships and contrasts drawn will add to the knowledge of our occupational system.

This paper is part of a larger study which contains much more data than is possible to present here (Peters, 1971). Therefore, after a brief description of the study's methods, the points most relevant to the work life of an actress will be discussed.

METHOD: PARTICIPANT OBSERVATION AND INTERVIEWING

In order to study aspiring actresses, I situated myself so that I would have access to actresses in the routines of their daily lives. During 1968 and 1969, I lived for over eight months in the Hollywood Studio Club, where eighty other young women were living. The residents were

39

aspiring singers, actresses (twenty-eight were interviewed), dancers, musicians and some non-show business employees. This situation was fortunate for me in two ways. The supervisory staff at the Studio Club was in favor of my plans for the study, and as a female of approximately the same age as the young women who lived at the Studio Club, I did not look conspicuous as "someone doing a sociological study." Besides living with the actresses, I did other types of participating which increased my understanding—"making the rounds" of a few agents, taking an acting class, and working one day on a feature film as part of an enormous crowd. On such occasions I took field notes.

The depth interviewing of twenty-eight aspiring actresses did not begin until after I had established a rapport with each actress. Also specific questions were not formulated until I became familiar with the argot and world view of actresses. Melville Dalton states:

> . . . the technique (participant observation) enables the inquirer to avoid questions which often cause ridicule behind his back and injure the research in unconsidered ways. (Dalton, 1964:75)

Among the questions asked were some I felt required much rapport during the interviews, because they involve the "self" an actress presents to those in her field who matter (see Goffman, 1959). These were the questions concerning age, sexual relations with men in show business, and acting jobs.

Age is a problem for any actor. The problem is compounded for actresses by the cultural peculiarities which disparage aging females. Many of the actresses stated that they never reveal their true age in a "professional" context. They broadcast a "professional age," which means actual age cut by two to five years. Everyone engages in this practice because the film industry will not generally hire actors who are older than the age for which a part is written. This adaptation to the sparse employment situation is fostered by actors' agents and others concerned with publicity. Several of the actresses in the study report their agents have specifically directed them to adopt a "professional age."

The question of sexual relations with men in show business may bring to mind the legend of the "casting couch." The real question being raised is exploitation of people both on the part of the actress and on the part of those who may have some power over her acting career. Answering with extreme candidness, they generally agreed that getting involved with a man who has some power over their careers is dangerous. A few suggested that "in the right situation" it would be a good way to further their careers, "if they could handle it."

It has been noted by others that there is a tendency among actors to embellish their answers to questions concerning the history and progress of their careers (see McHugh, 1966: 1–2). In a situation relating to employment, an actor is generally called upon to list his theatrical credits. Because of the intense competition in the field, actors must try to make their accomplishments sound better than those of competitors for a role and are likely to exaggerate their credits. One actor encountered during the study confessed that he tended to make the parts he had played sound much more important than they had actually been. It is most important for people to establish and maintain a positive image in show business circles. Reasons for this include: (1) the lack of prescribed criteria for judging the worth of an actor; (2) the penchant among show businessmen for "discovery" of actors with unique, charismatic qualities; (3) the great financial reward for the producers of a successful show.

What follows will deal primarily with the information derived from answers to questions on the meaning of a career in acting as well as daily activities and in-the-field observations.

ACTING AS A CAREER

One of the most salient features of acting is the lack of a prescribed route for entering the field and then for progressing in a logical pattern within the field. Acting is often called a profession, especially by persons in show business. Yet, it exhibits few of the characteristics of a profession, such as specified training and required credentials. Because careers are generally attributed to luck and "breaks," young actresses do not discern any particular set of steps to be followed on the way to making a career of acting. There are a few activities actresses can engage in without waiting for "breaks." These have consequences for the career, though they are not always necessary and predictable.

Training. One activity in which most actors and actresses engage is the study of acting. Contrary to my original conceptions of aspiring actresses in Hollywood, I find there is a tendency for these actresses not to identify themselves solely with Hollywood. They are quite cosmopolitan in that they travel between New York City and Los Angeles to seek acting jobs. Thus, there is a basis for considering acting in the United States as a unified occupation, not necessarily split between those who do stage work exclusively in New York and those who do film work exclusively in Hollywood.

New York City takes on special significance in the training of actors and actresses. While observing casting interviews for a television series

at a major film studio, one point came across very clearly. People doing the casting were much more interested in the possibility of hiring
actresses who had some training in New York; they were especially
pleased if the actress had worked in legitimate theatre. From what I
have gathered in other situations also, New York actors are generally
looked upon more favorably in Hollywood than are actors who have
been trained locally. One actress sums up the situation with the following words:

> New York actors are different, you know. I think that we are a little more
> sophisticated. We've done things, you know, like gone to voice teachers
> and stuff like that. A lot of actors out there just don't know all these tricks
> that you learn. And those teachers . . . in New York—that's where the
> teachers are.

Judging from conversations with people in production, it appears that,
all else being equal, the producer of a film or television show will prefer
hiring New York trained actors for the small parts, parts too small for
"name" actors to play. This is done mainly for economic considerations,
particularly in television, because shows are cast quickly and have to be
put together speedily. The better trained the actor, the better performance he can be counted on to give without taking up much of the
director's time. A common complaint among the actresses of the study
who had done film and television work is that there is very little direction. Whether or not a particular New York actor is actually more
capable than his Hollywood counterpart is generally not an issue to be
debated. The mystique of New York training is taken for granted, and
so the mystique is nourished in objective employment experience.

The mystique of New York training for an actor or actress is similar
to the imagery and appeal of having graduated from an Ivy League
college. In neither case is a person trained in such a setting necessarily
superior to persons trained in other settings. Yet, the persons themselves,
their prospective employers, and others with whom they deal will attribute to them a gratuitous superior ability and competence which
holds real social and economic consequences.

The world of show business is a particularly good setting for the
observation of social interaction on the basis of mystique, or notions
about people who have yet to prove themselves. One characteristic of
show business which may foster the growth of and action upon "fantas-
tically" conceived notions is the fact that there is no prescribed way to
build a career in acting or in any other phase of show business. The only
ultimate standard to which a person can refer is popularity with audiences. Who or what will be popular with the public is professed to be

incalculable. On the other hand, the agents of publicity are well aware that actors can be "sold" to the public. So what really remains incalculable is which actors will receive publicity on what basis.

Drama Classes. Every actress living at the Hollywood Studio Club during the period of the research had studied acting for several months at least, whether or not she had been to New York. The major way in which acting is studied is through classes run by drama teachers who allow anyone who can pay to enroll (usually the rate is about forty dollars per month, with two classes per week). Several of the actresses have been able at some time to qualify for admittance to classes of well-known teachers, who require stringent auditions and credits, as well as the usual fee. Some have studied acting at college and may have augmented this training with private classes in New York and/or Los Angeles.

The study of acting is one of the positive steps an actress or actor can take to help establish a career. However, the only training which may materially assist the actor or actress in getting a job (besides the intrinsic worth of the training) is training with a well-known teacher. This credential, which is part of the mystique, seems to carry weight in casting interviews.

Since no training at all is *required* for anyone to call himself or herself an actor or an actress, there must be other factors which are considered more crucial to pursuing a career in acting than drama classes. The factor which seems most crucial, about which most folklore is constructed, is acquiring an agent.

Agents. An agent, particularly in Hollywood, is a businessman (or businesswoman) who has access to information on when what producer is casting what roles for what shows. This information is not generally available to actors, and even if it were, they could not make appointments for casting interviews without the sponsorship of an agent. The problem thus becomes one of finding an agent who is influential enough with producers to have much information about shows being produced and to have sufficient weight to get his clients lined up for interviews. There is no question about the necessity of acquiring an agent. An actor must have an agent if he is to act professionally.

An agent is hired by an actor at the rate of ten percent of the actor's salary to be the actor's representative vis-à-vis people who cast shows. In practice, it does not work out that an actor has a free choice of agents. Even though it is the actor who pays the agent for representation, an actor must first be chosen by an agent. The agent does not want to be burdened with too many people to represent. Also, an agent prefers to have a "stable" of various "types" of actors so that he can send out one actor of each type to casting interviews which call for a particular type. Thus, his actors will not be competing against each other for the same roles. This is an ideal account of how the agent-actor system operates. One of the major abuses of the system reported by the actresses in the present study is an agent's sending out more than one actor for the same part thus increasing his own chances of making the ten percent commission. There are so many actors competing for agents franchised by Screen Actors Guild that the agents can pick and choose whomever they wish to represent.

Since acquiring an agent is one of the few tangible steps an actress or actor can take toward establishing a career, there is much concern about agents among the Hollywood Studio Club actresses. The two bases upon which agents seem to choose actors present problems to the actor. As mentioned above, agents think of actors and actresses in terms of "types." Secondly, agents seem to think of themselves as gamblers who take chances upon actors with "unique qualities," which are qualities indefinable. It is these two factors which show what an actor ought to do to attract an agent. Much lore is built around these two points and much socialization among actors themselves seems to center around these.

Discovery of Unique Qualities. The desire on the part of agents to discover someone who has those qualities which constitute a potential "star" behooves the actor or actress to appear unique to agents. I asked the question of the actresses in my sample, "Is there anyone after whom you model yourself as an actress?" The answer reveals a consistent consciousness of this requirement to be unique among actresses. I was told one could not copy anyone else; there would be no point in it and no satisfaction in it.

The situation in which I was made most aware of this "presentation of self" problem for the actress was when I asked advice on how to make the rounds of agents. I was told by several actresses: (1) Go to the agent's office after 6:00 P.M. so that his secretary will not be there, and (2) *Do something to make yourself look unique.* The latter direction was not spelled out in detail; it could not be. Somehow it involved being able to talk to the agent alone in a manner which would make him take notice.

If presenting oneself as unique were the only problem the actor had, it would still be difficult to deal with because uniqueness is so indefinite. However, when coupled with the second thing an agent is looking for—a definite "type"—the problem is compounded.

Casting for most roles in all productions is done by type. This is not always true for lead roles, where a particular actor's talent may be more crucial than his type. "Type" refers to such stereotypes as "the ingenue," "the chubby," "the he-man," "the girl next door," and so on. There are complex reasons for the development of type-casting, the most obvious of which is that audiences expect actors to "look their part." Also, it is efficient to be able to call in actors of a particular type for casting; otherwise it would take forever to cast every part in a show.

How does the Hollywood Studio Club actress deal with the expectation she should be a particular type? The answer is fairly clear-cut; she addresses herself to being a type, or maybe several types. A type is a reasonably tangible object to orient oneself toward. It is something concrete an actor or actress can develop as part of the process of making a career in acting. Actresses are able to classify themselves and to dress appropriately for the type they wish to convey. They go to great pains to present themselves as the correct type for a certain role in a casting interview. It is not only clothes, but also make-up and demeanor upon which they concentrate before going to an interview. A traumatic experience for an actress is not knowing anything about the role she is being interviewed for beforehand.

There is a structural inconsistency here with which the actor must deal on a personal level. There are demands from show business that the actor be both unique and classifiable as a type. Presumably, both of these attributes can mean a profit for everyone involved in a production. On the one hand, it is thought that an actor who has a unique quality will become a star and will thus make money on his "personality." On the other hand, an actor is useful to the extent he can be easily cast into certain types of roles, thus assuring everyone involved of a steady income. The actor himself does not have the power to resolve this conflict, as he is not in charge of productions. The resolution, then, has to be a pragmatic compromise and a desire that someone actually will discover his uniqueness even while he is playing stereotyped roles.

Creating a Career. The notion of a career in acting cannot be similar to the notion of a career in a more usual profession, which requires specific training, degrees, sponsorship, adherence to a set of ethics, etc. (see Barber, 1963: 669–688). Aside from becoming proficient as an actor and acquiring an agent, there are no steps and no formulas that actors are able to establish. Success and failure are almost always attributed to luck. This feeling of normlessness and unpredictability is described by one of the Hollywood Studio Club actresses who has had a modicum of success:

> Now all these people that are trying to break into show business are not going to have realistic answers, because they do not know how to get into show business . . . And all the people who have gotten some place in show business do not know how they did it either . . . And if I had it to

do over again, I would have no idea, even having gone through this. If I had all the knowledge I have now, and I was starting all over again, I would not know how to do it because there is no formula.

If any career in any occupation is sociologically analyzed, it can be demonstrated that there have been unpredictable contingencies which have contributed to whatever standard of failure or success apply to that career. The question is *why is such unpredictability institutionalized for acting, whereas in other professions the general assumption of predictability is made?* If this question could be answered, it would probably tell us why actors are given more license to break the rules of society than are most other people. Perhaps part of the essence of being an actor is to possess "charisma," or "starlike qualities," to employ a phrase commonly used by people in show business. If charisma is institutionalized and routinized (see Weber, 1964: 358–386), it is no longer a "gift of grace" possessed by a unique individual, placing him outside the realm of the ordinary. The answer might also tell us that standards of success in show business are quite different from standards in other occupations. It may be the difference between being a well-known, respected physicist and a Nobel laureate. The former and the latter could both be considered to have had successful careers. However, the actor may not feel he is successful unless he becomes, like the Nobel laureate, a "star."

Seventy percent of the Hollywood Studio Club actresses stated they would like to be stars. In a sense, stardom is more realistic a goal for an actress or actor than the Nobel prize is for a physicist. The less distinguished physicist is able to engage fully in his occupation without tremendous recognition. However, the only way in which an actor can gain power enough in his occupation to choose the roles he desires to perform is to be a star, to be in great demand. These distinguishing marks of the occupation of acting deserve greater study, because they would explain a great deal about the society which sustains such an occupation. It may be that people who live in a rather routinized society desire some extraordinary figures to emulate. One such figure may be the American actor. Others may include people in similar occupations who are exposed as specially gifted by the mass media (e.g., painters, musicians).

OCCUPATIONAL DIGNITY

Acting is functional in a positive sense for the self-esteem of the person who chooses to be an actor or an actress. During the course of the present study, many of the actressess stated they felt acting was fun, satisfying and fulfilling in ways that most occupations are not. The life of an actress is not dull and routine, although it may be insecure and offer few exciting roles. This element of life style is very important when considering the self-definitions of actors and actresses.

Only thirteen of the twenty-eight Hollywood Studio Club actresses had ever made a living from acting. The others survive by taking part-time or full-time jobs to which they are not dedicated. A few have inheritances. It seems to this observer that one of the most attractive things about the occupation of acting is its life style, even when at times that life style is lamented. To someone who assigns great value to the occupation of acting, who is proud to be an actor or actress, the idea of taking odd jobs while waiting for "a break" must seem better than working steadily at any other occupation. A person who calls himself or herself an actor or an actress can maintain dignity even when the financial struggle is extremely difficult, because it is legitimate to identify with the occupation of acting without making a living at it.

Dealing specifically with actresses now, it can be pointed out that there are very few prestigious occupations in which women stand an equal chance with men of succeeding to the point of winning some degree of eminence. Acting is the only occupation that comes to mind as not being composed predominantly of one sex or the other. And, it offers the successful female the same status and financial rewards it does the successful male. When a young woman identifies herself as an actress, she does not have to give up hope for being occupationally successful. If the actress takes a secretarial job, she is not compelled to identify with it as the best occupation she will ever have. She can maintain much higher hopes as an actress. This is the attitude I shall label *occupational dignity*.

Occupational dignity is the sense one can derive from identification with acting. This identification is functional for bolstering self-esteem, so that a person does not give up ambitions for success at great odds. Probably some of the same functions operate for male actors, though their occupational alternatives are not narrowly circumscribed by office work and school teaching. However, it is much better for a man to be able to think of himself as an actor than as a parking lot attendant or as a movie usher.

Examining the phenomenon called acting will reveal two features of occupations in the United States. First, future orientation toward success through a career is very important in this society. Actors espouse these deferred success values perhaps more than anyone else in the society, because it is they who must totally orient themselves to the fantasy of one day achieving success through stardom. There is no success for an actor unless he is well-known. What can be called a drive for eminence (see Turner, 1964: 284) is perhaps typical of all artists, at least of all performing artists. The unknown must look toward the day when he will be in a position to express himself grandly. This hope for the future keeps people striving and staves off rebellious discontent.

The second feature of the American occupational structure is revealed by the fact that there are far too many actors for acting jobs available. For those people who have chosen to gamble their lives in this occupation, life may be tolerable because of the dignity that hope for a "break" can bring. But if success in acting is so unlikely, then it would seem reasonable for most actors to give up. Yet just the opposite behavior is reasonable if one faces up to the quality of life the majority of regular jobs offer. There is much competition for the kinds of jobs (generally the professions) which lend dignity to their holders. Many jobs in this society are dull and menial. From this point of view it is quite understandable that actors view the occupation of acting as a salvation, as a repository of dignity and hope which few other people experience.

Jessie Bernard

The Housewife:
Between Two Worlds

There is no category of workers, male or female, which remotely approaches the category "housewife" in size. Housewives include at least half of all women sixteen years of age and over in the United States.[1] None of the work they do as housewives has economic, in the technical sense of market, value. Its societal value, however, is generally conceded to be literally incalculable. It is the purpose of this paper to explore the nature of this paradox in terms of a conflict between two paradigms—the economic and the societal. Much of our thinking about the housewife is handicapped by a gap between these two models, leaving us with policy choices based on incompatible assumptions, values, and goals. Either of these models alone is inadequate to deal with the problems generated by modern industrial trends, and the housewife remains caught between policies based on the two models.

After a brief overview of several versions of the basic conflict between two kinds of models—economic versus societal, status-world versus cash-nexus, pre-industrial versus industrial—the effects on the housewife of these opposing ways of viewing her work will be examined. For example, viewed from the outlook of the economic model, housewifery is not an occupation, the housewife is not in the labor force nor is she even in industrial society. Viewed from the outlook of the societal paradigm, the housewife is in a status "love-and/or-duty" relationship to the "clients" she works for. In the last section, proposals for integrating the housewife into modern industrial society will be examined.

INCOMPATIBLE MODELS

The economic and the societal models have been compared and contrasted by Mancur Olson, Jr. (1968: 114) who concludes that:

> . . . the economic and sociological ideals described [by the economic and the societal models] are not only different, but polar opposites: if either one were attained, the society would be a nightmare in terms of the other. . . . The important question is how much of the one ideal to give up in order to get more of the other when you can't get more of both. . . . The economic and sociological ideals, far from both being destroyed by their contradiction with one another, are in fact expressions of the most fundamental alternatives human societies face. . . .

A related contrast has been made between what Talcott Parsons calls the domestic and the occupational world in which the first is governed by particularistic status norms and the second, by universalistic, impersonal ones; the first is characterized by traditional norms, the second, by rigorously functional ones (Parsons, 1959: 261).

These two statements of the contrasting models are recent versions of a long tradition of social-science preoccupation with the revolutionary change in human relationships that came with the industrial revolution. Sir Henry Maine was among the first to analyze it; he characterized the preindustrial world as a status world and the industrial one then emerging as a contractual world. Others characterized it as a cash-nexus or money-mediated world.

The terms "status" and "cash-nexus" or "money-mediated" worlds are used here since they highlight the particular aspect of the two models considered most relevant to a discussion of the housewife. The housewife works in a status world in which motivation is expected to be based on love and/or duty rather than in a cash-nexus world in which it is taken for granted that motivation is based on wages, salaries, or other monetary incentives. The old saying, "I wouldn't do that for love or money" recognizes the contrasting motivations in the two worlds. The housewife is called upon to make all the adjustments demanded by the incompatible models.

The position of the housewife is an excellent starting point for a discussion of the difficulties involved in attempting to deal theoretically with the situation. Parsons, for example, has given us his version of how our society in the past has attempted to deal with the matter of incongruent paradigms: only one person in the family could be dealt with according to the economic model; applying the economic model to the domestic world would be disastrous, but applying the societal paradigm to the labor force would be equally so. So the husband was assigned to the cash-nexus world and the wife to the status world.

THE WORK COMPONENT OF HOUSEWIFERY

The actual, specific tasks involved in housewifery vary widely according to size of household, income of family, social class standards, facilities and equipment available, and no doubt many other relevant variables. They usually include at least shopping or "procurement," food preparation, cleaning, and laundering. These are all amenable to the same kind of job analysis as the components of any other kind of work. And, in fact, there is a long tradition of such analyses by home economists. In the nineteenth century, for example, the great state colleges of agricultural and mechanic arts had established, along with agricultural and engineering schools for men, schools of home economics for women. Household management was viewed as a perfectly respectable subject in colleges of home economics.

But not all of the efforts to glorify "women's work" succeeded. A woman could be trained to be ever so competent in household management, quite professional, in fact. But housework remained housework. No amount of scientific knowhow or romantic glorification in the women's magazines could finally hide the fact that it was low on any prestige scale. Little by little a change came over the colleges of home economics. Emphasis on the hard sciences increased while interest in domestic skills decreased. There was more physiology and nutrition, less food preservation and cooking; more chemistry of textiles, less sewing; more social psychology, anthropology, and economics of fashion, less tailoring. The schools were now, in brief, training professional women rather than housewives, producing domestic engineers who could design the most efficient arrangement of kitchen equipment rather than housewives.[2] These highly trained women went into the labor force rather than into the home. The women who went into the home still had to carry on the low-level work.

THE HOUSEWIFE IN THE ECONOMIC MODEL

The only component of housewifery that is recognized in the economic model is that of "procurement." The housewife does most of the shopping and marketing for food and clothing; she is therefore salient as a consumer. But as worker she has no place in the economic model: her work does not constitute an occupation; she is not in the labor force; she is not even in industrial society.

Housewifery Is Not an Occupation. The housewife does not, according to the economic model, have an occupation. For although running a household may fully occupy most of her waking hours, and even though what she does may be the hardest kind of work, it has none of the characteristics associated with an occupation (Bernard, 1971b: 74). Helena Lopata (1971: 139) states:

> . . . there is no organized social circle which tests a candidate and then admits or rejects her on the basis of proven skills. She enters the role "sideways," as an adjunct to the role of wife . . . In addition, the role is not easily located in the occupational social structure. . . . It lacks the basic criteria of most jobs. It has no organized social circle which judges performance and has the right to fire for incompetence, no specific pay scale, and no measurement against other performers of the same role or against circle members. It is vague, open to any woman who gets married, regardless of ability; it has no union and belongs to no organizational structure.

Why, then, is the housewife included in the present volume? She is included here because her work is, sociologically speaking, *sui generis.* It is wholly outside of the occupational world, a negative case that, by way of contrast, helps to highlight other occupations.

"To housewife" and "to husband" both once meant to economize, to manage with skill and thrift, one a household and one a farm. In such a sense the job of housewifery was, and is, the running of a household. The term as either verb or noun specifies the two characterizing aspects of housewifery as a job: it is done in a house and it is done by a wife. Merely having a house as the place of work does not, however, in and of itself set it off from other kinds of work. The same work done by a hired person of either sex is no longer housewifery but rather household management, housework or stewardship. What renders the housewife *sui generis* is that her marital status and hence her motivation is part of the job description; it is these aspects that remove her from the labor force.

The Housewife is Not in the Labor Force. The housekeeper or the steward is a member of the labor force, but the housewife who does identical work is not. The housewife does not inhabit the same world as do other workers.

The concept of the labor force came in with the industrial revolution. Before then there really was no such labor force as we know it today. Jaffe and Stewart (1951: 33) define the work force as including: "those persons—who voluntarily offer their services for hire in the labor market (in exchange for which they receive wages or salaries) and who thereby participate (or attempt to participate) in the production of the gross national product." The operant words are "voluntarily," "labor market," and "wages or salaries." So also is "production of the gross national product. But contribution to the gross national product is definitionally prohibited by the fact that housework is not paid for.

If paid for, the contribution of the housewife would vastly increase the gross national product. One study (Gronseth, 1970) reports it would increase our country's national income by almost two-fifths (38 percent) and a forensic economist (Soo, 1969: 271–284) has computed the value of the lost services to a man if his wife dies.[3] But since the housewife's work is not mediated in a labor market it does not count and including it in the labor force would not help economists understand the operations of the economy. "It would serve no purpose . . . to include housewives in a count of a country's working force," because their work, however socially desired, is extra-economic, so including them in the labor force "would have no relevance for the significant economic problems of our times" (Jaffe and Stewart: 14, 18). Again, since the housewife's work "is outside the characteristic system of work organization or production . . . for purposes of analyses of the functioning of the economy, as required for social policy decision" (Jaffe and Stewart: 14) including their extra-economic services would tell us nothing about the labor market or the way the economy was operating.

The Housewife Is Not in Industrial Society. Not everyone who worked in the primitive factories and mines of the eighteenth century was in the labor force; some were contracted by overseers of the poor who found this kind of employment an excellent way to deal with paupers. But for the most part, workers, especially adult males, were in the labor force voluntarily and were paid wages determined by the labor market. One may cavil at the adjective "voluntary" as applied to men in the labor force; but for most it was not forced, slave or indentured labor. One may cavil also at the wages paid, but for the most part it was in money. And one may cavil at the concept of market when the positions of hirer and hired were so unequal. Nevertheless, in the industrializing world men entered a cash-nexus, a world in which relationships were based on money. This was revolutionary and did revolutionize all human relationships.

Most women, however, remained at home, working as hard as ever at their domestic occupations. They did not enter the cash-nexus world mediated by money. They continued to live and work in the status world of the home in which one related to others on the basis of love and/or duty, not money.

The two worlds are widely different. The differences between a non-industrialized and a modern industrialized society are summarized by Jaffe and Stewart (1951: 28) this way:

Non-Industrialized World	Modern Industrialized World
Very low level of technological development	Very high level of technological development freeing many from the necessity of producing the needed physical goods
Almost no division of labor	Very highly developed division of labor
Each worker tends to own and control his means of production	Control of the means of production largely concentrated in a few persons or in the state
No exchange economy based on cash	Highly developed exchange economy based on cash
No notion of free contract; the culture determines the person's labor activities	Highly developed notion of free contract; the culture does not predetermine the individual's labor activities; rather he enters into free contractual relationships

Since the eighteenth century an increasing number of men have been moving into the labor force, the money-mediated or cash-nexus world. And in the twentieth century an increasing number of women have also moved into this world. But the housewife remains in the love and/or duty status world. Some people look back nostalgically to the time before the cash-nexus replaced the pre-industrial love and/or duty status world. Whether or not the money-mediated world is worse than the status world is moot. But one thing is certain: if half of the world is in a cash-nexus world and half is not, the half that is not is at a great disadvantage.

These characterizing aspects of housewifery—that it is not an occupation, that it is not part of the labor force, and that it belongs in a pre-industrial or status rather than in an industrial world—are not trivial or superficial but fundamental and widely ramifying throughout the institutional structure of our society. The exclusion of the housewife from the occupational world is more than merely a statistical artifact for the convenience of economic analysts. It reflects rather, as Talcott Parsons (1959: 262–263) tells us, a necessary accommodation of the family to the occupational world. The work of wives has to be separated from the occupational world because it operates on wholly different principles from that of work in the labor market. In order to articulate such different systems, only one marital partner can participate in the labor force and that one partner has to be the husband:

> . . . Broadly speaking, there is no sector of our society where the dominant patterns stand in sharper contrast to those of the occupational world than in the family. The family is a solidary group within which status, rights, and obligations are defined primarily by membership as such and by the ascribed differentiations of age, sex, and biological relatedness. This basis of relationship and status in the group precludes more than a minor emphasis on universalistic standards of functional performance . . . Clearly for two structures with such different patterns to play crucially important roles in the same society requires a delicate adjustment between them . . . To an important degree their different patterns can be upheld only by mechanisms of segregation which prevent them from getting in each other's ways and undermining each other. Yet they must be articulated. Broadly this problem of structural incompatibility is solved in the United States by making sure that in the type case only one member of the effective kinship unit, the conjugal family, plays a full competitive role in the occupational system. This member is the husband and father (Parsons: 263).

Since the focus of our discussion here is primarily on the housewife as housewife rather than on her labor-force participation, we pay here only passing attention to the ways in which, once more, "the woman pays." The woman worker in the labor market is, in effect, victimized by policies based on the conflicting models. Because the "delicate adjustment" referred to by Parsons calls for a view of women primarily, if not exclusively, as wives, a train of consequences follows. Employers can rationalize discriminatory practices as follows: (1) women have to devote most of their time and energies to their families; they are, therefore, only short-term workers, so there is no point in putting time or money into their training; (2) their domestic obligations will lead to much absenteeism; (3) they are only secondary workers in the family, working primarily for pocket money, so lower pay for them is justified. A great deal of anguish is, in fact, generated by working wives and mothers, torn between their obligations as defined in the status love and/or duty world and in the cash-nexus occupational world. It is generally assumed that all the adjustments required for accommodating these two incompatible worlds should be made by the housewife. Only now is it beginning to seem unfair and even now only an avant garde is beginning to ask why society should not make some of these adjustments. We shall return later in our discussion to several proposals being offered for integrating the two work worlds.

THE HOUSEWIFE IN THE SOCIETAL MODEL

Lip service is universally given to the contribution of the housewife to society. Her work in the home is accorded great importance. Still, in actual practice, it is taken for granted or enormously denigrated. David Riesman (1964: xxiv) has called our attention to the infrastructure that successful men depend on but which they rarely acknowledge. And the long controversy during the nineteenth and early part of the twentieth century about whether or not women should "work," i.e., enter the labor force, revealed the strong feelings associated with retaining their services in the home.

An analysis of housewifery reminds us of the highly artificial nature of the usual economic approach to work which includes only activity of a certain kind, based on certain presuppositions. It reminds us also of the uncertain accommodation between the economic system and other systems as they operate in our society. It reminds us also of the very considerable part of the consumption goods and services which are produced quite outside of the economic system. A strange anomaly emerges: we consume a great deal more than, technically speaking, we produce.

Not only in the home but also in the community, for in addition to housewifery, the housewife makes a contribution to the community in several other ways. It has been suggested, for example, that the beautiful yards of homes in the cities and suburbs constitute in effect public parks maintained at private expense but enjoyable to all. If we had to depend on tax monies for their upkeep we would probably not have them. A large part of such gardening and yard tending is done by housewives and garden clubs are one of the major activities of many well-heeled housewives. A great deal of the work of voluntary agencies is also contributed by housewives, work whose value we will only realize when, as is increasingly the case, they begin to demand pay for doing it.

The contrast between the societal and the economic paradigms has been highlighted in an unexpected area, namely blood donorship, by one of the most distinguished men in the field of welfare, Richard M. Titmuss (1971). He finds that the practice of paying blood donors leads to waste, inefficiency, higher costs, and poorer quality:

> . . . the commercialization of blood and donor relationships represses the
> expression of altruism, erodes the sense of community, lowers scientific

standards, limits both personal and professional freedoms, sanctions the making of profits in hospitals and clinical laboratories, legalizes hostility between doctor and patient, subjects critical areas of medicine to the laws of the marketplace, places immense social costs on those least able to bear them—the poor, the sick, and the inept—increases the danger of unethical behaviour in various sectors of medical science and practice, and results in situations in which proportionately more and more blood is supplied by the poor, the unskilled, the unemployed, Negroes and other low income groups and categories of exploited human populations of high blood yielders. Redistribution in terms of blood and blood products from the poor to the rich appears to be one of the dominant effects of the American blood banking systems (1971: 245–246).

The analogy between the contribution of the housewife and the blood donor is striking. Titmuss is arguing for a return to the non-market, the non-cash-nexus world.

But the determinative characteristics of the work of housewives lie in the way our society structures the living arrangements of families in separate, individual, privatized households. This pattern means that the work is isolating, a fact that has important effects on the woman herself. It means also that her "clients" or "employers" are in a non-economic relationship with her. But there are other characterizing aspects of housewifery. An analysis of housework made some thirty years ago, for example, singled out several especially significant characteristics, namely: (1) it is not, for most women, freely selected as an occupation, but with or without interest in it, it is or has been compulsory, not voluntary, however subtle the coercive pressures may be; (2) it has low status; (3) it is non-competitive; (4) the timing is not synchronized with the work world; (5) it is, as noted above, isolating; and (6) the housewife is in a non-economic relationship with her "clients."

Housewifery is Not Voluntary. The Jaffe-Stewart definition of the labor force specified that membership in it was voluntary. Not many women have an interest in housewifery. A generation ago, in fact, L. M. Terman and C. Miles (1936: 209–210, 215–216) reported that little over a third of a sample of women twenty-five to sixty-five years of age with high-school education expressed great interest in the domestic arts; a tenth showed little or none. Among college women the levels of interest in the domestic arts was even lower, fewer than a fifth (eighteen percent) showing great interest and only 8.6 percent, little or none at all.

Yet housewifery is prescribed for all. For although the marital vow taken at marriage does not commit the wife to housewifery, the pressures of the world she lives in, including the law, do. "The legal responsibilities of a wife are to live in the home established by her husband; to perform the domestic chores (cleaning, cooking, washing, etc.) necessary to help maintain that home; to care for her husband and children" (Schulder, 1970: 147). The courts jealously guard the husband's rights to his wife's services in the home. And the wife who insists on monetary payment for her services is looked at aghast. Some states expressly deny such payment. It is taken for granted that a woman will leave her job when she marries, if not immediately, at least soon thereafter, and almost certainly when she has children. Even if she continues to keep her outside job, the management of the household will be still defined as her responsibility. "The law allows a wife to take a job if she wishes. However, she must see that her domestic chores are completed, and, if there are children, that they receive proper care during her absence" (Schulder, 1970: 141).

Even, as is increasingly the case, the husband shares some of the household chores, he does this as a favor to the housewife, not as part of his genuine responsibilities. Only recently has this "forced labor" aspect of the housewife's job become an issue, raised primarily by the Women's Liberation Movement. In this non-voluntary characteristic, the work of the housewife violates the labor-force concept.

Housewifery Has Low Status. The lack of money payment for the work of the housewife contributes to the low regard in which her work is held. So also is the undeniable fact that it is menial work and in this country menial work has low status. "The homemaker is typically portrayed as someone who needs little intelligence, since the duties are routine and narrow in scope and since her home is not part of the social life" (Lopata, 1971: 141).

There has been a long and valiant history of heroic efforts to glorify housewifery. But not all of the efforts have been able to achieve that goal. A woman could be ever so competent, quite professional, in fact, but housework remained housework. And no amount of clamor about the dignity of labor could change the low esteem placed on it. No amount of scientific know-how or romantic glorification in the women's magazines or on television could finally hide the fact that it was, in the words of some of the radical women, "shit-work," and as such low on any occupational prestige and hence status scale.[4]

Housewifery is Non-competitive. Although competition may have damaging effects when too highly encouraged, as in the male professional rat-race or the factory worker's rate-busting, still when it is wholly absent the result, however tranquilizing, is boredom. Laboratory studies a generation ago showed that competition had a stimulating effect on speed and quantity of work done. Since the housewife is not in the work force and cannot be fired nor promoted there is little in the situation that creates competition. She adapts to this situation by creating it for herself. Advertisers understand this well. Television commercials show us housewives competing with one another about the relative whiteness or "tattle-tale grayness" of their laundry, about the relative shine of their kitchen dishes, about the polish on their furniture, about the taste of their coffee. If one bridge-club hostess puts whipped cream on the cake, the next one adds a maraschino cherry, the third, nuts, the fourth an ornament, and so on. The whole family has to keep up with the Joneses. There is also maternal competition, each mother trying to get her child to reach certain levels of development—first word, toilet training, crawling—before the others. Another adaptation to the boredom of non-competitiveness is the reverse: withdrawal. One characteristic also reported a generation ago was that in non-competitive situations irrelevant ideas tended to be more frequent. The housewife may therefore be more likely to daydream or let her mind wander, or escape boredom in television soap operas.

The housewife may adapt to the non-competitive nature of her work by overcompensating; she may be more compulsive. More than a century ago this was already being noted as a problem of housewives, much of their work being labelled as unnecessary (Fern, 1870: 40). A generation ago there was a popular play and moving picture, *Craig's Wife,* on the same theme: the compulsive household manager for whom the house was the major concern in life.

The Work of the Housewife is Isolating. The structure of living arrangements on the basis of separate, individual, privatized households has the effect of cutting the housewife off from contacts with fellow-workers.[5] In spite of modern means of communication and transportation, the housewife is functionally isolated from her peers. "Not only does the housewife lack the stimulus of functional contacts with other people doing the same work or working on a common project, but in addition she is practically isolated in her work" (Bernard, 1942 533–534). And isolation has been found "to encourage brooding; it makes for more erratic judgments, untempered by the leavening effect of contact with others" (Bernard: 534). Isolation also heightens one's sense of powerlessness (Seeman and Evans, 1962a: 772–782). It also renders one more susceptible to psychoses. These points will be elaborated below in our discussion of the pathogenic effects of housewifery as an occupation.

The Housewife Has Non-economic Relations with Her "Clients." The "clients" or "customers" or "consumers" of the services supplied by the housewife do not pay her for them. She performs them on the basis of love and/or duty. Although she cannot be fired, neither can she quit, short of breaking up her marriage itself. The relationship, thus, between the housewife and her "clients" or the "consumers" of her services is extremely delicate. None of the sanctions available to "buyers" and "sellers" in the labor market operates here.

The Timing of Housewifery Does Not Synchronize with that of the Occupational World. The peak loads of work for the housewife do not coincide with the work schedules of the outside work world. Her peaks come at meal times when other workers are not working and her work lulls come when others are working. Her leisure time is thus scheduled when adults to share it with, except other housewives, are not available. She tends, therefore, to have a one-sex social life, or none at all.

On the positive side of housewifery is its autonomy. The housewife has some say about when and how she will do her work. It is, further, one of the few kinds of work in which handicraft can still be engaged in (Bernard, 1942: 536).

THE HOUSEWIFE AS VICTIM: THE PATHOLOGICAL ASPECTS OF HOUSEWIFERY

All of our thinking about occupations, about work, about the labor force, about the labor market on one side and about marriage, family, child-rearing, and the home, and the policies based on such thinking are determined by the models or paradigms that guide them. There is an acceptance of the two paradigms—economic and societal—as given. There is little challenge of the presuppositions and assumptions basic to both of them, and such presuppositions and assumptions are intrinsic parts of the paradigms. The rejection of the housewife in one model and her preconceived role in the other mean that she is not viewed realistically in either.[6] Her plight is rejected as irrelevant in both.

We noted earlier some of the consequences of this conflict in models for working wives and mothers in the form of discriminatory practices by employers. Here, from a somewhat different angle, we note that the circumstances attending the work of housewives is pathogenic. The devastating overall effect of housewifery has been commented on for at least a century. It has long been noted that it cuts the housewife off from intellectual stimulation, and from satisfying emotional contacts; it is dehumanizing. This is how the housewife's position was described a century ago under the rubric "Hints for the Household":

Need of Change. Women need more change, more variety, than is to be found in the ordinary housekeeper's life. Year in and year out the great body of womankind in our country stay at home, faithfully treading their monotonous round of work and duty; no break in the drudging sameness of their lives only as sickness, or births and deaths, each in its own way, jars on the monotony for a time. We are more careless of ourselves than of our brittania and silver, for we are careful to keep them brightly burnished, but our intellects are dulled with lack of friction with others, and our minds narrowed for want of broader channels in which to widen. With all of us the dearest spot on earth is home, sweet home; yet do we not all admit that always staying at home leads to narrow, unhealthy views and nervous prostration? Change of air, change of surroundings, change of thoughts—oh, for more of it for our over-worked, nervous women! (Unsigned, 1886).

As late as the first third of the century, the Lynds (1929) were still noting how eager the women in Middletown were to talk, even if only with a researcher. Their wishful comments illustrated the continuing isolation of housewives. Still today commentators speak of the fundamental vacuity of the housewife's existence, of its emotional as well as intellectual poverty. Her isolated workshop is a prison that needs no walls. This is especially abrasive in the case of women who have been exposed to the stimulation of college life; "the emotional and intellectual poverty of the housewife's role is nicely expressed in the almost universal complaint: 'I get to talking baby talk with no one around all day but the children'" (Slater, 1970).

In the 1920's there was already a book on *The Nervous Housewife* and by 1963 Betty Friedan was still documenting the problem that had no name. By 1970, a public health survey provided clear-cut evidence that the "housewife syndrome" was, indeed, a reality and not a figment of the imagination. A fairly extensive research literature had shown that, as compared to unmarried women, married women showed up poorly as far as mental health was concerned (Bernard, 1972: Chapter 3). A great many aspects of marriage might well contrive to bring about this result. But the trauma of housewifery seemed to be among the most crucial. One study reported that whereas more working than non-working wives were neurotic, almost twice as many non-working mothers as working mothers were psychotic (Sharp and Nye, 1963: 316). And even the findings with respect to neurotic symptoms are controverted by other studies, one of which reported that "working mothers are less likely than housewives to complain of pains and ailments in different parts of their body and of not feeling healthy enough to carry out things they would like to do" (Feld, 1963: 344). The most spectacular documentation of the destructive effects of housewifery was provided by a Public Health Service study in 1970 which showed that housewives had far greater vulnerability to symptoms of psychological distress than did working women, three-fifths of whom are married. The "housewife syndrome" was far from a figment of anyone's imagination: "white women who were keeping house had higher rates than expected for eleven of the twelve symptoms" of psychological distress (United States Public Health Service: National Center for Health Statistics, 1970: 9). Housewifery seemed, literally, to make women sick. (See United States Public Health Service: National Center Health Statistics [1970b: 30–31], table 18, entitled Psychological Distress in the United States. This reports figures on various symptoms of psychological distress comparing working women and housewives. For example, working women are less likely than housewives to experience nervous breakdowns, trembling hands, nightmares, dizziness, heart palpitations and other related symptoms.)

Thus, although a wide variety of factors might be invoked to explain the poorer health of married as compared to unmarried women, the 1970 study seemed to pinpoint the work factor or housewifery as the most salient.

RE-THINKING THE SITUATION

It is becoming increasingly clear that the old functional differentiation of work by sex is being eroded. The assumptions that underlay the old paradigms are less and less valid, such, for example, that housekeeping was intrinsically a female function. Avant garde women are less and less inclined to take housewifery for granted as a life work. There has been a renewed interest in the problem in the current second-cycle of feminism in this century. The old definitions and conceptions are no longer accepted without challenge. Some of the thinking is a re-statement of the nineteenth-century ideas; some of it is revolutionary. One presupposes a continuation of present life styles; some envisage quite different ones. Only five lines of thought are discussed here: (1) return to the status world in as many ways as possible; (2) re-vamp our life styles by moving away from individual, privatized households to more cooperative or even communal living styles; (3) retain the present life style but make possible more sharing by husbands of functions presently performed by the housewife; (4) retain present life style but professionalize and industrialize housewifery, thus moving it into the industrial or cash-nexus world; and (5) pay for the services performed by the housewife.

Widen the Area of Status Relationships. Richard Titmuss (1971) views the cash-nexus world as dysfunctional. He thinks we should restructure our institutions to increase volunteer contributions rather than continue in the present course of expanding the cash-nexus world. He argues that the way a society organizes and structures its institutions encourages or discourages human altruism. Social systems may have integrating or alienating effects. And he would like to see the "theme of the gift" in the form of generosity towards strangers to spread. He would, in effect, turn back the clock of time and reverse the trend toward sucking larger and larger segments of our lives into the cash-nexus world.

Cooperative or Communal Living Arrangements. During the nineteenth century there was a considerable amount of criticism of the waste involved in separate, individual households, each with its own separate kitchen, its own separate heating and maintenance problems, its own procurement system, and its own garbage pails. Such an arrangement was contrary to all the tenets of efficiency. Scores of proposals were made for cooperative living arrangements of one kind or another, common dining facilities, shared housekeeping chores. But despite numerous attempts to establish such common, even communal living arrangements, they did not catch on. Families continued to prefer individual, private living arrangements, whatever the cost in efficiency and female effort. This is an interesting example of the family's imposing its preferences on the economy rather than the family's adapting itself to the economy. It is interesting also to contemplate what would have happened if the tenets of economic efficiency had won over the preference of families for private, individualized living arrangements. Many communal arrangements still imply that the housewifery involved would be done by women, but at least some of the weight would be lifted from the shoulders of the housewife. The entire responsibility for taking care of the living arrangements would no longer fall on her alone; there would be others helping, spelling her off, and overcoming the usual isolation.

Shared Roles. A third line of thinking with respect to housewifery has to do with the sharing of its responsibilities, not with other women but with husbands. The separate, individual, privatized household is still envisaged, but not as the responsibility of the wife alone. Both husbands and wives would have the option of performing both the provider and the housewife functions rather than having to specialize in one or the other. Such an arrangement would require more flexibility in the organization of industry with respect to hours of work. But such a reorganization is seen by some industrial engineers not only as feasible but even as profitable. An increasing number of plants are experimenting with flexible work hours. With genuine flexibility, both men and women would be able to hold jobs in the labor force and also to contribute to the work of the household (Bernard, 1971a: 272–275; 1971b: 21–28; 1972).

Industrialize and Professionalize Housework. None of the above plans would necessarily bring housewifery into the labor force. The communal or cooperative life style would not preclude such a move. If the members of the cooperative household choose to hire others to perform the housewifery work rather than do it themselves, that would bring it into the labor market and bring those who did the work into the labor force.

But the movement to industrialize housewifery does not presuppose any specific living style. Its major premise is simply that housewifery is technologically no different from any other kind of work and there is no reason why it could not be taken over by industry like any other service. A company would contract with households to perform whatever services were called for: keep the household clean; provide laundry service; provide meals; provide valet service for wardrobes, keeping them mended and clean; etc., etc. Such industrialized services are already coming into operation.

Industrialization requires "professionalizing." That is, workers have to be trained, learn how to handle the tools of their trade, work on time schedules and meet certain standards. In the case of women who do housework by the day, there has been a movement in this direction for some time.

Pay for Services of Housewife. More radical than any of these lines of thinking is one that proposes that the services performed for the economy be paid for, even if performed in the home by the housewife. From this point of view, the function performed by the housewife is one of keeping the work force in good condition. When or if the work environment is such that these services cannot be supplied by housewives, industry itself or employers must supply them. On a ship, for example, in a lumber camp, in a mining town, an exploring or scientific expedition, a military camp, or engineering assignment—in any work situation in which living arrangements must be taken care of by industry or employer or other personnel—the work traditionally done by the housewife is done by specialized personnel. When a corporation employee has to leave home, he is provided a per diem to pay for the maid, valet, and the meal preparation service his wife provides at home. It is, in brief, the work situation and not the work itself that determines whether it is done by housewives or by others and whether it is paid for or not. There is no logical reason why housewives should not be paid for services that are paid for when performed by others, why she should be obliged to perform them out of love and/or duty rather than for money.

The idea is not, actually, totally novel, although as presented in the past it has been from a male rather than from a female point of view.

The family wage system, for example, in a curiously biased way recognized the services performed by the housewife. A married man was paid more than an unmarried man since he had to support a wife. That blind spot was that the married worker was getting services from the wife for which the unmarried worker, male or female, had to pay. (Professional women often note laconically how much they need wives too.) The married worker was thus being paid to "hire" services for which he did not have to pay. (The part of the family wage that was meant for the care of children raises altogether different questions which are not relevant here.)

In general, the idea of a family wage has never been congenial in the United States where the emphasis has been on "equal pay for equal work" and women workers especially have objected to the idea that because a man was married he should be paid more. Still, in some cases there has been a curiously accepting attitude. Some fellowships allow extra funds for dependents, itself a kind of "family wage."

The logic of paying housewives for keeping the work force in good condition is not likely to appeal to either employers or to husbands. And certainly there are many hurdles to overcome. But, who knows, by the twenty-first century employers may be contributing to a fund to pay for the services supplied to their workers by wives in the home as routinely as they contribute to Social Security funds, or unemployment accounts. It may be simply a matter of getting used to the idea.[7] Such a system would require conceptualizing housewives as part of the labor force and counting their contribution to the gross national product. It would constitute a major shrinkage of the segment of social life for which the societal model was relevant, with what "unanticipated consequences" we cannot yet say.

NOTES

[1] "The majority of women continue to be homemakers, whether or not they also have jobs. In 1968, 41 million women were not in the labor force, and 35 million of these devoted their full time to housekeeping. Almost two-fifths of all married women and many single women as well are both homemakers and workers. During an average workweek in 1968, 50 percent of all women were keeping house full time, and about 42 percent were either full or part time workers. Most of the remainder were girls 16 to 20 years of age who were in school." (United States Department of Labor: Women's Bureau, 1969: 12). Two-fifths of all married women were both workers and housewives.

[2] This trend was in line with the same kind of trends in other types of work. Nurses have been upgraded to become "para-medical personnel" while the old servile components of their work are taken over by aides and other low-level workers. Social workers are relieved of the time consuming leg-work and free for more prestigious treatment services. So also with teachers who are assigned aides. The situation was not the same in the case of the house-wife. There just were not enough "aides" to turn the menial work over to when she became highly trained. Housework or domestic service declined from 51.2 per cent in 1870 to 6.3 percent in 1968. The implications of the disappearance of household service is one of the least researched aspects of the study of the family today.

[3] If a woman with secretarial skills, married and mother of three sons, died at the age of 41, when the youngest child was 11, her replacement value would be $105,546.

[4] A comparison of the work components in the housewife's job with similar work done in the labor force by Wilma Heide Scott found it to be on about the same level as a restroom or parking lot attendant, a public bath maid, pet show attendant, a hotel clerk.

[5] One of the most interesting examples of the effect of isolation is reported in a British study of apartment-style living among service men in Germany (Fanning, 1967). The incidence of psycho-neurotic disorders was almost three times higher among women living in flats than among those living in houses, but the most interesting finding was that psychoneurotic disorders increased the higher up the apartment was. The confinement of mothers of preschool children within the walls of the apartments added another irritant to the monotony and boredom of their lives. Even the children suffered; they had a higher sickness rate. (Hurtwood, 1968: 12)

[6] One of the few attempts to bring the two paradigms into some sort of relationship to one another was made by Charlotte Perkins Gilman, who wrote in 1898: "when a man marries a housemaid, makes a wife of his servant, he alters her *social* status; but if she continues in the same industry he does not alter her *economic* status. When he makes a servant of his wife, or she of herself by choice, whatever social, civic, mental or moral status may be, her economic status is that of domestic service. What she is entitled to receive from society for her labor is the wages of the housemaid. What she gets more than that is given her by her husband without any economic equivalent. She is supported by him on account of her sex." (Gilman, 1968: 177).

[7] After this was written, Senator Russell Long, Chairman of the Senate Finance Committee, was reported in the press as exploring the idea of admitting housewives into the Social Security system in order to make them eligible for retirement benefits: "Senator Long believes, in principle, that housewives deserve equal recognition for their work. But he is still stumped over how to finance a housewives' pension plan. One possibility would be to deduct the wife's social security tax from her husband's salary. Another idea would be to require husbands to pay their wives a weekly wage, from which her social security contribution would be deducted." (Anderson, 1971)

James M. Henslin

The Underlife of Cabdriving:
A Study in Exploitation
and Punishment*

I find cabdriving the worst experience a man can have to the implemen-
tation of neo-Darwinism. It is a world of enemies with the cab itself, the
armed weapon of the only friend that the cab driver has—himself.

Irving Louis Horowitz
—Private communication to the author

What is the work of the cab driver like? Many people appear to have
the idea that a cabbie's work is carefree. He hops into his cab, picks up
passengers at various locations, and delivers them to their destinations.
In the meantime he meets interesting people from all walks of life,
enjoys good conversation, and collects sizeable tips—roaming the city
as a sort of modern vagabond on wheels.

Such a view does contain an element of truth. The cabbie indeed
delivers people to places they want to go. He does meet many people,
of whom some are interesting and a few are even fascinating. He does
become involved in many conversations. And he does collect tips. But
there is much more to the work of the cabbie. And not all of it is
rewarding—or even pleasant. This paper emphasizes the punishments
and exploitation to which the cabbie is subjected, the brutalizing elements which are built into his job and go hand in hand with driving
a cab.

One must also understand the rewarding aspects of the cabbie's life

---

* This is a revised version of a paper read at the annual meetings of the
Midwest Sociological Society, St. Louis, Missouri, April 1970.

if one is to have an accurate or balanced picture of the cabbie's world. These rewarding aspects of the occupation are also crucial in the cabbie's life. They also shape his identity, mold the way he thinks of himself, and structure the way he views the world. For an analysis of the positive features of cabdriving, see Henslin (1967: 145–174; 1971).

This analysis of the underlife of cabdriving is based on data gathered by this participant observer who drove a cab in the City of St. Louis on a part-time basis for about a year. Neither the management nor the workers knew they were being studied. A hidden tape recorder was used to record: 1) interaction among cabbies before and after work, 2) messages transmitted over the cab's radio, 3) conversations with passengers, 4) conversations with cabbies at the cab stands, and 5) crap games which these cabbies played after work. At no time were people informed that they were being studied, nor did they indicate any awareness that they had a researcher in their midst.

Why the choice of participant observation? A major goal of many sociological researchers is to understand the subject's world from *his* point of view. This purpose goes under various names in sociology, such as verstehen, interpretative understanding, subjective interpretation, definition of the situation, uncovering underlying "background expectancies," or investigating the "socially-sanctioned-facts-of-life-that-any-bonafide-member-of-the-group-knows" (See Becker 1963; Blumer 1969; Bruyn 1966; Garfinkel 1967; Ichheiser 1970; Malinowski 1950; Schutz 1962, 1964, 1966, 1967; Thomas and Znaniecki 1918–20; Weber 1946, 1947, 1949; Whyte 1955). The assumption is that intimate familiarity with someone's world can lead to an understanding of that person's definitional process, and that we can thereby know the factors he finds important and better understand his behavior.

Those researchers who follow this goal ordinarily choose a method of research which least molests the phenomena they are studying. Participant observation is frequently chosen because it not only allows the researcher entry into the everyday world of his subjects, but also, when done correctly, minimizes disruption to interaction. Thus the researcher can have greater confidence that the data he gathers by this method is representative of the regularly occurring, ongoing interaction of the group he enters; that it is naturalistic and not an artifact of his presence (See Henslin 1972a).

If one attempts to understand life's experiences from the perspective of the other, the researcher must "get into" the symbolic system of those he is studying. He must know what members of that group consider important in any relevant situation. When he understands how the members of a culture define their situations, the researcher knows much of what goes into the decisions they make. He then has some understanding of what influences and buttresses their life style.

In this research, I entered their world as someone who knew little about cabdriving and cab drivers. Not having previously learned to accept the cab drivers' view of reality as reality led me to question fundamental aspects of their existence. I then sociologically analyzed parts of their world which they routinely and unquestioningly took for granted. (See Henslin 1972b.)

Not only did I gain information about the world of those I was studying, but more importantly, I directly experienced that world. I was thus able to understand the events in cabbie culture from the perspective of the members of that culture. For example, I not only learned *what* a "no-go" is (a location to which a cabbie is dispatched, but where there is no passenger when he arrives), but I also learned the *meaning* of a "no-go" for the cab driver, such things as the effect of the "no-go" on his income for that shift, the frustration which seethes within him, and his feelings of futility in dealing with his world.

This paper, then, is presented from the point of view of the cab driver, and is an examination of the major areas of his life which he sees as punitive. Relevant aspects of his work setting are examined, including problematic aspects of interaction with passengers, competition among cabbies, mechanisms of social control, the cabbie's equipment, and factors which are structured into the occupation that exert control over his life situation and lead him to work hard but to live in poverty.

THE CABBIE AND HIS PASSENGERS

The cab driver is constantly on the go, being dispatched throughout the city. He transports businessmen, shoppers, tourists, workers, drunks, prostitutes, and housewives to their destinations. As he deals with these people, the cabbie regularly confronts passengers who threaten his self, his routine, and sometimes his property or even his life.

The cabbie is frequently treated as a non-person, that is, people sometimes act as though he were not present. Passengers sometimes do not adjust their behavior for his presence—anymore than they would for the steering wheel of an auto. When intimate arguments are fought out in the cab between lovers, for example, it is as though the cab driver were merely a non-human extension of the steering wheel, a kind of machine which guides the cab. Such interaction in all its varied aspects —the tones and loudness of voice, the words used, the subjects spoken about—takes place as though the individuals were in private, with no third person present. The effect on the cabbie of some types of non-person treatment is a challenging of the self since others are not acknowledging his self but acting as though he did not exist.

The cabbie also regularly has passengers who in various ways challenge his control over the transaction. Some passengers berate him for not going fast enough or for missing a green light, while others withhold the tip as a sanction against something they did not like about the driver. The cabbie must also put up with persons who are "playing." (In "cabby-ese" this refers to those who call in and have a cab dispatched to a location where no one desires a cab.) Other callers are present when he arrives but refuse to enter the cab. Still others, "bucket loads," skip out without paying their fare. Other passengers demand services he is unwilling to provide, such as locating a prostitute or entering an area of the city which the driver considers to be unsafe after dark. To communicate some of the "flavor" of such problematic interactions, I shall illustrate the punitiveness of the belligerent and non-cooperative passenger. In an afterwork group, a driver related the following incident:

He picked up a passenger who said, "Take me to thirty-five." The driver asked, "Thirty-five what?" The passenger became somewhat angry and raised his voice, saying, "Just take me to thirty-five!" In exasperation, the driver said, "Well, thirty-five what?" The passenger then said, "Just start driving!" The driver began driving, and after he had driven a short while, the passenger told him to make a right turn, and the driver did so. A while later, the passenger asked, "Where in the hell do you think you're going?" The driver then said, "I don't know where I'm going." The passenger then said, "I told you to take me to thirty-five!"

At this point the driver covertly placed his hand on a hammer he carried in the cab and said, "Thirty-five hundred what? You just name me the street, and I'll show you what thirty-five hundred is on any street in St. Louis!" At this, the passenger finally named his street. When they arrived at his destination, the fare was $1.55, and the passenger handed two one dollar bills to the driver, who still had his hand on the hammer. He then tapped the driver on the shoulder, and said, "There you are, buddy. Take it easy."

In reaction to such passengers, cabbies frequently develop a veneer of hardness, an outward crust which helps deflect painful threats to the self. This veneer manifests itself in the commonly perceived belligerency of cab drivers—the shaking fist and the cursing mouth, or the "Don't-tell-me-how-to-get-there" attitude. These are part of the cabbies' attempt to maintain control over threatening passengers and a life situation over which he actually has little control.

The threat of danger is also a constant part of the cab driver's work.

Each day he drives his cab he lives with the knowledge that he might be robbed or murdered. This uncertainty of safety is constantly in the back of his mind as he picks up strangers as a routine part of his job. In the privacy of the cab, with these strangers at his back, he is literally at their mercy for his very life. This fear for his own safety constantly gnaws at him, and because holdup men are disproportionately black, both black and white cabbies tend to avoid black neighborhoods and black passengers—especially at night (Stannard 1971; Henslin 1972b).

Since the potential of danger is always present, many warning devices have been suggested. One was to install a mechanism to flash the cab's top lights when the cab driver stepped on a button. The flashing lights would supposedly alert pedestrians, motorists, and the police. But cabbies scoffed when the device was suggested, saying that the light would also alert the robber since he would be able to see its reflection as they drove past store windows. If this happened, the robber might retaliate physically, and cabbies felt that they would be in greater danger with this device than without it.

In spite of this continual and seemingly permanent danger of robbery and murder, cabbies are prevented by law from carrying weapons, even for self defense. Most drivers just take their chances, but some find substitute weapons:

> While we were waiting for the cabs to arrive, I noticed that one driver was carrying what looked like a small fishing tackle box. As he was putting something in this box, I saw a hammer and said, "Hey, watcha got that for?" The driver replied, "Ah ha! That's it! I use that! Cops can't get you for carrying a concealed weapon. And it will do the job. I just lay it right out on the front seat."
>
> Another driver picked up the small ball peen hammer, one with a regular flat nail-driving surface on one end but with a ball instead of the nail-pulling claw on the other, and hit the flat surface against his hand and said, "Yeah, that will do the job." The first driver took the hammer, gestured to the end with the ball, and said, "No. Hit 'em with this other end. It'll go way in."

Some drivers are not satisfied with weapons such as hammers or tire tools, and they run the risk of being arrested on a felony charge for carrying a gun. Cabbies, however, generally feel utter futility and defenselessness in the fact of this danger. This is well expressed by the driver who said: "You got ten guns—that don't do a fucking thing when . . . son-of-a-bitch puts that fucking thing in the back of your neck, there's not a fucking thing you can do."

COMPETITION AND CONFLICT

Besides problems with passengers, cabbies also are problematic to one another. The major reason for this is the intense competitiveness of cab-driving. Each cabbie, if he is to survive financially, directly competes with all other cab drivers in the city—both those from rival companies and drivers from his own company.

Intra-company competition regularly takes the simple but legitimate form of beating other drivers to a stand or getting one's own bid for "open" orders accepted by being faster at the mike than others. At other times competition with co-workers takes the more deviant form of being dissimulative when bidding for "open" orders, that is, lying about one's location in order to be eligible for the order. A more deviant form of intra-company competition, however, is "scooping" (stealing orders). It is possible to "scoop" or steal an order because all drivers can hear via their cab radio the location to which a driver is being dispatched. By also knowing the location of the stand from which the driver is being dispatched, a second driver can approximate the time it will take the first driver to arrive at the order. If he figures that he can get there first and still have enough time to pick up the passenger and be out of sight when the dispatched driver arrives, scooping is within his realm of possible action. The dispatched driver is then confronted with a "no-go." Since "no-goes" are punitive, scooping is a technique by which cabbies sometimes "pay back" or "get even with" other cabbies. Its use as a sanction is illustrated by the cabbie who said, "He's a son-of-a-bitch! Every chance I get, I scoop him!"

Inter-company competition is always keen, but it sometimes changes to conflict. Beatings, tire slashing, and other violence during periods of strikes and rate disputes are well-known. However, even during "times of peace" the "truce" is uneasy and regularly threatens to erupt in violence. For example, after work one Metro driver related:

> I was drivin' in Forest Park, and these three women flagged me down. I pulled over, and as they was gettin' in the cab I saw this Red Top Cab come beatin' down the road and the last woman wasn't in yet and she said, "Look! There's our cab now!" Red Top is an air conditioned cab, and so they wanted to ride with him. The women got out, and I said, "You better pay me somethin' for my stoppin' or else this bastard's gonna get his wind-shield knocked in." One woman gave me a dollar, and I left.

SOCIAL CONTROL THROUGH SARCASM, CENSURE, AND THREATS

While he is on the job the cabbie needs to deal not only with proble-matic passengers and competitive co-workers, but he must also drive for an extremely punitive management. Management regularly uses biting verbal techniques in order to keep cabbies in line. For example, in the early morning hours some drivers park at stands with the motors running and their radios on, and then lie down on the front seat and sleep, keeping mentally "tuned" for their stand to be called. When their stand is called they sometimes awaken in time to answer the call, but they frequently respond more slowly than usual, or are perhaps a bit sluggish in their speech. The following, which took place at 4:45 a.m., illustrates the dispatcher's generous use of (1) sarcasm, (2) censure, and (3) threats:

Dispatcher: "DeBaliviere Delmar." (The dispatcher is calling a "stand," places where drivers park to await orders.)
Cabbie: ((Gives his cab number and stand.))[1]
Dispatcher: "5560 Waterman."
Cabbie: ((Probably says, "Clear," meaning that he understood the order.))
Dispatcher: (1) *"Did I disturb you, junior?"*
Cabbie: ((   ))
Dispatcher: "Well, I'm glad to hear that."
Cabbie: ((   ))
Dispatcher: (2) *"Then quit laying down,* (3) *or you won't get the order."*

To understand the punitory nature of this combined sarcasm, censure, and threats, keep in mind first of all that this occurs *publicly.* These statements are being broadcast to all drivers, making the violator's positive reference group knowledgeable of the problem. Secondly, the regular dispatcher on the shift I usually worked was a woman. This means that males, who are already being ordered about by anyone who has the price of a cab, must undergo scorn or berating by a female in the "audible presence" of their fellow drivers.

Cabbies have not found an effective recourse to this ill treatment. Some drivers attempt to "get even" with dispatchers by "tying up the air." They keep the button on their microphones depressed in order to make it difficult for the dispatcher to give out orders. Not only is this action seldom successful, but were a cabbie to succeed in "tying up the air," he would also be penalizing his fellow cabbies by preventing them from receiving orders. He would end up being punitive toward those with whom he strongly identifies. With neither a legitimate nor an effective recourse open to get back at a dispatcher with whom he is having problems, a driver will sometimes withdraw—sitting in his cab, but angrily refusing to answer his radio. This, of course, is also a most ineffective sanction because he ends up harming himself, further lowering his already depressed income.

THE CABBIE AND HIS EQUIPMENT

In analyzing negative aspects of cabdriving, I wish to broadly apply the concept of punishment. The common sense idea of punishment refers to more than just persons as punitive agents. People frequently apply the term punishment not only to persons who are either purposely or inadvertently punishing to them, but also to experiences with material objects in which they feel that they are in some way humiliated, degraded or frustrated. We shall now examine this broader approach to understanding punishment and cab drivers, looking at objects which are punishing to cabbies.

The cab is obviously of extreme importance to the cab driver. He is so strongly identified with this vehicle that his name is but a diminutive of it—"cabbie." Moreover, as indicated by the quotation heading this paper, the cabbie's vehicle is a sort of armed weapon with which he approaches a hostile world. However, even his cab, with its equipment, is in many ways inimical to the cabbie.

Although the cab driver is supposed to "check out" his cab before he begins driving, he soon finds that factors militate against doing so. First of all, checking the cab for mechanical problems means that the cabbie loses time when he could be taking his first order. Secondly, he soon learns to avoid the garage men who repair the cabs since they become surly and sarcastic when they see anyone bringing a cab to the garage. The garage men are salaried, so cabs needing repairs represent only additional work for them. Finally, since cabs sitting in the garage also represent a loss of income to management, there is little encouragement from this sector.

The typical attitude is that as long as the cab moves when the accelerator is pressed it should be on the road. These cabs are on the go twenty-four hours a day, with one driver turning a cab in at the end of his twelve hour shift and another driver immediately taking it out again. When a motor burns out, another is merely shoved into the old chassis. With the combination of not checking the cabs and running them continuously, cabs, at least in the city of St. Louis, are some of the most unsafe vehicles on the road.

A dysfunctional consequence is that it is not uncommon for a cabbie to find himself without such "niceties" as signal lights and properly working brakes. Additionally, with the condition of the cabs on the road, breakdowns are not infrequent. When a breakdown occurs, the cabbie is stuck. He must await "Metro Safety," whom the dispatcher sends to either make on-the-road repairs or to tow the cab away. Even such a small item as a flat tire means a breakdown for the cabbie since it is the practice of Metro Cab Company to send drivers out with neither a spare tire nor tire changing tools.

His cab can also prove physically dangerous to the cabbie. The air intake of the cab is unfortunately located in front of the vehicle. In bumper-to-bumper traffic it directly sucks in the exhaust of the car in front. Those who live in urban settings all experience short periods of such exposure when they drive in rush hour traffic, but the cabbie is frequently in such situations for extended periods of time. In protest against the location of the mounting of the air vent, one Chicago cabbie refused to return his taxi to the garage. For this defiant act, however, he was summarily fired.[2]

The other major part of a cabbie's equipment, his radio, is also a punitive source for the driver. He sometimes receives an electric shock, especially when he is perspiring and resting his arm on the cab's door as he presses the button on his microphone. His radio is also likely to "go bad" at any moment, and to do so without warning. The new driver soon learns by painful experience that a variety of factors will cause his transmission to be too fuzzy or too weak for the dispatcher to receive, such as having too little water in the cab battery, parking too close to the curb, not warming up the radio, and even driving in a low area of the city. These occupational facts are ordinarily learned only through frustrating personal experience.

Radio silence is also threatening to the cab driver. When his radio is silent, the cabbie does not know whether anything is being broadcast or whether his radio is malfunctioning. He can check the source of radio silence by pressing the button on his mike and listening for a click to indicate working order, or he can call the dispatcher. These checks, however, tell him only if his radio is working *at that moment*. Should there continue to be silence, as happens during slack periods, the driver is again made uncomfortable, thinking that he might not be receiving orders which are being broadcast. In periods of radio silence drivers nervously respond to this tension, as indicated by the dispatcher saying such things as, "There's nothing wrong with your radio, Driver. I just don't have any orders." But this only gives a momentary reassurance since his radio can begin malfunctioning at any time, without warning.

HARD WORK AND POVERTY

In the midst of these varied problems, the cabbie works hard to make a buck. Sometimes even the weather and climate appear to conspire against him. In summer the cabbie swelters in heat since none of the rental cabs are air-conditioned. It is only when his cab is moving that he has air circulating to cool him. In winter, on the other hand, he not only suffers from heaters which are less than adequate, but he must climb in and out of his cab as he searches for a house number or picks up a package. Consequently, he cannot wear clothing adequate for the situation, and he is either too warm in heavy clothing or too cold in lighter clothing.

Cabdriving does not even allow normal release of bladder tension. If he is to make any money at all, the cabbie must be constantly listening to his radio, and doing so does not give him time to urinate. If he takes time out to use the restroom of a gas station or restaurant (to use a dark street is to invite arrest), he runs the risk of missing orders and lowering his income. On the other hand, if he takes time to relieve his bladder after he has received an order, it takes longer to arrive at the order and greatly increases the chances of a "no-go." And, of course, after he picks up the passenger, it would be both humiliating and awkward to, in effect, "ask permission" of his passenger to go to the bathroom! Consequently, bladder tension is a routine part of the cabbie's job.

Another physical need which cabdriving cuts into is sleep. St. Louis cabbies work an eleven or twelve hour day, six days a week. Since this is required to make a living, and the cabbie must also allow for driving time to and from work, the cabbie must either cut down his sleep or cut down on the amount of time he spends in non-work activities such as his family or recreation. Judging from the haggardly tired appearance marking these cabbies, most seem to make the choice of cutting down on sleep.

Although they work full time, usually six days a week, eleven or twelve hours each day, cabbies in St. Louis still live in poverty. One cabbie, for example, goes to the City Hospital when he is sick since there he can receive the free treatment which the city provides for indigents. This full-time working man considers himself to be so poor that he is in need of public welfare. I have also seen a cabbie begging other drivers for a dollar with which to buy breakfast, and another cabbie who did not know where he was going to sleep that night after work. In a single issue of *Taxi Union News* (March 1967), which focuses primarily on cabbies in Chicago, it was reported that food and clothing had been given to one cabbie who along with his eight children had been burned out of his home. Another cabbie had been put out of his home by the landlord. Still another cabbie had been placed in an industrial plant and his "family of five children were put back into their apartment after the furnishings had been placed in the street."

Above rental and gasoline expenses, St. Louis cabbies average approximately fifteen to eighteen dollars per twelve hour shift. From this pittance they must put away money for income taxes, which are not withheld since cabbies are "independent entrepreneurs." Nor do they even receive a check from which to withhold taxes. If they desire basic social security coverage, cabbies must pay at the higher "self-employed" rate since they are technically not employees of the company. Through this loophole in the law, their "employer" contributes nothing. In effect, cabbies are day laborers who end up with a variable but small amount of cash at the end of each working day. Cabbies struggle for existence without the benefits American workers have learned to take for granted: they do not enjoy employer-contributed pension plans, paid sick leaves, hospitalization, holidays, vacations, or even social security. Nor do they even have job security, but are subservient to the employment whims of management. Not surprisingly, this leads to a life situation which prevents cab drivers from planning ahead, giving them little security for either the present or the future.

There are indeed not many unionized occupations today where poverty characterizes workers who labor sixty-six to seventy-two hours per week under the punitive and degrading conditions I have outlined. How can this possibly be? How can a group of men be unionized and yet be so blatantly exploited?[3]

Cabbies themselves have not been in a good bargaining position. Alternative means of transportation are usually readily available, and if their collective demands bring too great an increase in fares, they may run out of passengers. More than this is involved, however. The major source of exploitation appears to be the capitalistic system under which these men labor. Management, regardless of any high-sounding ideological phraseology to the contrary concerning service to the public, has but one purpose—and that is profit. In order to turn the greatest profit, costs must be cut. Management, as we have seen, drastically cuts the amount it spends on the maintenance of its cabs. Safety features, also expensive, are almost non-existent. But the major source of cutting costs centers around the remuneration cabbies receive. By paying them little, management cuts its costs and remains competitive. By keeping them poverty-stricken and in physical need, management attempts to assure itself of a certain type of labor—a fawning, self-ingratiating type which is grateful for every "favor" it receives.

Central to management maintaining its dictatorial dominancy is the cooptation of the unions. Management has been able to manipulate cabbie unions to the point that union officials frequently appear to represent management more than they do workers. For example, management is able to successfully and regularly manipulate work rules to the detriment of workers. As a case in point, we can note "down time" refunds. During "down time" a driver is supposed to be refunded his cab rental for the period during which his cab is inoperable, being reimbursed about seventy-five cents an hour. This reimbursement is merely a negation of the amount which he would otherwise have had to pay during that period for an operable cab. It is not remuneration from management; nor does it represent a profit. Yet the cabbie ordinarily has to fight *as an individual* to get even this cancellation of rental fees.

When the interests of management and union officials coincide, it is ordinarily at the direct cost and detriment of cabbies. Collusion between the two does not appear to be uncommon, as one would infer from what took place in San Francisco in 1970. At that time a more dissident element of a major cabbie union attempted to vote its candidates into power. The establishment of the union refused to recognize the motion and hastily adjourned the meeting. In the following weeks the management of this cab company fired a dozen or so of its cabbies which of course included the dissident group who had attempted to gain control over the union.[4]

The nationally noted cab strike of 1970 in the City of New York was not, as commonly thought, an attempt to gain higher wages for cab drivers. It was, rather, a successful attempt to gain a higher fare structure for *employers*. Moreover, while higher profits were gained for the employer, wage *cuts* were "gained" for the cabbies. After the union's fifteen day strike, taxi fares went up from 45 cents for the first sixth of a mile to 60 cents for the first fifth of a mile, and from 10 cents for each additional one-third mile to 10 cents for each additional one-fifth mile. "Waiting time" charges were also increased at about the same proportion. But the drivers' commission on the total fare was actually reduced by 10 cents for each trip: 10 cents per trip is subtracted from the total bookings and held in "escrow" for "benefits" which no one has seen. Additionally, the commissions of "new" drivers were further reduced from 49 percent of "new" bookings to 42 percent (Miller 1972).

CONCLUSION

If from my presentation the reader comes to the conclusion that almost everything about cabdriving appears to be punitive, this is not too far from the truth. Although there are indeed compensations to this occupation, the cabbie is enmeshed in a hostile, exploiting, threatening, and punitive world. Some of the punitive and exploitative aspects of cabdriving are willfully inflicted on the cabbie, but most are built into the structure of cabdriving. The source of this exploitation and punishment does not arise primarily from individuals, such as passengers, managers, and fellow cabbies, but it originates especially from the structuring of the profit system within which the cabbie works.

In order to understand man, one must study the structure which helps determine the elements present in his world, and the situations or contexts within which man lives out his life. Cabdriving is structured such that it is exploitative to cabbies. This centers especially around its capitalistic context and focuses specifically on the nature of cabbies' shift work and the forms and amounts of remuneration which he receives. These men live a hard, exploited life—a life in which they are filled with frustration and in which they are continually manipulated by both their physical and social environments. It is difficult to escape the view that cabbies are captives within an extremely exploitative and punishing system. It is probably not that the men directing the system are invidious. It is rather, that the system itself is invidious, pitting man against man for the sake of profit (See Veblen 1953: 137).

If sociologists desire to understand the everyday or common-sense experience of man, interaction in occupations should be a focal point since they demand such a huge part of the waking hours of people in our society. Man's everyday experiences in his occupations greatly structure his perception of the world. If, for example, we are to understand such a common thing in our society as why cabbies feel they are punished, we must understand both the structure of the occupation and the cabbie's reaction to or perception of his place in that structure.

NOTES

[1] The cabbie's response to the dispatcher cannot be heard by other drivers. The double parenthesis indicates these responses. Where the responses are patterned, I have indicated the typical response, placing it within the double parenthesis.

[2] It should be noted that in this case Yellow Cab Company was forced to pay the "offender" ten months' back wages. This decision was won through arbitration, and the union claimed that because of it they now had "greater protection and a higher degree of job security than ever before." (For details, see Taxi Union News, 3, January and April 1967.)

[3] This situation may be different in other parts of the country, such as New York where the number of cabs allowed on the street is limited and where the demand for cabs is exceptionally high. New York cabbies are also exploited, however. See the relevant item in the conclusion to this paper.

[4] My thanks to George Toussaint for this information.

Clarence E. Tygart

The Clergy

Sociologically, the clergy is a most strategic occupation. Clergy deal with ideas as a large part of their work and many of these ideas have relevance for political issues. Thus, the study of clergy affords an investigation of a classical sociological problem, i.e., the effects of an individual's ideas on his behavior. This paper will assess the relative importance and interrelationships of ideological and structural influences for the behavior of clergymen. The clergy behavior analyzed will consist primarily of attitude toward and involvement in political issues.

Discussion will focus on issues and movements which were topical in the 1960's and continue into the 1970's. Few social scientists or general populace would disagree that the Vietnam war and civil rights issues dominated public controversies of the last ten years. Less topical issues could also serve as tests for theoretical propositions. However, any usefulness of sociological studies for future historians largely would be ignored. Also, studying the topically trivial little serves the general public in providing information on pressing problems.

THE HISTORICAL CONTEXT OF MODERN UNITED STATES CLERGY

Alba Edwards (1943), a pioneer scholar in the study of occupations, suggested that the history of the occupational structure singularly reveals the most knowledge about the history of that society. It was previously suggested that the clergy was a sociologically strategic occupation; the clergy also has central importance for the study of history. The history of the clergy enables insights into the nature and development of professions, and the study of professions is a key concern in occupational sociology.

Antecedents of the modern clergy appear in pre-literate societies. The priestcraft of pre-literate societies most aptly reveals the necessary prerequisites for the development and continuation of a profession: 1) a service is performed which people generally feel is of great importance; 2) the general population feels incompetent to assess the quality of the service; and 3) sometimes uncertain and undesired outcomes occur when the service is performed. To illustrate the third prerequisite, the sick sometimes die whether the "professional" attending is a medicine man of the "African bush" or a "Johns Hopkins M.D."

Of crucial importance for laity acceptance of the professional explanation for the outcome of his service is whether such explanations are viewed by the populace as fitting into the context of general knowledge. The explanations of the priestcraft of a pre-literate society concerning the nature of illness and death are convincing for the laity because of harmony with general knowledge. If food supply results from spiritual forces, death readily can be traceable to the individual's having offended a spirit.

In medieval Christian Europe literacy and membership in the clergy were largely one. A glance in a dictionary reveals that the words "clergy" and "clerical" share the same derivation. The derivation of "clergy" is from a word which meant "learning" or "knowledge"; and "clerical" translates to: "Of, belonging to, or characteristic of a clergyman."

Because of their control of education, the clergy probably served as the founding profession in Western civilization, and the rise of the other early professions largely developed out of the clergy. Historically, a member of a profession was one who professed publicly as having received a divine calling to serve in his vocation. By professing a divine call to his vocation, the professional was also professing his religious faith *per se*. To this day, some religious denominations (mostly Protestant sects) require their clergy to publicly profess having experienced a divine call in order to enter the clergy.

The medieval European Christian church as the singular creator and transmitter of knowledge furnished a pervasive religious definition of phenomenon which was accepted by the general population. While man's earthly existence was harsh, the clergy offered a means of achieving a utopian existence after physical death. However, the likelihood of a given individual's obtaining after-life utopia was not certain and virtually impossible without the church.

While some medieval clergy engaged in largely theoretical pursuits of various specialties, such as law and medicine, the interrelated forces of developing industrialization, capitalism and the nation state engendered needs for applied knowledge. The demands of the nation state appear to be the most powerful determinant of early professionalization. For example, Carr-Saunders and Wilson (1933), in their history of the development of the professions in England, suggest that law was one of the first professions to establish itself apart from the clergy. Apparently, clergy began to specialize in civil law apart from canon law to the extent that these specialists began operating outside the church. As practitioners began to form professions apart from the clergy, modes of analysis started differing from religious explanations. For example, in civil or criminal law, the offenses were committed against the state or other individuals instead of the Deity. Religion became but one knowledge context competing with such alternative contexts as science and pragmatism.

The sphere of services solely performed by clergy continually shrank. The clergy no longer furnished the services of medicine, law and education. Probably of no less importance than the clergy's loss of medicine, law and education was the disappearance of church control of recreation and entertainment. The holidays of the Middle Ages were "holy days" and the entertainment was under the direction of the church.

As the clergy's structural position in society changed and the dominance of religious ideas in the culture diminished, the structural changes seem to have exerted the first important impact for clergy role performance, especially in the United States. Because of the separation between church and state in the United States the church lost an assurance of financial support as well as a surety of membership. The necessity for clergy to "sell religion" developed which was reflected in the evangelical conception of the Protestant clergy in America.

The mission of the evangelical clergy was leading individuals to an affirmation of Christian doctrine and, consequently, salvation of souls. Thus, the principal concern was other-worldly, as was the case for the medieval Catholic Church of Europe. However, unlike the medieval church, the church for the evangelical clergy was only a voluntary association of the saved. The evangelical clergy went among the "unsaved" and actively sought converts while in the medieval church the laity usually came to the church. The evangelical conception of the Protestant ministry shows considerable continuity from early colonial America until the present. The "revival" phenomenon of the middle 1800's of the American frontier is elaborately described by historians writing of that period. The Reverend Billy Graham is one of the best known examples of a present-day evangelical clergyman.

American ideals of democracy and decentralized local control had effects for the clergy. The laity of a religious denomination exerted great influence on the behavior of their clergy. The organizational structures of various Protestant denominations afforded varying degrees of autonomy for the local congregations. Baptists and other more sectarian denominations invested almost complete control in each congregation. The local laity of these denominations usually selected (and continue to do so today) their clergymen and "informed" them when they no longer desired their services. The more formally structured denominations, such as most branches of the Methodist Church developed the policy of the bishop appointing pastors. However, even in denominations where pastors were appointed, seldom would an appointment be instituted which might offend large segments of the laity of that congregation.

One of the previously-mentioned essential prerequisites for the existence of a profession became undermined for the clergy with entrenchment of laity power. The clients had obtained the authority to judge the competency of the professional. Even with eroded professional authority, the evangelical clergyman performed his services within a general cultural context largely harmonious with the religious ideas he espoused. The general cultural explanation for the misfortunes which man experienced consisted primarily in conflict between good, which emanated from God, and the evil of Satan, a corrupted spiritual being. With industrialization and technological growth, scientific ideas became prominent. Religious ideas no longer had primary domination of the cultural framework. Science increasingly challenged religious explanations. The Old Testament told of a divine creation of the universe, while Charles Darwin suggested the scientific explanation of an evolutionary process.

The new competing intellectual cross-currents received two polar reactions from Protestant clergy. The conservative-fundamentalist faction emphasized preserving the evangelical mission of religion. The liberal clergy sought to update their religious ideas and concept of clergy mission in the light of the scientific changes. Theologically liberal Protestant clergy suggested a very important concern with present-day human existence. This concern was not greatly tempered by an emphasis on preparing individuals for an existence after physical death as was the case for conservative or fundamentalist clergy. The liberal Protestant clergyman, was, therefore, intellectually confronted with the human suffering accompanying the rapid industrialization of the United States during the latter 1800's and early 1900's. Hopkins (1940), writing of this historical period, concludes that clergymen were among the leading critics of the maladjustments from industrialization. Organizations were formed for the "advancement of the interests of labor." Some clergy became political activists and a small minority joined the Socialist Party. Many clergy working for societal reform began to advocate the scientific study of society for assistance in finding diagnosis and remedies for social ills. Clergy were active in promoting organizations to advance the scientific study of society.[1]

The clergy's disagreements among themselves as to the proper amount of concern and involvement of the clergy in social issues became quite pronounced. In the transition to the examination of contemporary research of clergy disagreements among themselves as to the proper attitudes and behavior concerning political issues, the reader may view the contemporary research from the standpoint that such cleavages are not new for United States clergy.

CONTEMPORARY RESEARCH: IDEOLOGY

The recent investigations of relationships between Protestant pastors' theology and political preferences were largely initiated by the research of Benton Johnson (1966, 1967). Johnson's operationalization of theology was to ask respondents to classify their theology in terms of one of four alternatives: liberal, neo-orthodox, conservative or fundamentalist. Only neo-orthodox theology has not been discussed previously.

About the beginning of the 1900's, neo-orthodoxy arose as an attempt to mitigate some of the liberal criticism of conservative theology's lack of concern for social problems. While not rejecting science and supporting social reforms, neo-orthodoxy is, nevertheless, skeptical of the liberal theological assertion of the goodness and perfectability of man. For neo-orthodoxy, theology is to remain an autonomous discipline.

Johnson (1966) investigated the association between respondents' classifications of their theologies and political party preferences among a sample of Methodist and Baptist pastors in Oregon. Stronger relationships between theology and political party preferences existed for pastors than had been found among laity. About two times the percentage of conservative pastors preferred the Republican Party compared with liberal and neo-orthodox pastors. Johnson (1967) further investigated theology of pastors and positions on six public issues. Liberal and neo-orthodox pastors were more liberal than theologically conservative pastors on all issues.

Hadden (1969), replicated and extended Johnson's findings with data from a national sample of clergymen from six Protestant denominations: 1) American Baptist, 2) American Lutheran, 3) Episcopalian, 4) Methodist, 5) Missouri Synod Lutheran, and 6) Presbyterian. The relationship between ministers' theology and political party preference for each of the six denominations confirmed Johnson's findings. Fundamentalists and conservatives were almost two times as likely to prefer the Republican Party than neo-orthodox and liberals.

METHODOLOGY

In the Tygart study (1969), questionnaires were mailed to 120 pastors randomly drawn from the church directories for the Los Angeles area supplied by each of five denominations (total sample was 600): Roman Catholic, Protestant Episcopal, United Church of Christ, United Methodist and American Baptist. The overall response rate was fifty-four percent. The smallest response rate was from Roman Catholics, with thirty-six percent. Protestant Episcopal pastors returned the highest number of questionnaires, sixty-seven percent; and the total Protestant return rate was fifty-seven percent. As in the Johnson and Hadden research, respondents were asked to classify their theological beliefs in terms of one of four categories: liberal, neo-orthodox, conservative and fundamentalist. Only four respondents failed to classify their theology in one of the four categories.

FINDINGS

Table I shows the strong relationship between theology and the index of liberalism-conservatism [2] as well as the differences among the religious denominations concerning theology (tables at end of paper). United Church of Christ and United Methodist had the largest percentages of theologically liberal pastors. American Baptist and Roman Catholic had the largest percentages of theologically conservative pastors. American Baptist and Roman Catholic were the only denominations having fundamentalists, with fifteen percent and five percent respectively of each denomination so classifying themselves. Anglican pastors displayed greater divergency regarding theology than the other denominations. As the column margins of Table I indicate, liberal and conservative theologies each comprise thirty-seven percent of this sample; neo-orthodox and fundamentalist categories twenty-two percent and four percent respectively.

Johnson (1967) speculated that the greater the proportion of liberal and neo-orthodox theologians within each denomination, the greater their propensity to endorse liberal political positions. Table I shows support for this speculation. For liberal and neo-orthodox theologies, United Methodists give the largest percentage of liberal political preference followed by the United Church of Christ. Also, as expected from

their relative proportion of liberal and neo-orthodox theologies, Episcopal (Anglican) pastors occupied the median position in terms of liberal
political preferences.

Thus, the evidence is convincing that pastors' theological self-
identifications are related to their political attitudes. An almost commonsense expectation would be that theology is related to political
activism. However, only my study (1970) systematically investigated
the relationship between theological self-identification and activism
along with political preference. Quinley (1970) related pastors' theology
with Vietnam war policy preferences, e.g., advocating increased United
States military efforts or immediate withdrawal. The relationships
found by Quinley were similar to my findings. Liberal and neo-orthodox
theologians were more than three times as supportive of a policy of
American withdrawal from Vietnam than were conservative and fundamentalist theologians. Quinley also investigated protest involvement
and found much involvement; fifty-one percent of his sample reported
some form of social protest activism and ten percent had demonstrated.
Unfortunately, Quinley did not report the relationship between theological self-identification and social protest activism for his sample.

Tables II and III indicate a strong association between theology and
social protest participation.[3] Liberal and neo-orthodox theologies ac-
counted for almost all the social protest participation. Also, when controlling for denomination, the effects were similar as was the case for
liberalism-conservatism.[4] Generally, the greater the proportion of liberal
and neo-orthodox theologians within each denomination the greater
their propensity to participate in social protest movements.[5]

SOCIAL STRUCTURE (OCCUPATIONAL COMMUNITY)

Structural effects have received much less attention from sociologists
studying the politics of clergy than ideology. Church laity has been the
structural effect most frequently investigated. The evidence (Hadden
1969; Hammond 1966) shows that clergy who are more structurally
removed from the church laity are more leftist in their political views
than are clergy more immediately responsible to the laity. However, as
with much sociological research, it is difficult to ascertain whether the
social structure has the greater influence for the increased political left-
ism or whether clergy predisposed toward leftist views are disproportionately drawn into certain structural entities.

Since the formal professional power of clergy has waned, an inquiry
was made on the effects of informal association with other clergy on
clergymen's political domain. The classical utilization of the concept of

occupational community was in a study of internal politics of the International Typographical Union by Lipset, Trow and Coleman (1953). The legitimacy for the drawing of an analogy between clergy and printers concerning the effects of occupational community involvement for social and political issues is increased by both occupations having "odd hours." Lipset concluded that shift work was a prime reason for the development of occupational communities. Recreational associates are greatly limited to those who have the same hours "off the job." Additionally, many non-clergy might feel a reluctance to engage in friendship activities because they feel that clergy is an occupation somewhat apart from the general society.

Participation in printers' formal social organizations and informal social relations were the two indexes of involvement in the occupational community. Formal social organizations included benefit societies, war veterans, sport organizations and others composed mostly of printers. Informal social relations were concerned with having friends who were printers and engaging in informal social relations with printers when not at work.

Because several denominations were investigated, participation in clergy formal organizations was not probed. Denominations differ on the formal organizations available to clergy. Thus, the finding that certain clergy were more involved in formal clergy organizations might be mostly due to differential opportunities. Since respondents of this study were residents of an urban complex, the opportunities to engage in informal relations with other clergy were available to almost all. At least two types of occupational communities among clergy are possible. One is a community of clergy of the same faith and the other consists of clergy of different faiths. Respondents were asked how many of their five closest friends were clergy of their faith and how many were clergy of other faiths. Respondents also were asked how often they met socially with clergy of their faith as well as clergy of other faiths.

Table IV gives the frequency distributions for the two items used to measure intra-faith occupational community. The column margins show the extent of involvement in intra-faith occupational communities for the entire sample. Roman Catholic pastors are the most active in the community from the standpoint of number of closest friends and frequency of informal social relations. Most clergy displayed some involvement.

Table V gives the frequency distribution for the two items used to measure inter-faith occupational community and the column margins show the extent of involvement for the entire sample. There were almost no consistent differences among the denominations as to number of best friends among clergy of other faiths. Roman Catholic clergy have fewer informal social relations with clergy of other faiths than the other denominations. Pastors generally were less involved in the inter-faith than in the intra-faith community.

A peripheral adjunct of the concept of the occupational community is the contacts with clergy of different race and religion from that of the respondent. Contacts have a less restrictive referent than occupational community because contacts may include interaction other than "social," e.g., recreational and/or friendship. A persistent research finding shows that equalitarian contacts with Negroes are associated with more favorable attitudes toward Negroes and civil rights activities. For example, Jeffries and Ransford (1969: 323–324) concluded:

> The results of this study show that the presence or absence of the experience of equalitarian social contact with Negroes is an important factor in the way Whites in the samples reacted to the Watts riot. To summarize the relationships (that held up well through control analysis) it was demonstrated that those lacking contact were more aware of the presence of Negroes after the riot, were more fearful of Negroes, cited more outside-agitator explanations, evidenced more feelings of increased social distance and place greater reliance on punitive solutions to urban disorders than those having contacts.

This study emphasized equalitarian contacts when respondents were asked the number of conversations they had with clergy of other races during a specified time. Partial analysis of these data indicates support for the Jeffries' study because interracial contacts were higher for the theologically and politically liberal denominations.

Regarding relationships between involvements in occupational communities and civil rights activism, no variable explained more than one percent of the variance. The correlation between interracial clergy contacts and civil rights activism showed a positive relationship of moderate strength ($r = .42$); seventeen percent of the variance is explained. The data show that the degree of association between interracial contacts and civil rights activism is stronger for the theologically and politically liberal denominations than the more conservative ones.

INDEPENDENT EFFECTS OF IDEOLOGY AND SOCIAL STRUCTURE
FOR POLITICAL BEHAVIOR

The findings of the present study indicate that aspects of the social structure have much less effect for politics than religious ideology.

However, research which systematically investigates the effects of social structure while controlling for ideology is meager. Religious denomination is primarily the structural effect reported when attempting to measure the independent effects of ideology and structure.

These data enable an analysis of the independent effects of ideology and social structure.[6] A "Multiple R^2" was utilized in analyzing the independent effects of each variable in predicting civil rights activism. As expected from the lack of zero-order relationships, all four measures of occupational communities explained a total of only one percent of the variance. However, theology which had been such a powerful predictor of civil rights activism on the zero-order level added an independent effect of three percent to the R^2 total. Interracial clergy contacts explained eight percent of the variance, a decrease from seventeen percent on the zero-order level. The index of political liberalism-conservatism explained thirty-eight percent of the variance. The combined independent effects of all variables considered in predicting civil rights activism explained fifty percent of the variance.

CONCLUSION

The evidence suggests that ideology is much more important than social structure in clergy political attitudes and involvement. Clergy who define their theology as "liberal" or "neo-orthodox" are considerably more likely to express liberal political opinions and participate in civil rights and anti-Vietnam war activities than clergy who describe their theology as "conservative" or "fundamentalist." Concerning social structure, involvement in clergy occupational communities had no effect on the political activism of clergy. Greater frequency of contacts with black clergy increased participation in civil rights activities. About half of the relationship between interracial clergy contacts and civil rights involvement remained after allowing for the effects of theology and political liberalism-conservatism.

The clergy has declined in Western civilization from the cradle of learning to an occupation which is presently struggling for survival as an individual entity. The clergy has reacted to this decline largely in terms of two polar strategies. The conservative and fundamentalist clergy advocate a lack of involvement in societal struggles while liberal theologians give societal involvement priority over traditional religious concerns for other-worldly existence. Parallels from the clergy can be drawn for the present dilemma facing college and university academicians. One position advocates a lack of direct involvement in societal issues and urges research and knowledge for their own sake. The counterposition emphasizes "relevance," i.e., direct involvement of academicians *qua* academicians in societal issues.

The clergy and the academicians have lost much of the most essential prerequisites of professional power: the client's acceptance of the professional's right to define what constitutes the client's best interests, and the professional's exclusive right to define professional competency. Boards composed largely of laity control the finances of most schools and churches. Local laity "hire and fire" clergy, and students "evalute" professors.

A sociological irony is the propensity of social systems to be weakened and even destroyed by their successes. Marx's well known critique of capitalist society asserts that the downfall of capitalism will result from economic advancements stemming from capitalism. The clergy formed the basis for the development of the professions which have enormously advanced scientific knowledge and technological change. This advanced technological society presently constitutes a difficult environment for the functioning of the church and clergy. Mass education has achieved a population which often feels competent to judge the work of professionals and threatens to undercut the academician who helped make mass education a reality.

TABLE I

Theology and Political Liberalism-Conservatism Among
the Five Denominations

| Theology | Political Liberalism-Conservatism | | | | N |
	"Liberal" %	"Mixed" %	"Conserva-tive" %	Total %	
United Methodist					
Liberal	87.5	10.4	2.1	100	48
Neo Orthodox	50	50	—	100	14
Conservative	28.6	57.1	14.3	100	7
Fundamentalist	—	—	—	—	—
Total %	73.9	23.2	2.9	100	69
United Church of Christ					
Liberal	61.9	35.7	2.4	100	42
Neo Orthodox	75	16.7	8.3	100	12
Conservative	16.7	83.3	—	100	6
Fundamentalist	—	—	—	—	—
Total %	60	36.7	3.3	100	60
Anglican					
Liberal	60	40	—	100	20
Neo Orthodox	54.5	45.5	—	100	22
Conservative	16.2	45.9	37.8	100	37
Fundamentalist	—	—	—	—	—
Total %	38	44.3	17.8	100	79
American Baptist					
Liberal	100	—	—	100	3
Neo Orthodox	44.4	55.6	—	100	9
Conservative	2.1	42.6	55.3	100	47
Fundamentalist	—	20	80	100	10
Total %	11.6	39.1	49.2	100	69
Roman Catholic					
Liberal	50	50	—	100	6
Neo Orthodox	18.2	81.8	—	100	11
Conservative	—	9.5	90.5	100	21
Fundamentalist	—	—	100	100	2
Total %	17.5	57.5	25	100	40

TABLE II

Theology and Civil Rights Movement Participation Among the Five Denominations

Theology	Participation %	Non-Participation %	Total %	N
United Methodist				
Liberal	85.4	14.6	100	48
Neo Orthodox	78.6	21.4	100	14
Conservative	28.6	71.4	100	7
Fundamentalist	—	—	—	—
Total %	78.3	21.7	100	69
United Church of Christ				
Liberal	69	31	100	42
Neo Orthodox	66.7	33.3	100	12
Conservative	50	50	100	6
Fundamentalist	—	—	—	—
Total %	66.7	33.3	100	60
Anglican				
Liberal	65	35	100	20
Neo Orthodox	81.8	18.2	100	22
Conservative	37.8	62.2	100	37
Fundamentalist	—	—	—	—
Total %	57	43	100	79
American Baptist				
Liberal	66.7	33.3	100	3
Neo Orthodox	77.8	22.2	100	9
Conservative	19.6	80.4	100	46
Fundamentalist	20	80	100	10
Total %	29.4	70.6	100	68
Roman Catholic				
Liberal	33.3	66.7	100	6
Neo Orthodox	50	50	100	10
Conservative	19	81	100	21
Fundamentalist	—	100	100	2
Total %	28.2	71.8	100	39

TABLE III

Theology and Anti-War Participation among the Five Denominations

Theology	Participation %	Non-Participation %	Total %	N
United Methodist				
Liberal	62.5	37.5	100	48
Neo Orthodox	42.9	57.1	100	14
Conservative	28.6	71.4	100	7
Fundamentalist	—	—	—	—
Total %	55.1	44.9	100	69
United Church of Christ				
Liberal	34.1	65.9	100	41
Neo Orthodox	50	50	100	12
Conservative	16.7	83.3	100	6
Fundamentalist	—	—	—	—
Total %	35.6	64.4	100	59
Anglican				
Liberal	45	55	100	20
Neo Orthodox	31.8	68.2	100	22
Conservative	8.1	91.9	100	37
Fundamentalist	—	—	—	—
Total %	24.1	75.9	100	79
American Baptist				
Liberal	33.3	66.7	100	3
Neo Orthodox	11.1	88.9	100	9
Conservative	6.4	93.6	100	47
Fundamentalist	—	100	100	10
Total %	7.2	92.8	100	69
Roman Catholic				
Liberal	16.7	83.3	100	6
Neo Orthodox	—	100	100	11
Conservative	—	100	100	21
Fundamentalist	—	100	100	2
Total %	2.5	97.5	100	40

TABLE IV

Religious Denomination and Intra-Faith Occupational Community Involvement

Of Your Five Closest Friends, How Many Are Clergy of Your Faith?

	None %	One %	Two %	Three %	Four %	All %	Total %	N
American Baptist	11.8	20.6	35.3	19.1	7.4	5.9	100	(68)
United Methodist	11.6	18.8	21.7	26.1	14.5	7.2	100	(69)
Anglican	20.0	26.2	28.8	12.5	6.2	6.2	100	(80)
United Church of Christ	17.2	19.0	37.9	17.2	5.2	3.4	100	(58)
Roman Catholic	7.0	2.3	20.9	27.9	14.0	27.9	100	(43)
Total	14.2	18.9	29.2	19.8	9.1	8.8	100	(318)

How Often Do You Meet Socially Clergy of Your Faith?

	Almost never %	2 or 3 times a year %	Once a month %	3 or 4 times a month %	2 or 3 times a week %	Total %	N
American Baptist	14.7	27.9	44.1	8.8	4.4	100	(68)
United Methodist	13.0	18.8	50.7	15.9	1.4	100	(69)
Anglican	32.9	30.4	24.1	12.7	—	100	(79)
United Church of Christ	23.3	46.7	28.3	1.7	—	100	(60)
Roman Catholic	11.6	18.6	18.6	41.9	9.3	100	(43)
Total	20.1	28.8	34.2	14.4	2.5	100	(319)

TABLE V

Religious Denomination and Inter-Faith Occupational Community Involvement

Of Your Five Closest Friends, How Many Are Members
of the Clergy of Another Faith?

	None %	One %	Two %	Three %	Four %	All %	Total %	N
American Baptist	41.2	27.9	19.1	8.8	—	2.9	100	(68)
United Methodist	50.0	25.0	16.2	5.9	1.5	1.5	100	(68)
Anglican	51.3	23.1	16.7	3.8	5.1	—	100	(78)
United Church of Christ	37.5	12.5	21.4	21.4	5.4	1.8	100	(56)
Roman Catholic	76.7	7.0	7.0	4.7	—	4.7	100	(43)
Total	49.8	20.4	16.6	8.6	2.6	1.9	100	(313)

About How Often do you Meet Socially Clergy of a Faith Other than Your Own?

	Almost never %	2 or 3 times a year %	Once a month %	3 or 4 times a month %	2 or 3 times a week %	Total %	N
American Baptist	33.3	37.7	24.6	4.3	—	100	(69)
United Methodist	36.8	44.1	13.2	5.9	—	100	(68)
Anglican	50.0	22.5	22.5	5.0	—	100	(80)
United Church of Christ	46.7	38.3	11.7	3.3	—	100	(60)
Roman Catholic	64.3	21.4	9.5	2.4	2.4	100	(42)
Total	44.8	33.2	17.2	4.4	0.3	100	(319)

NOTES

[1] Many seminaries began courses in "Christian sociology." Early academic professorships in sociology and related fields were often occupied by clergy. Thus, not only is the clergy an important occupation sociologically and historically, as I previously suggested, but much of the very foundations of sociology as a scientific discipline was provided by the clergy.

[2] In order to obtain a single measure of political liberalism-conservatism an index was employed. Respondents who described themselves as liberal on the political orientation self-identification item and scored liberal on at least nine of the issues utilized were classified as "liberal." Expressing no party preference did not keep a respondent from being classed as "liberal" or "conservative." "Conservative" was a conservative political orientation self-identification and conservative on at least nine of the ten issues. A residual category termed "mixed" consisted of middle-of-the-road political orientation and/or those who did not otherwise qualify for the other categories.

[3] Civil rights and anti-war activism were measured by:

Please check *all* the following in which you have participated. If you have not participated please check the "None" category.

_____(1) None
_____(2) Contributed money
_____(3) Belonged to anti-Vietnam War Organization(s). Please specify organization(s) ....
_____(4) Attended rallies
_____(5) Participated in demonstrations
_____(6) Other (Specify)

[4] The extent of political liberalism-conservatism among Protestant pastors is comparable to the findings of Hadden's (1969) national study. The Hadden study did not include Roman Catholics.

[5] The almost complete absence of civil rights and anti-war activism found for Roman Catholic pastors in the Los Angeles area might not be representative of Roman Catholics nationally. The lesser degree of social protest activism by Anglican pastors compared with United Methodists and United Church of Christ conflicts with popular news media depiction of Anglican clergy as the most politically active denomination.

[6] In the statistical analysis the recommendations of Labovitz (1967, 1970) were generally followed. The data which were usually ordinal were treated as if they were interval level of measurement for statistical purposes. None of the categories were collapsed in computing measures of association. The "Pearsonian r" was used as the bivariate measure of association with "Multiple R" and "partial r" utilized in multivariate analysis.

Analysis

Cultural and Societal Control

The occupational studies in this section demonstrate that societal norms and values influence occupational group and role autonomy. While we are unable to compare these disparate occupations directly, we can examine how these work roles cope with controls generated from outside the occupation. Although occupational control can come from many sources, these papers report on the formal and informal social processes which derive from the society's need to regulate autonomy in the work world. The following occupations are compared on the basis of how group and role autonomy vary and how diverse occupations cope with similar problems of regulating work: law (woman lawyer); acting (actress); cab driving; the clergy; and the housewife. The societal norm by which woman's primary role is associated with the home and non-work can be examined with interest by comparing the three studies in this section that include women in occupational roles. Simpson and Simpson (1969) and others have compared women in occupations within the same skill level on several work-related variables. They conclude that women who work have a high turnover level, and low commitment to work and that women in general have accepted the societal value of primary identity with non-work role obligations. However, Simpsons' findings are mostly on women in what Etzioni calls semi-professions (1969) and not women in the traditional professions such as law.

Davis (1964) has studied the patterns of female and male academic achievers in college. In his breakdown of students into female and male *high* and *low* performers, he concludes that even though women college students were more likely than men to be high academic performers, the *high* female academic performers were only slightly more likely to indicate future plans for graduate or professional study than the male *low* performers. This study further supports the idea advanced earlier that the primacy of the female role over the career and scholarly role has to some degree been accepted by women even though they have demonstrated ability to proceed further. However, these studies do not reflect definitions of women that seem to be emerging with the new feminist movements.

THE LAWYER (WOMAN)

In the world of work some occupations are structured such that members with undesirable status are not able to move upward in the elite positions. Epstein, in her study of women lawyers, reports that the group processes of recruitment, promotion and job selection are formally and informally regulated with the clear purpose of eliminating women and other nondesirables from attaining membership in key positions in the occupation of law. Her findings that women lawyers are restrained from obtaining important law positions are in harmony with the widely held cultural belief that women should not be in authority over men of the same education, age and social class. It further reflects the norm that women generally do not belong in the elite professions that require women to compete with men of similar abilities. But this is not necessarily restricted to the occupations called professions. Industry has long held the policy that women should not be in the position of foremen over a male crew (Caplow, 1954).

Thus, in this occupation, societal control encourages the prevalence of ambiguity as a process of curtailing women from obtaining entry into the key law firms at any level. Epstein's findings in this regard are of interest. The possible choices of employment were apparently limited for the women in her sample. Few women were able to obtain employment in key law firms and in work other than matrimonial and real estate law. However, these women did not feel this was necessarily inappropriate treatment nor an injustice to them. She hypothesizes that the social control systems of the professions and the larger society interact in a harmonious way such that role members consider non-entry into the elite positions as acceptable. Thus aspirations are reduced without any regret despite equal skills and expertise. In addition, the women indicated their worthiness for these positions and yet accepted work not requiring their special skills. Epstein's findings and those of the Simpsons seem to coincide with the cultural value placing women in an inferior status set in terms of work roles. They argue that women are less ambitious than men for advancement on the job and less inclined toward the kinds of competition that the struggle for advancement may require. Epstein, however, shows that women in the profession of law have considerable difficulty in passing the first step of obtaining employment in any important law firm. Thus, advancement and promotion are secondary concerns if women cannot obtain necessary entry at any level. Many would argue that such placement of women is inappropriate since men in important key organizational positions do have many duties which involve representing the organization to the public. If the cultural norm states that women do not belong in elite professions nor in elite positions, ambiguity as a means of social control in law is in harmony with the social control system of the larger society.

Today we are beginning to observe changes in this cultural norm and we will perhaps see changes in several occupations and industries. However, these changes will come slowly until there is tolerance in the society for women in authority positions in the work role. As Epstein notes, the current normative occupational structure is functional to the degree that social interaction is easy and competition among males and females at work is reduced. But changing this aspect of the role network will likely affect other work and non-work related roles between males and females. The conflict is likely to be covert since control coming from cultural norms and social values requires some degree of support from existing institutions. In work and non-work roles women will need to develop a set of ethics whereby autonomy and discretion seem appropriate.

But more importantly, the acceptance of women into elite professions and positions in organizations requires tolerance by male members of these professions. They regulate the opportunities that allow mobility into the key positions. The degree to which change can result will be determined significantly by male acceptance of competition with women. However, another condition is required. The "consciousness" of women must be raised so that unification occurs and women help increase this tolerance.

The above discussion while not examining direct group and role autonomy does support indirectly the cultural norm that the public is less willing to grant autonomy to women than to men, since the woman's primary attachment is supposed to be the family. In fact, the Simpsons (1969) state that women are more willing than men to accept the bureaucratic controls imposed upon them in semi-professional organizations because of their strong attachment to the family. In their analysis of the semi-professions (nurses, librarians, school teachers, and social workers) they conclude that women are unlikely to develop an ideology of professional autonomy and colleague control. Because they are less intrinsically committed to work than men, they are also less likely to maintain a high level of specialized knowledge and more strongly attached to their clients than men are. This may be the case in the semi-professions which are primarily located in organizations where all role autonomy is limited. This position can also be advanced for professions employing women such as law, medicine, and university teaching. Some movement toward professional and colleague control can be seen in several disciplines such as sociology, and psychology and several others where special associations and groups are being formed to act as checks on the larger professional body. They are trying to remove the ambiguity in activities that act to regulate the entry of women into the professions and colleague groups. At this time, we can conclude that in the profession of law, women at the group and role level have little discretion and control over work behavior. Men and women start out equal but the control system does not reward talent and hard work if connected to a negative status set. Women holding this status set have gone along with the control system where rewards and punishments are different for males and females. This control seems to be limited to recruitment, promotion and other position-related items. The autonomy to determine how work will be performed was not addressed in Epstein's paper. Yet, this would seem to be an important aspect to investigate since all professions to some degree regulate role activities, but how the tasks once assigned are to be completed or how the case is to be solved must be determined at the role level if specialized expertise is to continue to be a factor separating out some occupations from others.

ACTING (THE ACTRESS)

Any woman can call herself an actress whereas this is not the case with the woman lawyer. One similarity in the two occupations, however, is the prevalence of social control by ambiguity in such processes as recruitment, employment and occupational success. We recognize that more successful actresses may have autonomy. But there is little autonomy in the occupation of acting at the group and role levels.

Many occupations attempt some regulation of new members into the group. However, Peters found in the occupation of acting there appears to be little control over selection by the occupation. Furthermore, no standard procedures, and no required credentials exist to qualify the actress for particular roles. Thus, it is difficult for an aspiring actress in the United States to know what training and preparation are necessary. This ambiguity serves to keep members in the position of continually striving for success.

In obtaining employment control is retained by actresses who magnify the importance of previous work experiences, credits and accomplishments. In addition, the development of a professional age, somewhat lower than the chronological age, provides actresses further control in finding employment. Nevertheless, there is no sure established route of success.

Ambiguity, as a means of social control in this occupation, is illustrated in Peters' findings that there is no prescribed way to build a career in acting. It is not possible to calculate what steps a career should follow or what training activities are relevant to employment or chance of future success. The extent to which the actress needs to study acting to qualify for admittance to the occupation or establish a career is not acknowledged. However, the mystique of studying with a well-known teacher is defined by Peters as an important factor in obtaining parts during casting interviews.

One step that seems to be quite unambiguous is the actresses's acquisition of an agent to represent her in the industry. Agents are aware of what companies are casting for various roles and the requirements for these parts. Since this information is not available to actresses, the need for an agent is obvious. This control by the actress is minimized since the agent is generally the one to choose the client.

Ambiguity as a means of social control in the occupation of acting is further demonstrated in the mystical quality of what constitutes success or "making it." Here again at the group level little autonomy prevails in defining success. Several factors might explain this but of importance is the societal determination of success in the form of audience participation. This stimulates a competitive environment in the occupation creating many types of innovative techniques at the role level. In this aspect of the occupation, the structure of the industry becomes significant. The agent, casting personnel, producers, and directors all to some degree determine the actresses' success. Due to the fact that a majority of these positions are held by white males, opportunities to use sexual politics have been described as a means of gaining some degree of control over future success. The notorious "casting couch" is known to the lay public, but is considered sometimes to be risky in the occupation. This practice is apparently used by both men and women aspiring to be actors. Peters does suggest that unclear standards of success and failure do occur equally as often for men as for women.

There are other means by which this occupation is controlled. Problems in promotion and advancement are different in this occupation from many others as there is no direct career line established. That is, an actress never knows if she has "made it." These ambiguous communications of success and failure are proliferated by the occupation since this reflects the values of the larger society, competition, future success orientation and achievement. For the actresses, prestige lies in the occupational dignity associated with a sense of future success, even though they work in other occupations. This is in contrast with Epstein's findings of the women lawyers who indicated that they experienced prestige in the community for having been a lawyer but not necessarily committed to future success in law.

In sum, this study of aspiring actresses suggests that the occupation of acting at the group and role levels has only minimal autonomy to determine work expectations and rewards. Control does emanate from the society at large, the employing industry, producers, directors, and agents. The organization of the acting occupation into a guild apparently has not resulted in providing increased autonomy for the occupation. Except for some respects, acting is a low status occupation. Actresses support cultural values of non-competitiveness with men for scarce resources. Women lawyers, on the other hand, are potentially disruptive of the social system by violating societal values.

THE HOUSEWIFE

Any woman can become a housewife by one act—marriage. Social interaction in work roles is easier when women are not competing with men for places in scarce work markets, such as in the occupation of law. There is no union for housewives that controls working conditions, fringe benefits, financial rewards and promotion since by an economic definition housewifery is not an occupation. No occupational group establishes the ideology and standards, nor determines the role boundaries. Dependence on others is reduced as well as social control because of the isolating nature of the role. However, if we consider housewifery at the role level we are aware of the similarities and differences between this non-work role and many work roles. For example, in terms of preparation, skills and requirements for entry, the role of housewife is similar to that of acting. Definitions of success and failure are not clearly established and any women can enter the occupation.

Bernard does not define housewifery as an occupation. She reports that housewifery has little autonomy since the law defines occupational duties and freedoms. Using our broad definition, housewifery can be considered an occupation. Status and membership in the occupation are tied completely to the status of the husband. This is functional in maintaining societal order since menial role tasks of housewifery hold low status. Societal processes do operate to influence the housewife to perform in line with the role expectations that the husband's status carries.

Societal values of achievement, competition, orderliness, and security are all supported in this occupational role. Mass media uses of extensive advertising and other activities reinforce the societal need to regulate this significant role. Intensive competition, for example, serves to support the capitalistic system with its emphasis on procurement. The housewife who competes with other housewives becomes like the professional gatekeeper of secrets or medieval guildsmen. Whether in cooking or other role tasks, housewives maintain their specialized expertise by withholding knowledge from others. Evidence of this intensive competition in housewifery, acting or in cab driving provokes the question as to whether societal needs are served in this process. Also, the problem arises as to what positive and negative effects competition has on the occupational group, role and society if competition is too highly encouraged.

Varying forms and degrees of autonomy can be observed as part of the housewife role. As suggested by Freidson (1970), autonomy by default can be very significant for various occupations with high degrees of skill as well as for those with little skill. The cab driver and housewife fall into this position. No one evaluates the housewife, and no supervision of the work role occurs because of the nature of the work situation and the specific duties. The range of duties to be performed varies with the size of the family, income, etc., from meal preparation to elaborate entertainment. The degree of energy and amount of time to be invested in these role tasks and how they are to be completed varies from very little to almost total involvement. The housewife can be a ratebuster or have no pride in work. Role autonomy in these areas is almost total since there are no universal standards of performance and few occupational do's and don't's set up by the occupational group.

Bernard examines the differences between the economic and societal models which have dominated Western thinking on this occupation and reviews several possibilities for resolving this conflict. Two of these alternatives, professionalizing and industrializing housewifery, and paying for the services performed by the housewife provoke many questions. One of these is how will the occupational group and role be regulated by societal, organizational and client control. Since this is a low status occupation, incentives for work productivity such as group autonomy may be less when this role is industrialized than when performed by the housewife. The development of unions, where present, may further prohibit the client from firing low performers since the standards of performance would be controlled by the union. Paying the housewife by putting this occupational role in the labor force might result in more autonomy for the occupation than industrializing it. This would permit standards of performance to be determined at the role level and raise the status of the group by separating it from the husband's. Further ideas along this theme will soon emerge as societal changes reflect the changing role of women today.

THE CAB DRIVER

The social control of the cab driver is interesting to examine because it would appear that at the role level this occupation is autonomous. Freidson (1970) suggests that the cab driver, like the housewife, has autonomy granted to him by default since there are no significant others to evaluate role performance. While this may be true for individuals, this is inconsistent with the findings Henslin presents in his participant observation study of the cab driver's role. At the role level, autonomy is minimal since the societal norm is that all persons must be served regardless of perceived threats to the physical security of the cab driver. But, as Henslin suggests, the cab driver has learned to cope with this form of control by putting up the "on call" sign between him and his potential client, or pretending to talk on the cab radio. In addition to selecting his own clients, the driver can maximize his chances for survival by carrying some form of weapon to protect his individual and occupational livelihood. This does provide the driver some degree of control when the prevailing norm in the occupation is the service ideal.

Other occupations that support the service ideal have mechanisms whereby clientele are selected. For example, in nursing, occupational specialization allows nurses to select the patients they find acceptable even though the normative position of service to all requires that everyone be cared for (provided they can pay).

Like the actress, anyone can call himself a cab driver. This may be one reason for the low status the occupation holds in the work world. Licensure is not difficult to obtain for anyone who can drive and is able to pay for a license. Renting the necessary equipment can be accomplished by negotiating employment in the established cab companies. Skills required are minimal and work in this role can be found relatively easily. Despite the simple requirements of this occupational role there are many sources of social control that limit its autonomy.

Henslin argues that the capitalistic profit value in our society helps to reduce role autonomy since members, as in acting, must compete intensively to obtain work. This form of control is further extended to the management in the industry. Dispatchers are able to use censure, sarcasm, and threats of no work to make the cab driver conform to role expectations. Failure to conform results in no work. This results in worker being pitted against worker.

Occupational group autonomy is limited by the setting of the work which does not allow attention to physical or body activities such as eating, elimination of body wastes, etc. These activities are regularly performed in most occupations with minimal effort. The nature of the work setting prohibits such activities from being routinized in this occupation. Furthermore, limited opportunities are not provided in the structure of the occupation for achieving fringe benefits that most American laborers take for granted. Pension plans, hospitalization, etc., are matters that many labor unions have been able to provide for their workers. It would appear that the cab unions in this study were not able to negotiate as well as desired. In fact, Henslin suggests that the real power of the union to succeed with management is apparently very poor since the degrading conditions continue. The dominant business values of American society are reflected in the management of the occupation where they reduce costs by not fixing faulty equipment. Workers must take what they can get with the clever able to make a marginal living as a cab driver. This is similar to the structure in the occupation of law for women where only the outstanding obtain key positions. But, in general, they have little role autonomy and few opportunities to rise.

In summary, any job to the cabbie is good since he is grateful for what he can get. Henslin suggests evidence for the point made by Taylor (1968) that management is able to influence the unions more than the unions are able to influence management. This works against the workers in their attempts to achieve any needed rewards and autonomy. Henslin reports that in this occupational study management limits role autonomy and continues to manipulate work rules. But of more significance to him is the exploitative aspects built into the structure of the profit system in which the occupation survives. In this regard, the acting union seems to be on a parallel in terms of obtaining control for the occupation. Societal norms and values generate pressure upon the occupational groups in the work situation to maintain harmony between the several systems. Even though the occupational role of cab driver is quite distinct from actress or lawyer, similar adaptive processes and similar societal constraints do exist. This constraint serves to regulate the autonomy of each group and role.

THE CLERGY

Like the cab driver, actress, housewife and woman lawyer, clergymen in contemporary American society have limited autonomy in the work role. Today, in modern church organization, the influence of the laity in determining what is taught in the pulpit and in church school has greatly increased. Instruction in the above areas must match the best interests of the prevailing local clients, as they define this position. Tygart's review of the history of the clergy is instructive since it demonstrates how the influence of ideas and knowledge have altered the autonomy of the clergy profession and clergyman role. Early development of this profession reflects its control of education and how other professions emerged from the clergy. In addition early professions required a public calling to service in a particular vocation. Tygart notes that some religious denominations still require members to admit publically commitment to a calling.

Public acceptance in the past of clergy expertise and professional position has been very significant in acceptance of clergy power. However, as new knowledge and ideas developed in the early professions, religion began to be in competition with science and other bodies of knowledge. Accompanying this new knowledge was a decrease in clergy power and control over behavior in the society and determination of values. The dominance of religious ideas in American society and culture has reduced with an accompanying change in the structural arrangements in the Church. Tygart suggests that the separation of church and state was most crucial since it contributed to a loss of financial support and assured membership. This was seen in the United States in the phenomenon of "selling religion" and in the evangelical flavor of the Protestant clergy in the United States. Today this is visible with the Reverend Billy Graham and his religious crusade.

Decentralization of authority and local control of the Protestant church has resulted in local laity participation in selection of clergymen. The increase in laity control and power in decisions affecting the profession and role of clergymen did function to reduce the autonomy accorded the clergy. This idea that Tygart makes is important. We could compare this process with other contemporary developments such as the rise of technology and industrialization. The prominence of a scientific ethic will continue to arouse the public's level of participation and evaluation as seen in many occupations and consumer movements.

As Tygart indicates, the cultural importance of religious ideas was challenged by the rise of science and education. The polar reactions to this phenomenon among the Protestant clergy as he studied this was the division into the conservative-fundamentalist and the liberal factions. The former attempted to preserve the evangelical function of religion by retaining the sacredness of religious ideas oriented to another world. The liberal Protestant clergy revised their religious ideas to include and reflect scientific changes and embraced secularism. Tygart finds that religious ideology has more impact on clergy's political attitudes and social activism than some aspects of social structure. That is the liberal clergy indicated more concern and action with social protest and political issues than the conservative-fundamentalist. Thus their concern with social issues emphasized how to live in the modern world rather than preparing members for life after death. In doing this they relinquished some of their autonomy.

Tygart's study of the clergy has suggested that the occupation has changed from a profession to an occupation struggling for survival. Encroachment by various specialists such as funeral directors, counselors of many varieties and laity control have usurped the functions and autonomy of the clergyman. In terms of autonomy in the occupation and role, clergymen are attempting to innovate and regain their influence on the larger society. Several parallels can be drawn from this study in examining other occupations. For example, in occupations such as medicine, law and dentistry, we are beginning to see some movement in the direction of encouraging laity participation and evaluation of the profession and professionals. However, the opposite movement to keep expertise secret and reduce laity control by not permitting client participation is occurring in the same professions simultaneously. Thus, when technological and scientific norms are advanced and accepted by a large segment of the society, changes will occur in some of these professions and occupations since the public will use the same objective scientific approach to eliminate unnecessary occupations and incompetent members. This may be a result of the fact that the occupation is no longer needed in the society or a result of changing social values and cultural norms. The clergy has reacted by division in the profession; other occupations may follow this pattern. However, of specific importance in studying the clergy has been the combination of several forms of control removed from the occupation. Cultural control on the values of religion, organizational control by laity in financial decisions in the schools and churches, lack of consensus or organization of the occupation as seen in the split between conservative and liberal, all contribute to a continued trend towards almost total lack of occupational autonomy. Innovation and some autonomy will likely exist only at the role level.

2

THE ORGANIZATION

Introduction

Organizational Context

It has indeed been documented that most occupations today find their viability and permanence in complex organizational structures, with elaborate hierarchies, largeness of scale and other features of the ideal type bureaucracy examined by Weber. Usually it is assumed that organizational purposes are distinct from the purposes of the occupational groups and roles that occupy it. The pronounced interface between occupations and organizations today demonstrates the need to examine, theoretically and empirically across occupations and organizations, how each controls the other. The occupational studies discussed in this section are, by their structure, predominantly influenced by the work setting of the bureaucratic environment. We are primarily interested in how organizational settings and environments create and sustain particular occupations. Because organizations are primarily in need of control, such that authority over member flows down rather than up, the way specific occupations and roles are granted autonomy and power at each level is important to study. To some degree, this determines the viability of both organizations and occupations.

These papers examine the types and degree of control exercised by the organization on the occupation to alter its autonomy. Organizational control of role performance may be extensive as in the case of the jail school teacher role where survival of the organization (security of the jail) is predominant in regulating all goal activities. Mennerick reports that the larger system, including the decisions of the judicial system do impact on what standards and techniques of teaching the teacher can use and other decisions affecting work. Variations of behavior may be instituted, however, at the role level, so each teacher can define what to do in the teacher-client relationship. While Mennerick does not directly address the idea of autonomy, he does examine external and internal organizational controls affecting the jail school teacher.

Organizational control over occupations is not absolute. Samuels views autonomy as a variable that is a characteristic of all occupations. Her study of elementary school teachers indicates that as the size of the school district increases, teacher autonomy in certain matters decreases. That is, as size of school district increases, standardization of materials increases so that organizational resources might be adequately dispersed. Loether's paper on college professors suggests that autonomy does vary in the different organizational contexts in which work is performed. Autonomy for the teacher at the university level is much higher than that of the elementary school teacher. Even at the university level autonomy is not absolute. This study of the university professor parallels to some extent changes in an occupation due to conditions outside the organization of the occupation. In the case of the university Loether suggests structure of the college system was unable to or not desirous of providing a work environment conducive to productivity for all members of the occupation of university teaching. Using the typology of professional role orientation this analysis does provide more precise knowledge on what attitudes and behavior might be characteristic of some members of the occupation—not necessarily all.

Lengermann, while studying a different occupation, is asking some of the same questions as others in this section. For example, what influence does type and size of organization have on the maintenance of professional autonomy. Because he is examining data on the perceptions of certified accountants working in these varying types of organizational structures, we can only raise the question as to the real effect of organizational structures on professional autonomy. His data do indicate that organization setting is an important variable in perceived autonomy. However, hierarchical position provides even more precise understanding of group and role autonomy.

The impact of different organizational structures is further examined in Miller's analysis of scientists and engineers. His findings provide evidence to support the hypothesis that the organizational context is crucial to professional work performance. His comparison of the laboratory and other organizational subdivisions demonstrates that varying forms of organizational structure result in varying forms of autonomy and professional performance. How to match professionals, organizational goals and organizational structure is not answerable since all the necessary data for evaluating this question have not been collected. However, some factors such as level and type of education, work specialty (e.g., development, design, pure research, etc.) and preferred organizational structure seem to fit together in a predictable pattern. This pattern is directed at providing optimum group and role autonomy.

George A. Miller

Aerospace Scientists and Engineers: Some Organizational Considerations*

During the decade of the 1960's, aerospace scientists and engineers emerged as a very visible and important group of workers in contemporary society. They represent dramatic examples of the increasing incorporation of professionals into bureaucratic organizations and therefore provide the student of social organization with a valuable source of information concerning the conflicts inherent in the professional-bureaucratic dilemma. This paper will examine the basis for, and factors that may modify some of this conflict. Specifically, it will be argued that the degree of conflict experienced by these professionals is influenced by the length and type of professional socialization they have received. Moreover, it will be argued that the type of organizational structure in which these professionals perform their work is a major factor affecting the way in which they react to their work.

Today the typical professional works for a salary in a large bureaucratic organization, and the evidence indicates that the process will continue at a greater pace in the future. For example, employment trends over the past half century show that clerical and professional workers have shown striking proportionate increases, whereas skilled workers have increased more slowly, and managers, proprietors and officials have remained about constant. Significantly, the largest increase within the professional ranks has been among the professions related to

* This research was supported in part by a Public Health Service Fellowship from the National Institutes of Health. Financial assistance was also provided by a grant (No. 2377) from the UCLA Committee on Research and by a Summer Faculty Fellowship from UCLA.

114

industry—chemists, electrical engineers and designers (Gross, 1964: 642). Etzioni (1964: 3) argues that the factory of the future will employ more men in its laboratories than in its shops. He notes that Dupont already employs more Ph.D.'s than Yale or Harvard, and General Motors employs twice as many of these professionals as does Princeton University. In the United States engineering has become the single largest professional occupation, and the largest concentration of engineers is found in electrical equipment firms and the aerospace industry (Perrucci and Gerstl, 1969: 1, 2). Moreover, the organizations in which these professionals work tend to be very large; almost seventy-five percent of these engineers are employed by organizations with over one thousand employees (Lebold, Perrucci and Howland, 1966: 243).

A study conducted by the Bureau of Labor Statistics (United States Department of Labor 1970a) reported that the employment of scientists and engineers in private industry exceeded the one-million mark for the first time in 1967. Both proportionately and absolutely, this was the largest increase for any year on record. Of the total number of scientists and engineers employed by private industry, the report further shows that approximately forty percent were engaged in research and development (R&D) activities. Another study (Bureau of Labor Statistics, 1970b) focused upon those scientists and engineers with the Ph.D. degree. The results indicated that of those employed by private industry, eighty percent were engaged in R&D and they constituted about one-third of the total number of all scientists and engineers with the Ph.D. degree. Finally, the report indicates that between 1968 and 1980, requirements for scientists and engineers with the Ph.D. degree in private industry are expected to increase by more than fifty percent.

However, since the organizations employing these professionals tend to be heavily involved in government contracts for defense and space exploration, contract awards and cancellations can and do bring sudden shifts in the needs for the employment of these professionals (Seidman, 1969: 222). Major contract cancellations during the 1963–64 period (one year prior to this study) resulted in large-scale layoffs in the Seattle area (United States Arms Control and Disarmament Agency, 1965), the San Francisco Bay Area (Loomba, 1967), and the Greater Boston Area (Mooney, 1969). Although these layoffs were small in comparison to the current unemployment rate among scientists and engineers (Cordtz, 1970; Rose, 1970; Burck, 1971), these layoffs did result in long periods of unemployment, frequent downgrading of jobs, loss of seniority, geographical relocations, and other hardships for these professionals.

It has been suggested that the growing interdependence between professions and bureaucratic organizations has been facilitated by similarities in the principles that govern both professional and bureaucratic modes of practice. As Parsons (1939: 476) and Blau and Scott (1962: 60) have argued, both modes of practice stress rationality, universalistic standards, affective neutrality, and expertness as basic institutional values. However, while some of these principles are congruent, others are not. These latter have created conflicts for both the professional and his employing organization. Kornhauser concludes that most conflicts between the scientist or engineer and his employing organization stem from the basic dilemma of autonomy versus integration. Professionals must be given enough autonomy to enable them to fulfill their professional needs, yet their work activity must also contribute to the overall goals of the organization (Kornhauser, 1962: 195).

Organization implies the coordination of the diverse activities necessary for the achievement of organizational goals. Such coordination requires some mode of control over these activities. How to coordinate the very specialized work activity of professionals and how to coordinate their activities with other functions of the organization is a major problem for organizations employing professional personnel. This problem arises from the fact that the organizational mode of control often differs markedly from the type of control deemed appropriate by the professionals. Whereas organizations tend to be structured hierarchically with control over work being centered in the line, professions tend to be organized in terms of a "colleague group of equals," with ultimate control being exercised by the group itself. This conflict between hierarchical and colleagual control is one of the basic conflicts between organizations and professions. Scott (1964: 500), for example, has commented on this problem as follows:

> So reluctant are most professionals to submit to the authority of any man, but especially a 'layman,' that in those instances where they possess sufficient power to control the conditions of their work they resist hierarchical regulation of any but the most peripheral aspects of their performance.

As the above quotation indicates, there is also a problem concerning the basis of authority. In most bureaucratic organizations there are two differing criteria for the legitimation of power, technical knowledge and incumbancy in office. As Gouldner and Gouldner (1963: 414) have noted, the difference lies in the two kinds of directives that may be issued concerning the performance of work activity: "Do what I tell you because I know best, or do what I tell you because I'm the boss."

In addition to the conflicts stemming from differences in the type and degree of control, conflicts between professionals and their organizations also arise over problems associated with differences in the kinds of incentives provided (Kornhauser, 1962). Previous research has shown that the incentives most sought after by scientists and engineers are: (1) freedom to publish the results of their research, (2) funds for attending professional meetings, (3) freedom and facilities to aid in their research, (4) promotion based upon technical competence, and (5) opportunities to improve their professional knowledge and skills (Riegel, 1958: 12, 13; LaPorte, 1965: 33, 34). It is more common, however, for the organization to slight professional incentives in favor of organizational incentives such as promotions in the line, increases in authority or position, and increases in salary. This is the case because organizational incentives have proved satisfactory for other employees in the past, and differing incentive structures are viewed as competing sources of loyalty (Kornhauser, 1962: 135).

As a consequence of these and many other conflicts, sociologists have focused attention upon the professional-bureaucratic dilemma, and the results of these studies often paint a dismal picture of the professional caught up in the huge organization. One such study was conducted by Moore and Renck (1955: 66), who argue:

> Because of the central position of technology in modern industry, it would seem that professional employees, including engineers and natural scientists, would be a satisfied, well-integrated group. Evidence from attitude surveys conducted by the Industrial Relations Center of the University of Chicago, however, indicates that these employees tend to be chronically frustrated and dissatisfied. Factors in the morale of professional employees revolve primarily around a fundamental conflict which exists between the expectations and values of professional employees and the opportunities which they have to realize their ambitions and interests as professionals in the industrial setting.

In fact, Moore and Renck found that industrial scientists and engineers were only slightly more satisfied than factory production workers and were less satisfied than foremen, salesmen, skilled workers, and management.

Although it is clear that conflicts exist between professionals and their employing organizations, it is also clear that organizational administrators are not unaware of these problems and conflicts. The research to date suggests that these organizations are attempting to become more professional and flexible. Moreover, as Kaplan has observed (1965: 93), there seems to be an implicit assumption in many studies of industrial scientists and engineers that these professionals would rather be engaged in basic research somewhere other than in an industrial setting. "It is hard to imagine that this can be so," he notes, "since so many scientists do in fact work for industry, and industry admittedly is not dedicated to basic research as a main goal."

Professional Socialization. One of the major reasons for professionals' frustration and dissatisfaction with the organization stems from the discrepancy between their educational training and the actual work environment encountered when they leave graduate school. Orth (1965: 141) has described this problem:

> Professional training in itself, whether it be in medicine, chemistry, or engineering, appears to predispose those who go through it to unhappiness or rebellion when faced with the administrative process as it exists in most organizations. Scientists and engineers *cannot* or *will not* . . . operate at the peak of their creative potential in an atmosphere that puts pressure on them to conform to organizational requirements which they do not understand or believe necessary.

Kornhauser (1962: 138) argues that the strength of professional loyalty and identification can be expected to vary by the *type* of training received by the professional. He notes that professions differ in their selectivity of recruitment, intensity of training, and state of intellectual development, and that all of these factors affect the nature of the person's orientation. In this respect, a number of studies report that the orientations of engineers are closer to those of management than are those of scientists (Becker and Carper, 1956; Shepherd, 1961; Kornhauser, 1962; Goldner and Ritti, 1967; Ritti, 1968).

In addition to differences in the type of professional training received, differences in the *length* of training undergone are important. Those professionals who receive the Ph.D. degree should develop stronger professional loyalties and identifications than those persons with M.A. or M.S. degrees. This greater length of training also represents a greater investment on the part of the professional, and it is reasonable to assume that he will expect higher rewards from the organization in return for his services. The research findings to date support this argument (Glaser, 1963; Wilensky, 1964; Hagstrom, 1965; Orth, 1965). These studies show that professionals with the Ph.D. degree are more professionally committed than are those with the M.A. degree, who are more organizationally oriented.

The effects of educational training upon professional commitment generally occur before the professional becomes a member of the organization, and there is evidence that without positive reinforcement a strong professional commitment will not be sustained. Perrucci and Gerstl (1969: 98), for example, note:

The early professional socialization of the student engineer provides an important, but partial, set of influences upon the professional values and activities of the practicing engineer. If professionalization is viewed as a process, then the forces that influence a practicing engineer to behave in a more or less professional manner must be operative throughout his career. A student whose professional socialization has led him to subscribe to, and actively support, professional values might find such early commitments extinguished after a few years working in an organization that pays little more than lip service to the professional interests and needs of its engineers.

Organizational Structure. Just as there are important differences resulting from the length and type of professional socialization received, there are important differences in the types of organizational contexts in which these professionals perform their work activities. Hall (1967: 478) makes the important point that just because a professional works in a bureaucratic organization does not lead automatically to the conclusion that he experiences conflicts. This is the case because organizational departments or units differ in both their organizational structure and goals. Hall argues that rather than assume that conflict is inherent it is necessary for the researcher to demonstrate that it exists.

Comparative organizational analysis shows that the greater the organization's dependence upon research, the more the organization will evidence high professional incentives and low organizational control (Kornhauser, 1962: 149). Moreover, structural variations within an organization may also be apparent, and the type of organizational structure of the unit in which the professional works has a very important influence upon his reaction to his work.

For example, one method for resolving conflicts between professional goals and organizational objectives is to separate organizationally the different types of work performed. Units are therefore established that are devoted to basic or pure research, and these are administratively independent from other units in which the more applied and technical activities are performed. In this way, the organization as a whole is able to engage in both long-term exploratory research and immediate product development (Kornhauser, 1962: 198).

This process is illustrated in an important study conducted by Glaser (1963). In the organization he studied, the goal of the organization was to produce scientific knowledge. Scientists who were strongly motivated to contribute to scientific knowledge (i.e., evidenced a high professional commitment), were in agreement with the organizational goal and no conflict developed. In addition, the strongly motivated scientist also performed many of the administrative functions of this organization. Glaser concluded that in this particular organizational setting, high sci-

entific motivation tended to make scientists both hard-working professionals and also hard-working organization men.

Not all aerospace scientists and engineers, of course, work in organizational units that are devoted to pure or basic research. Moreover, it
appears that the organization selectively recruits professionals to work
in its various units. One major factor in this differential recruitment is
the length and type of professional socialization the potential employee
has received. Lebold, Perrucci, and Howland (1966: 248), for example,
found that organizational units whose main function was basic research
employed relatively large numbers of doctorate engineers and scientists.
Similarly, Marcson (1960) describes how the basic research laboratory
he studied made a special attempt to impress upon the recruit that basic
research was being conducted at the laboratory. The recruit was introduced to distinguished scientists who had made fundamental contributions to the field of science, and emphasis was placed upon the fact that
none of the separate laboratories were engaged solely in applied research.
Marcson noted that this strong emphasis on stressing the nature of basic
research was necessary if the laboratory was to compete successfully with
other organizations and universities in recruiting their best graduates.

Finally, in a study conducted by the Bureau of Labor Statistics
(1970b: 8), it was concluded:

> The most effective inducement for attracting Ph.D. scientists and engineers
> to a specific firm revolves around the overall 'image' of the particular firm
> or its research laboratory, especially its ability to provide an opportunity
> for professional development. Specifically, the most effective inducement
> for attracting Ph.D. scientists and engineers, according to the firms inter-
> viewed, is the opportunity to perform work of an advanced theoretical
> nature in the area of the individual's particular field of interest. An integral
> component of this inducement is the opportunity of working in association
> with authorities in a particular field in the proper scientific environment.

PROBLEM

This chapter will focus upon two significant varieties of work experiences for aerospace scientists and engineers that the previously reviewed
research findings have shown to be related to conflicts stemming from
the professional-bureaucratic dilemma. Interest will be focused upon:
(1) differences in the types of role orientations manifested by these
professionals, (2) differences in the nature and importance they ascribe
to various satisfactory and unsatisfactory work conditions they encounter
in their work. It will be argued that the way in which these professionals
react to their work is significantly affected by differences in their profes-

sional socialization experiences and the type of organizational structure in which they work. It will be suggested that the strength of professional commitment shown by these professionals is strongly related to the type and length of professional socialization they have received. Further, it will be suggested that those persons with high professional commitments should experience greater conflicts than those with low professional commitment. However, it will be argued that the organization selectively recruits professionals with differing lengths and types of educational training into units with different structures and goals, with the result that much of the potential conflict is mediated by the organizational differentiation of work tasks.

Research Setting. Data were gathered during the summer of 1965 from scientific and engineering personnel employed in two units of one of the largest aerospace companies in the United States. The largest of the company's several units was the "Aero-Space Group," which contained a missile production center, laboratories, testing facilities, wind tunnels, and many space-related facilities. The organization had also established a "Basic Science Research Laboratory" which operated relatively independently of all other laboratories and units of the company. The principal product of the laboratory was the scientific and engineering information made available to other divisions of the company by means of consultation programs. The laboratory had three major objectives: (1) to carry on research programs that would put the company into direct and effective communication with the larger scientific community; (2) to choose and maintain a staff of competent specialists who would provide consulting advice in their chosen fields of specialization; and (3) to engage in exploratory and basic research in fields where new discoveries will be of value to the company's overall operations.

These two units represented a sharp contrast in the nature of the work situation for the professionals involved. Professionals working in the Basic Science Research Laboratory shared an environment more like that of the university, whereas those working in the Aero-Space Group were more representative of persons engaged in traditional research and development work and functioned primarily as staff personnel within the unit.

Subjects. Subjects for this research were nonsupervisory scientists and engineers selected from the Basic Science Research Laboratory and the Aero-Space Group. All subjects held the degrees of M.A., M.S., or Ph.D., in science, engineering, or mathematics. Twenty different types of engineers were represented, ranging from aerospace to nuclear engineers. Scientists included astronomers, chemists, and physicists. General, applied, and theoretical mathematicians were also included. Subjects within the two units were selected by the following criteria:

1. All Basic Science Research Laboratory personnel ($N = 66$)
2. All persons in the Aero-Space Group with Ph.D. degrees ($N = 74$)
3. All persons in the Aero-Space Group with M.A. or M.S. degrees in science or mathematics ($N = 164$)
4. A 50-percent random sample of all persons in the Aero-Space Group with M.A. or M.S. degrees in engineering ($N = 236$)

In the analysis to follow those persons with degrees in mathematics are included with those having degrees in science and both are labeled "scientists." The engineering personnel are treated as a separate group of "engineers." This distinction will serve as the empirical indicator of *type* of professional socialization. *Length* of professional socialization will be defined empirically in terms of whether the professional holds the Ph.D. or M.A. degree.

Data were gathered by means of a mail-back questionnaire sent to the homes of the study participants. The questionnaire was anonymous, and a postcard was included for the subjects to sign and return after they had returned the questionnaire. This procedure allowed for subsequent follow-ups in the case of nonrespondents and two such follow-ups were undertaken.

Seventeen of the original 540 subjects had either moved from the area or the addresses provided by the company were incorrect, leaving 523 potential subjects. Of this total, eighty-four percent returned their questionnaires and eighty percent were completed sufficiently to be used in the analysis.

RESULTS

Organizational Differences. The two organizational units were selected because of differences in their structure and stated goals. As previously indicated, the goals of the laboratory were more concerned with pure or basic research, whereas the goals of the Aero-Space Group were more concerned with traditional research and development work. Therefore, the laboratory should be characterized by less organizational control and more professional incentives than the larger unit.

Professionals working in the two units were asked questions related to their perceptions of the degree of organizational control in evidence and the amount of professional incentives provided by the organization. Two indices of organizational control were used: the type of supervisor with whom the professional worked, and the amount of freedom permitted the professional to choose the type of research projects in which he was involved. Two indices were developed related to the incentive structure: a general index of the amount of professional incentives made available by the organization, and an index based upon the degree to which the organization encouraged specific types of professional incentives (cf. Miller, 1967).

The results indicated that the professionals in the two organizational units perceived striking differences in both the degree of control over their work and the amount of professional incentives provided by the organization (Miller, 1967: 765). For example, seventeen percent of those working in the Aero-Space Group said they worked for a "Directive" type of supervisor, as compared with only two percent of those working in the laboratory. Conversely, forty percent of the Aero-Space Group workers described their immediate supervisor as being "Laissez-Faire," as compared with seventy-eight percent of those working in the laboratory. Regarding the amount of freedom in their research choice, forty-two percent of those in the larger unit, as compared with only eight percent of those in the laboratory, said they had low freedom of research choice. Conversely, fourteen percent of those in the larger unit and eighty-six percent of those in the laboratory indicated they had a high degree of freedom in selecting the types of research projects in which they were involved.

Concerning differences in the incentives provided by the organization, forty-four percent of those in the larger unit said the general professional incentives provided were low; not one person in the laboratory indicated this to be the case. Conversely, only eighteen percent in the larger unit described the general incentives provided as being high, as compared with ninety percent of those working in the laboratory. Finally, forty percent of those in the larger unit described the degree of company encouragement of specific professional incentives as being low, as compared with only four percent of those in the laboratory. Conversely, seventy-six percent of those in the laboratory described company encouragement as high, as compared with thirty-two percent of those working in the larger unit.

Role Orientations. Having established perceived differences in the structures of the two units, interest was focused upon the effects of professional socialization and organizational structure upon the type of role orientation manifested by the professionals (Miller and Wager, 1971). The central question of interest here was whether professionally trained persons are becoming "organization men" or whether organizationally employed persons are becoming "professional men" (Kornhauser, 1962).

A five-item cumulative scale of professional orientation was developed consisting of items like: "In the long run, I would rather be respected among specialists in my field outside the company," or "In the near future, I would most like to publish a paper in the leading journal in my profession, even though the topic might be of minor interest to the company." Similarly, a five-item cumulative scale of bureaucratic orientation was developed. Examples of the types of questions asked were: "Being able to pursue a career in management is very important to me," and "I would like to assume a position with more managerial responsibility."

Path analysis was utilized as a method to assess the relative importance of professional socialization and organizational structure in affecting type of role orientation. The results indicated that the professionally oriented respondents were more likely to be trained as scientists and to possess Ph.D. degrees, whereas the bureaucratically oriented were more likely to be trained as engineers and to possess the M.A. or M.S. degree. The data showed that length of educational training produced two-thirds of its total effect upon type of role orientation directly, without any mediation by the organizational unit variable. Similarly, most of the total effect of type of educational training was direct—particularly in the case of bureaucratic orientation. These results indicate that these professionals were socialized in their schools to have different role orientations.

However, the data also indicated that the organizational context in which the professional performs his work *did* affect his commitment to both professional and bureaucratic values. The findings showed that type of organizational unit had relatively strong independent effects upon type of role orientation. Specifically, those persons working in the laboratory were more professionally oriented as compared with those persons working in the larger unit who were more bureaucratically oriented. The findings indicated further that Ph.D's and scientists were more apt to work in the laboratory, and engineers and those with master's degrees were more likely to work in the larger unit. Since almost none of these respondents had been employed in both units or had returned to school to receive a more advanced degree, the effects of the two organizational units occurred *after* the professional had been recruited to the organization. These effects reinforced the preorganizational role orientation and were opposite in direction for the two units.

These findings, therefore, strongly suggest that the type of role orientation shown by these professionals was largely the result of differences in the length and type of educational training they had received. Moreover, the effect of the organization was to reinforce, rather than to change or otherwise manipulate these orientations (Miller and Wager, 1971: 161).

Work Conditions. The conflicts inherent in the professional-bureaucratic dilemma should be reflected in the types of satisfactory and unsatisfactory work conditions felt to be most important to these professionals, and in the differences in the descriptions reported by those with different educational and organizational experiences. Therefore, the respondents were asked to describe the single most important satisfactory and unsatisfactory work conditions they actually encountered in their work. A classification scheme was developed that accommodated almost all of the descriptions obtained (ninety-four percent of the unsatisfactory descriptions and ninety-five percent of the satisfactory descriptions). In addition, five lay judges were able to classify these responses in the same manner as the author with about ninety percent agreement for both types of work conditions (cf. Miller, 1971).

The results showed that over one-half (fifty-nine percent) of the total sample mentioned either freedom in, or the intrinsic nature of, their work as constituting the most satisfying aspects of their work. Moreover, this percentage remained about the same for Ph.D.'s (sixty-three percent), M.A.'s (fifty-seven percent), scientists (sixty-three percent), engineers (fifty-four percent), and Aero-Space Group workers (fifty-five percent). However, a major difference was observed among those working in the laboratory, with eighty-two percent of these professionals mentioning these two work conditions as being their most satisfying. In the case of the unsatisfactory work conditions, sixty percent of the total sample described either their physical work environment or the organization of their work as being their most unsatisfactory work conditions, and this percentage remained very much the same for Ph.D.'s (fifty-eight percent), M.A.'s (sixty percent), scientists (sixty-one percent), engineers (fifty-nine percent), and Aero-Space Group workers (sixty-two percent). The major difference was again evident among laboratory workers, where only thirty-three percent mentioned these two work conditions.

Consistent with the argument developed thus far, it is believed that the differences in the descriptions of work conditions observed between the two organizational units is the result of the fact that the two units are devoted to very different goals and selectively recruit different kinds of professionals in order to achieve these goals. If correct, no systematic differences were observed because most professionals *for whom the conflict would be greatest* worked in an organizational unit whose structure and goals minimized such conflict.

For example, although freedom was ascribed the highest importance for all groups, seventy-one percent of those in the laboratory mentioned this one work condition as being their most satisfying (forty percent more than among Aero-Space Group workers). Freedom to pursue one's own research is, of course, a major component of a professional orientation and is consistent with the structure and goals of the laboratory. It was among the unsatisfactory work conditions that most of the differences between these two organizational units were most apparent. Whereas physical work conditions was the most unsatisfactory work condition mentioned by the sample as a whole, laboratory personnel ranked it next to last in importance. This was because those working in the laboratory enjoyed excellent physical facilities as compared with those working in the larger unit. In fact, the physical surroundings of the laboratory appeared much more like a university than an industrial organization.

Professionals in both units ranked the organization of their work as being their second most important unsatisfactory work condition, although the reasons for this were different. Those working in the larger unit disliked the interruptions, cancellations, and reorganizations associated with their work. On the other hand, those in the laboratory disliked the fact that part of their official work duties was to provide consultation to others in the organization. Examination of these descriptions showed that they were dissatisfied with the time and effort they had to give to others. For most of them, they regarded this aspect of their work as undignified and unnecessary—providing information that most of the persons could have found out for themselves by spending more time in the library. Finally, the time they had to spend with others in consultation took time away from their research. Again, these descriptions are consistent with both a professional orientation and the structure and goals of the Basic Science Research Laboratory.

CONCLUSION

The results of this research strongly suggest that differences in the type of organizational structure in which the professional performs his work is of crucial importance in understanding the way in which he reacts to his work. Moreover, the very different structures and goals evident in the laboratory and the larger unit, as well as the consequences of this for the work experiences of the professionals involved, raise questions concerning the empirical generality of many studies to date which have focused on the laboratory rather than the larger unit in their analysis. These findings suggest that caution should accompany attempts to generalize across units within an organization, as there may be as much structural variation within a particular organization as there is between different types of organizations.

It has also been suggested that some of the conflict inherent in the professional-bureaucratic dilemma can be mediated by the organization's selective recruitment of professionals into units with structures and goals that are "compatible" with professionals' educational training and commitments. It should be noted, however, that the professionals working in the laboratory were a very small minority of the total number of professionals employed by the organization. Examination of other divisions devoted to specific development and production functions (e.g., military and commercial aircraft divisions), showed a much higher concentration of engineering personnel with B.A. or M.A. degrees. The laboratory, on the other hand, was the smallest of all the company's divisions, the ratio of Ph.D.'s to non-Ph.D.'s was the highest, and it was the only division with the stated goal of basic research. Thus, these professionals were very different from the majority of the professionals working in the organization, and this fact is important for an understanding of the way in which aerospace scientists and engineers may view their work in the future. For example, while the evidence is increasingly clear regarding the appropriate organizational structure necessary for basic research, recent events involving the aerospace industry in particular suggest that many of these companies are moving in just the opposite direction. Cordtz (1971: 106), for example, notes that many of these companies are shortening the time span within which research is expected to lead to profits, are creating closer linkages between the laboratory and their marketing and production departments, and are spending much less money on basic research. If this trend continues, the uniqueness of the laboratory will lessen and its structure and goals will become more like those of other units in the organization.

Joanna J. Samuels

The Effect of School District Size on Teacher Autonomy

The purpose of this study is to investigate the relationship between school district size and the professional autonomy of elementary school teachers. It is hypothesized that teachers working in large districts will experience lower levels of autonomy than teachers employed by small districts because of the need for control and coordination in large, complex organizations. With increased size it is expected that the autonomy of subordinate members i.e., teachers will decrease.

There are two components of professional autonomy. The first component is concerned with the individual practitioner's control over his decisions and work activities within a particular work setting, or his freedom to deal with his client. The second is concerned with the autonomy of the occupational group or profession to control its decisions and activities in the community in which it functions, or its freedom to direct the activities of the profession (Engel, 1968: 37).

The first component of professional autonomy, the individual practitioner's control over his decisions and work activities, is examined in this paper. The practitioner in this case is the classroom teacher. His decisions and work activities are defined by his role as professional educator in the school setting. His "clients" are his pupils. The classroom teacher has been described by Wayland (1964: 612) as a functionary in an essentially bureaucratic system—a replaceable unit whose most significant aspects of work are determined for him.

128

LACK OF AUTONOMY

As a group, public school teachers have not enjoyed a high level of professional autonomy. Most of the decisions which are important in an educational setting are not determined by the profession.

Lieberman (1956: 91) discusses what kinds of decisions should be made by teachers as a group if education is to be considered a profession. Among the decisions he believes should be made by educators are: subjects to be taught, materials and textbooks to be used in teaching, criteria to be used in deciding which students should be admitted, retained, and graduated at all levels, the forms to be used in reporting pupil progress, school boundary lines, the qualifications for entrance into teacher training, the length and content of teacher training programs, the standards for entry into and expulsion from education, the standards of professional conduct, and the power to judge if and when practitioners have violated these standards. Lieberman concludes that educators do not make these decisions. Lieberman admits that getting the public to value and respect professional autonomy in education will not be an easy task. He believes a different attitude on the part of laymen can be expected only after educators themselves understand the need for professional autonomy and are alert to every opportunity to strengthen it.

There are many factors at work in our society which operate to set limits on the decision making of teachers as a professional group. A few historical elements responsible for the lack of teacher autonomy in the public school have been lack of teacher competence (Wayland, 1962: 44–45), lay control (Clark, 1962: 160; Bailyn, 1960: 44; Lieberman, 1956: 106), and business values in education (Callahan, 1962: chs. 1, 2, 10). Some contemporary factors contributing to the low autonomy of teachers are the high proportion of women in education (Lieberman, 1956: 242–243, 253; Rossi, 1962: 82–83; Caplow, 1954: 245–246), high teacher turnover (Mason, Dressel, and Bain, 1959: 382; Charters, 1956: 253–255; Wayland, 1964: 607), the structure of the local school system, and societal and educational factors which press for an informal national school system (Wayland, 1962: 46–51).

For many teachers personal professional autonomy may not be important. While our value system exhorts us to aspire toward security based on excellence in some productive activity and to seek major satisfaction in work (Gilman, 1962: 74), not all groups look to the job for a justification for living. Some, perhaps the majority, prefer to accept instruction, direction and orders without question and even resist being placed in situations where they are required to evaluate or otherwise exercise

independent thought (Scoutten, 1962: 86). Riesman (1955: 334) expects to find among teachers whose origin is in the lower edge of the
middle class or the upper edge of the working class "very little zeal either
for geometry or for children, but only moderate zeal to rise one notch
in the occupational and social class system." In any case the vast majority
of teachers in the sample reported themselves satisfied with teaching.
But for those teachers and prospective teachers who value personal
responsibility and professional autonomy in a job, classroom teaching
may appear less attractive than other occupational alternatives. Among
the teachers surveyed in this study, those who valued freedom from
supervision in a job were significantly less likely to describe teaching as
"satisfying" than were teachers who did not rate freedom from supervision as important. For them classroom teaching may become only a
step toward preparing for other jobs allowing a higher level of individual
autonomy such as school administrator, professor of education, or educational researcher.

One factor which may affect the individual teacher's autonomy in the
classroom is the increasingly large size of public school systems. Reports
of the effects of organizational size and complexity on the autonomy of
employees can be found in the literature on bureaucracy.

In a simple organization most of the limitations placed on the autonomy of an employee evolve from the leadership prerogatives assumed by
his boss. In a large, complex setting many leadership functions can be
built into the organizational structure. Behavior can be controlled and
coordinated by rules and regulations. Autonomy of the individual may
decrease regardless of the leadership style of the boss (Charters, 1964:
180–181).

Large organizations are characterized by specialization of staff, stratification of authority, many rules, and impersonalization (Blau, 1956:
17–19). The larger and more complex an organization becomes, the
greater the necessity for coordination and cooperation. Management
must build up an elaborate hierarchy of many supervisory levels and
institute a variety of formal controls. As size increases, the number of
persons who actively contribute and the extent of their contribution can
decline significantly (Corwin, 1963: 69). Terrien and Mills (1955)
found that size of school districts in California was directly related to
the proportion of administrative personnel. The larger the district, the
larger was its administrative component.

Today school systems are complex bureaucratic organizations, and
demographic trends are pushing for even more bureaucratization. It has
been estimated that within the next ten to fifteen years there may be
only 4,000 to 5,000 districts remaining in the entire United States,

whereas in 1965–6 there were more than twenty-five thousand school districts. Recognizing the problems inherent in the increasing size of school systems Woodring wrote:

"As a school system expands, the multiplying echelons of administrative authority increasingly separate the policy makers from the classrooms. The many administrative directives made necessary by organizational complexity make it even more difficult to adopt instruction to individual children, who, unlike the products of industry, are not interchangeable units. The teacher caught up in a vast system is prone to lose his professional status and to accept the role of an employee. While he may eventually resign himself to the fact that he must teach a rigidly prescribed curriculum, punch a time clock (as New York City teachers do), and take orders from above, he responds by becoming hostile toward the administration." (1965: 51)

METHOD

Independent Variable: Size of School District. The main independent variable considered was size of school district. To insure that size of school within a district was not confounded with school district size, two analyses were made to test for this relationship. The first analysis indicated no significant relationship between school size and school district size. Nearly as many large elementary schools were located in small districts as in large districts (Samuels, 1966: 88). The second analysis indicated no relationship between school size and various indicators of professional autonomy (Samuels, 1966: 87–91).

School district size was measured by the average daily attendance (ADA) of children in grades K–8. All fourteen school districts participating in the study were located in southern California. All were publicly supported, unified school systems, located in metropolitan areas.

Thirteen of the districts with ADA's ranging from 2,431 to 83,101 were grouped into four categories based on size.[1] Five districts were included in the "small" category. In this category the average ADA was 2,856 with a range from 2,431 to 3,467. Five districts ranging in size from 4,626 to 9,005 with an average ADA of 6,578 made up the "medium-small" district size category. Two districts, one with 15,172 ADA and the other with 15,410 ADA (average ADA = 15,291) made up the "medium-large" category. One district with an ADA of 83,101 was designated as the "large" category.[2]

The average yearly expenditure for the thirteen districts did not vary greatly. The average expense per pupil was $520 for the small districts, $432 for the medium-small districts, $474 for the medium-large districts, and $457 for the large district. A fourteenth district which was small (ADA = 2,636) spent so much more for the education of each pupil ($834) that it was not included in the general analysis but was analyzed separately as a deviant case.

Sample. The entire population of first through sixth grade regular classroom teachers from every elementary school in each of the small and medium-small districts was included in the sample. In the medium-large and large districts, elementary schools within the districts were selected at random to provide the other half of the sample.[3] All regular classroom teachers within each school selected were included. Data were collected by means of questionnaires sent to the home address of each member of the sample. A total of 1,125 useable questionnaires was returned by teachers representing the staffs of 231 elementary schools. Average percent of return was fifty-nine. Rate of return was not related to district size.

Dependent Variable: Teacher Autonomy. Professional autonomy of the elementary classroom teacher was the dependent variable. Professional autonomy was defined as the freedom an employee has to exercise his competence in the performance of tasks required of him by his occupation. Questionnaire items elicited data for three dimensions of autonomy.

Scope For Decision-Making. The first dimension of autonomy is teacher's scope for decision-making. Decision-making involves the discretional content of a job. Where scope for decision-making is great, an employee is authorized, required, and expected to use his own discretion or judgment as he proceeds with his task, overcoming obstacles by choosing what he considers the best of all alternative choices available to him at each stage of his work (Jaques, 1956: 34). Decision-making is brought into play when methods are not prescribed or predetermined.

Standardization of Instructional Resources. The second dimension affecting a teacher's autonomy is the extent of standardization or routinization in his work activity. If much of the content of his task has been routinized and his methods and resources are standardized, then fewer problem-solving activities are required (March and Simon, 1963: ch. 6). When alternatives are circumscribed, the scope for decision-making is reduced. For example, teachers' testbook manuals which accompany required textbooks provide detailed lesson plans and methods of presentation of the material. Extensive use of these suggestions reduces the need for search and problem-solving by the teacher. Many of the teachers' manuals have been developed by experts in the subject matter field. Use of the manuals reduces the need for expertise on the part of the classroom teacher. "Packaged curriculums" can demean the teacher and his role in instruction; in fact, the package may be designed so that it is as "teacher proof" as possible (Wittrock, 1965: 3; Sizer, 1965: 53–54; O'Neil, 1968: 12).

Product Versus Process Evaluation. The third dimension of professional autonomy is the type of review utilized by the school administrator to evaluate teacher success. Where methods are specified and evaluation focuses on methods rather than on outcomes, teachers have little opportunity to exercise discretion (Simon, 1944: 28). On the other hand, when methods are left to the discretion of teachers and *results* are reviewed and evaluated, more opportunity for autonomous decisions is available (Blau, 1956: 62).

FINDINGS

Scope For Decision-Making. Among the items included as indicators of scope for decision-making were seven statements which referred to situations involving professional autonomy which teachers might experience in the classroom. The responses of teachers within each of the four district size categories are reported in Table I (see end of paper) under statements one through seven.

When the responses to statements one through seven in Table I are examined, it can be seen that the larger the district, the less likely teachers are to perceive their classroom setting as providing opportunities for decision-making. Responses to statement eight support Wilensky's (1964: 148) assertion that whenever organizational routines gain ascendance, salaried professionals may lose sight of client welfare.

Statement nine deals with teachers' perceptions of the style of supervision employed by their principal. Principals perceived as being strict were assumed to allow teachers less professional autonomy than those perceived as not strict. A separate analysis of responses to seven autonomy indicators showed that teachers who perceived their principal as being "usually" or "always" strict experience significantly lower levels of autonomy in the classroom than did teachers who perceived their principal as being "rarely" or "never" strict (p < .01; Samuels, 1966: 92–103).

The responses to statement nine in Table I show that teachers in larger districts were more likely to perceive their principals as being "always" or "usually" strict. Because strictness of principal was found to be associated both with size of district and with low levels of autonomy, the question arose as to whether teacher autonomy was related primarily to organizational factors associated with district size or merely to the fact that strict principals happened to be found more often in larger districts. To answer this question the effects of size of district on autonomy were analyzed with the variable of principal strictness controlled.

With principal strictness held constant, a strong relationship between large district size and low professional autonomy persisted (p < .001; Samuels, 1966: 104–110). These data thus support the hypothesis that as school district size increases, the autonomy of teachers to make professionally relevant decisions decreases.

Provision of Standardized Instructional Resources. The second dimension of autonomy examined the extent of standardization or routinization of the teacher's work activity. It was assumed that if the tasks to be performed in teaching were preplanned and standardized by professionals other than the teacher, scope for decision-making would be constrained.

To provide a census of instructional resources available to teachers in districts of different sizes, teachers were asked to respond either "yes" or "no" to each of 130 questions. The format of the questions was as follows:

My district of county provides:
1. Adopted textbooks
2. Adopted supplementary textbooks
3. Teacher's textbook manuals
4. Workbooks and/or follow-up materials
5. Basic subject guides
6. Grade-level guides
7. Instructional bulletins
8. Pre-planned teaching units
9. Audio-visual resources
10. Consultants, supervisors, resource persons
11. Educational television
12. Special teachers
13. Workshops

. . . in the following subjects:

1. Language arts
2. Reading
3. Writing
4. Spelling
5. Social studies
6. Arithmetic
7. Natural sciences
8. Art
9. Music
10. Physical education, rhythm and dance [4]

Responses to the 130 questions were broken down by school district size categories and an index of standardization was computed. The index number represents the average percentage response across ten subject matter areas within a given instructional resource. A large index number (average percentage) indicates a greater density of directives from the district to the classroom teacher and implies less scope for decision-making within the classroom.

The findings in Table II (see end of paper) indicate that the availability of seven of the thirteen types of instructional resources was positively associated with district size. The larger the district, the more likely it was to provide teachers with basic subject matter guides, grade-level guides, instructional bulletins, preplanned teaching units, audio-visual resources, consultants, and teacher workshops.

Little differentiation by district size is revealed for textbooks, supplementary textbooks, and teachers' textbook manuals. This finding is to be expected for two reasons: (a) textbooks are provided by the state and teacher's manuals automatically accompany the classroom text, and (b) textbooks are generally considered to be essential aids in teaching. Neither availability of workbooks and follow-up materials nor provision of special teachers varies directly with increasing size of district. Educational television is negatively associated with increasing size. Nevertheless, the availability of seven of the types of resources is associated in a positive way with increasing district size. It was found that not only were some resources more available to teachers in larger districts, but also teachers in larger districts tended to use these resources more often than teachers in the smaller districts (Samuels, 1966: 82–84).

Furthermore, although there was little difference in the availability of adopted textbooks, supplementary textbooks, and teacher textbook manuals, teachers in the larger districts tended to use these materials more often than did teachers in the smaller districts (Samuels, 1966: 86).

It is obvious that by providing teachers with resources in various subject matter areas and by standardizing the task and by restricting teacher autonomy, school districts are attempting to facilitate good teaching and learning. One might expect that in districts where a large variety of resource materials is available that teachers would be free to choose among the materials available and to use them in diverse ways which would maximize their opportunity for instructional decision-making, thereby increasing their scope for professional autonomy. However, the data did not support this point of view. All of the teachers had some resources of all kinds at their disposal but the responses of those who reported having the greatest selection of such resources did not indicate any particular freedom in their instructional role.

Teachers in large districts clearly experience less professional autonomy than teachers in small school districts, perhaps because of the profuse array of standardizing materials and services provided for them by their districts. If lack of autonomy were simply the result of inadequate teacher preparation or failure to recognize the need for autonomy, then through improved teacher education and desire for greater autonomy teachers might increase their scope for decision-making. On the other hand, if one of the major barriers to professional autonomy is the structural organization of school districts, then neither recognizing the problem nor increasing the educational preparation of teachers would aid in the professionalization of teachers in so far as their instructional role is concerned.

Product Versus Process Evaluation. The third dimension of autonomy studied how teachers were evaluated by their principals. One of the important products or outcomes of teaching is pupil gain in achievement. When the evaluation of the teacher is determined by student achievement, teachers are left relatively free to use methods of their own choice which *work*, that is, which produce the desired learning outcomes. When the evaluation of the teacher is based upon process criteria, that is, how subject matter is presented and how closely the teacher follows approved teaching methods, the teacher must focus on *means* rather than on the goal of student achievement and cannot realistically be held responsible for learning outcomes. Under conditions of process evaluation, teachers will be less free to exercise their own discretion in using techniques which they have found most suitable for the needs of their particular students.

To learn what factors teachers thought were most important to their principals in arriving at his evaluation of them as teachers, the method of paired-comparisons was used to obtain a ranking of four evaluative criteria. These criteria were the academic achievement of their pupils, their teaching methods, their classroom control and discipline, and their relations with other members of the staff. The data were analyzed to determine whether district size was associated with particular evaluative criteria.

It was found that regardless of the size of the district in which teachers worked, more than fifty percent of all teachers agreed that classroom control and discipline were the most important criteria in teacher evaluation. Second most important was the teaching methods used by the teacher. Pupil's achievement was ranked third, and the least important criterion was judged to be staff relations.

Teachers, then, feel they are judged by process criteria, that is, by their teaching methods rather than by the achievement of their pupils.

This finding may explain why from sixty to ninety percent of the teachers in the study chose their methods according to what their principals or districts preferred, thereby reducing their scope for decision-making in the classroom. In the area of discipline, however, the opposite situation exists. Most teachers used techniques which they had developed through experience. No one method can be a surefire producer of "good citizenship," so to maintain order in the classroom the teacher must use varying personal techniques.

Not only does the principal encourage the teacher to handle classroom problems independently, he is believed to evaluate the teacher's performance in terms of how successful she is in maintaining classroom control and discipline. This finding confirms Gordon's belief that classroom disorder is taken as a visible sign of incompetence. Ability to control, he says, is equated with ability to teach (1955: 5). The less willing a principal is to support the institutional authority of a teacher, the more likely that the teacher will absorb conflict in his classroom role and the more likely he will be to resort to personalized leadership (Waller, 1961: 195). To maintain discipline the teacher is free to use his own methods; he is encouraged to handle discipline problems himself and he will be evaluated by the behavior of his pupils, a product criterion.

The data suggest the possibility that greater scope for decision-making may lie in the area of classroom control and discipline than in the area of subject matter teaching methods.

The data on product versus process evaluation found no relationship between evaluative criteria and district size. However, with regard to the other two dimensions of autonomy, the results supported the hypothesis. Firstly, as school district size increased, the autonomy of the teacher to teach the way she thought best and her freedom to make other educationally relevant decisions decreased. Secondly, the larger the district, the more likely it was to provide teachers with instructional materials and services and the more likely teachers were to use them.

However, since both district size and provision of instructional resources are correlated with autonomy, these two variables are confounded and one does not know whether autonomy is affected more by size or by the provision of many standardized resources. One can argue that it is not size itself, but rather the provision of resources that is related to reduction of autonomy.

This hypothesis is given support through the analysis of the deviant case, a small but wealthy district providing many instructional resources for its teachers. The analysis of the deviant case demonstrates that small district size does not guarantee professional autonomy.

THE DEVIANT CASE

The deviant case was described earlier as a small district which was excluded from the general analysis because its average support per pupil exceeded by over three hundred dollars the average support per pupil in each district size category. The amount spent in the deviant district for public education is an indication of the affluence of the community and also of the concern for education felt by its citizens whose levels of education and occupation are very high.

As seen in Table I, teachers from the deviant district reported having less scope for decision-making than teachers in small districts on all nine measures. They reported having less scope for decision-making than teachers in medium-small districts on all nine measures. They reported less scope for decision-making than teachers in the medium-large districts on seven of nine measures. Teachers in the deviant district did, however, report greater opportunity for decision-making than did teachers in the large district on seven of the nine measures.

Variables other than district size must be sought to explain why such low autonomy levels exist for teachers in the deviant district. The hypothesis that it is the profuse array of standardized instructional resources provided for and used by teachers which actually constrains their scope for decision-making was tested by comparing the amount of resources provided teachers in the deviant district with the amount of such resources provided teachers in the other district size categories.

In Table II it can be seen that the deviant district did in fact make available to its teachers a very large amount of various kinds of instructional resources.

The deviant district provided twelve out of thirteen types of resources more often than other districts of corresponding size; it provided twelve out of thirteen types of resources more often than the medium-small districts; it provided eleven out of thirteen types of resources more often than the medium-large districts; and it provided eight out of thirteen types of resources more often than the large district. And, in fact, teachers in the deviant district used these resources more often than did teachers in the same size and larger districts (Samuels, 1966: 124).

Low autonomy levels and the availability of numerous instructional resources are associated in both the general analysis and in the deviant analysis, a finding which supports the hypothesis that districts which provide teachers with a great many resources, whether for goals of coordination and control, or simply for the achievement of more consistent high-level student performance, may actually be reducing the teacher's opportunity for professional decision-making. Provision of such materials can be either a bureaucratic consequence of size of district or a product of the affluence of a wealthy district which can afford to provide any resource which might produce high pupil achievement.

It seems likely that teachers in the immediate future, regardless of their instructional competence or the wealth or size of the district in which they work, will be provided with an increasing amount of standardized instructional resources developed by professionals outside of the classroom, and even outside the school system. Educational publishing houses, mass media, commercial educational research organizations, and institutions of higher education are rushing to provide the hard and soft ware that will be bought by school districts for classroom use. The instructional role in classroom teaching is not likely to provide teachers with greater opportunities for individual professional autonomy. Both size and affluence of school districts will operate to constrain teacher autonomy.

TABLE I
SCOPE FOR DECISION-MAKING

Statement	District Size Categories (in percentages)				Chi-Square Levels of Significance	Deviant District[b]
	Small	Medium-Small	Medium-Large	Large		
1. Teaching in your district is a good job for someone who likes to be "his own boss." (percentage who agree)	78% (137)[a]	72% (300)	50% (119)	26% (73)	p < .001	35% (13)
2. I feel free to teach each subject in any way I think best. (percentage who agree)	95 (167)	89 (375)	76 (181)	39 (111)	p < .001	78 (29)
3. In your district teachers never have to follow procedures which conflict with their own professional judgment. (percentage who agree)	44 (78)	31 (130)	23 (54)	17 (47)	p < .001	22 (8)
4. Teachers in your district must refer most non-routine decisions to someone else higher up for a final O.K. (percentage who disagree)	50 (88)	38 (159)	32 (75)	21 (60)	p < .001	21 (8)
5. I am allowed to teach only those subjects which are included in the course of study. (percentage who disagree)	86 (152)	70 (294)	49 (118)	41 (116)	p < .001	42 (16)
6. I am expected to follow suggested instructional sequences and unit plans as closely as possible. (percentage who disagree)	68 (119)	55 (231)	33 (78)	11 (32)	p < .001	21 (8)
7. I choose my teaching methods according to what the district or my principal prefers. (percentage who respond "rarely" or "never")	39 (68)	29 (123)	20 (48)	10 (27)	p < .001	26 (10)
8. I choose my teaching methods according to what I believe best for my pupils. (percentage who respond "always")	63 (111)	53 (224)	49 (118)	37 (105)	p < .001	42 (16)
9. My principal is strict with teachers. (percentage who say "always" or "usually" strict)	18 (32)	32 (135)	34 (81)	36 (102)	p < .001	39 (15)

[a] Number of respondents   [b] Excluded from statistical computations

TABLE II

SCHOOL DISTRICT SIZE AND AVAILABILITY OF INSTRUCTIONAL RESOURCES

(in percentages)

Instructional Resources	Small	District Size Categories				
		Medium-Small	Medium-Large	Large	Deviant District
1. Basic subject guide	53.34 [a]	61.03	62.95	77.96	62.29
2. Grade-level guide	50.95	56.56	75.58	97.16	78.53
3. Instructional bulletins	28.06	24.67	29.94	44.50	51.99
4. Preplanned teaching units	8.96	12.99	9.75	35.63	18.47
5. Audio-visual resources	65.69	72.95	76.23	92.53	83.76
6. Consultants	32.68	29.06	59.53	91.25	90.16
7. Workshops	26.12	48.07	63.58	58.47	60.13
8. Adopted textbook	67.84	72.58	73.26	70.95	74.54
9. Adopted supplementary textbooks	36.29	35.77	31.28	32.93	54.53
10. Textbook manuals	71.22	76.47	79.19	76.84	79.36
11. Special teachers	19.37	11.72	10.69	14.95	39.64
12. Workbooks or follow-up materials	28.38	18.43	17.94	22.98	34.77
13. Educational television	30.29	35.65	12.23	4.14	27.54

[a] Index number = average percentage response across ten subject matter areas

NOTES

[1] Figures were those for 1962–1963, the latest available figures from the California Department of Education (n.d.) for the fiscal year ending June 30, 1963.

[2] Twenty-five superintendents of publicly supported, unified school systems located in metropolitan areas within a single state were contacted and asked to allow teachers in their districts to participate in the study. Eight superintendents of "small" districts were contacted of whom six agreed to cooperate; nine superintendents of "medium-small" districts were contacted of whom five agreed to cooperate; four superintendents of "medium-large" districts were contacted of whom two agreed to cooperate; four superintendents of "large" districts were contacted of whom one agreed to cooperate. Because the sample of school districts could not be randomly selected, findings from this study may not be generalizable to the universe of school districts or teachers in California or to districts or teachers in other states.

[3] In order to obtain an adequate teacher sample from the smaller districts, it was necessary to include all the teachers from each elementary school in each of the smaller districts. In the larger school systems, schools were randomly selected to provide the necessary sample size.

[4] All of these are subjects in which instruction is required in California elementary schools.

Lewis A. Mennerick

The County Jail School Teacher: Social Roles and External Constraints

The roles associated with the status of teacher are numerous: director of learning, disciplinarian, judge, friend or counselor, and model of middle-class morality. Variations in the fulfillment of role expectations may be due to the teacher's personality, his social and educational background, and the particular school setting. Considering the school setting, role expectations will likely vary according to the level of the school, the type of school (private, parochial, public), and particular schools of the same general type (inner city, suburban, rural). In short, the school setting and the larger setting in which the school functions may be influential in determining which roles will be emphasized and how role expectations will actually be fulfilled. An extreme example of the influence of the external setting was found in the case of the Metropolitan County Jail School.[1] Teachers in the Metropolitan County Jail School face some very tough conditions within which to realize the ends teachers are supposed to achieve: to teach, to maintain order, to help students. Thus, the school's external environment—the judicial system, the community, and especially the jail complex within which the school is situated—influences jail school teachers in a variety of ways.[2] In this paper, I will discuss the role of the jail school teacher as teacher, emphasizing the ways in which the external environment influences the fulfillment of role expectations. Also explored will be the ways in which jail school teachers cope with the overall problem of being only minimally successful in their teaching.

143

METHOD AND SETTING OF STUDY

Metropolitan County Jail is located in a large northern city. The jail population, which includes both sentenced misdemeanants and non-sentenced inmates awaiting trial, averages approximately eighteen hundred inmates with an annual turnover of roughly twenty-three thousand inmates. The school consists of an academic section with four classrooms and a vocational section with a print shop, wood shop, shoe shop, and craft shop. The school is located in the basement of two cell-blocks and has a normal daily enrollment of approximately one hundred-fifty students. And although the jail population is composed of adults of all ages, school attendance is limited to inmates, seventeen to twenty. The teaching staff consists of ten full-time teachers and an assistant principal, supplied by the Board of Education.

I participated in the activities of the jail school in the role of researcher during a period of approximately one and one-half years. I observed the teachers, inmates, and jail personnel as they went about their activities in the school. During this time I engaged in many conversations with people in the jail, especially with the teachers. Attempting to learn as much as possible about what goes on in a jail school, I listened to what was said and raised questions to clarify points or to elicit information on specific topics. In the present paper, I use excerpts from my field notes to document and illustrate the analysis. The name and position of the person speaking and the date of the field work accompany each quote.

THE JAIL SCHOOL TEACHER

The principal role of the teacher is to teach: to transmit knowledge to his pupils. In the jail school, the teaching tasks involve a blend of instruction in academic, vocational, and social matters. Yet the teaching role in the Metropolitan County Jail School is influenced greatly by the school's external environment: the courts, the community, and especially the jail complex within which the school is located. More specifically, two aspects of the jail school's environment greatly constrain the activities of school personnel: the external control of the recruitment of students and the jail's emphasis on security.

External control of recruitment. Most teachers in most schools have little direct control over the number and kinds of students they get.[3] Jail school teachers are no exception. Upon entering the jail, all males between the ages of seventeen and twenty ordinarily are assigned to the school tiers. They automatically become students in the jail school.

The school has no control over the length of time an inmate will attend, it has no control over the level of educational attainment or the social background of the students. Rather, the students are provided by the courts and the jail. And the kinds and number of students the school actually gets has various consequences for school personnel as they attempt to fulfill the teacher role.

A major characteristic of jail school inmates—as well as other jail inmates—is that they will be in the jail for a relatively short period of time. While convicted misdemeanants may be sentenced to the jail for up to one year, most jail school sentenced inmates are present for only a few months. And while non-sentenced inmates—those being temporarily detained while awaiting trial or transfer to another institution—may be held in the jail from a matter of minutes to several months or even longer, most are in the school for only a couple of weeks.[4] The teachers have no way of knowing how long the boys will remain in jail and accordingly in the jail school. The relatively rapid turnover of both sentenced and non-sentenced inmates in the jail school influences various aspects of the teaching situation: enrollment and classification procedures, curriculum, and teaching techniques.

One consequence of rapid turnover is seen in the initial process of enrolling students. Incoming inmates are not systematically tested, nor are past school records checked to determine the student's proficiency. Rather, they are assigned to either the academic or vocational section largely on the basis of non-academic criteria. Non-sentenced inmates are always assigned to a classroom in the academic section rather than to one of the shops in the vocational section. Rapid turnover and unpredictability of length of stay of non-sentenced inmates is less disruptive for the classrooms than it would be for the shops. Security is also a factor. The sentenced inmates are convicted misdemeanants and are considered more stable and trustworthy than the non-sentenced inmates who may include persons accused of such violent acts as murder, rape, and armed robbery. Accordingly, only sentenced inmates are allowed access to the shops and to the numerous tools which might be used as weapons.

Within the academic section, non-sentenced inmates are assigned to a particular classroom largely on the basis of their own report of the grade level in which they were last enrolled. Thus, students in any given classroom are supposed to be of the same grade level. As a consequence, teachers are confronted with students who are diverse in terms of grade level. (Grade levels range from a few boys who dropped out before entering high school to an occasional boy who is attending college, with most students falling into the ninth to twelfth grade category.) The biggest problem, however, is that almost all students are below the academic norms for boys their age, with dramatic individual differences in proficiency in any given subject.

> . . . You know, almost all of these boys are high school dropouts. Oh, occasionally, we'll get one or two who are still enrolled. But most of them are dropouts. We try to help them as best we can. But most of them are just too far gone. They're too far behind in their schooling and they just don't care. . . . (Teacher-Richardson; 5-11-67)

Each teacher must determine the subject areas in which his students are deficient and/or interested. Some teachers give new students a short quiz in a particular subject area. Others merely talk to the new student and observe his work over a period of time. Thus, the teachers' teaching activities are greatly hampered by the diversity of background of the students, by the fact that most students are far behind in their schooling, and by the lack of systematic knowledge of the students' achievement and aptitude.

A more basic consequence of the rapid turnover is found in the teaching plan used by the teachers. The rapid turnover precludes the use of a conventional lesson plan involving an outline with daily or perhaps weekly designations of topics or subjects to be covered. Jail school teachers have adapted to the constraint of rapid turnover by using a "bits-and-pieces" teaching technique. The technique consists of two basic components: short-term assignments that can be completed in one or two days, and individual tutoring. For example, the teachers use materials such as *Junior Scholastic* or *Science World* magazines or short sections from standard textbooks. The students read a short article and then answer questions dealing with what they have read or discuss the material as a class project. Or the teacher may use a multiple-page list of spelling words. The students first write each word a specified number of times and then write a complete sentence containing the word. These assignments are short. And for the most part, they allow boys to leave the class as they are released from jail and new boys to be enrolled without classroom activities being greatly disrupted.

> The teacher said, "Well, this morning we'll be using this magazine." He handed me a copy of the magazine, entitled *P.E.: Practical English*. Then the teacher continued, "Yesterday, they worked on some exercises in here. Today we'll go over them and correct their answers. You see what we do here isn't anything like in a regular school. The kids are just coming and going too fast." He shuffled through his class cards and said, "You see here. These two boys are gone today. What is it? The eleventh? And they came

in on May ninth. So they've been here three days and now they're gone. I've had a couple of boys here since November, but they are few and far between. So we just try to help them as best we can. But you just can't do anything like in a regular school."

I said, "Well, how do you go about deciding what you will teach each day? Do you make a study plan of some kind?" The teacher replied, "No, we really don't use a lesson plan like other teachers. It would just be too difficult; so you just have to go from day to day and decide what to teach as you go along. . . ." (Teacher-Richardson; 5-11-67)

In addition to the short-term assignments, each class views educational movies for about one hour every day or every other day. Students are often given ten or fifteen minutes of "free" time to look at magazines or to write letters to friends and family. And teachers spend varying amounts of time tutoring individual students, usually in arithmetic or in reading. Finally, primarily because of the rapid turnover, the teachers do not systematically evaluate their students in terms of grades and report cards.

While the role of teacher as teacher is most drastically affected by the rapid turnover of students and by their diverse but usually retarded educational background, the school and the teachers are also affected by the external control of the number of students. It is the courts that control the supply of inmates for the jail and accordingly for the jail school. In the academic section, the consequence is great fluctuation in the number of students present on any given day. For example, a teacher may have five students one day, fourteen the next, and eight the next day, depending on how many young persons are arrested, how many make bond, how many have their court cases continued, and so forth. Thus, even though the school system has officially established class size at fifteen students per teacher, jail school teachers never know from one day to the next how many new students will enroll or how many old students will have been released or transferred. An even more drastic consequence of the external control of the supply of inmates was evident in the vocational section. Changes in sentencing procedures— so that young offenders would be sentenced to other institutions—forced the school to close one shop and threatened the existence of the entire vocational section, for lack of students. Although no teachers were transferred or fired during my period of observations, some teachers were concerned that their jobs might be in jeopardy if the number of young men housed in the jail did not increase.

Emphasis on security. The second major source of constraints influencing jail school teachers' fulfillment of their teaching roles lies in the school's lack of priority within the jail and the jail's concomitant emphasis on security and custody.[5] The major concern of jail officials is to maintain a secure institution: to make certain that prisoners do not escape and to control violence on the tiers where the inmates are housed. School activities are subordinate to this overriding concern. However, while there are bars on the windows and the inmates are frisked when leaving the school, security within the school is seldom constraining or disruptive. Rather, the teachers are affected when security-related activities elsewhere in the jail affect school activities: when inmates are not allowed to attend school and when inmates are troubled emotionally by activities outside the school. The constraint derives from the fact that the school exists in a much broader maximum-security milieu.

The emphasis on maintaining order affects the school must directly when the inmate students are not allowed to come to school. Each morning those inmates (both school inmates and other inmates) scheduled to appear in court are brought down from the tiers to the basement corridor where they are processed prior to being moved from the jail to the courts. While this movement—referred to as "court calls"—is in progress no other inmates are allowed in the basement corridor. Depending on the number of inmates being moved and the number of guards on duty, the procedure may be quite time consuming. And the problem is that the school inmates are not brought down to the school from the tiers where they are housed, until all court calls have been completed. The result is almost daily delays—for from a few minutes to an hour or more—in the start of school.

The school is also affected when jail personnel attempt to maintain order on the tiers. For example, because of conflicts between white and Negro inmates, the two groups were segregated, with the whites on one tier, the blacks on another. More importantly, the separation continued while the inmates attended school. Thus, one group of inmates attended school only in the morning, the other group only in the afternoon.

> . . . Don't get me wrong. This is not segregation—it's for their own protection—and it's not to say that the Negroes don't gang up on other Negroes, because they do. But there were so few white boys on each tier that they didn't have a chance. White inmates even refused to come down to the school with the others—they were scared. . . . So now we have to figure out a way to bring the two tiers down separately. The jail has to protect the inmates from each other. . . . A big burly boy can make a lot of trouble for another boy. . . . And like I said, all kinds of things from fights to sexual abuses go on in the cells without the guards finding out. . . . (Principal-Meyer; 10-5-67)

Other sources of trouble on the tiers include fights between opposing juvenile gang members, cliques, or individuals. And when unable to determine who is responsible, the guards often punish all inmates on the tier by putting the tier on "ban." They deny the inmates such privileges as using the television set, seeing the weekly movie on the tier, purchasing cigarettes and extra food from the commissary, and attending school. When the inmates are placed on ban and are not allowed to attend school, the school ceases to function: sometimes for a couple of days, sometimes for longer. Custodial personnel, not teachers, decide when the inmates may or may not attend school. In short, the school is most directly and obviously affected when security-oriented decisions made by individuals outside the school prohibit or interfere with the students attending school.

The school is also affected when disorder on the tiers is not controlled. Because of overcrowding of inmates, insufficient number of guards, and the physical structure of the tier which allows numerous areas where inmates can gather without being observed by the guards, trouble on the tiers is not always controlled. Accordingly, the teachers are also affected when fights on the tiers, concern with their court case, or other problems affect the students emotionally.

> The next boy to enter the office was a six foot Negro dressed in dark checkered, tight, tapered slacks and a black, long-sleeved turtleneck shirt. He said, "I want to go to the infirmary." The principal replied, "Is your name on sick call?" The inmate said, "No. I've got venereal disease. And it's bothering me real bad this morning. I was down there [the infirmary] last night and they said they'd give me some pills." The principal asked, "Didn't they give you any penicillin?" The inmate responded, "No, they said I'm allergic to it—so they were going to send me some pills but I never got them. They've [the other inmates] been jumping me up on the tier. And it's real bad this morning. Can't I go to a doctor?" A few minutes later, the student replied to a question by saying, "They've been jumping me. I don't know why. I didn't do anything to them. I shouldn't be in here. I didn't do anything. But they won't leave me alone. Last night they beat me with what they called a 'shit stick' and I'm not going up [to the tier] again." (A "shit stick" is a heavy duty brush with stiff bristles used for cleaning toilets.) (Principal-Meyer; Inmate student; 10-10-67)

Thus, teachers define their students as being troubled by many problems, unrelated to their school work, and expect less of them academically.

> Most of the work here is remedial. And with the turnover, it's mainly on the individual level. You can't lecture much because these boys are full-up

with that. At the most, you can keep their attention for half an hour or an hour. You may have a boy who's really enthusiastic one day and the next you can't reach him. Maybe he's had trouble—been in a fight. (Teacher-Scott; 10-9-67)

ADAPTATIONS TO THE PROBLEMS OF BEING A JAIL SCHOOL TEACHER

Thus far I have discussed ways in which the role of jail school teacher is influenced by virtue of the fact that the school has no control over the types or number of students it gets and the fact that the primary concern of the jail (upon which the school is dependent) is security. Conditions prevent teachers from receiving many of the rewards commonly associated with successful teaching. And the teachers are aware of the problem of measuring how successful, how effective, they have been with their students. There are no grades or progress reports; there are no follow-up reports on the students after they leave the jail. The teachers seldom know whether they are accomplishing anything, whether or not they are helping the boys either academically or socially. Nevertheless, the teachers believe that they do help a few boys.

. . . In my own way I think that I do help a few of these boys. Most of them are just too far gone, but occasionally you will find one who seems to profit. I think that if I can just help one boy a month, I'm doing well. . . . (Teacher-Richardson; 5-11-67)

Adaptation: shift the responsibility for failure. Thus it is difficult for the teachers to measure the outcome of their teaching efforts. Depending on your point of view, the teachers are either minimally successful in that they do help a few boys or they are maximally unsuccessful in that they do not help most of the boys. But given that they can accomplish so little—that they can help only a few boys academically—the jail school teachers, like some teachers in Indian reservation schools and inner city slum schools, devise explanations that locate the reason for that failure in ways that suit them (see, for example, Becker, 1952: 453–456; Wax, Wax, and Dumont, Jr., 1964: 67–71). Part of the explanation places the responsibility on the public schools and the individual student.

. . . You know, almost all of these boys are high school dropouts. Oh, occasionally we'll get one or two who are still enrolled. But most of them are dropouts. We try to help them as best we can. But most of them are just too far gone. They are too far behind in their schooling and they just don't care. I think the real problem is in the regular schools. I taught in the public schools . . . , and the problem is that too many of the teachers just don't care. They don't want to take the time to help these boys—especially in the schools in the ghettos. You know, it takes patience and time. And just too many of the teachers are not willing to help these guys. (Teacher-Richardson; 5-11-67)

So, neither the boys nor the public schools care. The boys are so far behind that it is difficult to accomplish anything in such a short period of time.

Another element in the explanation is the boy's home life. The students come from poor homes. Most live on the south side. Their world is limited to that area of the city. And they have not received the proper amount of discipline and attention at home. If they had, they would not have dropped out of school and would not have gotten into trouble with the law.

> . . . A lot of these boys lack a strong father image—many of them don't even know their fathers or their fathers haven't been around enough. . . . They need someone to discipline them. But they also need to know that there's someone who cares for them—maybe for the first time. . . . (Teacher-Lee; 12-19-67)

A final element in the teachers' explanation of their failure is the jail itself. School activities are subservient to the jail's emphasis on security; school activities are delayed when inmates are being transferred to the courts and completely halted when school inmates are being disciplined. Furthermore, the rapid turnover of inmate students makes normal school activities impossible. Given these numerous constraints, the teachers reason that it is a wonder that anything gets accomplished.

> ". . . because we really don't get much of anything done here. There's just so much turnover that you can't do what you would like to do." (Principal-Meyer; 2-21-67)

Thus, Metropolitan County Jail School teachers do not explain their failure solely in terms of the students' lack of native intelligence or his state of cultural deprivation. Granted, they concede that many of the boys are not too bright and that they often lack a proper (middle-class) environment at home. Yet part of the blame is fixed on the public schools, the reasoning being that if the public schools had done the job they were supposed to do, the tasks of the jail school teachers would not be so difficult. And finally, it is not merely the boys, their families, or the public schools which are to blame. Rather, it is the jail itself—the almost unsurmountable conditions with which the teachers must cope as they attempt to execute their teaching duties. Thus, the teachers' explanation for failure incorporates several interrelated elements.

Regardless of the number of factors involved, the jail teachers' explanation for failure appears to serve the same function as other explanations which focus exclusively on intelligence quotient or cultural deprivation. The primary function—intentional or not—is to shift the source of failure away from the school (see Sexton, 1967: 58–62). For example, failure among the disadvantaged is sometimes attributed to the student's low I.Q. Thus, the source of failure is shifted from the school to the individual. Similarly, when cultural deprivation is the primary explanatory variable, it is the student's culture and his own family, rather than the school, which cause the failure. Such explanations—and especially the cultural deprivation and "Vacuum Ideology" explanations—serve other functions. Wax and his colleagues, for example, concluded that the "Vacuum Ideology," prevalent among teachers and school administrators on the Pine Ridge Indian Reservation, serves as a rationalization for the educators' failure. Since school officials view the Indian home and the mind of the Sioux child as "meager, empty or lacking in pattern," they can reason that it is miraculous that the school is able to teach him anything. Furthermore, since the Indian child is presumed so deficient in experience, the Ideology ". . . serves to justify *any* activity within the school as somehow being 'educational'" (Wax, Wax, and Dumont, Jr., 1964: 70). The jail school teachers' explanation for failure appears to serve similar functions. The teachers' explanation rationalizes the school's lack of accomplishment. Given the failure of the public schools, the inmate's family, and the inmate himself, and given the constraints imposed on the school by the jail and the courts, it is miraculous that the jail school is able to accomplish anything. Viewed from this perspective, helping only a handful of boys a year constitutes effective teaching. Similarily, given these same conditions—and especially, given the fact that the boys are so far behind academically—anything can be considered useful teaching material.

Adaptation: the role of teacher as agent. Metropolitan County Jail School teachers adapt to their very limited teaching accomplishments by devising explanations that locate the reason for that failure in ways that suit them. But they adapt in another way too. Being unable to gain many of the rewards commonly associated with successful teaching, the teachers emphasize another aspect of the teaching role. They emphasize helping the boys: by providing information, and to a lesser extent favors. How much the teachers can do for the inmates academically or socially is always questionable. However, there is no question that they do help the students resolve many important, immediate problems. The teachers define some students as bewildered and confused when they first enter the jail. More generally, they define students as having many things other than school to think about. And the teachers realize that they can do various things to help alleviate these problems. The teachers serve as agents for the students.

> . . . The unsentenced boys are another story. But it didn't used to be that way. Now all they think about is getting out—calling their parents—talking to a social worker—getting a personal bond. Anymore, the teachers just serve as their agents. They are always wanting you to make a telephone call for them or to help them get a personal bond. They come down here and that's all they can think about: how to get out. . . . (Teacher-Scott; 5-26-67)

Also of importance is the teachers' conception of the school as being separate from the jail—as being the inmate students' "isle of reprieve."

> . . . You've got to keep the school separate. The teachers here aren't just jailers. These guys [the students] know that—and they know that teachers can do a lot of things for them. And we do do a lot of things—finding out if the've got a warrant and when their court date is. These boys can get pretty shook up. . . . (Principal-Meyer; 10-27-67)

So in lieu of grades or other types of rewards for the students, the teachers provide information and small favors.

> No, it would be impossible to use grades. But the teachers do a lot of things for the students. I always let them get magazines [which are kept in the classroom] for a while after they've done their assignment. And, too, you talk friendly to them—give them a break. We do a lot of favors. They're supposed to see a social worker if they've got any questions about their case. But the social workers are always busy and then too, their [request to see a social worker] slip may be lost. That happens sometimes too; so they ask us to look these things up for them sometimes. (Teacher-Murphy; 10-26-67)

The favors which jail school teachers dispense are of two types: practical favors and "treats." Being captive in the jail, inmate students do not have access to many items ordinarily considered necessities. And if they do have potential access to these items, they may have to wait for a day or two until they can actually acquire the item. Or they may not have the money to buy the item if it is something available only from the jail commissary. Accordingly, the teachers often provide students with various small favors: bandaides, shoe strings, needle and thread, or paper to take up to the tier for writing letters. These are small, yet important items, which the inmates need but which may not be readily acquired elsewhere.

Other favors may be referred to as "treats." For example, teachers often give the students ten or fifteen minutes at the end of the period to look at magazines or write letters. Similarly, three of the four teachers in the academic section allow the boys to smoke in class. Some teachers occasionally give an inmate a cigarette. Also, on occasion, teachers give inmates passes so that they can take books from the school back to the tier to read at night.

The second type of assistance provided by the teachers is information, usually related to the inmate's court case. This information may be of several types. The most common is the inmate's court date—the date he is scheduled to appear in court. When a new inmate enrolls in the school, the principal usually makes certain that the inmate knows his court date and amount of bond. The principal may also tell the boy about the possibility of being released on a personal bond—a recognizance bond. And quite often the principal gives new inmates request forms to see a public defender and/or a social worker.

> This is the actual [request to see a public offender] form. The inmates are supposed to be able to get them in the cell block. Then they fill them out and give them to the guard. But sometimes if you ask an inmate if he has filled one out, he may say that he didn't know about it—or that he did and gave it to the guard. And the guard may have just thrown it into the waste basket. That's not to say that the inmates always tell the truth, but it wouldn't surprise me. So we keep some copies down here and give them to the inmates whenever they need them. . . . (Principal-Meyer; 5-16-67)

Other problems arise when the inmate forgets his court date, the date is changed, or the guards fail to get the inmate from his tier on the day he is to appear in court. In these instances, either the principal or the teachers inquire about the matter. Similarly, the teachers may also provide public defender and social worker request forms for the students. They may ask particular students if they know their court dates and they may explain various aspects of the judicial system—for example, grand jury, true bill, recognizance bond—to the students. Thus, the teachers provide a variety of standard information for the students. However, other requests for information are more unique.

> The inmate said to the school principal, "I wonder if you could help me. I want to appeal my case." Meyer asked, "Have you been sentenced?"

The boy replied, "Yeah. For nine months." The principal asked, "Where?" The inmate said, "Pennyton. But I want to appeal it now." Meyer said, "What are you in for?" The inmate said, "Petty theft, but there were four of us." Meyer said, *Nine months* for petty theft? Did you have a lawyer?" The boy said, "Well sir, the priest at the school . . ." Meyer asked, "What school?" The boy replied, "All Saints. The priest said he would get one, but the lawyer didn't show up. So the judge tried us all together. I don't know what happened with the lawyer." After a few minutes of additional discussion with the inmate and the school psychologist, Meyer said, "We can't do anything for you here. . . . What you'd better do is to write to the priest right away. . . . I'll give your request [form] to our legal department, but that may take awhile. They only have two men helping out and I don't know how long it'll be before they can get to it. So you'd better try every avenue you can. Write to the priest right away." As the boy stood there he nervously fidgeted with his shirt. (Principal-Meyer; Psychologist-Mitchell; Inmate student; 10-10-67)

While most of the information requested by the inmates is information related to their court cases, other requests are sometimes made: for example, when a discrepancy occurs in an inmate's account with the jail commissary or when an inmate who is supposed to be on the sick call list is not called. Similarly, the teachers often inquire about the condition of inmates who have just returned from the infirmary or who complain, while in class, of not feeling well.

The teachers can and do provide much information. In some instances, however, this can cause problems. For example, some teachers usually do not ask the inmate about his offense, for fear the inmate will think that the teacher can help with his court case—intervene on his behalf. Similarly, the teachers make it clear that they are not lawyers. They provide only general information, such as court date or amount of bond, for the inmates; they do not provide actual legal consultation. In other instances, inmates cause problems when they are constantly seeking information. This is especially true of sentenced inmates who think they may have another warrant for their arrest pending. (If there is a warrant against an inmate, the inmate will not be released after he has served his sentence in jail. Rather, he will be turned over to the authorities who have issued the warrant.) Similarly, because sentenced inmates often make mistakes when trying to compute their "good time" allowance, the principal usually computes it for them.

Metropolitan County Jail School teachers, as a source of information and favors, serve an important function for the inmates. Because of the overcrowding of inmates and the lack of social workers and public defenders, the teachers provide much information which probably would otherwise not be provided. However, the staff-inmate ratio is low enough in the jail school to make such interaction possible. The teachers provide inmates with information and to a lesser extent inmates provide teachers with information concerning what is happening elsewhere in the jail—for example, when trouble develops on the tiers or when inmates are transferred to a different tier. Thus, while the teachers never know how much good they are doing for the boys academically or socially, they do know that they are helping them by providing favors and information. In many conventional schools, bandaides, candy, a needle and thread, free time to look at magazines, and court dates would be trivial or irrelevant. However, in the jail school, they are important.

SUMMARY AND CONCLUDING COMMENTS

Teachers in the Metropolitan County Jail face conditions that make it difficult for them to realize the ends teachers are supposed to achieve. The school's external environment is a major source of constraints. Individuals and organizations outside the school determine the kinds and number of students the teachers will have to work with. And given the rapid turnover of inmates, and the students' heterogeneous but retarded educational backgrounds, the teachers are forced to adapt their teaching activities accordingly. The external control of the number of students also has consequences for the teachers; for even at the time of the study, they were faced with the possible extinction of the vocational section of the school. The school and teachers are also influenced by their low priority within the larger jail organization. The jail administrators' primary concern is security. The teachers are affected both when security is enforced and order maintained and when it is not—when trouble arises on the tiers. In virtually all instances, it is the school and the teachers who must adapt. Finally, given that the teachers can accomplish so little, they devise explanations that locate the reason for that failure in the public schools, the individual inmate student, the student's home, and in the jail itself. Teachers also cope with the problem of lack of evident accomplishment in teaching by emphasizing the role of teacher as agent.

Thus far we have been concerned with ways in which the school's environment constrains the activities of jail school personnel and with ways in which the teachers cope with the larger problem of being only minimally successful in their teaching tasks. Under these circumstances, what keeps these teachers on the job? Why don't they seek other types of work, other types of teaching positions? In the past especially, jail school teachers have viewed the jail school teaching position as one offering high job security. Similarly, because the school operates twelve months a year, the teachers are assured a larger, more stable annual salary than teachers in conventional public schools. Finally, while the teachers confront many problems that are unique to the jail situation, they do not confront some of the problems that teachers in conventional schools face. Because the jail is a maximum security institution, jail school teachers seldom meet the parents of their students and thus are not burdened with the problems inherent in teacher-parent relations.[6]

More generally, however, the teachers continue to teach in the jail school, in part at least, because they have made the necessary adaptations that make the job more manageable than it first appears to the casual observer. Certainly, jail school teachers do face conditions that make conventional teaching difficult. Yet having taught in the jail school or in similar types of schools for several years, they have learned to cope with these difficult situations. To cope with problems in the teacher-student relationship, jail school teachers, like workers in other service occupations who confront problems with their clients, define their students as falling into a variety of types. The resulting typology helps the teachers anticipate and attempt to cope with a variety of potential problems caused by the inmate students.[7] Similarly, school personnel have devised ways of dealing with the inherent conflict between custody and treatment.[8]

Thus, jail school teachers remain in the difficult teaching situation of the Metropolitan County Jail School for several reasons, ranging from job security and financial reward to the fact that they have learned how to deal with the problems which they confront. But perhaps the most important implication to be drawn is that even when confronted with an extremely problematic work situation, many workers will remain in that situation. They will stay provided that they are able to bring a degree of order to what they are doing and are able to justify to themselves and to others that their work is in some way worthwhile.

NOTES

[1] The field work upon which this paper is based was conducted while I was a research assistant to Professor Howard S. Becker at Northwestern University and was supported by National Institute of Mental Health grant, number R12 MH 9222. I thank Professor Becker for his advice and encouragement in this research and writing. For the complete study, see Lewis A. Men-

nerick, "The Impact of the External Environment on a County Jail School" (1971b). Finally I thank Professor Kenneth C. W. Kammeyer for reading an earlier draft of this paper.

[2] In the present analysis, I view the jail school as a distinct subsystem within the larger jail organization. Accordingly, everything outside the school —including the jail itself—is part of the school's external setting or environment.

[3] I have discussed external control of recruitment in much greater detail in another paper: "External Control of Recruits: The County Jail School," *American Behavioral Scientist* 16 (September/October, 1972): 75–84.

[4] The average length of stay of the 489 non-sentenced inmate students who were released between September 30, 1967, and February 15, 1968, was nineteen and one half days. However, the average drops to fourteen and one half days when the twenty-five inmates who had been in the school the longest are excluded. Approximately one half of the inmates were in the school for periods ranging from one to ten days. The mode is seven days. Because a large number of sentenced inmates were transferred out of the jail during the period upon which these computations are based, no computations have been made for sentenced school inmates. However, teachers estimate that the present average length of sentence is approximately three months.

[5] I have discussed security as a constraint in much greater detail in another paper: "The County Jail School: Custody-Security as a Constraint," unpublished paper.

[6] One might also suggest that the teachers remain in the jail school because they lack the ability or the qualifications to transfer to other types of schools. Yet, the jail school teachers meet both the general requirements for teaching in the school system and the special requirements of additional graduate level study required of all teachers who teach in the system's "special" schools. Further, several of the teachers have Masters degrees.

[7] For a much more detailed discussion, see my paper, "The County Jail School: Problems in the Teacher-Student Relationship," *The Kansas Journal of Sociology*, 7 (Spring, 1971a): 17–33.

[8] For a much more detailed discussion, see: "The County Jail School: Custody-Security as a Constraint," unpublished paper.

Herman J. Loether

Organizational Stress and the Role Orientations of College Professors

American colleges and universities are in the throes of a crisis, perhaps more serious than any in their history. They are accused of being the seedbeds of revolution, criticized for their impersonality, singled out as major perpetuators of institutionalized racism and decadence, and besieged by financial problems. Their very legitimacy has been threatened from both the right and the left of the political spectrum.

The extent of concern is reflected in the appointment by President Nixon of a Commission on Campus Unrest and the release by the Carnegie Commission on Higher Education of a massive, eighty volume report designed to diagnose the ills and prescribe the cures for American higher education.[1]

Many of the current problems are undoubtedly related to the sheer press of numbers. Each year the number of college and university students increases. During the decade between 1960 and 1970 the number of students enrolled in degree programs increased from three and a half to over seven million. (Bureau of the Census, Statistical Abstract of the United States, 1970: 126). The percentage of high school graduates going on to college increased from fifty-three percent in 1960 to sixty percent in 1969. (Statistical Abstract: 126). Even though the leveling off of the birth rate promises to relieve some of the pressure on the nation's elementary and secondary schools, the fact that the percentage of young people going on to college is continuously increasing casts doubt on the possibility that enrollments in higher education will stabilize very soon.

The course generally chosen in the face of enrollment pressures has been to expand existing colleges and universities rather than build new ones. Consequently, many schools have grown to almost unmanageable proportions. The school with more than twenty thousand students is ever more common and several public colleges and universities have in excess of forty thousand students. Faculties of departments sometimes become so large that the departments are not administratively manageable as single units.[2] Undergraduate classes of fifteen hundred students are not uncommon. Concern over the size and impersonality of classes led a committee of the University of California to recommend in 1970 that each lower division student be given the opportunity to take at least one small class per year.

Increasing size is, however, only one factor of several that account for the current crisis. The roots of the crisis are embedded in the organizational stress arising out of the conflicting pressures on colleges and universities (some internal, others external) to move, on the one hand, toward collegial model of organization and, on the other, toward the bureaucratic model.

BUREAUCRATIC VERSUS COLLEGIAL TRENDS

The traditional concept of the college or university has been the *community of scholars*. That is, a collegial organization composed of academicians who have dedicated their lives to knowledge and who devote their time, unhampered, to scholarly activities and teaching. Under such an arrangement decision making power rests with the faculty. Whatever administrative apparatus is necessary is subordinate to the faculty and exists to serve faculty and students. Such organizational models existed in early European universities. Many colleges in the United States prior to the Civil War fit this model. The only administrative officer of the college was the president and the few necessary administrative decisions were usually made by the president and faculty in general meetings. (Demerath, Stephens and Taylor, 1967: 18). In isolated incidences today and, with few exceptions, in small colleges, the collegial model of organization may be found. It is, however, the exception rather than the rule.

The collegial model has generally been favored by academicians because it fits the image they have of themselves as professionals, beholden to no one and subject to no restrictions beyond those that they impose upon themselves.[3] Although they have never been free professionals like doctors and lawyers, professors have characteristically seen themselves as possessing commensurate professional status. By the very nature of their "craft" they have been compelled to function within an organization but have sought to keep the organizational influences on them to a minimum.

Colleges that lend themselves to the collegial model are characterized by small size, private sponsorship, relative autonomy, emphasis on a classical curriculum, and lack of specialization by faculty members. Given such conditions, the total faculty of the college can function as a unit without the need for an elaborate administrative structure.

The dominant forces in American higher education, however, have tended to undermine the collegial model of organization. If organizational styles can be put on a continuum with the collegial model at one end and the bureaucratic model at the other, then American colleges and universities can be characterized as moving toward the bureaucratic pole. This shift may be attributed to a number of factors.

1. A peculiarly American concept of higher education has emerged from a combination of the British college model, the German university model, and some ideas attributed initially to Benjamin Franklin and Thomas Jefferson (Perkins, 1966: 15). According to Demerath, Stephens, and Taylor (1967) the contemporary university,

> emerged from the desire of mid-nineteenth-century educators to combine three conceptions of an institution of higher learning: (1) the British concept of a college for the making of educated gentlemen, which characterized American institutions before 1876: (2) the German concept of a graduate university pursuing knowledge for its own sake, which was introduced with the founding of Johns Hopkins and was gradually accepted by the larger privately controlled colleges of the time; and (3) the American concept of a university supported by the people and justifying itself by serving their needs, the idea that is associated especially with the great state universities.

> As a fourth concept, or perhaps a variant of the third, the contemporary American university is also regarded as an integral part of an advanced technological society. That is, it is seen as a source of socio-economic momentum and of scientifically trained manpower (1967: 18–19).

The British concept was first to appear in the United States when graduates of Cambridge and Oxford established colleges in the Colonies (among them, Harvard College). The college with the classical curriculum, designed to educate clergymen and gentlemen, dominated until after the Civil War.

The idea that a university should be supported by and serve the needs of the public was introduced formally into American higher education by the Morrill Land Grant Act of 1862. The Morrill Act turned public land over to the states to be used for funds to establish colleges. The Act directed that these colleges, "would teach courses in agriculture, the mechanic arts and military science in addition to other scientific and classic studies" (Lockmiller, 1969: 127–28).

The Morrill Act stimulated the development of state institutions of higher education throughout the United States—institutions that embodied the ideas of Franklin and Jefferson that education in practical studies should be made available to the people.

Last to appear was the German concept of the graduate research institution engaged in the pursuit of knowledge. This idea was introduced with the founding of Johns Hopkins University in 1875. It gradually transformed many colleges into universities (Harvard, among them) and was adopted as a model for many new schools (e.g., University of Chicago).

The combination of these three diverse concepts of higher education produced institutions much too complex for the collegial model of organization. The need to coordinate activities and goals led unswervingly toward bureaucracy.

2. The development of state and municipal colleges and universities supported by public funds has led to the notion of accountability. This has reduced the autonomy of institutions of higher education. Budgets are generally submitted to legislatures for approval and anticipated expenditures must be justified in terms of their returns in practical benefits to the public. The necessity for colleges and universities to get involved in complicated accounting procedures has led to the growth of bureaucratically organized business management practices that must be articulated with the academic sector.

3. Public funding and control has also led to pressures on colleges and universities to open their doors to an ever expanding number and range of students. The philosophy behind this is that activities supported by public taxes should be accessible to the taxpayers. Furthermore, business and industry increasingly demand educated workers. Consequently, enrollments have spiraled upward, and colleges and universities have expanded accordingly. As size increases, the collegial model of organization becomes impractical and, again, the trend is toward bureaucracy. The need to coordinate activities, to keep records for thousands of students, and to solve problems of logistics almost dictates a bureaucratic shift.

4. The explosion of knowledge and the ever accelerating pace of scientific development has led to increasing specialization of academi-

cians. The classical educated man with expertise in many fields is extinct. Academicians have been forced to become more and more specialized in order to keep current in their fields.

The effect of this specialization has been to complicate the organization of the college or university. The department has become the basic organizational unit. Bureaucratic superstructures have been erected to coordinate the activities of the various departments and articulate departmental curricula. It is no longer feasible for a total faculty to sit down with a college president and make the necessary administrative decisions. It is difficult enough for departments to make policy decisions with respect to their own curricula and day-to-day operations.

Basically, increased specialization has led to decentralization of the academic function and centralization of the administrative function. It is the job of central administrators to keep the whole, big, complicated mess operating as much like a single organization as possible.

For these and other reasons colleges and universities have moved closer to the bureaucratic pole of the organizational continuum; simultaneously, however, some characteristics of collegial organization have been preserved. As Demerath, Stephens, and Taylor (1967: 21ff) point out, the modern university is actually a mixture of collegial and bureaucratic organization. The major thrust of bureaucracy is in the administrative area, while the major stronghold of collegium is in the academic area.

ORGANIZATIONAL STRESS

The bureaucratic and collegial mix characteristic of the contemporary college or university is, in fact, a mix rather than a blend. This mix is, furthermore, an inevitable point of organizational stress. On the one hand, the forces of bureaucracy impinge on the collegial organization; and on the other hand, academicians resist bureaucratization and seek to advance the collegial structure.

A common belief among academicians is that the pressure to bureaucratize comes from the academic administration of the institution because of a basic disagreement with the faculty about goals. Edward Gross (1968: 538) however, found that academic administrators and faculty members shared basically the same perceptions of appropriate and desirable goals.[4] The really serious disagreement about university goals was between faculty and academic administration, on the one hand, and legislatures and state governments, on the other (Gross: 541). Legislatures and state governments saw as important goals: keeping down costs, satisfying area needs, accommodating as many students as possible, and training students for specific careers.[5] With respect to the goals perceived by faculty and academic administrators, Gross says,

> . . . the intellect of the student is emphasized and the importance of the student's developing objectivity about himself is also emphasized. Students are to be trained in methods of scholarship, whereas student taste and student careers are to be de-emphasized. Direct service consists essentially of serving as a center for ideas, and preserving the cultural heritage, and not the land-grant goals. Pure rather than applied research is emphasized, and furthermore, when the faculty have power, they tend to be elitist in trying to select students. As could be expected, the will of the faculty is one of the important goals and strong effort is made to see to it that the university is run democratically and the professors themselves have a good deal to say about running the university (1968: 541).

Gross's study leads one to conclude that the university goals perceived by faculty and academic administrators are congruent with the collegial model of organization while those perceived by legislatures and state governments are congruent with the bureaucratic model.[6]

The organizational stress emanating from the collegial-bureaucratic mix is cogently illustrated by the reward system for faculty members. College and university faculty are rewarded by being granted tenure and by being promoted. The bureaucratic forces tend to reward members of an organization for contributions to the organization. Thus, teaching performance, committee work, and other direct services to the organization are stressed by those who see the bureaucratic model as proper. On the other hand, those who stress the collegial model favor rewards for contributions to one's discipline such as scholarly publications and research.

In those institutions where reward systems are controlled by collegial forces such as faculty or faculty oriented academic administrators, faculty members who publish and do research get more rewards. When reward systems are controlled by bureaucratic forces, faculty members who work hard at their local duties reap more rewards.

FACULTY ROLE ADAPTATIONS

In many colleges and universities power struggles ensue between bureaucratic and collegial forces for control of the reward systems. In such situations the faculty member is faced with the problem of defining his role so as to make his relationship with the organization viable. Four distinct role adaptations that have been adopted by faculty members in the face of organizational stress have been identified.

A number of sociologists have identified two very different faculty roles variously called *academic men with professional orientations* and *academic men with organizational orientations*, (Lazarsfeld and Thielens, Jr., 1958) *scholars and educators* (Wilson, 1964), *itinerants* and *the home guard* (Slocum, 1966), and *cosmopolitans* and *locals* (Gouldner, 1957–58).

Gouldner contrasts the role orientations of cosmopolitans and locals as follows:

1. Cosmopolitans: those low on loyalty to the employing organization, high on commitment to specialized role skills, and likely to use an outer reference group orientation.

2. Locals: those high on loyalty to the employing organization, low on commitment to specialized role skills, and likely to use an inner reference group orientation (Gouldner: 290).

The cosmopolitan casts his lot with his discipline and there he seeks recognition and rewards. His college or university is merely a base of operations that legitimizes his claim to the title of academic man (and also a source of income). Of course, he is not adverse to the reception of rewards from his local organization; but if they are not forthcoming, he will move to another college or university that will offer rewards in keeping with his reputation in his discipline. The local casts his lot with his college or university. He identifies with it and immerses himself in its affairs. His ties to his discipline are tenuous or even nonexistent. Any recognition and rewards coming to him come from his local organization.

Caplow and McGee (1958) have commented on the consequences of cosmopolitan and local role adaptations and have identified a third possible role type.[7]

> Today, a scholar's orientation to his institution is apt to disorient him to his discipline and to affect his professional prestige unfavorably. Conversely, an orientation to his discipline will disorient him to his institution, which he will regard as a temporary shelter where he can pursue his career as a member of the discipline. And he will be, as a matter of course, considerably more mobile than his institutionally oriented colleagues. In a handful of great universities, where many of the departments believed to be the best in their fields are found, a merger of orientations is possible. There a man may simultaneously serve an institution and a discipline and identify with both. But tensions exist between the two orientations everywhere. (1958: 85).

Stewart (1968: 128) has labeled the type who simultaneously identifies with and serves both his local organization and his discipline the *local-cosmopolitan* and has added a fourth type which she calls the *indifferent*.

The local-cosmopolitan, in effect, recognizes that both bureaucratic and collegial forces exist in the contemporary American university or college and plays his academic role in a manner designed to satisfy the requirements of both.

The indifferent, on the other hand, is oriented neither to his local organization nor to his discipline. He does not distinguish himself through his efforts in behalf of his college or university, but neither does he publish or do research. Many of these indifferents establish reputations among their colleagues as "deadwood." It is a curious role stance which they adopt, not likely to endear them to either the bureaucratic or the collegial factions and likely to minimize their chances for rewards. This role adaptation may result from frustration, exasperation, or sheer inability to cope with the organizational stress arising from the bureaucratic-collegial mix.

Given the existence of these four role adaptations, it should be possible to assess the state of the bureaucratic-collegial struggle for power in a particular college or university by studying the role choices made by faculty members and the distribution of rewards among faculty members in the various role categories. If the bureaucratic forces are dominant, then the local role should be that most frequently adopted and rewards should be distributed most frequently to those playing local roles. If collegial forces are dominant, then cosmopolitan roles should be more frequently adopted and the cosmopolitan should reap the rewards. If there is a balance of power between bureaucratic and collegial forces, then the local-cosmopolitans should be numerous and should benefit from the reward system. The indifferents should fare badly as far as rewards are concerned no matter what the state of the struggle; but, in the college or university in a state of demoralization the indifferents may be relatively numerous.

A CASE STUDY

The author collaborated on a study of a state college for which data were available to test the above notions.[8] The setting of the study was a very large urban campus of a state college system administered by a chancellor and an appointed board of trustees. Rigid line-item budgets approved by the state legislature and the governor were the life-blood of the system in general and the college in particular. An elaborate bureaucratic structure had developed to administer the affairs of the college. The faculty was engaged in a struggle to get as much control as possible, and to develop some semblance of a collegial organization in the face of threats from the chancellor, the trustees and the legislature.

Faculty members were under pressure from these parties to adopt goals essentially like those that Gross (1968: 541) found espoused by legislatures and state governments; while they, themselves, espoused typical faculty goals such as academic freedom and primary responsibility for managing their own affairs and the affairs of the college.

In the midst of this power struggle it was revealed that the chancellor's staff had made errors in budgeting faculty salaries. An appeal was made to the legislature for an emergency appropriation to maintain the level of faculty salaries for the remainder of the academic year. The legislature, already disturbed at what it considered lack of forcefulness on the part of the trustees and the chancellor's office, balked at making any such appropriation. Under directions from the trustees, the chancellor's office "solved" the problem by reducing the salaries of associate professors and full professors by one and eight-tenths percent.

Within two months after the salary cut the researchers distributed a questionnaire to the 694 full-time members of the college faculty. The questionnaire included items about the college administration, salaries, teaching loads, research opportunities, facilities, etc. In addition, background information such as age, sex, rank, years of service, degrees held, tenure status, organizational memberships, and scholarly activities were solicited. Finally, respondents were asked about their plans for staying with or leaving the college. After two follow-ups, 542 questionnaires (seventy-eight percent) were returned and analyzed. The data were considered to be of unusually good quality and comparisons on selected known characteristics with non-respondents led the researchers to conclude that there were no serious biases.

Role Adaptations. A ten item scale dealing with commitment to the college was combined with an item on the future of the college to produce a measure of each respondent's orientation toward the college. Items dealing with publications, research grants, and other forms of scholarly productivity were combined to produce a measure of each respondent's orientation toward his discipline. These measures of orientation toward college and orientation toward the discipline were combined to produce four types of faculty role adaptations:

1. The Cosmopolitan: measured low on orientation toward the college (low commitment to the college and pessimism about its future) and high on orientation toward the discipline (high scholarly productivity and research grants).

2. The Local: measured high on orientation toward the college (high commitment and optimism about the future of the college) and low on orientation toward the discipline (lack of scholarly productivity and research grants).

3. The Local-cosmopolitan: measured high on orientation toward the college and high on orientation toward the discipline.

4. The Indifferent: measured low on orientation toward the college and low on orientation toward the discipline.

Analysis of the questionnaires of the 542 respondents resulted in classification of eighty-seven (sixteen percent) as cosmopolitan, 229 (forty-three percent) as locals, 138 (twenty-five percent) as local-cosmopolitans, and eighty-one (fifteen percent) as indifferents. The other seven respondents (approximately one percent) were not classifiable because of incomplete data. The fact that the local was the most frequent role type of the four suggests the dominance of the bureaucratic forces in the struggle for control of the college. A correlated and confounding variable that must be taken into consideration, however, is the relative competitive position of the college in the academic labor market, i.e., the college's ability to attract other than the local type.

Role Types and Personal Characteristics. Faculty members did differ significantly on certain personal characteristics. Of the four types, cosmopolitans were those most likely to have doctorates (seventy-nine percent) while locals were least likely (thirty-two percent). Seventy percent of the local-cosmopolitans and fifty percent of the indifferents had doctorates. The local-cosmopolitans were older and had served the college the longest. The indifferents were younger and held less than five years of service. Twelve percent of the cosmopolitans were above fifty and forty-five percent were twenty to thirty. Thirty-two percent of the local-cosmopolitans had ten or more years of service with the college as compared to twenty-eight percent of the cosmopolitans, seventeen percent of the indifferents and fourteen percent of the locals.

The concentration of indifferents in the younger age category and the category of less than five years service to the college suggests that some of their number may have been "late starters" who had not established themselves by the time of the study. It may also have been the case that indifferents had a high attrition rate and were, therefore, under-represented among those with more years of service to the college. Generally speaking cosmopolitans and local-cosmopolitans were more likely to be joiners of professional organizations than either locals or indifferents.

Role Adaptations and Rewards. If the attainment of tenure and promotion are identified as rewards in the academic arena, then it is obvious from the data that those faculty members playing either cosmopolitan or local-cosmopolitan roles most frequently reaped the rewards. Seventy-nine percent of the cosmopolitans and eighty-one percent of the local-cosmopolitans were tenured, compared to forty-six percent of the locals and forty-seven percent of the indifferents. Furthermore, sixty-three percent of the cosmopolitans and seventy-one percent of the local-cosmopolitans were in the higher ranks (associate professor and professor) as compared to thirty-nine percent of the locals and thirty-five percent of the indifferents.

While the preponderance of locals among the faculty members seemed to indicate that the bureaucratic forces had the upper hand and controlled the fortunes of the college and its faculty, the preponderance of cosmopolitans and local-cosmopolitans among those tenured and of higher ranks appeared to contradict such an interpretation. The fact that professors were rewarded for their scholarly contributions even when their orientation toward the college was minimal (cosmopolitans), seemed to indicate, rather, that the reward system of the college was more heavily influenced by collegial forces.

The apparent contradiction in these findings can be resolved logically, however, if, in fact, the ranks of the locals were swollen by a number of younger faculty members whose productivity indices were low because they had not had sufficient time to develop their scholarly inclinations. The facts that fifty percent of the locals were young and forty-nine percent had less than five years service to the college would tend to support this interpretation.

Attitudinal Reactions to Organizational Stress. The composition of the college faculty at the time of the study reflects past recruiting practices and the operation of the rewards system previous to the time that the data were collected. The assumption was made that when the data were collected respondents' answers to attitudinal questions would reflect more directly the state of affairs at the college than these "factual" data.

Respondents were asked: "Considering your life-situation here as a whole (including your family life, job, finances, leisure, opportunities, etc.) how would you say it compares to most other individuals in similar academic positions elsewhere?" Interestingly enough, the two role types with the most positive attachments to the college (the locals and the local-cosmopolitans) were *least* likely to consider their present life-situations better than those of others. The two role types with minimal attachments to the college (the cosmopolitans and the indifferents) were *most* likely to consider their life situations comparatively better. Thirty-five percent of the locals and twenty-five percent of the local-cosmopolitans considered their life situations better; sixty-one percent of the cosmopolitans and forty-four percent of the indifferents considered theirs better.

In contrast, when respondents were asked, "Would you recommend this college to a friend seeking an academic position?" only seventeen percent of the cosmopolitans and nineteen percent of the indifferents said yes compared to seventy-five percent of the locals and eighty-three percent of the local-cosmopolitans. Along the same lines, respondents were asked, "If you were starting over again, knowing what you do now, would you still accept a position at this college?" To this question twenty-one percent of the cosmopolitans and thirty-one percent of the indifferents said yes, compared to eighty-two percent of the locals and eighty-two percent of the local-cosmopolitans.

It is curious that cosmopolitans and indifferents, when asked to compare their life situations with those of others in similar academic positions elsewhere were most likely to feel that their life situations were better; but, at the same time, would not recommend the college to a friend and generally would not accept a position with the college if they were starting over again. One explanation for this combination is that favorable life-situations existed in spite of their position with the college, not because of it. Perhaps, the location of the college in a desirable metropolitan area offered compensation sufficient to outweigh their dissatisfactions with the college itself.

As a crucial test of their reactions to the organizational stress arising from the state of the bureaucratic-collegial mix in general and the salary crisis in particular respondents were asked if they had any intentions of leaving the college. Sixteen percent of the cosmopolitans said that they were not considering leaving, twenty-nine percent said they were considering leaving, and fifty-five percent said they were leaving. For the locals the corresponding percentages were forty-one, forty-one, and eighteen; for the local-cosmopolitans they were sixty-two, twenty-three, and fifteen; and for the indifferents they were eight, forty-six, and forty-six percent. It is significant to note that the cosmopolitans and the indifferents were those most likely to be leaving the college. It is conceivable that some of those classified as indifferents were so classified because they had already decided to leave and, therefore, scored low on orientation to the college.

The fact that a higher percentage of cosmopolitans were leaving than any other type is consistent with the characterization of them as the most mobile of the academicians. When their local situation becomes intolerable they can move because they are in demand in the academic labor market. The fact that fifty-five percent intended to leave seems to indicate that the plight of the college was viewed as being desperate.

If there is truth to the assertion that the most effective college teacher is one who is an active scholar, then those intending to stay would seem to be a mixed blessing. Local-cosmopolitans may add strength to a college faculty, but in this case they were outnumbered about two to one by the locals. This would seem to bode ill for the academic reputation of the college. Strong faculty members attract other strong faculty members. This is a function usually performed by cosmopolitans, but in this case the majority of the cosmopolitans were in the process of leaving. Thus, the job of attracting active faculty members was left up to relatively few local-cosmopolitans and even fewer remaining cosmopolitans. Once the locals get the upper hand at a college, the college is likely to become more vulnerable to bureaucratization. The champions of collegial organization are usually the cosmopolitans and the local-cosmopolitans.

For the first time in the history of the college collegial forces had made successful inroads in their battle to capture control of the reward system as evidenced by the distribution of rewards among those in the four role types. Current attitudes among the faculty indicated, however, that the campaign of the collegial forces had been dealt a serious setback by the salary crisis and the deepening sense of mistrust that the legislature felt toward the state college system and its administrators. The legislature announced its intent to exercise tighter control over the whole state college system. The college in particular and the system in general appeared headed inexorably toward the bureaucratic pole of the organizational continuum.

The college studied here is but one case in the whole arena of American higher education. The indications are, however, that the trend toward increased bureaucratization in higher education is widespread and is likely to continue into the future. Perhaps the growing popularity of professors' unions and demands for collective bargaining are indicative of the forms of active resistance professors will use in their power struggle against the forces of further bureaucratization.

NOTES

[1] Publication of these volumes by McGraw-Hill appeared early in 1970.

[2] The psychology department of one midwestern university has grown so large that it has been divided into sections representing the major specialties in psychology, each administered by a section chairman.

[3] An example is the code of ethics adopted by the American Association of University Professors.

[4] The primary goal from the perspective of both academic administrators and faculty members was the protection of the faculty's right to academic freedom.

[5] At one state college a state auditor counted the number of chairs in each classroom, multiplied by the number of teaching hours during the day, divided by the number of classes in a full student load, and reported back to the state that the college could accommodate seven thousand students rather than the two thousand students actually enrolled.

[6] Perhaps, the belief, on the part of many faculty members, that academic administrators disagree with them on university goals and ways to implement those goals stems from their lack of understanding of the necessity for administrators to act within the constraints of their offices, thereby implementing the wishes of legislatures and state governments.

[7] Their balanced type, contrary to their statement, is not limited to a "handful of great universities."

[8] Other members of the study team were Donald G. McTavish and Joseph Phelan.

Joseph J. Lengermann

Professional Autonomy in Organizations: The Case of CPAs

Certified Public Accountants carry out their professional work in a variety of work settings: sole practice offices, professional firms of both small and large size, and non-CPA organizations. CPAs therefore provide very appropriate data for examining the issue of professional autonomy in bureaucratic organizations. Professional autonomy lies at the center of the tensions produced when two quite different sets of principles for organizing work activity (the bureaucratic and the professional) are combined in the same work setting. Despite the traditional image of the independent professional, the trend is for more and more professionals to carry out their work as part of a highly coordinated set of activities within large organizations. The American belief in large organizations, the advanced specialization and sub-specializaton in professional knowledge and expertise, and the universal reliance upon expensive technology in carrying out professional work have all contributed to this trend. In the case of CPAs, this trend has been especially strong. Their functions are closely tied into government and business. Since both government and business corporations are large and widely dispersed, it has become advantageous for CPA firms to become larger and larger, with some of the national firms having as many as five hundred partners and eighty branch offices. As many as fifty partners and seven hundred professional staff may be found in the central office alone. Paul Montagna (1968) has indicated that CPA firms are professional organizations which are more centralized and less bureaucratic than most organizations, but such large size alone necessitates considerable reliance upon bureaucratic principles and procedures in order to coordinate the diverse activities of so many members. If professional autonomy becomes an issue when professionals work in organizations, CPAs certainly are among those professional groups for whom this issue is especially salient.

Professional and bureaucratic modes of organizing activity do of course share several important principles (e.g., rationality, achievement). However, strain results from crucial differences in principles of authority and of identification. The organization expects its members to look to the organizational hierarchy, procedures, and rules to guide decisions and behavior; the professional looks to his professional body of knowledge and the opinion of his professional colleagues as providing the most crucial guidelines. The organization also expects its members to identify their own goal with the goals of the organization, to be loyal primarily to it, and to develop career goals according to organizational advancement lines. The professional is concerned primarily with the pursuit of professional activities in their own right and may view the organization as merely a context or means for pursuing those activities. As for career advancement, the professional may see this not so much in terms of organizational promotion as in terms of recognition and reputation within his professional colleague community both within and outside any specific organization. The very notion of being a professional means the possession of expertise based on a special body of knowledge and includes the assumption that it is the professional's prerogative to use his own expert judgment in decisions about his professional activity. Therefore, when organizational members are professionals, the usual tensions caused by an organization's effort to integrate its members as completely as possible can be intense.

The focal questions are: can this important prerogative of professional autonomy be maintained within organizations? Or is it seriously compromised in a "bureaucratization" of professional decision-making and activity? What influence does type of organization (professional firms vs. non-professional organizations) and size of organization have on these questions? What are the mechanisms that might increase the possibility of maintaining professional autonomy in organizations? These are the general questions tested on data collected from 373 CPAs from the state of New York who work in the following types of work organizations: sole practice office, local CPA firm, regional CPA firm, national ("Big Eight") CPA firm, and non-CPA organization.[1] Details on the methods used in collecting and analyzing these data are found in an appendix at the end of this report.

Even in the course of background interviewing during the questionnaire construction phase of this study, it became clear that CPAs themselves think that type of organization and size of CPA firm crucially affect their CPA work experience. While most of the CPAs agreed that professional autonomy was greater in sole practice work and in small firms, CPAs from large firms persistently stated that the best CPA work was done in large firms and that this was where the most promising young CPAs orient themselves. These survey data indicate that CPAs in large national firms come from higher social class backgrounds, possess higher educational qualifications, and receive much higher financial rewards than do CPAs in local firms or sole practice offices. These also show the attractiveness of carrying out CPA work in large organizational settings.

But what are the costs of this in terms of the important professional characteristic of professional autonomy? By professional autonomy we mean the freedom or prerogative of professionals to carry out their professional work activity according to their own collective and, ultimately, individual judgment in the application of their profession's body of knowledge and expertise. Similar to Gloria Engel (1970), this study is concerned with the "work related autonomy" of the individual professional.

According to popular stereotype and much of the theoretical and research literature, we can expect professional autonomy to be considerably lessened in large organizations due to bureaucratic procedures necessitated by size and complexity. These data show that CPAs themselves believe this to be the case. The questionnaire asked them to rate six different CPA work situations as "poor," "average," or "excellent" in terms of the extent to which they allow their members to have "freedom to exercise one's own professional judgment in carrying out one's work."

Results show the percentage of CPAs who think the "opportunity for professional autonomy" is "excellent" in the various CPA work situations declines from eight-three percent for the sole practice office to fifty-nine percent for local firms, to thirty-four percent for regional firms, to twenty-seven percent for small offices of national firms, to twenty-three percent for large offices of national firms, and to twenty-five percent for non-CPA organizations.

It remains to be seen whether these beliefs of CPAs about the relative opportunity for professional autonomy in various CPA work settings (and particularly their negative judgments against the national firm setting on this dimension) are accurate when compared to the data on actual levels of professional autonomy in these various work settings. When the levels of professional autonomy actually experienced by CPAs in the various work settings are examined these beliefs seem to be born out at least initially—except that professional autonomy in non-CPA organizations is lower than in the national CPA firms. For each of three measures of professional autonomy, the same pattern is present: the percentage of CPAs possessing high levels of professional autonomy decreases consistently as the degree and size of organization increases. Sole practice CPAs show the highest professional autonomy with seventy-seven percent considering themselves completely free to exercise professional judgment. Only four percent feel they receive less professional autonomy than they desire. This is as expected since in their case organizational factors such as size, complexity, and bureaucratic hierarchy are almost entirely lacking. Since non-CPA organizations are neither organized for the primary purpose of carrying out professional CPA activity nor directed by CPAs as such, it is not surprising that this kind of CPA work situation is lowest in professional autonomy. Only fifty-two percent feel completely free to exercise their own professional judgment, twenty-six percent receive less professional autonomy than they desire, and a full eighty-three percent feel that their superiors, rather than their clients or professional peers, constitute the group most necessary to please if they are to be rewarded.

The more interesting question is what happens to the professional autonomy of CPAs who work in professional organizations (CPA firms). How does the size factor of such firms affect professional autonomy? According to our data, professional autonomy in the local and the regional firms is somewhat lower than in sole practice but not considerably so. There is less difference between these firms and sole practice on professional autonomy than between these firms and national firms. The professional autonomy level in the national firm setting is better than, but close to that found in the non-CPA organization setting. Only fifty-nine percent of national firm CPAs feel completely free to exercise their own professional judgment, seventy-three percent feel that their superiors constitute the group most necessary to please, and twenty-three percent receive less professional autonomy than they desire. At this point, therefore, these data seem to support the previously discussed beliefs of CPAs themselves (consistent with popular stereotype and much of the professionals-in-organizations literature) that there is considerable reduction of professional autonomy both in non-CPA organizations and in the very large professional CPA firms.

Before accepting this conclusion, however, it is necessary to consider an additional factor, hierarchical position level. To accurately understand the relationship between size of firm and professional autonomy, it is necessary to control for the position level variable because: (1) our data show a strong positive relationship between position level and professional autonomy;[2] (2) the proportion of CPA firm members at low position levels becomes considerably greater as size of firm becomes larger.[3] These facts have important implications for understanding the relationship between size of firm and professional autonomy. The positive relationship between position level and professional autonomy remains consistently strong when we examine it separately for the local, regional, and national types of CPA firms. However, the previous negative relationship between type of firm and professional autonomy ceases to exist when we examine it separately for the four position level groups (juniors, seniors, supervisors, and partners). It would seem that our previous finding—that regional firm CPAs have somewhat less professional autonomy than local firm CPAs and that national firm CPAs have considerably less professional autonomy than either local or regional firm CPAs—is due not to the factor, size of firm, but to the spurious effect of differences in position level. A more accurate conclusion would be that while larger firms have greater numbers and proportions of their members at lower position levels (and subsequently at lower levels of professional autonomy) than do the smaller firms, equivalent proportions of CPAs at equivalent position levels experience equivalent levels of professional autonomy regardless of whether they are in the smaller or the larger firms. This conclusion which denies any direct relationship between size of firm and professional autonomy is therefore contrary to the beliefs of CPAs themselves and much of the literature on professionals-in-organizations. It is, however, quite compatible with the findings of James Sorensen's (1967) study of national firm CPAs which indicate that job satisfaction and professional orientation vary significantly according to position level but not according to size of office.[4]

These findings are contrary to the expectations of CPAs themselves that size of firm relates negatively to opportunity for professional autonomy. The findings can legitimately be accepted as reason for some lessening in the concern of CPAs and other professional groups over the supposed threat to professional autonomy entailed by large professional firms. They do not, however, entirely discount all threat to professional autonomy in such large firm work situations. Due to the extremely strong positive relationship between position level and professional autonomy, there are still large numbers and proportions of CPAs in large firms who experience very little professional autonomy. This positive relationship is to be expected since hierarchical position gives authority to make decisions and thus increases the opportunity to act according to individual professional judgment. Because the strength of this relationship is so strong it suggests that junior level CPAs must improve exclusively on their attainment of a bureaucratic characteristic—that of hierarchical position. This could easily lead to disillusionment and withdrawal from the firm or even the profession, or at least to a diminishing of proper professional concern for wanting to maintain professional autonomy. Our data do in fact indicate a negative relationship between length of time in the firm and attachment of importance to the value of professional autonomy. Sorensen (1967) also reports that professional orientation decreases with increases in both position level and years of experience in national CPA firms. Even granting that in a professional organization such as a CPA firm there is likely to be a closer correspondence between pofessional expertise and position level than in other organizations, professional values would be better fulfilled if professional autonomy depended on more profession-related factors than promotion to higher hierarchical position.

In our research we have explored the contribution of individual "exchange strengths" as such possible profession related resources for maintaining professional autonomy. The exchange strengths we believe are important for this are: (1) high value of the professional member to the organization; (2) great difficulty for the organization in replacing the professional member; and (3) good realistic job alternatives for the professional member. A review of the conditions which exchange theorists believe affect power and independence in exchange relationships (See Gouldner, 1959; and Blau, 1964) and a review of the conceptual and empirical literature on professionals (See Lengermann, 1969; and Miller, 1967), suggests that professionals are more likely than most members of organizations to be in a favorable position as regards their exchange relationships with organizational superiors. Therefore, they ought to be able to use these exchange strengths to influence their mode of participation in the organization so as to safeguard their prerogative of professional autonomy. A high involvement in what Goode (1957) has called the "community of professionals" seems to be the general characteristic which helps professionals both to possess such favorable exchange strengths and apply them toward a professional type reward such as professional autonomy.

How does this theory of exchange strengths as profession-linked resources for professional autonomy check out in the case of CPAs? Tables 1 and 2 (see end of paper) present the appropriate data for both lower and higher position CPAs working in various organizational settings.

These data generally support our theoretical expectations about the positive contributions of exchange strengths to professional autonomy. Although chi square levels do not show statistical significance in every case, gamma measures of association are positive in every instance. The percentage of CPAs with strong exchange strengths who also have excellent professional autonomy is in every instance higher than it is for CPAs with weak or medium exchange strengths. Our theoretical expectation is verified in the case of the non-professional organizations, both for the lower and the higher position level groups. Such verification is less apparent, however, in the case of CPA firms. Note that the relationship between exchange strengths and professional autonomy is weakest for the lower level CPAs in firms, precisely the group that stands in most need for such a resource for professional autonomy because of their disadvantage due to the previously discussed strong relationship between position level and professional autonomy.

Although such data are generally in support of the advantage of exchange strengths to professional autonomy, a second reason they are somewhat disconcerting is that a rather low percentage of CPAs were found to possess strong sets of exchange strengths. In terms of our strict measure of this variable, only twelve percent of CPAs in firms and seventeen per cent of CPAs in non-CPA organizations are in the "strong" category. In terms of the broad measure, only slightly higher percentages appear: twenty-one percent of CPAs in firms and fifty-five percent of CPAs in non-CPA organizations. Closer analysis shows that the CPA groups which tend to be "high" on the first two exchange strengths (the higher position groups) tend to be "low" on the realistic alternatives exchange strength, and that those CPA groups which tend to be "high" on this third exchange strength (the lower position groups) tend to be low on the first two exchange strengths of value to firm and difficulty of replacement. Thus, relatively few CPAs possess a "strong" total set of exchange strengths.

This lack of exchange strengths among most CPAs is contrary to what the literature on professionals suggests and makes us examine empirically whether or not CPAs fulfill the condition of "professional community identification" which underlies the relevance of exchange strengths to professional autonomy. Three separate measures of this condition were used and our data clearly indicate that professional community identification is weak or absent among most CPAs, with only forty-two percent expressing a loyalty preference for their profession over their present organization, only eighteen percent looking to their profession rather than to their organization as their more primary reward source, and only seven percent considering their career track as being primarily within the profession as such. If we now control for the presence of this professional community identification, we find that for those few CPAs who do possess this condition the relationship between strengths and professional autonomy becomes quite strong, as can be seen in Table 3 (see end of paper).

Note, first of all, in column one of the table that by itself professional community identification relates hardly at all (and usually negatively) to professional autonomy. Its positive contribution comes only in conjunction with exchange strengths. Note also the gamma measures of association under the two "Total Set Exchange Strengths" headings. The gamma values under the "PCI Present" heading are, for each of the seven CPA groups considered, stronger in every instance than the comparable gamma values in Tables 1 and 2 and considerably stronger in every instance than the comparable gamma values under the "PCI Absent" heading in Table 3. Note too that the presence of professional community identification adds the greatest increase in the positive directionality of gamma values, precisely for those lower level CPA groups who otherwise have the greatest difficulty in maintaining professional autonomy.

Earlier it was shown that the factor of organizational setting does affect professional autonomy but that it does not threaten it as much as popular stereotype and much sociological literature leads us to expect. The bureaucratic factor of hierarchical position, however, was found to relate so strongly to professional autonomy within organizations that exchange strengths were examined as a hopeful profession-related source of improving professional autonomy at all levels. If the possession of exchange strengths is coupled with the possession of a professional community identification, the possibility of professional autonomy is considerably improved in all organizational settings and at all position levels. These findings suggest to a profession such as Certified Public Accounting the utility of implementing or increasing those conditions which are likely to provide its members with stronger exchange strengths and greater professional community identification.

Preliminary analysis of our CPA data (see Lengermann, 1969) indicates that possession of these factors is favored by certain professional activities (such as participation in professional conferences and extensive professional reading) and by certain work experiences (such as intensive specialization and spreading one's work experience over multiple CPA work situations). Data also indicate that CPAs, especially lower level CPAs, engage minimally (if at all) in such professional activities and work experiences. There seem to be certain structural characteristics in the CPA profession which operate not only to reduce such activities and experiences but also subsequently reduce professional communuity identification, reduce access to the three major exchange strengths, and ultimately reduce professional autonomy among CPAs. Two such characteristics seem to be the practice of within-firm socialization rather than university based professional school training, and the tradition of effectively discouraging mobility of CPAs from one firm to another. Each of these structural characteristics of the profession leads to the practical identification of one's own firm and its organizational traditions with the CPA profession itself. This results both in a compromise in the very notion and concern for professional autonomy, and in a decline in those exchange strengths which our study found to be positively associated with the maintenance of professional autonomy. This exchange strength perspective and our data certainly support the policy of those CPAs who wish to replace the in-firm apprenticeship requirement with a university-based training program. This not only will socialize new CPAs into a more direct identification with the profession as such, but also will develop a network of peer group contacts which will facilitate the possibility and acceptability of greater inter-firm mobility. Opportunity for professional autonomy is then likely to increase in all CPA work situations. Whether or not leadership groups within the CPA profession as presently constituted are in fact desirous of such potential increase in professional autonomy for its members, is of course a quite separate empirical question.

BRIEF METHODOLOGICAL APPENDIX

Data used in this report came from a survey study of CPAs in the state of New York during the summer of 1967. Three hundred and seventy-three mailed questionnaires were completed and returned. A stratified random sample was drawn of CPAs and prospective CPAs according to the principal CPA work situations: sole practice offices, local and regional CPA firms, national ("Big Eight") CPA firms, and non-CPA organizations. The 373 completed questionnaires represent a response rate of forty-nine percent. A telephone follow-up indicated that this sample is more representative still because many of the non-respondents were no longer in CPA practice. Because of the prominence of New York City as a financial center, New York State has far more CPAs (17,019 as of 1965) than any other state and is in the forefront of developments within the CPA profession. This makes it an appropriate group of CPAs to select for study, but it should be remembered that our sample therefore contains a higher proportion of "big city" CPAs than would be found in most other states. The questionnaire method of collecting data was selected because a broad spectrum of data representing several types of CPAs and containing information about numerous aspects of the CPA's professional attitudes, experience, and activity was considered important.

Because of the questionnaire method of collecting data, our measures of major variables such as professional autonomy, professional community identification, and exchange strengths are restricted to the self-reported judgments of the respondents. To obtain data on the beliefs of CPAs about opportunities for professional autonomy in various work situations, respondents were asked to rate six different work situations (listed in Table 2) as "poor," "average," or "excellent" in terms of the extent to which they allow their members to have "freedom to exercise one's own professional judgment in carrying out one's work." Our primary measure of actual professional autonomy is the respondent's rating of his own job as "poor," "average," or "excellent" according to the extent that it actually provides him "freedom to exercise his own professional judgment in carrying out his work." Two secondary measures of professional autonomy were also used: a negative measure indicating whether or not it is more necessary to please "superiors" rather than "clients" or "professional peers," and a measure indicating "negative discrepancy" on professional autonomy if the respondent rated his actual reception of professional autonomy lower than its personal importance to him. Since the secondary measures showed essentially the same results as did the primary measure, we have focused on the latter in the report.

Respondents working in CPA firms provided information on various characteristics of their own firm, including several dimensions of its size. Responses on "number of branch offices in the entire firm" were collapsed into a three category breakdown (1; 2–44; and 45–98). Responses on "number of professional staff in own specific office" were collapsed into a three category breakdown (1–19; 20–99; 100–800). Analysis results for both these variables were basically similar when more than three caregories were used. The data results summarized on footnote 4 are based on the more simple three category breakdown.

Our measures of exchange strengths are based on the respondent's own estimates of his "value to firm," "difficulty of replacement," and "realistic job alternatives." Realistic job alternatives were interpreted in two ways: (a) being wanted by other work situations; and (b) both being wanted by other work situations and seeing those situations as attractive. These individual exchange strengths were then combined into a measure of the total set of exchange strengths, with the primary (strict) measure utilizing the "b" interpretation of realistic alternatives and a secondary (broad) measure utilizing the "a" interpretation of realistic alternatives. Only those individuals were rated "strong" on a total set of exchange strengths who were in the highest categories on each of the three individual exchange strengths.

Our analysis utilized two statistical techniques—chi square and gamma. Chi square is taken as a test of whether or not a relationship between two variables can, within certain probability limits, be judged to exist. A significant value of chi-square indicates that the distribution of observed frequencies is non-random, not due to chance. The Goodman and Kruskal gamma is used more extensively in this report. It can be considered a "proportional reduction in error" measure for ordinal data and can be interpreted as the proportion by which "error can be reduced by virtue of the association between the two variables being considered" (Costner, 1965). It ranges in value from —1 to +1. When it is positive, anticipate the same order on the dependent variable for a given pair of observations as their order on the independent variable. When it is negative, anticipate the opposite order on the dependent variable for a given pair of observations as their order on the independent variable.

TABLE 1

Combined Set of Exchange Strengths (S) Related to
Professional Autonomy (P.A.)*

Control Groups	(N)	Total Group % with excellent P.A.	Weak Exchange Strs. % with excellent P.A.	Mediocre Exchange Strs. % with excellent P.A.	Strong Exchange Strs. % with excellent P.A.	chi square	gamma
All CPAs	(315)	62	57	59	78	> .10	+ .23
All CPAs in firms	(215)**	63	61	62	74	> .10	+ .12
Low Level CPAs in firms	(108)	50	52	47	57	> .10	+ .02
High Level CPAs in firms	(100)	81	83	79	92	> .10	+ .18
All CPAs in Non-CPA Organizations	(66)	53	50	45	91	< .025	+ .58
Low Level CPAs in Non-CPA Organizations	(28)	36	50	20	83	< .10	+ .60
High Level CPAs in Non-CPA Organizations	(38)	66	50	62	100	< .05	+ .69

* A brief note on the meaning of chi square and gamma is contained in the methodological appendix at the end of the report.

** Cases in the "low level" and the "high level" groups do not total 215 because seven respondents did not indicate their position level.

TABLE 2

Combined Set of Exchange Strengths (B) Related to
Professional Autonomy (P.A.)*

Control Groups	(N)	Total Group	Weak Exchange Strs.	Medio-cre Exchange Strs.	Strong Exchange Strs.	chi square	gamma
		% with excel-lent P.A.	% with excel-lent P.A.	% with excel-lent P.A.	% with excel-lent P.A.		
All CPAs	(315)	62	58	57	74	< .10	+ .26
All CPAs in firms	(215)**	63	62	60	75	> .10	+ .19
Low Level CPAs in firms	(108)	50	50	48	58	> .10	+ .07
High Level CPAs in firms	(100)	81	80	79	88	> .10	+ .22
All CPAs in Non-CPA Organizations	(66)	53	40	45	70	< .05	+ .48
Low Level CPAs in Non-CPA Organizations	(28)	36	50	21	50	> .10	+ .40
High Level CPAs in Non-CPA Organizations	(38)	66	33	58	91	< .10	+ .74

* A brief note on the meaning of chi square and gamma is contained in the methodological appendix at the end of the report.

** See note for table 1.

TABLE 3

Summary of Gamma Values Reflecting Relationship Between Exchange Strengths and Professional Autonomy as Affected by the Presence or Absence of Professional Community Identification (P.C.I.) *

Control Groups	(N)	Prof. Community Ident.	Total Set Exchange Strengths (STRICT)		Total Set Exchange Strengths (BROAD)	
			PCI Absent	PCI Present	PCI Absent	PCI Present
All CPAs	(315)	− .11	+ .14	+ .39$_a$	+ .17	+ .43$_a$
All CPAs in firms	(215) **	− .04	− .03	+ .36	+ .11	+ .39$_a$
Lower Level CPAs in firms	(108)	+ .05	− .31	+ .34	− .24	+ .44
Higher Level CPAs in firms	(100)	+ .13	+ .20	+ .25	+ .18	+ .45
All CPAs in Non-CPA Orgs.	(66)	− .27	+ .43	+ .86$_a$	+ .15	+ .84$_a$
Lower Level CPAs in Non-CPA Orgs.	(28)	− .41	+ .46	+ .93$_a$	− .03	+ .87$_a$
Higher Level CPAs in Non-CPA Orgs	(38)	− .16	+ .44	+ 1.00$_a$	+ .73	+ .86$_a$

$_a$ = chi square significant at .10 or less.

* A brief note on the meaning of chi square and gamma is contained in the methodological appendix at the end of the report.

** See note for table 1.

NOTES

[1] The data gathering aspect of the study was carried out during the summer of 1967. The study was financed by a National Science Foundation dissertation grant. Computer time was granted by the Computer Science Center of the University of Maryland.

[2] The percentage of firm CPAs feeling complete freedom to exercise professional judgment rises from 33 percent at the junior level, to 65 percent at the senior level, to 68 percent at the supervisor level, and to 90 percent at the partner level. Gamma measures of association for the relationship between position level and the three measures of professional autonomy are + .64, + .61, and + .69.

[3] Forty-nine percent of our sample CPAs in local firms are partners, compared to fifty-five percent in regional firms and only twenty-five percent in national firms. Only eight percent of our sample CPAs in local firms are juniors, compared to twenty-seven percent in regional firms and thirty-nine percent in national firms.

[4] Use of more quantitative measures of size and complexity (number of branch offices run by a firm and number of professional staff in specific branch office) not only supports the point about lack of a negative relationship between size and professional autonomy, but suggests a U curve effect, with professional autonomy being lowest at the middle ranges of CPA firm size while almost as high at the upper size ranges as at the lower size ranges. For more detailed data and discussion, see Lengermann (1971).

Analysis

Organizational Control

Occupations are to some degree modified by the work setting in which they are performed. Hughes (1958) distinguishes three occupational models which are later discussed by Freidson (1970: 107–108): science, professions, and business. The papers in this section approximate these models and provide insightful comparisons of the models within organizations. Scientists and engineers (science), university professors (professions), and accountants (business), are occupational roles that are today generally performed in large, complex organizations. Interdependence of organizations and occupations is necessary for the survival of each. Problems in this interdependence have been studied by many sociologists (see Zald, 1971, and the Overview in this volume for references).

Features of complex organizations such as identity, structure, work setting and goals are examined in terms of their impact on occupational group and role autonomy. For example, to some degree organizational identity imposes varying requirements upon occupational groups and roles. The teacher's autonomy in a prison primarily concerned with physical security is likely to be less in some respects than the role autonomy of a teacher in a public school. Scientists and engineers working in aerospace industries experience more autonomy than similar professionals in government laboratories but less than those in university laboratories which require professionals to be self-regulating (Vollmer, La Porte, Pedersen, and Stewart, 1964).

The piracy of the United States Navy ship Pueblo in 1968 illustrates how decision-making problems can emerge within an organization with divided authority generating from the organizational identity and structure. This ship was set up as an organizational unit to collect classified information. Within this structure existed a special unit of administrators specifically responsible for the protection of collected classified data. These members, the ship commander and the officer directly responsible for the mission, all shared the decision of what to do with the classified documents after it was apparent that the ship was under seizure. A delayed decision resulted from disagreement between the two administrators as to what action should be taken to protect or destroy the data. However, even though the eventual decision was made to scuttle the ship, resources were not available to destroy the data. The commanding officers testified that budgetary limitations set by the parent agency prior to the ship's embarkment prevented the organization from having the resources necessary to carry out their missions. This example demonstrates two difficulties for role members in complex structures: problems in organizational effectiveness which develop from a split authority (especially in a time of crisis), and problems in maintaining budgetary balance and resources to promote organizational effectiveness.

Organizational control over occupational roles is likely to be minimized if group autonomy is high because this protects the role from influence of organizational constraints. However, role autonomy is not axiomatic for any occupation because the organization is the primary bastion of power; this is not absolute power but variable and shared with occupations. Knowledge of the sharing process (exchange) between the occupation and organization is required for an understanding of how occupational roles may be to some degree self-regulating.

SCIENTISTS AND ENGINEERS

American industry and organizations are characterized by rapidly expanding technology which requires continuous performance by highly skilled scientific and engineering specialists. The survival of this technical knowledge today rests to some degree on how organizations utilize available specialists who provide the resources for scientific and organizational advancement. As long as an emphasis in American society and culture remains on progress associated with rapid industrial expansion, the interdependence of organizations and specialized occupations will continue to expand. Kornhauser (1962), Stewart (1968), and Miller in this volume indicate that the interdependence of the two forms of social organization is a definite trend with some degree of permanence. The advancement of science and technology in American society requires autonomy for the innovators. If societal values are contrary to the perpetuation of technology, then the associated occupations may decline in significance and degree of self-regulation. Some examples of this have been seen in the "space race" between the American and Russian governments. While the implications of this issue and of the trend are not explored in this volume, they provide challenging issues for the student of occupations and organizations.

Miller, in his study of scientists and engineers in this volume, delineates several characteristics unique to the work setting of research and development (R&D) scientists and engineers. For example, the unit primarily concerned with basic research did provide a work environment similar to that of a university laboratory. Type of supervisor (directive or laissez-faire) and freedom to choose the type of research project in which involved were used by Miller as measures of professional control and incentives. Specialists (professionals) in the university-like work setting were able to choose their projects and were more likely to be satisfied with the supervisory style (laissez-faire) than professionals in the larger structure.

Even though we know the appropriate structure for accomplishing basic research goals, the structure for other specialist areas such as design and development have not been designated. The question has been raised in other studies of professional socialization whether or not *length* and *type* of professional training result in a multiple or a universal role orientation among technical specialists. These factors have been considered to be of unparalleled importance in the status of professional growth and development. However, while these are significant, Miller concludes that reinforcement in the work setting is necessary for maintaining the socialized orientation. In addition, Miller demonstrates (as does Stewart, 1968, and Loether in this volume) that several role orientations are likely from combinations of these variables and attitude toward the employing organization. However, organizational placement (work setting) of technical specialists will to some degree modify and change the orientation and commitment. This can be viewed as a form of subtle organizational control (socialization) that may result in altered commitments and changing role orientation.

University training and preparation for work for scientists is more limiting than for engineers in terms of immediate work productivity. Generally, an engineer with a Bachelor's degree is able to enter an organization and be productive by contributing to goals and solving problems immediately without organizational training. Managers have told this author (Stewart, 1968) during research studies: "Engineers can do something when you hire them. Scientists have to be trained. Even though in the long run scientists may pay off better for the organization, you have too many months of non-productivity while you train them. Sometimes you don't get anything at all and it has cost the organization plenty to have a guy sitting around non-productively." However, in this same study of aerospace scientists and engineers, the author found that the single most important item for 99 percent of the sample (N = 250) was freedom to determine *how* the task should be done, not *what* the task or goal should be. These professionals accepted the position that, within reason, organizational goal priorities needed to be established by management. But autonomy (discretion) at the role level was necessary for all technical specialists to determine the means to accomplish established objectives. This was the raison d'etre for technical specialists in organizations—their esoteric knowledge and expertise.

The occupations of science and engineering are constantly changing. Miller notes that the structure of organizations in which occupations are carried out are changing as well in the balance of control maintained and permitted for occupations to be self-regulating. Sometimes changes may occur in the wrong direction. This author conducted a longitudinal study of the relationship between organizational change and professional attrition of aerospace scientists and engineers (Stewart, 1968). Specialists committed primarily to the profession (cosmopolitans) did associate changes in the organization's structure from *functional* groups to *project* groups as removing opportunities for professional autonomy, growth and development. As indicated by Hughes (1958) in the science model, pursuit and communication of knowledge are key work requirements for these technical specialists. Since their colleagues are considered the consumers of scientific findings, organizational structural arrangements that prevent open communication are negatively viewed by scientists and some engineers. Solomon (1968), who supports Hughes, maintains that students should study occupations in process. This idea should be further extended to include that today in order to study occupations in process (survival is an important process), it is necessary to examine the interaction process between organizations and occupations. Structural changes occur in both occupations and organizations which interact with each other, and thus modify the constantly shifting balance of control between the two. As indicated in the perspective of this book, this interaction between the two forms of social organization—occupations and organizations—is modified by social-cultural control and client control. Miller's study is significant since he indicates that while *type* and *length* of professional training are important in occupational group and role regulation, the impact of organizational structure is more pervasive in affecting the commitment to both professional and bureaucratic values.

TEACHING

The educational process can be studied at many levels. Teaching at the elementary school level generally provides less group and role autonomy than at secondary or university levels (Samuels and Loether in this section). Teaching at any level in the jail system is different from either elementary or university teaching. Thus this discussion compares the occupation of teaching as it is affected by the varying work settings in which it is integrated. This type of comparison could be applied to other occupations. For example, it is likely that the physician functioning in a prison setting has limited role autonomy since the prison goal of physical security restricts provision of some types of equipment. It is also likely that prison budgetary limitations restrict allocation of funds for such secondary goals as medical care. Whether the physician is able to provide good medical care (even if his autonomy is low) is, however, an empirical question. Physicians as an occupational group obviously enjoy extensive autonomy to regulate the occupation. But to some degree the work setting of this "model" occupation does modify role autonomy.

The Elementary School Teacher—The Jail School Teacher. A comparison between the public school and the jail school teacher serves to illustrate how the organization in which an occupation is performed modifies role autonomy. Many items for comparison could be selected but the topics of goals, structures and client relationship will be considered in this section. The goal of the public school is to educate all students who attend; the goal of the jail is to provide security (control) to the public from public offenders of various types. Thus any decisions in this latter organization must serve this first goal of control. Decisions in the public school are coordinated by a group of administrators who are responsible for educating the society. The secondary goals of each of these organizations entail a reversal of the primary goals. The public school must maintain order; the jail school must provide some education. The role of teacher in each of these organizations must coincide with those of the organization or continuous conflict will result. Samuels, in her study of public school teachers, found that the teachers perceived little professional autonomy in most areas of their work, except maintaining order and discipline. The teacher must solve this objective herself. Furthermore her subjects indicated that teacher performance evaluation was carried out on the basis of how teachers could meet the secondary goal of discipline and control. Secondary in this evaluation was the method (process) the teacher used to carry out the teaching objective. The last criterion of evaluation was the student product (first goal, education). The jail school teacher, however, is probably not evaluated on the basis of how he accomplishes the first goal of control, because this function is determined by the administration. The administration decides who will go to school and punishes prisoners for cell misbehavior by withholding the privilege of school attendance.

The methods of instruction used by these two roles also differed because of the organizational setting. Samuels reports that the teachers in the public school generally chose the method most often favored by their principals even though this was not what they thought was best. (This example of reduced use of autonomy is somewhat similar to the female lawyers who elected to accept inferior positions and assignments). Mennerick indicated that the work setting in the jail school, while not ideal in terms of the resources it provided, did allow the teachers autonomy to determine what methods and resources they would use to carry out their objectives. In addition, the teacher could determine *what* to teach, *how* to teach it and *whom* to teach. Special tutoring could be given to pupils whom the teacher decided should receive it. For the public school teacher no such autonomy exists, not at least in the larger school districts. Samuels found a positive relationship between school district size, provision of standardized resources in instructional materials and perceived autonomy. Educational publishing houses, primarily concerned with profit, have been commissioned to provide standardized material for many districts. While to the teachers this is viewed as reduced autonomy, to the public school organization this is viewed as providing equal educational opportunities for all students at all levels. This latter view is more consistent with the societal values on education than teacher autonomy.

Another area on which the two teacher roles can be compared is the client-teacher relationship. For the jail school teacher the encounter between client and teacher varies from a single tutoring experience to the full classroom experience, which for him is generally smaller than it is for the elementary school teacher. The jail school teacher may overlook infractions of the rules by his students for many reasons. The temporariness of the contact suggests that the problem will soon go away, so there is not permanent threat to the teacher's control. The elementary school teacher, on the other hand, must live with the problem for the entire school year; she must teach students in the class and show no partiality to any individual. The jail school teacher may have the student removed if the student becomes unmanageable; this reinforces the prison view that the student is a troublemaker. Going to school is a different experience for the elementary school student than the student in jail. For the latter it means getting away from the confinement of his cell; space to move around, contact with other prisoners and opportunity to exchange news and stories. Thus the motives for attending school might serve to regulate student behavior. Apparently jail school teachers value autonomy in the client relationship which suggests that the dilemma between professionals and organizational loyalty is more inclusive. This identity is more likely a tripartite relationship composed of: occupation, organization and client. For the jail school teacher satisfactory encounters with students are more immediate and perhaps more rewarding than the amount of knowledge imparted.

In sum, the degree of autonomy for the teacher role varies depending upon the organizational setting in which it is carried out. The public school system with its primary stated goal of teaching is likely to continue standardizing more of its instructional materials and methods of teaching performance because the populations which it serves are stable from year to year. However, the organization such as the jail which has security as its primary objective, is not likely to provide extra resources for the secondary goal of teaching unless pressured from the larger society. The occupation of teachers is not at this time strong enough to impose standards of excellence, etc. upon the prison system. These standards must come from a change in societal values as to the educational rights and privileges of persons labeled as offenders. At this time teaching is organized in several ways with some groups attempting to strengthen bargaining unions and others trying to improve the power of professional associations. This latter group is important for public awareness because it is the ultimate constituency for granting license and mandate to teachers. They vote the school bonds; they elect the school boards. It would appear that public acceptance of teacher autonomy is waning for reasons suggested in Samuels' paper. If this is true and school systems continue to enlarge (as survival becomes the most important goal), problems such as competition for scarce resources will result. Under these circumstances of increased standardization autonomy for teachers is not likely to increase despite the further organization of the occupation.

For the jail school teacher it is more difficult to evaluate what changes in autonomy will occur. If societal values result in pressure on the prison system to provide better education, then it is likely that standardization of the instructional resources will develop. If this should occur, then teacher autonomy in the jail setting might be reduced, especially if changes are made whereby students are evaluated on what they have learned. At this time, however, it would appear that the bargaining position of the teachers in jail schools is greater than in the elementary level because the supply and demand may be out of proportion. Also, being a teacher in a jail may be considered a low status position in the occupation. Data on these ideas are not available in these papers.

University Teaching. Loether describes the varying work environments (bureaucratic and collegial) of colleges and universities as these have evolved in the United States. The need to coordinate university activities and goals became necessary as increasing expansion occurred. Many view this continued shift to a bureaucratic university environment as automatically reducing the autonomy of professors. In the past, a high degree of academic freedom existed in all collegial work settings and few decisions required the time and expertise of faculties as to the management and administration of static programs. Contemporary universities are organized with the department as the basic organizational unit that administers and coordinates most faculty activities. Departmental decisions are coordinated by administrative branches in the organization that are separated on the basis of function. For example, recruitment of faculty, while initiated at the department level, is not totally a department function or decision. Depending upon the specific organizational arrangements, a series of deans and sometimes vice-presidents must meet and accept the candidate. This is not always a *pro forma* procedure.

Recruitment becomes an organizational decision, rather than primarily a departmental decision because contemporary universities today face one serious problem—survival. Thompson (1967) states that survival and coping with uncertainty are the predominant concerns of all organizations. In the university, sources of uncertainty are many: numbers of students, sources of funding, dissatisfied public, demanding faculties and students for academic standards, and apathetic alumni. According to Loether the numbers of students is increasing, but this trend may not continue if college graduates are "over-educated" for employment in the labor force. Many argue that the function of the university is to educate, not to train persons for the labor force. Trade and vocational schools are set up for meeting these needs. One mechanism that an occupation uses to maintain control is the training of its recruits. Whether an emerging occupation has control over training location of new members might be explainable by the origins of the emerging occupation. Nurses and physicians obviously want to control the new specialties, nurse specialist and physician's assistant. Thus it becomes important for the occupation to locate curriculum in an organization that permits this autonomy.

University survival today is linked to the degree it can control uncertainty (elimination is not likely) of funding problems. From an organizational perspective, every faculty promotion or expansion in the organization is only possible if there is money for the position. The justification for many faculty decisions then becomes financial (survival) rather than academic. Organizationally it is sound that the administration has decision-making power to determine how much expansion should occur. However, to return to the point on recruitment, the autonomy of professors is encroached upon when the organization rather than the faculty selects the new colleagues. This is similar to the problem faced by other occupational roles where the method to carry out an assigned task is usurped by the organization, rather than permitting the occupation to make decisions based on expertise, judgment, and varying skills.

Because of the predominance of government activity in education, universities and colleges continue to compete for these funds not only for expansion (innovation) but also for survival. The need to innovate programs requires that the organization provide incentives for the faculty to increase their skills in entrepreneurial functions. It is at this point that the interaction between occupational roles and organizational managers is a delicate balancing process, a negotiation of exchange strengths. Faculty need to be rewarded for developing and selling ideas and programs that bring support to the university, e.g. training programs. Sometimes these programs provide faculty with the opportunity to pursue their own interests. In Loether's study of college professors, reward was given in terms of promotion and tenure to those who engaged in research grant activity. If professors want continued autonomy and control in the university they need to increase the number and types of new programs they develop, as well as research activities. As in industry, the entrepreneurial role for the professor is an important function in providing organizational survival and occupational role autonomy.

The development of new programs today appears to reflect an inter-disciplinary approach, especially in the areas of social science. Concern with developing social issues, domestic and international, has stimulated experts from many disciplines to combine their academic efforts in search of knowledge for purposes of social action. In industry too, it has been necessary to some extent for management to organize occupational roles into projects rather than functional groups because highly specialized diverse technologies require intensive coordination to produce a product (Stewart, 1968). New programs, technologies, and social conditions may require occupations to widen their contact and interaction with each other to promote team products. The pressure of survival in universities may necessitate a pragmatic change among occupations for control to remain at the group rather than the organizational level. This would require more interaction between departments on several levels.

Loether found that the cosmopolitans receive the rewards that the college offers in promotion and tenure. However, despite these findings these members are leaving the organization. The question is raised as to why professionals would leave when they are receiving the desired rewards. While Loether's explanation is tenable—that professionals find their whole life situation better than most in spite of their work arrangements—other explanations are possible. As mentioned earlier, the dilemma between organizational and professional loyalty could be extended to include loyalty to the client. That is, perceived student quality might be an important factor in the cosmopolitans' decision to remain or leave. Although there are not data to address this point in Loether's paper, good students are a necessary resource to carry out research and participate in training programs. In addition, relationships between the professor and student (client) are part of the reward structure of teaching which suggests that the encounter between professor and student is an important aspect of faculty consideration when selecting a university position.

Another explanation for Loether's discovery of cosmopolitan exodus may lie in the administration action to reduce salaries for associate and full professors. This is not an endorsement of confidence, especially when cosmopolitans comprise these levels. In addition, while in the past professors have accepted low salaries for the privileges of academic environments today the university is a different work environment. Salary becomes a significant rewarding feature, especially for those who have already received promotion and tenure. It is probably easier for the professor to accept financial deprivation when he is located at a prestigious organization.

Furthermore, professors may view salary reduction as a beginning decline in professor autonomy. If this were true, the decision to leave while they still have bargaining power in other universities is not surprising. The degree to which professors perceive this as a universal phenomenon and not just an isolated case at their own college, would also contribute to their decision to leave.

CERTIFIED PUBLIC ACCOUNTANTS

The development of large scale organizations and business is not possible without sound accounting systems and principles of business management. Early bookkeeping procedures grew into complex record keeping such that specialized knowledge of rules, procedures, tax and corporate law requirements all contributed to the need for the development of certified public accountants. Lengermann, like Samuels, found a positive relationship between organizational size and professional autonomy. However, further analysis of this relationship shows that level in the organization (hierarchical position) is a likely factor in determining exchange strengths that members can use in improving their autonomy and position. Loether also finds that the cosmopolitans in his sample were in the higher ranks and had more autonomy than those in the lower. Again the question arises: in what areas is autonomy withheld from professional role members? One problem with all the findings to this point may lie in the measure used to assess autonomy. Lengermann and others (Miller in this volume) have used freedom to exercise one's professional judgement in carrying out one's work. If this item is perceived by professionals to include opportunity to select assignments, as well as how to carry out tasks once assigned, then autonomy measures need to be operationalized more clearly so that managers and role members are using the same measures. Also, researchers may need to clarify with professionals the dimensions of autonomy. From an organizational perspective, partners and supervisors, having an overview of the organization and its problems, may assign accountants to business accounts randomly or because of specific expertise. However, junior level accountants are not as likely to have specialized expertise based on business experience. Thus additional variables to be explored in this autonomy measure are length of time in position number of years certified and also length of time in the organization. (Lengermann mentions this in his study.)

Organizational managers are not likely to promote nor give autonomy to members they deem undesirable for any reason (see Epstein for another example). But there is some inconsistency here with Lengermann's results because he found that the CPA firms discouraged mobility between firms, yet did not provide professional incentives for persons to remain. Thus the accountant became loyal to a particular CPA firm and only secondarily to his occupation. The predominance of locals (see Loether) at the junior level would be high under such socialization conditions in an organization. Using such a philosophy (discouraging mobility, few professional incentives but encouraged organizational identity), management is able to accomplish its goals as inexpensively as possible.

Like Miller in his study of scientists and engineers, Lengermann concluded that the nature of the work setting does affect professional autonomy but less than current sociological literature on organizations and professions would indicate. The variable of hierarchical position in the CPA firm was very strongly related to professional autonomy. Lengermann combined exchange strengths with professional identification and found that professional autonomy is considerably improved in all organizational settings and at all position levels. The inconsistency mentioned earlier in lack of professional incentives in an organization suggests that organizational control rather than occupational role control will be stabilized under these conditions.

As in the other occupational roles studied in this section, the client-accountant relationship may provide a source of satisfaction not found in other aspects of the work or organization. Although data are not available on this factor, a tripartite orientation may be considered in this occupational role (profession, organization and client). Service to the client is still part of the professional-client relationship even though the professional may be based in a large organization. The nature of the encounter between the accountant and his client does serve to reinforce to the accountant his expertise, specialized abilities and professional identification. This may improve client service. The organization must share some autonomy with professional groups and roles if the organization is to survive. This will vary from occupation to occupation and from organization to organization. The conditions under which the organization will grant this autonomy to groups and roles will vary from occupation to occupation. The interaction is certainly affected by the degree to which society values the occupation, accepts it and the degree to which the occupation is organized with the intention of self-regulation.

3

THE OCCUPATION

Occupational Context

The degree to which societal and organizational controls are effective in modifying autonomy is to some extent regulated by the organization of the occupation. For some occupations unions and professional associations serve to regulate work activities and conditions of employment. The organization of the occupation in determining who will be recruited, what preparation and skills are required for entry vary with many occupations. As already noted in a previous section, the housewife, actress and cab driver are not carefully recruited by the occupation such that the member comes prepared with a particular body of knowledge and skills separate from lay information. For some occupations the tasks that are to be performed do not require a specialized expertise in order to function at the role level. This would appear to be the situation in the occupation of saleswoman in that anyone with average ability and intelligence can perform the function. However, as Dalton shows us, variations of performance and control do exist at the role level. The innovator in this occupation is the ratebuster who manages to obtain considerable autonomy in all aspects of her work. Since the task of selling is a close intimate process between seller and client, careful control over this interaction is not always possible.

Brewer, in his study of the wiremen, also demonstrates how the informal structure operates to allow the worker more autonomy than he would find in a formalized occupation. This occupational role is different in that rewards are tied to the role of wireman in a particular structure but the nature of the structure does not encourage the wiremen to organize into a specific occupational group.

The study of musicians in an orchestra indicates further evidence for differentiating autonomy at the group and role levels. While the musician must conform to a limited degree to the conductor, because of the organized task, autonomy at the role level can be exercised in how the task is performed. Even though autonomy does exist and is granted by the occupation, some control is necessary for team success. This is further illustrated in Federico's study of the ballet dancer. This occupation, in terms of the tasks to be performed, requires that the dancer relinquish his artistic autonomy. Perhaps the phenomenon of ratebusting in these two occupations would result in removal from the group beyond the point of social ostracism as seen in the saleswoman. The ballet dancer who outperforms the rest of the team is risking considerable sanction and reduced privilege to exercise role autonomy.

Of further interest in this section are the baseball players described by Charnofsky. Because of the task and need for team success, they experience very little autonomy at the group and role level. That is, the physical nature of the task requires that the ballplayer structure all aspects of his work and non-work activities around his specific task of playing ball. Not only the task but also the organization of the occupation is such that the coaches, managers, etc., all determine to some extent how the occupation will be directed and what changes will occur in terms of how and when the game will be played.

A new occupation not very widespread in terms of recognition, prevalence and utility is the petroleum landman. Bryant's study suggests that this occupation developed because of the societal need to regulate land use for petroleum exploration. The skills required for the occupation are not obtained easily and not well-known to the public. Public acceptance of the occupation does exist since the group has autonomy and control to determine the skills and knowledge to carry out the role. Thus what seems to have happened is that autonomy developed at the role level and became organized into autonomy at the group level. To some, Bryant included, this indicates professionalization of the occupation.

Nursing is a complex occupation to compare in terms of group and role autonomy. There is so much role differentiation and division of labor in the occupation that it is difficult to compare all types of nurses with each other. For example, nurse specialists appear to have considerable autonomy at the role level as well as more prestige and status than non-specialists. Of significance in this occupation is Bulloughs' position that complexity and role differentiation have been developed by the occupation itself. Nurses at the role level have autonomy to select the patients they will care for and the degree of involvement and care they wish to provide. Nursing is one occupation where the student can examine rather closely the impact on group autonomy of the continued differentiation of roles. Colleague control is difficult to exercise if the occupation does not define clearly who are colleagues.

As in nursing, the reference librarian is in close interaction with the client. The nature of this encounter is examined by Shosid who indicates that the nature of the task is most significant in regulating the predictability of the encounter. Much differentiation has occurred in librarianship but this is not explored specifically in her paper. Like the nurse and others, the librarian has some autonomy to select what kinds of clients she wants to serve. In the specific organizational setting this autonomy is reduced since the service ideal of other occupations applies in this encounter.

Khleif's paper on the psychiatric resident illustrates the socialization process and how occupational skills are acquired. He studies how the beginning resident, a recognized professional, is stripped of his authority and automony in the physician role and how this is reestablished later in his training. This paper shows how the occupation itself regulates, trains and indoctrinates its members to certain ideologies and consequent performances. It also illustrates how control by the profession protects the role from criticism and influence of other levels of control. Thus, medicine is a perfect example of the benefits and autonomy to be accrued by the profession that is well organized in all aspects from selection of recruits at entry to total control of their training and performance. Few occupations in American society can match this degree of organization within the occupation.

Melville Dalton

The Ratebuster: The Case
of the Saleswoman

This is a case study of the female high performers on commission selling in the boys' department of a chain department store, Lassiters,[1] which has a total of 127 employees. The term ratebuster [2] probably originated in the 1920's in settings where industrial engineers had introduced wage incentive systems. These plans are thought to offer workers the opportunity to earn money in addition to their guaranteed basic wage. Such systems are based on stopwatch study of the time and motions that are considered by production engineers to be most efficient in doing the job. When a wage incentive is introduced the great majority of workers respond cautiously to the inducement and work out a general plan of response. They set a level of production that will make them a "safe" amount of bonus but will not exhaust them. They avoid "showing each other up," or doing anything to cause the engineers to "tighten" the rate so that making any bonus becomes very difficult. The person, if any, who does not go along with this position, and instead produces "too high" threatens to "bust" the rate and is therefore called a ratebuster. The presence of a ratebuster disrupts the existing fabric of production formalities that is already weakened by the introduction of a wage incentive. Fortunately for the group view and the rate, there are few ratebusters. I found only nine in a group of over three hundred industrial workers (Dalton, 1948); in another plant but one worker out of 231. The ratebuster, at least the male, is so perversely socialized that his relations with the group are largely a matter of indifference to him. Persons with this bent—individualistic, competitive, acquisitive, eager to succeed, in terms of whatever is defined as success—can probably be found even in unexpected crafts at nearly any time,[3] at least in the Western World.

The technical details of wage incentives in industry and commission selling differ, but those persons to whom such inducements have the greatest appeal show characteristic behavior and a similar personality type in both cases.

METHOD

Mike Masters, head of the boys' department at Lassiters, lived as a neighbor in my block. His help in getting confidential data for me was indispensable. Knowing of my interest in the human operations of industry and business, he told me of his saleswomen—some of whom I already knew slightly—and of his problems. He invited me to the store emphasizing that he had "some real saleswomen." After more talk with him about the differences and similarities between commission selling and industrial piecework as incentives, I expressed an interest in doing some research on the type of person who was a high seller. I began making regular visits to the store where I observed the saleswomen and talked with them at their convenience.

Conversation with the women and my observations suggested that two of the group were making high commission. The other women made noticeably fewer sales and spent considerable time getting out stock, tidying up, rearranging, and so on. This appeared to be one of Masters' problems: having two saleswomen making most of the commissions. I encouraged the saleswomen to talk about their selling. It became clear from what they said that Masters favored one of their group because of her high selling and that the amount of her sales may have been in part influenced by the favoritism.

To broach the subject I was most interested in, I talked to the saleswomen about male workers on incentive pay. This stimulated comparisons. However, I did not comment on the conflict surrounding the ratebusters in industry or on the attitudes of their fellow workers toward them (Dalton, 1948).

THE SALESWOMEN

Of the six people in the boys' department only the head was male, and he made sales only occasionally. Two of the women were high sellers—Mrs. White and Mrs. Brown. Mrs. White was fifty-nine years old, large physically and somewhat taciturn. She had worked at Lassiters for fourteen years. Mrs. Brown was a small active person, thirty-two and had been with the store for eight years. Masters told me that when she started in the store she was much taken with Mrs. White and copied and improved upon Mrs. White's selling techniques. Then, too, Mrs. Brown had the insights that came from close personal experience in out-fitting her son. Over a period of several months they developed a rivalry. For the last six years of so, according to Masters, they were coldly polite to each other when it was necessary to speak. Masters regarded exis-tence of this hostility as one of his major problems. His professed ideal was that the women should all be circulating among the customers, busy all the time and cordial to each other.

The other three salesgirls were Mrs. Bonomo, thirty-five, a quiet amenable person, in the department for four years; Mrs. Selby, forty-eight, an employee for five years, who took things as they came without being much disturbed—though judging from her behavior and remarks she made, she disliked Mrs. White much more than she did Mrs. Brown. Mrs. Dawson, at twenty-two, was the youngest member of the depart-ment. She had dubbed Mrs. Brown and Mrs. White "saleshogs." She had worked there less than two years. She liked Mrs. Brown despite the epithet she had given her. Mrs. Dawson had two years of college, the most schooling in the department.

The saleswomen received from $1.75 to $2.25 per hour, depending on how long they had been in the department. Records of sales (dollar-volume) for the department were kept for the past year and varied from month to month. These records established the quota for the current year. Once this was equaled, the women started drawing com-mission pay at the rate of five percent. Commission was paid separately once a month.

Before describing the selling tactics of Mrs. Brown and Mrs. White, the ratebuster types, it is instructive to note the average daily sales established over a six month period [4] by the five saleswomen. Mrs.

Saleswomen	Average Daily Dollar Sales
Mrs. Brown	227
Mrs. White	153
Mrs. Bonomo	119
Mrs. Selby	110
Mrs. Dawson	101

Brown with $227 average daily sales is over twice as much as Mrs. Daw-son and Mrs. Selby, nearly twice as much as Mrs. Bonomo, and $74 more than the second ratebuster, Mrs. White. Masters assured me that Mrs. White had slowed up noticeably in her selling over the last two years, but in terms of dollar sales and her constant challenge to Mrs. Brown she should still be classified as a ratebuster, or as a ratebuster in decline.

Lassiters had an employee credit union. Masters had access to the complete membership which was seventy-six. He gave me *rank only* of the five saleswomen based on the individual amounts deposited in the credit union. (He was so shocked when I requested the total savings of each of the saleswomen that I gladly accepted the partial data.) Mrs. White stood third in the store, and Mrs. Brown was fourth. Mrs. Selby ranked forty-ninth and Mrs. Bonomo was sixty-sixth. Mrs. Dawson was not a member. These data alone do not tell much, but they do indicate that Mrs. White and Mrs. Brown were among the top investors, and that commission was important in their behavior.

RATEBUSTER TACTICS

Mrs. Brown apparently had more personal relations with customers than anyone in the boys' department. She learned from Masters when specially-priced merchandise was coming in. She telephoned customers she knew well and made arrangements to lay away items of given size and style that were scheduled to go on sale. When she had filled these private orders there was little of the merchandise left for the general public when the official sale day arrived. These sales by telephone constituted about fifteen percent of her total sales. Relatively new customers who bought heavily a time or two she filed in her retentive memory and took steps to acquaint them with her special services.

Among her repeat buyers was a working woman with four sons who treated their clothing roughly. Every six weeks this woman came in to buy nearly complete outfits for the boys. This included shirts, underwear, socks and blue jeans, which amounted to what the sales force called a "big ticket" of about $120.

Mrs. Brown had another woman customer who did not believe in having the younger boys of her five sons wear the older boys' outgrown clothing. She did not come in much oftener than once a year to buy complete outfits, usually just before Easter, which could run to two hundred dollars or more. Mrs. Brown acted as though she had an exclusive right[5] to these customers, and several others that she knew who had only two sons. When Mrs. Brown expected these people she would skip her lunch hour for fear she might miss them, or ask Masters to make the sale and ring it up on her cash drawer in case the woman came when she was out to lunch. He was glad to do this. When business was very good, whether she expected specific customers or not, she ignored the coffee breaks (ten minutes each morning and afternoon) and the lunch hour, leaving the selling floor only long enough to eat a sandwich in the dressing room.

She also had a practical monopoly on sales for boys on welfare. These boys had to be presented by an agent on the welfare organization the first time they did business with the store. Masters turned the welfare customer over to Mrs. Brown and forever afterwards [6] she made the sales. In some cases the welfare officer brought the boy, or boys, with their only clothes on their backs, to buy a complete outfit with extra socks, handkerchiefs and underwear. (Shoes were not sold in the boys' department.) In any case, Mrs. Brown took care of the sales then and afterwards.

Mrs. Brown's housekeeping area was just inside the entrance from the parking lot. She watched this approach closely. When she was not busy, or was talking to the other members of the department, she could break off instantly—even when she was telling a joke—and move toward the door. If she did not recognize the person she formed some judgment of him based on the affluence of his dress and his bearing. If the customer had a boy along, she judged whether he would be hard to fit. In her own words, she had a theory that "the kids who are tall and skinny or short and fat are hard to fit." [7] Thus she made quick appraisals of everybody who moved toward the department. If she approached a customer and learned that he was not as promising as he looked, she often brought the person to one of the other saleswomen and presented him with a statement of what he wanted as though—according to the women—she was giving them an assured sale. She made no revealing comment on the matter, but she seemed at the same time to be putting a restraint on her rivals.

Mrs. Brown's most galling behavior to the group was her practice of getting sale claims on as many prospective buyers as possible. She thus deprived the other saleswomen of a chance at the buyers. For instance, as she was serving one person, she would see another coming through the door—which she nearly always faced even when busiest. Quickly she would lay a number of items before the first person with the promise to be back in a moment, then hurry to capture the second customer. If the situation were right, she might get her claim on three or four buyers while two or more of the saleswomen were reduced to maintaining the show cases, and setting things in order so as not to appear idle. Mrs. Brown was able to do this because her own housekeeping and stocking area (assigned by Masters) lay between the entrance to the store and the other sections of the boys' department. Only Mrs. White would challenge her by intercepting a patron. The rivalry between them never came to a visible break. As noted earlier some of the other saleswomen resented Mrs. Brown's behavior and privately called her a "sales hog." She was not called that by Mrs. Bonomo and Mrs. Selby who thought—as they said—that Mrs. Brown in action was a "show in itself."

A standard device was used by Mrs. Brown, for ends not intended, with the understanding and collaboration of Masters. On very slack days she frequently left the store shortly after one or two o'clock to do "comparative shopping," that is, to compare the selling prices of items that Lassiters sold with the prices that other local stores charged for the same or similar items. Sometimes Mrs. Brown actually did this, but often she would attend a matinee, or go home to catch up with her housework, or just take a nap. (Her time card was punched out by Masters at the official quitting time.) In any case, to the favorable implications of "comparative shopping," the further obvious inference was made that her absence from the store allowed the other salesgirls to make more commission. (Actually, business was so slow on some days, because of weather, etc., that it was not possible for any of the saleswomen to earn bonus pay.)

Mrs. Brown's conduct may suggest total indifference to the group. But possibly because she was a female in our society, she was not as nonconformist as the grim ratebusters in industry. Some of these could work for years without exchange of words with people, only a few feet away, that they knew hated them. To a degree Mrs. Brown was concerned about her group. Every week or so she would buy a two pound box of choice chocolates from a candy store near Lassiters and bring it in to share with the group. She could have bought a less expensive grade of candy at Lassiters. Sharing of the candy was almost certainly calculated (she ate little of it herself) but it appeared spontaneous and was received without hesitation. The saleswomen could not direct an unqualified hostility toward her.

She had another uncommon practice which made her stand apart from all of Lassiters' employees. Despite her determined assault on the commission system she did not use her right to a discount on items that she might buy for herself or members of her family. She took her fifteen-year-old son to a local independent department store to buy his clothes. She vigorously declared that "I don't want anything that [Lassiters] has." She was emphatic to the group—and implicitly condemned them —that she did not want to participate in the common practice of getting legal price reductions in addition to the regular employee discount by buying items at the end of a season. For example, an assortment of women's purses would be delivered to the selling floor. This was the "beginning of the season" for that batch of purses. The saleswomen with friends in the purse department would look at the display and select ones that appealed to them. These were laid away until the "end of the season" when they could be bought at the sale price which was further reduced by the regular discount. Mrs. Brown would have nothing to do with such items. She clearly did not want it said that she was taking advantage of her job.

A likely interpretation is that she sensed she was rejected and widely criticized for her methods and high bonus pay. She feared that some envious salesperson would report any borderline activity on her part to top management. Her own explanation implied that her esthetic taste could not be satisfied by the merchandise at Lassiters. In effect she downgraded the status of the store. As part of this complex she also implied that she was morally somewhat above the group. Also she may have been posing to hide her possible guilt feelings about her treatment of the group.

Although the aim of this paper is not to deal with morale problems, it was glaringly clear that Masters damaged group feeling by routing welfare customers to Mrs. Brown, and by ringing up some of his sales on her cash drawer. His tacit approval of her behavior discouraged the other saleswomen from attempting to control her.

CONCLUSIONS

Ratebusters are few in number because the role calls for a person who (1) is indifferent to his work group as shown by his defiance of their social restraints on his production, and who (2) has great capacity for enduring ostracism. Male ratebusters seem to have more intense and prolonged resistance to the group than females do. But fortified by religious conviction some women have been quite resistive.[8]

On might validly generalize from a single case if that one were selected with enough care. But how can one know, when ratebusters are so few and widely dispersed? On the basis of only two cases it would be ridiculous to generalize. In the absence of an adequate sample and the difficulty in getting one we may make a series of hypotheses.

In the selling situation, female ratebuster types have a strong memory for faces and personalities. They develop and act on simple hunches about the marks of potential buyers. For example Mrs. Brown and Mrs. White both agreed that men are easier to sell to than women. They also believe that "men who dress well" are more likely to "dress up" their sons.

The female ratebuster justifies exclusive access to certain customers; she in effect *chooses* customers. She skips her lunch periods and coffee breaks to make large sales. She seeks strategic positions on the selling floor that enable her to watch major entrances and approaches of customers to the department. She talks with buyers and other saleswomen and still alertly maintains this watch.

Almost simultaneously she commits several customers to let her serve them. This has the effect of keeping the other saleswomen from making sales when business is slow. When mistaken in her impressions of a prospective patron, she sometimes frees herself and pretends a charitable gesture toward the group by taking the person to another saleswoman.

The female ratebuster on commission selling is likely to be a social climber who strains after name symbols in clothing, appliances, furniture and so on. Somewhat like the male ratebuster in industry, she identifies more with groups outside than in the firm.

The industrial ratebuster experiences no visible pain in working outside the group rules because he considers himself a member of other groups. But the female ratebuster in selling cannot functionally or socially live with impunity outside the group rules. She does not have her work brought to her as the industrial ratebuster does. She must go get the work. She must—as would of course the male on commission—present a genial front and interested manner to the customers. But she must not be offensively eager if she is to win the customer as a "steady" who will wait for her if she is busy. She circulates among the group to economize time in the long run—to be sure of getting a response to questions she may need to ask about an elusive item or some size of stock. Then, both as a demand of the role and as a woman in our society, she cannot show the surliness that she may feel. She anticipates offense in the group and seeks to limit it in ways appropriate to the situation. She wants to have at least a semblance of good relations with the group, and yet qualifiedly works outside the group rules. She wants no open break with the group and maneuvers the situation to avoid it.

NOTES

1 The name of the store and those of its personnel are fictional.

2 This term is used in industrial research. See F. J. Roethlisberger and W. J. Dickson (1939: 522) and B. B. Gardner, (1945: 154). John Zadrozny, (1959: 277) defines the ratebuster as "a workman who constantly strives to produce more than his quota." Another term, "grabber" was used by the saleswomen in a study by George F. F. Lombard (1955: 90–94). At Lassiters ratebuster saleswomen were called "saleshogs."

3 For example, Lope de Vega, a Spanish playwright, (1562–1635) wrote

some eighteen hundred plays during the creation of which the charge was made by Cervantes (who wrote less than fifty dramas) that Vega was a "monster of nature." By Vega's own admission, in over a hundred different instances he wrote plays and brought them on the stage all within twenty-four hours.

Luca Giordano, an Italian artist, (1632–1705) painted so many pictures in so short a time and acquired such fame during his lifetime that his rivals accused him of working eight hours a day—which was unthinkable—and on holy days. He acquired the nickname of *Luca Fa-presto* (Luke Work-fast).

[4] Masters gave me these figures based on an average of 44 hours a week and including the back-to-school buying months of August and September 1969.

[5] Probably she was encouraged by the customers to think that way; certainly some customers waited for her to be free to serve them.

[6] The other saleswomen knew about this and resented it. Grateful to Masters for allowing me to observe and talk with the saleswomen, I naturally did not ask him why there was no sharing of such sales among his force. I inquired, but there was no voiced conception of a "day's work" among the saleswomen. This general practice of informal rewarding is not uncommon in industry where it is sometimes done even with the knowledge and cooperation of individual officers of the union. (Lassiters was not unionized.)

[7] Alteration of coats and trousers was done free by the store's tailor. But measuring and marking and the extra trying on were time-consuming. In the extreme cases this was futile. In any case Mrs. Brown avoided customers with "odd size" boys unless she knew them to be liberal buyers and worth her time.

[8] Max Weber did a study of work performance and variation of production in the German textile industry. Among other things he found two Pietist girls who were high producers. They resisted pressures of the unions to lower their production and were very stiff-necked and harsh toward their co-workers. See "Schwankungen der industriellen Arbeitsleistung," pp. 136–174 in *Zur Psychophysik der industriellen Arbeit*, pp. 61–255 from *Gesammelte Aufsätze zur Sociologie and Sozialpolitik*, Verlag von j.C.B. Mohr Paul Siebeck) Tubingen, 1924.

John D. Brewer

Informal Occupational Specialization:
The Case of the Wireman

To understand occupations, it is increasingly necessary to understand bureaucracy (Hall, 1969). And to understand bureaucracy, it has always been necessary to go beyond the formal organization to investigate the informal (see Blau, 1955 and Dalton, 1959). For example, there were 431 occupations listed in the detailed occupational classification of the census of Great Britain in 1841. More recently, the Dictionary of Occupational Titles (1965) listed approximately twenty-five thousand occupational titles. Bureaucracies are among the major administrative channels through which this very high degree of contemporary occupational specialization has been formally established and maintained.[1] But in response to organizational and individual needs that are unmet by the formal structure of bureaucracy, occupational roles that will be found in no dictionary are constantly being enacted.

These informal occupational specialties are a key aspect of the much studied informal organization of bureaucracy, but they are a relatively unexplored aspect of the occupational structure. It is more often noted that modern industrial organization suffers from an over-specialization of occupational roles. This is dealt with officially by human relations practitioners who initiate programs of job enlargement to improve employee morale. Unofficial practices by alienated workers on assembly lines and elsewhere include trading jobs to break the monotony and gain greater control over work (see Friedman, 1961). However, paradoxically, while highly specialized work creates needs for variety, highly varied work creates needs for specialization. The skills required for the different aspects of varied work are almost always unevenly distributed

215

among the members of the occupational group. Uneven distribution of skill poses managerial problems of assuring competent performance of all aspects of the job. It provides also openings in the formal bureaucratic structure through which workers may gain greater control over their work.

This paper describes one such case of informal specialization and considers some of the conditions under which individuals' informal behavior becomes socially organized into informal roles. It is clear that though there is informal behavior in all formal organizations, only a small portion of this behavior is incorporated into socially defined and regulated role relationships. Much informal behavior remains at the level of either individual action or purely interpersonal relations. Yet other behavior is governed by the operation of informal norms and processes of social control that apply to all the members of a work group. Informally organized occupational roles exist only when a substantial number of organization members agree that the regular and exclusive performance of a particular subset of work is grounds for conferring special rights and obligations upon certain workers vis-a-vis their superiors and fellow workers. Cases of this type are of particular significance sociologically because they graphically illustrate the processes by which social actors as well as social planners shape the structure of work roles.

THE CASE OF THE WIREMEN

The wiremen are electrical construction workers who perform an occupational specialty that is widely but not officially recognized within the light and power company in which they work. The electrical construction departments of light and power companies are responsible for the installation and maintenance of the electrical equipment upon which the operations of the company depend. The linemen who work on the high voltage overhead lines are, of course, the most publicly visible electrical construction workers. The men in this paper do the less dramatic but almost equally dangerous job of building and maintaining local electrical substations. Although this work requires a wide variety of construction skills, all workers within the department are formally classified as one or another grade of electrical mechanic. They generally work in crews of four, supervised by a crew leader who is in turn supervised by a roving foreman. Much of the work involves cooperative or interdependent labor. Crew assignments are temporary, usually only for the duration of the particular job at hand, and are made by a router or scheduler in the home office. The absence of permanently constituted work crews and the absence of formal specialization in the work force provides a high level of flexibility in the allocation of labor to meet the high variability in labor and skill requirements for particular jobs. The work of the department is not so standardized that all jobs can be handled efficiently by four-men teams. Often even different phases of the same job require work crews of quite different sizes. Nor is the mix of skills required so standardized that an elaborate division of labor can be economically maintained within the department.

However, despite the absence of formal specialization, certain workers within the department do become specialists in the particular work of wiring small, intricate circuits. Whenever extensive wiring of this type is to be done, one of the several men in the department known as wire-men is assigned to the job. All of the men in the department are in principle qualified to do wireman work and all are formally obligated to do so if called upon when a wireman is unavailable. Wiring is quite different physically from most of the other work in the department and is widely regarded as requiring special skills, aptitudes, and inclinations. Many men find wiring unpleasant and tedious or claim to lack the skill to do it well. A typical comment is that it is "more like watchmaking than like construction." Workers who become known as wiremen are men who show their ability and indicate a preference for wiring.

Specialization, whether formal or informal, serves not only to fix responsibilities for specific duties but also to establish at least by implication the duties for which the specialist is not responsible. On jobs to which wiremen are assigned it is understood that wiring is their major responsibility and that except in emergencies they are not asked to do much other work, especially the heavier or dirty work. Moreover, most crew leaders report that if possible they avoid asking wiremen to do heavy, dirty work even when a wireman is assigned to do a job that requires no intricate wiring. However, interviews with wiremen them-selves reveal that a major attraction of the role is the greater control over work and work relationships which wiring gives them; it was not, as one might think, a particularly strong intrinsic satisfaction that they feel in wiring as a type of work and not any particular aversion to other aspects of construction work. The wiremen could usually work inde-pendently of the crew leader and the rest of the crew. If he performed other work he worked under the nearly constant supervision of the crew leader and in almost continuous contact and interdependence with other crew members.[2]

A CONTRASTING CASE: THE "CONCRETEMEN"

Wiring is, of course, not the only work activity requiring special skills that are not formally specialized. Work that requires general rather than electrical construction skills (e.g., laying concrete) is usually either contracted out, or if the skills are required frequently enough (e.g., carpentry or painting) they are handled by crews of craftsmen who formally specialize in the work and who service the electrical crews when needed. However, during the period of the research, there was severe pressure within the company to cut back on labor casts and use available men whenever possible to avoid the added cost of contracting out. Some of the electrical construction workers were in fact skilled at laying concrete either from their prior training and experience in other construction work, or from having been previously assigned by chance to projects on which they had had the opportunity to observe outside contractors do this type of work. But there was no evidence of an informal role of "concreteman" as there was a role of wireman. The title concreteman is used for convenience by the author. Within the construction department, it was simply known and said that certain men had had experience working with concrete. One or more of these men would be assigned to jobs on the basis of this, which they either refused assignments, or reported that they agreed only after protest. The concretemen often complained that if they did accept assignments their work was less satisfying in a variety of ways than their usual work (e.g., "That's the kind of work that I started here to get *away* from."), but that they received little special consideration in return. But even those men who reported liking the work itself said that they were often reluctant to do it, because of tensions on the job.

Laying concrete, unlike wiring, is a cooperative rather than a solitary activity. Therefore, the one or perhaps two men in the crew who are concretemen are constrained either to do more work than their fellow workers, or to attempt to exercise control over their co-workers. The specialization of the wiremen increases the autonomy of all members of the crew. Recruitment of concretemen has the opposite effect. In the effort to forestall the resulting conflicts, formal organization gives way to interpersonal relations. Special care began to be taken by the routers in making crew assignments of concretemen so that when possible only workers and supervisors who are reputed to work well together are assigned to these jobs. No such care is taken to select wiremen, and jobs involving wiremen's services are not known as particularly conflict-producing. The new policy temporarily ended the conflict. But it did so at the costs of violating the universalistic, bureaucratic operating principle of the interchangeability of personnel. This violation limits the flexibility of work assignment which the varied operations of the department require. Moreover, the policy puts further strain upon interpersonal relations by making manifest previously latent patterns of hostility and conflict among departmental members. It opens the way to later conflicts within the network formal and informal exchange relations within the department.

SPECIALIZATION AND EXCHANGE

"Exchange cannot take place unless there is specialization, for there would be nothing to exchange; but specialization without exchange would be useless, for the tailor would starve and the farmer go naked. *Exchange without specialization is impossible; specialization without exchange is silly*" (Boulding, 1955: 552). Exchange relations are institutionalized in roles which in varying degrees of specificity and detail define the terms of the exchange as rights and obligations of the actor. Formal bureaucratic specialization of work roles identifies in advance of actual role performance people who are willing and able to carry out particular organizational tasks, sets a contractually agreed upon value to their labor, and assigns them the official responsibility for these tasks (Weber, 1947: 329–336). In principle, at least, these formal arrangements remove an important set of matters from the arena of daily negotiations and possible conflict; each supervisor and each subordinate need not bargain over what work the latter will do for what wage. But the cost of this planninig is to reduce organizational flexibility.[3] The structure of formal work roles is rarely adequate to meet the actual operational needs of the organization, and of the individuals who perform organizational roles. These unmet needs re-open the door to on the spot bargaining between organization members and to conflict among them should their bargaining give way to coercion and attempts at exploitation.

The bargaining over unmet needs is sometimes organized into the informal systems of interpersonal exchange which have been frequently described in studies of formal organizations.[4] Blau has given a general description of the processes of informal exchange as they occur between supervisors and subordinates:

> Every privilege the manager is granted and every rule he is empowered to enforce increases the capital on which he can draw to make subordinates indebted to him. By not using some of his power, he invests it in social obligations. The advantages subordinates derive from his pattern of supervision obligate them to reciprocate by complying with his directives and requests. (Blau, 1964: 206)

Social relations based upon favors and obligations develop among peers as well as superiors and subordinates. In either case, the key attribute is that both the giving and return of favors is voluntary. If the giver openly asks for his due the relationship is destroyed. These considerations suggest that interpersonal exchange can serve as a mode of socially organizing informal specializations only when the pressure to secure the benefits of exchange is moderately low. For example, the man whose job hinges upon subordinates' or fellow workers' cooperation is less likely to have the patience to wait for them to recognize their obligations than the man who expects only moderate consequences for his own future as the result of their actions.

Similarly, the more sources of supply for a particular service that a man has available and the less competition that there is from other men for the same service from the same sources, the more patient he is likely to be. In the case of wiring, all superiors require the service at some time, but only some subordinates were willing or able to provide it. This placed those workers who were able, but unwilling in a position where they were likely to be pressured to provide the service whether they wanted to or not. At the same time, those workers who are both willing and able are potentially in a very favorable bargaining position. The development of an informal specialization controls this potentially explosive situation. The rewards that the wiremen can derive from their special abilities are assured but also limited by the social definition of their role. They can lay claim to exemption from unpleasant work, but can not hope for a special recommendation in bonuses or promotion. Moreover, by openly though unofficially, designating certain men as wiremen, the chances that their benefits will be seen (through either ignorance, or willful misunderstanding of the informal structure) as favoritism are reduced. Public designation also served as an announcement that any man with the same skills can claim these benefits as his due. The relationships between the wiremen and their superiors differ in important ways from the interpersonal relationships of exchange described above.

Notably, the crew leader does not excuse wiremen from other work as a personal favor, but rather because they are wiremen, whose role obligations as commonly defined within the department do not call for them to do this other work. Nor do the wiremen perform their informal specialty out of a sense of obligation to the particular crew leader; they simply perform their duties. This lack of particularism is illustrated by the fact that a crew leader most often asks only for a wireman to be assigned to his crew and does not ask for any individual worker by name.

Informal norms may serve similar functions with respect to informal services that are performable by all rather than just a few workers. For example, the non-routine nature of much of the electrical construction work meant that there are many jobs which simply do not fit the formal schedule of lunch and rest breaks, when it is impossible for the whole crew to quit work for an hour or for even fifteen minutes. Under these conditions, regular lunches and rests are forgotten. Men stop individually just long enough to eat a sandwich quickly or eat while they work. But when this occurs, it is expected that at the earliest opportunity the crew leader will informally reimburse the men for their efforts by letting them leave the job early to beat the rush hour traffic, or by taking a longer than usual lunch break the next day, or by going to a nearby restaurant for coffee and doughnuts (for which the crew leader usually paid) instead of making their own coffee at the work site. The superior who too frequently failed to reciprocate, or did so grudgingly, would soon find himself unable to command compliance easily when a difficult job came along. Similarly, subordinates who refused to cooperate with the crew leaders with an unofficial service (flexible scheduling) experienced difficulties from other workers when doing their work. At the same time, the arrangement avoids conflict by more or less equally distributing a work burden which might otherwise be foisted upon the most exploitable workers or eagerly picked up by the most opportunistic.

A NOTE ON METHOD

The wiremen were found by accident during a period of approximately six months that I spent doing fieldwork in the light and power company. The research was heavily focused upon the inter-personal relations between supervisors and their subordinates.[5] My method was to observe systematically the verbal interactions between superiors and subordinates while they were at work, classifying each interaction in terms of a pre-established set of categories which described different aspects of the process of supervision. The data collected in this way were later statistically analyzed. I hoped to give greater depth to this analysis by providing extensive descriptions of the less quantifiable aspects of work life in the company as background against which to interpret the statistical data. As often happens, the background proved to be as sociologically interesting as the foreground.

One day near the end of my research while observing a crew leader and his men, I noticed that one member of the crew was treated quite differently from the others. He went directly to work wiring an elaborate circuit box and worked uninterrupted the entire day, except for lunch and coffee breaks. During the same time the rest of the crew worked in close contact with the crew leader, moving from one aspect of the job to another under his direction and surveillance. When I inquired, the crew leader explained simply: "He's a wireman." He went on then to describe the position of the wireman much as I have explained it here. Interviews with other supervisors, workers, and wiremen substantiated the description. Having previously observed the conflicts, interpersonal negotiations, and almost ritualized exchange of favors that accompanied other deviations from formal work roles, I was amazed to find such a complex and important set of informal activities carried out so smoothly that I had nearly missed observing them at all.

CONCLUSION

The work roles in modern industrial organizations that perhaps have been most often described are the very specialized ones that are carried out in relative social isolation and that are parts of elaborate, highly formalized divisions of labor. The prototype is, of course, the assembly line worker. These work roles produce the now familiar problems of alienation and the equally familiar informal adjustments to these problems.[6] There are, however, many different types of industrial work roles. The electrical construction workers, like many workers in craft based industries and like many maintenance workers in mass production industries, perform a wide variety of work activities, work in interdependent work teams, and have a large measure of flexibility in determining who performs what task when. As the accumulated knowledge of industrial sociology would suggest, these attributes of their work were major sources of job satisfaction to them. However, the same attributes (variety in their work, social contacts on the job, and flexibility) which they valued highly when they compared their work to, for example, factory work, were also major sources of role problems. A diversity of work activities can be stressful as well as stimulating. Close social relations at work may sometimes be important sources of social support and other rewards of sociability, but they may also be suffocating and filled with tension. Similarly, flexibility in job assignment may prevent monotony but it also deprives the worker of the security of closely specified duties.

The case study data presented in this paper illustrate both the nature of the role problems and nature of the informal adjustments to them that occurred in one company. In the case of the wiremen, the informal adjustment provided a solution that was apparently satisfactory to the participants. But the contrasting case of the concretemen cautions against the optimistic conclusion that occupational or organizational role problems necessarily generate informal social structural solutions which eliminate the tensions and conflicts. In the case of the concretemen, the locus of strain was shifted only from the level of their interpersonal relations. No intermediate level of informal role structure developed. A plausible and possible explanation is simply that concrete laying jobs are neither as frequent, nor as consistent a part of the departmental work load as wiring jobs. However, a more interesting explanation may be derived from the previously discussed differential effects upon work autonomy of specializing wiring and concrete work. An informal role of concretemen would in effect have been a new leadership role in the crew, because of the interdependent nature of the work. Autonomy at work is one of the most scarce resources in all work settings and is particularly scarce in hierarchically organized bureaucratic settings. This fact makes it exceedingly unlikely that consensual validation from the work force would be forthcoming for an informal role that significantly limited work autonomy. But, at the same time, it is equally true that not all workers feel an equal need for autonomy; and that for some, other needs are more pressing. Hence, while few workers would agree in principle to any structural arrangement that might limit their control over their work, some might—and did in the construction department—agree to temporary individual arrangements.

NOTES

[1] On the development of formal role differentiation within organizations, see Peter B. Blau and Richard A. Schoenherr, (1971).

[2] On close supervision and heavy downward communication in electrical construction crews, see John Brewer, (1971: 475–484). On interpersonal strains in interdependent work crews, see Leonard R. Sayles, (1958: especially 83–91).

[3] For an analysis of rigidity and conflict within French bureaucracies, see Michel Crozier, (1964).

[4] For example see the description of "the exchange of good turns" in William Foote Whyte, (1948). See also the description of unofficial reward systems in industry in Melville Dalton, (1959: 194–217).

[5] The results of this research are reported in John Brewer, (1970: 341–347).

[6] On informal adjustments to alienating roles, see Erving Goffman, (1961: especially 173–207).

Norma J. Shosid

Problematic Interaction: The Reference Encounter*

Librarians are inevitably associated with the institutions within which they work. Libraries are both employer and work setting for almost all librarians. As Hughes (1962: 40) notes, "when we say 'librarian' we say 'library.' The word 'librarian' makes no sense without the fact of the library." So accepted is the tie between librarian and library that its implications for work interaction tend to be overlooked.

The occupational world of librarians is divided into work activity, subject area, and type of library. A given librarian may be identified, for example, as a reference librarian, a science librarian, or a university librarian. Professional groups and library school courses are organized along all three dimensions. Evidence is mixed (Naegele and Stolar, 1960: 57; Parker, 1962: 55–57) as to primary area of identification, but there is some evidence (Naegele and Stolar, 1960: 75; Edmunds, 1971: 270; Sinclair, 1971: 197) that it is to *type* of library.

This makes sense for the librarian. The service the librarian may give is affected by the library's financial resources, staffing policies, provisions for special service, and by the overall scope and size of the collection. These factors all tend to be defined by the *type* of library.

Although librarians are supervised by other librarians (Goode, 1962:

---
* This research was supported by Grant Number MH 16505 from the National Institute of Mental Health.

The author is especially grateful for the guidance of Ralph Turner in the writing of this paper. Marion Schulman, by suggesting examples of the reference encounter and by reading an earlier draft of this paper assured that the librarian's reality was not totally lost in the sociological perspective.

224

12), very few libraries exist as independent agencies. There are public libraries, school libraries, corporate libraries, museum libraries, hospital libraries, prison libraries. For each type of oganization, there may exist a related library. No library, whether it be the Library of Congress in Washington, D. C., or the public library in Pasadena, California, can escape completely from the need to satisfy its governing institution.

Variation in size, number and dispersion of units, complexity and specialization of internal division of labor, and geographical location of libraries influence the librarian's work environment and occupational ideology. This influence is particularly strong in that a large proportion of librarians have not undergone a common socialization experience in the university graduate schools of library science. The lone librarian in a small company library is going to be affected differently by structural variables from a librarian working in the reference department of a large academic library.

Even the apparently casual one-to-one relationship of the reference encounter is bounded by the library's purposes, clientele, regulations, and physical setting.[1] This simple institutionalized ritual is pervaded by problematic aspects. The unscheduled nature of the encounter and its open-endedness are created by organizational variables. Mutual establishment of the participants "status categories" (Hughes, 1958: 56) or "social identities" (Goffman, 1963: 2) is essential to establish service provided. Yet, establishment of status is made difficult by just that open-endedness and lack of schedules. These factors make measurement of service difficult.

UNSCHEDULED NATURE OF THE ENCOUNTER

The reference encounter is fleeting and unscheduled with changing participants. It resembles the salesperson-customer relationship. The library inquirer, however, is seeking information or advice, a situation closer to the professional or semi-professional encounter.

When the encounter begins the librarian does not know who the inquirer is; the process by which the inquirer decided to come to the library; or the inquirer's library knowledge, subject expertise, and needs. Hutchins (1944: 23) emphasizes that the librarian has at best a few seconds to establish these facts. The timing of the encounter is determined by the inquirer not by the librarian. In certain libraries, the inquirer may send in his request ahead of the personal visit. Occasionally, from previous experience or third-person recommendation, the inquirer will ask for a specific librarian. Ordinarily, neither participant knows beforehand with whom he is going to speak. The librarian does not know even generally what the subject matter of the interaction will be.[2]

Given these uncertainties, the librarian could be expected to lack the feeling of security and confidence which Scheff (1968) imputes to the interrogator as opposed to the client. The interaction becomes one in which the participants are continually "testing inferences about the role of alter" (Turner, 1962: 23).

Either party may initiate the reference encounter. The subsequent patterns of cue behavior, recognition, and interpretation during the interaction will be affected (Shosid, 1966). Situational cues affecting the initiation include: Is the librarian at a desk which labels him "librarian?" Is he standing or sitting; alone, apparently engaged in interaction, performing some activity? Is he visible at all? Has the inquirer just entered or been present for some time? Does the inquirer approach the reference desk?[3]

Weyer (1930: 98) advises the librarian:

Library opinion and practice seem delicately balanced as to the niceties and proprieties of accosting those other shy or self-sufficient persons who either flutter vaguely about in the offing or who go straight to catalog, shelves, or vertical files with an air of long having been initiated into the mysteries. Some reference workers appear to regard both these with equal suspicion for having ignored the authentic approach to the temple and as equally certain to come to grief. The best maxim in such cases is 'Offer help, unless sure it is not required or desired.' Let no doubting Thomas ask for sure signs that it is not required. The practiced reference librarian will infallibly detect them even in the proud and confident person who fearlessly tackles the card catalog. As his operations slow down, assurance disappears, a vague uncertain look steals into the face, and the watcher will shortly recognize the psychological moment to intervene with 'Are you finding what you want?' And, if there should be doubtful cases, risk the asking.

OPEN-ENDEDNESS IN THE REFERENCE ENCOUNTER

The librarian does not have "control" of the setting which Goffman (1959: 93) says affects the "information the audience is able to acquire." To use his terms, front region and back stage (Goffman, 1959: 107, 112), loss of control over the front region (Goffman 1959: 137) "leaves the performer in a position of not knowing what character he will have to project from one moment to the next, making it difficult for him to affect a dramaturgical success in any one of them."

It will be difficult for the librarian to conceal the evidence of his "dirty work" and to present his work as a finished-product (Goffman,

1959: 44). In some cases, if very little effort was actually required to complete the information search, this fact cannot be concealed. In other cases, the inquirer watches while the librarian proceeds from step to step. Opportunities for hiding the amount of work exist, but the possibilities vary greatly from one interview to the next.

The physical structure and layout of the library, then, affects both original initiation of the encounter and patterns of interaction within it. For example, consultation of the card catalog is basic to reference work. If the card catalog is at a distance from the reference department, in another room, or the other end of the library, it becomes problematic whether the librarian will, during the course of the reference encounter, take that long walk. If the reference department is physicially adjacent to the card catalog, the likelihood that the inquirer will consult a reference librarian and that the librarian will consult the card catalog is higher.

Certain types of occupational identification symbols (Goffman, 1951: 296) which are found in other organizations are lacking in libraries. The librarian may be at a desk, but the desk may or may not be publicly labeled "reference." It is unlikely that formal "credentials" (Goffman, 1951: 296) will be displayed. Even the furnishings of the reference area can affect the interaction. Some libraries have substituted an office-type desk and chairs for the traditional counter-high reference desk. The purposes of the changes were, apparently, to make the situation more comfortable for the inquirer and to establish an atmosphere closer to the traditional client-professional setting. The new setting is suitable to long direct interaction, but it can be awkward for the quick question and for periods when the librarian rises to go elsewhere leaving the inquirer at the desk. Neither party may be sure when the interaction begins whether to sit or stand. The inquirer may expect the interaction to take only a few seconds. The librarian may find himself rising just as the inquirer is lowering himself into a chair. Since the librarian often is unable to estimate the length of time it will take to answer the question, the inquirer may be left waiting at the reference desk. At the same time, the inquirer may resent being asked to leave and return later.

Reference librarians probably spend only a small part of their time doing reference work, i. e., locating information or describing use of library material. Depending on the library, other tasks include record keeping, compiling indexes and bibliographies, checking out books, arranging displays, reading lists of new books, familiarizing themselves with new reference works, etc. These activities are often conducted in the same place as reference work. Thus, the reference question may appear to be an interruption. These other activities are also much more easily measured by supervisors than are reference encounters. Unless the inquirer complains or conveys praise to supervisor or administrator the librarian's performances remain virtually invisible.

The librarian busy with an inquirer may be interrupted by the telephone or by another inquirer. The presence of other people visibly waiting to be helped may affect both librarian and inquirer by creating a feeling of lack of privacy or of a need to rush through the interview. Librarians are advised not to leave the inquirer unoccupied for too long while the librarian is away getting information lest the inquirer thinks he has been forgotten (McColvin and McColvin, 1936). In practice, librarians may leave the inquirer with irrelevant material just to leave him with something. The inquirer may simply assume the librarian did not understand the request or is stupid. In one sense, librarians have professional autonomy. For a given inquiry, most librarians would be found working alone unless they specifically request assistance from colleagues and/or supervisors. However, if the librarian does wish to consult a colleague, he frequently must do so in the presence and hearing of the inquirer. The librarian must be willing to exhibit ignorance publicly.

ESTABLISHMENT OF STATUS IN THE REFERENCE ENCOUNTER

The need to establish relative status is present in all interaction (Form and Stone, 1957; Glaser and Strauss, 1964). The participants may differ in their awareness of the identity problem (Glaser and Strauss, 1964: 678) which is probably the case in the reference encounter. Each will interpret the behavior of the other during the interaction according to the role with which he identifies the other and himself. Hutchins (1944: 28) lists as the first purpose of the interview "the establishment of cordial relations" with the "classification of the problem" taking second place. Miller (1964: 19) found the same pattern in the auto salesman's approach to a customer. Freidson (1961: 192) pointed out that even in the doctor-patient relationship, the class identification of the participants affects the interaction.

Accurate establishment and communication of status for the librarian is made crucial: (1) by the existence of organizational rules which delineate those who are entitled to service and to what amount and level of service they are entitled; (2) by the probability that the inquirer's judgment of the encounter and the librarian's adequacy will come from agreement on status and need; and (3) by the librarian's practical need to commuunicate with the inquirer, to learn what type, level, and form of information the inquirer wants and can use. By defining an inquirer as especially in need, the librarian may give better service to someone than organizational rules would dictate.

McColvin and McColvin (1936: 192–194) say the librarian should have the ability to

> draw out of readers the exact nature of their enquiry, . . . inspire confidence without giving the slightest impression of superiority or know-it-all-ishness . . . treat all and sundry according to their own valuation and manner, as collaborators and friends, while still preserving a real balance (which should seldom be made apparent) between the importance of an enquiry and the amount of trouble that the exigencies of the service make it possible to take.

The variety of roles in which the librarian may place the inquirer during this process are indicated by the numerous terms found in library literature: patron, client, reader, inquirer, library user, visitor. The last is descriptive of others who come to the library as well as of the inquirer. The phrase "library user" is awkward although its shortened form "user" adds a racy note to articles on reference work. Client and patron have contradictory subjective meanings.

The library may set limits to the amount of time which can be spent on a given inquiry, denote what classes of people are entitled to what level of service, forbid assistance with certain types of questions, etc. A public library may forbid circulation of certain material to children, a school library may refuse to assist a student in answering homework questions, a university library may answer an inquiry for a faculty member, but not for a student. Differential treatment is apparently accepted by the inquirer (Naegele and Stolar, 1960: 114).

> One librarian recalls that a faculty member remarked that he had been especially impressed by the service he had been given since the librarian, at the time, had not known he was a faculty member.[4]
>
> An inquirer asked the dimensions of the Winfield Scott, a steamer sunk off Santa Barbara, California. The librarian found the details as requested. The inquirer then proceeded to ask for the same information about another sunken ship. At this point the librarian became "suspicious" and began probing. She elicited the information that the inquirer's hobby was treasure hunting. Further assistance was denied on the grounds that the purpose was not one which would legitimate the amount of work necessary to satisfy fully the inquirer's requests.

This encounter took place in an academic library. In a public library, the request might have received different treatment. Many public libraries, on the other hand, have rules against any assistance for people who are trying to answer puzzle contests. "Idle curiosity" in such instances may be defined as a more legitimate purpose than the pursuit of profit.

All libraries serve a broad range of statuses. While this commonsense observation is seen most clearly in the public library, it is true also of the academic. Apocryphal stories abound among academic librarians about the assistant professor mistaken for a mere student and the dire consequences for the librarian following such a *faux pas*.

The interest of the question for the librarian will affect the amount of time and effort he puts into answering it (Naegele and Stolar, 1960: 76). "Interesting" questions appear to be those which strike the librarian as new, different, difficult or having subjective or objective importance. As is common in other service relationships, the librarian and the inquirer may not agree on a problem's importance or interest. There is continuing degate among librarians as to whether the inquirer should be given the information he wants or told how to go about finding it. Library rules usually say, but in practice the librarian exercises his discretion. The degree of complexity in directing the person to finding the answer himself, not rules or theory, may determine the librarian's actions.

Given Scheff's (1968) propositions about negotiating reality and Hall's (1968: 98) findings on the service orientation of librarians, consensus can usually be reached if the inquirer is able to state his need in ways the librarian can concede to be legitimate. As we have seen, the average reference librarian works unsupervised in the encounter and is able to exercise a form of Mechanic's (1962a) "power of lower level participants." Differences in treatment are rarely brought to the attention of other inquirers.

Form and Stone (1957: 513) indicate that, in the middle class, blatant exchange of status is disapproved and more subtle cues are utilized. The library is very much a middle-class institution, and librarians are overwhelmingly middle-class. The problem of redefining the client's role as he perceived it is not peculiar to the reference encounter but is common in professional situations (Moore, 1970: 101). Moore refers to the "oversocialized" and the "undersocialized" client, both of whom must be oriented to the "proper" client role. It is doubtful that the librarian is considered a professional with the right to ask probing questions, and the librarian's attempts to question the client may be perceived as illegitimate.

The inquirer is to some extent in a no-win situation. A supersensitive librarian may react negatively to even a mild self-identification, yet feel tricked if there is none. If the inquirer advances an identification, the librarian may judge this to be a claim for special service. If the inquirer does not identify himself when such identification would facilitate service, the librarian will wonder why the inquirer tried to conceal his identity. Concealment of purpose may not be deliberate on the part of the inquirer. The librarian tends to assign intent. Some inquirers learn to "work the system." In one corporate library, the rule was that company employees were to be given assistance only on work related problems. Since the corporation also maintained an incentive program which encouraged employees to enroll in educational courses, employees often wanted library assistance in their homework. Most rapidly learned to conceal their purpose.

The inquirer is placing himself in the role of one seeking help. Homans (1961) assumes that ordinarily the person of lower status asks for help and advice from the person of higher status. Moore (1970: 103) says that "dealing with putative equals puts a strain on the professional-client role relationship." In some libraries, the inquirer may frequently see himself as of higher or equal status to the librarian. The institutionalized nature of the professional interaction is intended to alleviate the strain. Where roles are more problematic, as in the reference encounter, the strain would be expected to be greater.

Status is of course relative to the situation. A professor asking for assistance in an academic library on a matter related to his own specialty and the same person asking at the nearby public library branch for assistance on a matter related to his gardening hobby may be treated differently, and may not feel that his difference is unjust. Involvement of self in the request appears to be a variable. The closer the request for information on a subject to the person's self-conception, the more sensitive the situation.

While the problematic question for the librarian is the status of the inquirer, for the inquirer it may become the status of the librarian. The inquirer may perhaps overgeneralize from one library situation to another. Insofar as the type of treatment remains the same, this may not be too severe a problem. If it is different, and if the inquirer expected the role of "librarian" to be the same, initial interpretation of cues and evaluation of outcome will be affected. Inquirers may not be aware that there is a reality to negotiate, an element which Scheff (1968) considers integral.

In this paper, librarian has implicitly been defined as a person who is called a librarian by the institution in which he works or one who calls himself a librarian or both. Not all librarians would agree that all persons falling into this category are in fact librarians.[5] Lack of consensus on the part of librarians does not make the inquirer's task of establishing correct role relationships any easier.

An overwhelming majority of librarians are female. Sex of inquirer may affect both status and deference patterns in the interaction, and it may affect them in contradictory fashion. If a man is in the position of seeking assistance from a woman in matters relating to his professional or occupational competence, there may be a tendency to activate general societal male-female relationship patterns. This may interfere with task orientation. A male librarian has other problems in establishing a viable role, similar perhaps to those of the male elementary school teacher.

MEASUREMENT OF SERVICE

The inquirer has no way to judge if the service was as fast or as efficient as it might have been. If information was given, it may or may not have been complete or factually correct. Yet, the inquirer may feel more capable of judging reference service than of judging other professional services he receives. This would be especially true in those instances where the subject matter involved the inquirer's own expertise.

Librarians lack objective criteria by which to measure their work. Hieber (1966) found that librarians have not even agreed on how to classify questions much less on how to evaluate the performance of answering them. Criteria which have been used include: level of library expertise needed to provide the information; level or amount of subject knowledge needed to answer the question; format in which the information is provided; time required to obtain the answer or time spent in the interaction; and provision of information or directions on how to locate the information.[6] Since many libraries require librarians to keep numerical counts by type of question, the categories used may structure the way the interaction is perceived by the librarian.[7]

There may be no "answer," i. e., the information which the inquirer wants may not exist. This "answer" is often unacceptable to the inquirer, and the librarian may be left with a feeling that perhaps there really is an answer and he has failed in not finding it.

A woman called a public library in Texas wanting to know how to get on the bridge from California to Hawaii as she was planning on driving to the latter state. On being told there was no such bridge, the woman's conclusion appeared to be not that there was no such bridge, but that the library's staff was too incompetent to locate it.

Knowing the identity of the inquirer may cause the librarian incorrectly to assume the real question is being presented and that the item requested exists.

A professor of political science asked an academic librarian for an atlas of the United States census. Knowing that the inquirer was a faculty member and knowing his area of specialization, the librarian assumed such a work existed. At the same time, she knew that the Bureau of the Census had published no such item in recent times. Trying a compromise, she found an atlas which included maps showing population shifts in the United States. The professor's response was, "I wanted tables with budget figures." Following a series of questions and answers, the librarian handed the inquirer the *Historical Statistics of the United States* which turned out to be what he needed.

There are other problems in evaluating service. What starts out as a simple informational inquiry may end up a "real" reference question:

Inquirer: I see that you have *Music Index* only from 1949. Librarian: That's right, it began in 1949. Inquirer: What do you have before that. Librarian: Well, what sort of thing do you want? Inquirer: Jazz. Librarian: Well, perhaps we have something that will help. (Locates *Encyclopedia of Jazz* and gives it to Inquirer). The *Music Index* would list any articles on jazz and also in the card catalog there will be many books on jazz. Inquirer: (After looking briefly at the book he has been handed) I was looking for *periodicals*. Librarian: Any special aspect? Inquirer: Popular songs of the 1920's. Librarian: Popular songs aren't exactly jazz. If you want, we have other books that might be helpful. Inquirer: Well, what I'm doing is . . . in *Tender is the Night*, there are popular songs mentioned and I want to identify them. Librarian: (Locates three books on popular songs covering the period of the novel) These may help. Inquirer: What about words. Librarian: There may be the libretto if the songs were from musicals, or sheet music, or records. If any songs are still unidentified after you look in these books, let me know and perhaps we can find them in something else.

Alternatively, the presented question may be far more complicated than the actual question:

The inquirer asked for a list of all the senators from Arkansas. The librarian, after some effort, located a list of all the senators ever elected or appointed from Arkansas. The inquirer said, "Oh, all I want is Senator Fullbright's address."

Sociologists (e.g., Becker, 1951: 136; Goffman, 1959: 11; Miller, 1964: 19) have suggested that the person providing the service feels it essential to be in "control" of the interaction. Hutchins (1944: 24) says that in a reference encounter, the librarian can take over by careful manipulation even though the inquirer thinks he is in control. However, as has been noted the effects of certain structural variables are such that the role of librarian and the role of inquirer are more subject to variation and to interactional role creation than is usual in institutionalized situations. Attempts by the librarian to establish control will therefore be more difficult than a more structured interaction. One would expect that generally, the more tentative and subject to variation the roles, the greater the difficulty in establishing such professional control.

Retrospective judgment of service provided may be affected by the relative statuses established during the interaction. The judgment by each part of the other's role adequacy is directly affected if, as Turner (1968: 555) suggests, "Role behavior tends to be judged as adequate or inadequate by comparison with a conception of the role in question." Obviously, if a librarian makes a mistake in identifying the inquirer, he will be, by his own standards, providing less than adequate service. The judgment of the inquirer as to the quality of service will also be affected by the relative statuses established during the interaction.

There is overlap and lack of clarity between the role of the librarian and the role of the inquirer. Freidson (1961: 183) found that it is usual for the client to first treat himself and then to approach the professional for assistance. The librarian more than others in professional or semi-professional positions appears to regard the encounter as a senior-junior colleague collaboration. At times, the librarian seems to expect the inquirer to possess a level of library expertise which, if the inquirer had it, would have obviated the necessity for consulting the librarian in the first place. For the librarian to tell the inquirer how to go about answering a question, rather than telling him the answer, means the inquirer is learning how to be a librarian. The same "tools" and the same kinds of knowledge are expected to be utilized. One measure of service may be how well the inquirer learns to be a librarian.

In controlling the situation, the librarian is attempting to define the question during the negotiation stage of the interaction, and to define the type of service which the inquirer should receive. This definition will affect the satisfaction obtained and the judgment of both parties as to the satisfactory quality of the service. If the inquirer expects to be provided with the information by the librarian, but is given only guidance as to how to find the information, there will be a lack of consensus on roles. If the inquirer attempts to change the librarian's definition of the situation, the librarian may resist or may feel relieved of the responsibility for satisfying the inquirer.

Unlike some similar service or professional relationships, the reference encounter is usually expected to be a one-shot affair. The involvement of participants would be expected to differ from one where an ongoing relationship is anticipated. The inquirer may be surprised if the librarian attempts to schedule additional encounters. The librarian may engage in referral either to specific material or to another library. He commonly has no way of knowing whether the advice was followed. What is more to the point, he has no institutional or professional sanctions to force the inquirer to follow the advice or to report back to him except in rare instances. The outcome of the encounter is unmeasurable in part because it is unknown to the librarian.

Turner (1968: 554) suggests that "an actor's behavior is without clear meaning until he settles on a particular role in interaction and allows himself to be identified with it. The individual whose behavior cannot be fitted into an identifiable role will be regarded as violating the terms of interaction." Given the possibilities of misidentification and/or disagreement, one or the other or both parties to the reference encounter may judge the other inadequate, whether or not the instrumental task of information giving is accomplished.

In the short run, the progress of the interaction will be hindered if the participants attempt to correct felt misidentification. Resources will be allocated to alter casting and staking claims rather than to instrumental aspects of the encounter. Among long term consequences is the possibility that the inquirer may not return to the library in the future even when he needs or would be helped by the services it could provide. He may mislearn the role relationship of librarian and inquirer with consequent effects on future interactions. Effects on the librarian include possible lowering of self-esteem and a tendency to rigidify role relationships, both detrimental to "service."

CONCLUSION

The reference encounter is, for a semi-professional interview situation, at an extreme high in its problematic aspects. It is hardly surprising that Weyer (1930: 235) found "intelligence, accuracy, and judgment" rated as the most important traits for a reference librarian, with "professional knowledge" running a poor fourth. The definition of judgment in the survey included just those abilities involved in negotiating the problematic aspects of the encounter.

The lack of a generally accepted measure of service provided comes from several sources aside from the nonexistence of objective measures. Agreement is complicated by lack of consensus both within librarianships and between librarianship and its public on what reference service is and on what the roles of librarian and inquirer are. There exists a lack of clarity between the two roles. Turner (1962: 36) suggests that: In institutional contexts, the additional normative element that designates a priori what role each individual must play is introduced to insure the required division of labor and to minimize the costs of exploratory role-setting behavior. In the case of the reference encounter, there are reasons to suspect that much of the situation's ambiguity is in fact created by institutional variables.

NOTES

[1] A reference encounter is created when an inquirer wants an answer to a question and hopes to obtain the answer from someone in the library. There is no theory of reference nor agreement on the mechanics involved (Gwinup, 1971: 232). The librarian has rules of thumb for discovery of what is needed, location of the information or of a source in which the information may be found, and communication of the results to the inquirer. The reference librarian's expertise consists of (1) skill in questioning and (2) knowledge of "how to use the library" and awareness of available "tools" (e.g., reference books, bibliographies, indexes).

[2] While one might expect librarians to welcome preliminary phone calls, some librarians claim that the preparation which results is usually wasted. A telephone encounter severely limits identification cues. That the librarian often feels uneasy about telephone-established claims for service is evidenced by the practice of some librarians who attempt to check surreptitiously the claims of organizational or status affiliation.

Some libraries now place non-librarian personnel at the reference contact point to receive the initial inquiry and answer the simple ones. More complicated questions are referred to the librarian. This approach, obviously patterned on the professional model, may cut down on problematic aspects of the encounter for the librarian. It may be expected to add another problematic aspect for the inquirer as he goes from library to library.

[3] The use of the pronoun "he" in reference to the librarian glosses over an element of the interaction since, even in libraries, sex is sometimes relevant (Shosid, 1966). According to the 1960 census, only fourteen per cent of all librarians are men. Additional data suggest that the probability of a given reference encounter including a male librarian is much lower (Shosid, 1970).

[4] Examples of the reference encounter were drawn from the author's expe-

rience and observation and from information obtained from practicing reference librarians.

[5] The American Library Association says a librarian is someone who holds a master's degree from an accredited library school, but it does not limit membership in its organization to such people. The inquirer has a tendency to consider anyone who works in a library a librarian.

[6] The first criterion is sometimes related to expertise in a particular library and sometimes to generalized expertise. The former type is usually called a directional question, and it could often be answered just as well by the janitor.

[7] How many libraries keep what type of reference statistics is unknown. Hawley (1970: 143) found that of fifteen libraries surveyed, eight did and seven did not keep records on reference inquiries. They are usually used as quantitative measures of service and/or of staffing needs, the reference equivalent of book circulation records.

Robert R. Faulkner

Making Us Sound Bad: Performer Compliance and Interaction in the Symphony Orchestra

This chapter presents an empirical view of compliance in the orchestra as a work organization. The description and analysis which follows focus on the extent to which musicians willingly comply with conductor's directives and the range of activity viewed as legitimately controlled by him. Although there are many kinds of events which comprise the daily work of orchestra performers, here I shall deal only with those centering around the making of music as a focused encounter (Goffman, 1961b) between conductor and player. The reason for this is that a major factor in players' views of routine versus exemplary events, of "having an experience" as opposed to merely "experiencing things" (Dewey, 1958), is the nature of their interaction with the man on the podium. As a practical organizational achievement between one man and one hundred subordinates, making music together (Schutz, 1964) depends on a set of shared legitimating beliefs supporting the amount and kind of control exercised by the maestro. I shall argue that compliance as obedience to the commands and directives of the conductor is subject to reconstitution and appraisal by organizational subordinates. From the viewpoint of the performers, the question of whether an order will be accepted and serve as a basis for behavior is problematic.

The orchestra must be viewed as more than a pattern of roles and statuses. It is a network of interacting human beings, each transmitting information to the others, sifting their transaction through an evaluative screen of beliefs and standards, and appraising the meaning of conduc-

238

tors' action. At the center of recurring patterns of authority between superiors and subordinates lie those conditions of interaction which either generate or thwart the emergence of consent. In looking to the musician's participation in orchestra interaction, it must be appreciated that these professionals perform under many conductors, establish definitions of their work experiences, and thereby affect each others' understandings about music and music-making. From the moment a conductor first steps onto the podium, these players are prepared to judge the suitability of his demands and make critical decisions on the basis of the conductor's expressive signs. Not surprisingly, they have a detailed stock of cliches and customs for divining what is expected of the conductor. Psyching-out the maestro becomes a favorite art and, at times, finding out what he is all about turns into a delightful game on the concert stage.

Howard Becker's work (1963) on the conflict between commercial musicians and their clients is especially relevant here. He focuses on certain aspects of performers: 1) shared conceptions and understandings of playing commercial music, 2) routine run-ins with "squares," and 3) strategies for defending themselves against the presumptuous attempts of outsiders to control the use of their unique artistic gifts. Like most members of special occupational worlds which emphasize expertise and esoteric skill, his players constructed a mystique about the proper use and outrageous abuse of their art. They also developed a set of occupational rules governing how far others could intrude into their personal and occupational space. Clients' attempts to influence the pros' performance—the bases of their special expertise—were viewed as insulting; their right to direct behavior in the sacred realm of making music were seen as coercive interventions and violations of collective honor.

Becker does not devote attention to the question of control over work and presumptive authority in other musical settings. However, the problematics of work in the orchestra bear some close parallels to his conceptualization. Many of the problems confronted by the orchestra player are caused not by outsiders or by a lay audience, but by the conductor himself, a musician. That is, some of the most difficult demands and kinds of musical "interference" come from conductors who are presumptuous enough to claim expertise in the prescription of performance style and use of skills, and who intrude into the hallowed sphere of solo work. Like the jazz and commercial studio scene, the orchestral world has a set of routines and customs which define the extent of legitimate authority over a range of role behaviors. This especially touchy and potentially explosive issue of skill domain gave rise to some of the most articulate conceptualizations of player prerogatives and conductor obligations to be found in these interviews. *Compliance is problematic because a musician does not automatically grant a conductor the right to conduct his total role performance.* Some conductor directives are viewed as culturally unacceptable; they are unwarranted and illegitimate intrusions into the individual musician's expressive territory and sphere of professional skill. This "zone of acceptance," to use Simon's term (1965: 12; see also Barnard, 1938: 167–169), is therefore a particularly critical domain of both work and the self (Hughes, 1971: 283–347). The underlying collective sentiments justifying noncompliance arise most clearly from perceived threats to the identity of players as high powered professionals. If for no other reason, such a feature of work interaction should draw the attention of students of work organizations to patterns of authority in artistic organizations.

METHOD

This study is based on seven months of observation and forty intensive interviews lasting from one to four hours with members of one of the top fifteen symphony orchestras in the country. During the orchestra season, rehearsals were attended, and tape-recorded interviews were conducted either after work or later in the musician's home. All the section principals, a majority of the organization's brass players, and a sample of woodwind and string instrumentalists were interviewed. Some re-interviewing was also done in order to generate a complete comparison of successive conductors and for analyzing the musician's evaluation of them. Open-ended questions encouraged the musicians to define various conductors and work experiences, and to discuss factors which they felt could make their work difficult, unpleasant, and at times degrading. I aimed at soliciting cathetic-evaluative orientations towards work, colleagues, and conductors. Musicians are frank respondents when it comes to the generalities of making music, but getting at their troubles with particular conductors was difficult and at times required some unorthodox interviewing tactics. These consisted of beginning the questions about their work by asking the musicians to define the ideal conductor; once the interview was under way, some leading questions forced them to compare the merits and defects of several of the conductors with whom they had worked during the season (see Rose, 1945; Dexter, 1970). This elicited detailed interpretations of work situations in which the fracture between ideals and reality was most obvious, in which role-expectations were violated, and where performer tensions and complaints were viewed as "caused" by certain forms of interaction between musician and conductor. Finally, this interviewing strategy gave the respondent an opportunity to instruct the interviewer in the nature of his work. My pretense of not fully understanding some of the covert attitudes and expectations forced musicians to expose sentiments and define expectations of conductors more openly than they otherwise would have for an outsider (Becker, 1970: 60–61). The sections which follow present excerpts from these taped interviews which are exemplary in their collective imagery, representativeness, and articulation of players' outlooks concerning their travails and work contingencies.

MUSICIANS AND MAESTROS

Following Becker (1963: 79–83) and Hughes (1971), the culture of an occupational group arises, in part, in response to some set of problems faced by its members. In the orchestra as a work group, members assign a central role to the transmission of role-related information and interpretive knowledge from the maestro. From the perspective of principal players, it is the determination of how a musician should play his part which can lead to considerable antagonism between performer and conductor. While performers complain about ambiguity and equivocation of directives in making them sound unconvincing, they also note that a conductor can seriously limit their own spontaneity and artistry by demanding that they play his way and only his way. This is especially true with performers who have the responsibility and opportunity to play audible solos and to translate many of the conductor's commands into their own inimitable way of playing. They openly express their dislike of maestros who "get in your way" or "tell you how to play each note." While this issue is a persistent work contingency for the ensemble player, section leaders face this issue more directly. They are in charge of seeing that the section understands the directives and is able to carry out the commands. They agree that the conductor has mastered the important demands of his role to the extent that he provides players with a sum total of information and leeway.

Musicians claim that they are able to make quick, keen, and accurate on-the-spot assessment of the faces, fronts, and talents on the podium throughout the season. They see themselves as highly skilled craftsmen who intimately know the orchestral literature. They have lived with the music for years, performed it under a variety of conductors, and in general feel they should be the recipient of a surplus of understanding from a conductor. For these players, unwarranted attempts on the part of the conductor to extend directives into their own sphere of professional expertise was viewed as "going too far" (see Simmel, 1950: 321) and as illegitimate. In this type of interaction between musicians and the conductor several respondents described the situation: "the guy can make you sound bad."

The principal of one of the brass sections talked about the disagreeable way in which conductor directives could interfere with his own conception of how the part should be played. He discussed several conductors and then turned to one he especially disliked.

> With this guy, you would play this solo and, well, I know this thing pretty well, I've practiced it and worked on it for years. This guy would stop the whole show, the whole orchestra and say, "Well, take a breath here" and do this and do that. Then he'd start tearing the thing apart. Well you get so you want to say screw it, you don't feel like playing anything for the guy. I say he was wrong, he still is wrong. He doesn't allow a soloist any leeway for individual finesse in their playing. I think his problem is that he wants to control everything. So I think you would end up sounding bad, you would end up sounding unconvincing. You try to do what he wants, but with some the things are just wrong. T. worries about the ensemble and lets you play, that's great. He has confidence, but the lesser ones are continually bothering you. There is a right area for the musician to perform, the tempo . . . a good conductor you can trust, and he trusts you.

An older reed player with years of orchestral experience and the reputation of being one of the best musicians in the orchestra voiced a familiar theme about "sounding bad" and the jettisoning of quality playing under inadequate conductors whose own repertoire of ideas were "stifling," and who ended up getting in the way of well-conceived styles of solo playing. It is felt to be improper for a conductor to probe intrusively into a player's expressive territory.

> I'll tell you one thing I hate more than anything is a conductor who makes you sound bad. I can't stand conductors who, well like Y., he's very pedantic and stifling as my own playing is concerned. You never really know what he wants and then he'll try to tell you how to do it, like a big solo that I've spent my whole life working on and thinking about. To me, they get in your way and you sort of have to do it their way, but this is hard on you, especially the conductor who tries to make me play a way that is different than what I do naturally. You can't just change your years of work on this kind of thing to make it fit into his straitjacket. The great conductor won't do this.

The musician views directives such as these with the bias of an expert worker. That is, he tends to emphasize his own expertness and unique talents in making judgments about how things are to be played. Thus, "doing it his way" can be viewed as forced compliance which is outside a player's zone of acceptance.

> It's very difficult when a conductor asks me do something that's diametrically opposed to my own musical conception. It is very, very tough because I like to feel that I am putting my own personality into the part also. Now if you really did not like what he said, you would try to do it his way up to a certain point.

As a principal instrumentalist expressed it:

> I think that while you are playing you have to feel that this is the way I want to play it. If you're not convinced of that, if the conductor does not know what he wants or is not convinced of his own way, you can not be convincing to an audience.

As a professional and musical craftsman, he shows a strong reluctance to be directed in the technical particulars of how to produce a given effect on what is, after all, his instrument. He feels that he ought to be free to utilize skillfully his gifts, and that there is a personal zone or sphere which should always be left to his own discretion. Because of the highly individual matter of musical interpretation, it is easy to see why some directives are viewed as coercive and, at times, as a type of personal tyranny. Moreover, this perspective can lead to a particularistic bias on the part of the musician. Some respondents implicitly make a distinction between performance outcomes which make the individual sound bad as opposed to those in which the collective ensemble perform poorly. Unlike the majority of jazz musicians, orchestra players acquire a viewpoint which can lead to their being satisfied with their own solo playing but not terribly concerned about nor dissatisfied with their colleagues' performance. Not surprisingly, these players note that such particularistic dispositions are intensified when the imputed expertise and personal gift of a conductor are remarkably undistinguished. Under these maestros a sort of orchestral anomie sets in. As one young reed player put it, "With these guys you end up playing for yourself, there is no particular reward for being attentive because the guy up there does not know what he's doing."

Paradoxically enough, when asked if they had to comply with conductor directives, both ensemble and principal desk players showed a predisposition to endorse the conventionally acceptable. They shrugged and affirmed that their role obligation was to follow conductor instructions. These obligations to comply were thought of as legitimate demands because, in the words of several respondents, "He is the boss, you have to do it his way," or simply, "It it his show." Despite this facile affirmation, a very different picture emerged when the musicians were questioned more closely about some of the particulars of obedience. Thirty-two of the forty interviewed musicians said "you had to do it his way" but each expressed some ambivalence towards such categorical generalizations. Modifying or conditional statements were elicited which indicated that these demands were legitimate only insofar as they meshed with musicians expectations about performance. This was the "leeway" expectation, which said in effect that players with orchestral solos should have an opportunity for self-expression. When work was performed under stultifying or "strait-jacket" conditions—under too close supervision and instruction—or when musicians felt that discipline was being exercised for its own sake, they resented it and reported that they became angry with conductors.

This blending and blurring of obedience and technical obligations can best be understood in the light of a musician's stance toward his area of discretion. He feels he must be free to carry out the artistic directives of the conductor. He has clearer expectations about working than about obeying. He feels that conductors ought to provide a collective framework within which the performer is free to execute his craft.

Obedience is problematic. There is in the performer's attitude toward conductors, for instance, something akin to the "Yes, we do it his way, but . . ." sentiment found in other studies of compliance zones (compare with Schein and Ott, 1962). Respondents drew a line between unenthusiastic compliance and covert rebellion, as is reflected in these typical responses: "You are supposed to do it his way, but sometimes you only do it up to a point." As for the performer's tactics for getting back at the conductor, "You do it his way during rehearsal, your way during the concert." (The latter statement is not endorsed by all players, nor is it true all the time for those who do endorse it; it does, however, indicate a tendency frequently found throughout the orchestra.)

These statements indicate that the boundaries of the acceptance zone are constantly being redefined by the musician: the greater the feeling that the conductor is both expert and sensitive to his own needs, the more inclusive the range of behavioral demands with which he will comply. While mere compliance with directives about how the music is to be played is the musician's role obligation, enthusiastic playing is much harder, if not impossible, to coerce. Musicians distinguish between joyless submission and eager participation. This dichotomy appears not only in discussions of the process of playing, but also in its outcome;

submission results in "mere playing," while enthusiasm leads to "making music."

Two occupational cliches deal with this: statements that the conductor "can not force us to play" imply that lack of compliance can be a real outcome of the conductor-performer relationship; effective resistance to demands that are perceived as illegitimate is implied in the carefully vague statement that "we have our own ways of playing." The role conceptions implied in these statements deal not only with the organization of tasks, but also with the musicians' definitions of their own prerogatives. The following excerpts illustrate beliefs about conductors, as well as some of the consequences for performance. Asked whether he had to play his best all the time, this player, like thirty-four of his colleagues, couched his answer in conditional terms: "It depends on the conductor." He went on to discuss "ways of playing."

> I try to play my best all the time. The only time I do not play my best is when I am tired or something or I am bored to death with the conductor. I hate amateurism and incompetence. But I cannot play badly.
>
> Q. You cannot play poorly?
>
> I can play, how shall I put it . . . ? I can plan differently. You see there are ways of playing. In other words, if I do not like a conductor, if I do not like anything about him or I think he's wrong, then if the part says fortissimo, I will play a half harder than that. I will not give my all. On the other hand, I will not play wrong notes or things like that. In other words, there are ways a musician can play. First of all, if you play indifferently then it does not mean anything musically. Then you are just mechanically playing and that is what it amounts to around here at times.
>
> Q. . . . the notes are correct, but . . .
>
> . . . the notes are correct , but you are not listening to the intonation too carefully. You are not listening to the ensemble, you do not care too much about constant adjustment. He is not doing anything and no matter what, it will not come off. Why do it then?

As for compliance and playing under oppressive conductors, one player agreed that some are "impossible to play for." I asked him if he could spell out the scope of work behaviors which are legitimately controlled by conductors.

> Q. You said a conductor can go too far?
>
> Yes. Some of them do not let you play, this is my big gripe. B., now he would ask for things that would make you sound bad. It is hard to name these things but who wants to sound bad? He would ask for unmusical things, you just have these things that go against your grain. He would be

telling you—almost every note—how to play. M., on the other hand, worries about the ensemble and balance and you play your part the way you want to play it. I guess sometimes you feel, just play it—nothing more.

One musician's answer nicely reflects the juxtaposition of the themes presented here—the imputed expertise of authority, the conception of compliance, and the consequences of these for the performers' levels of effort. His exemplary response articulates the disjunction between ideal and real, the stock of knowledge players have about conductors, their internalized standards of quality performance, and their experiences of personal challenge and making great music under inspired leadership.

There are ways of playing, like I said, if you can ignore them it's better. Some of these jokers offend us so much that you just have to play and forget it, right? We all look at one another and just . . . you shake your head, just play, get your check and that's it.

Players' beliefs about and conceptualizations of the zone of acceptance point to a number of conditions under which they feel obliged to dissociate themselves from full compliance with conductor directives. There are instances in which an individual who complies with what are seen by others as incompetent role directives is defined as "odd;" he is seen as unable to discriminate between "routine" and "exemplary" maestros, and as grossly violating orchestra ritual. If *role distance* is viewed as a performer's expressed dislike toward the prescriptions defined by conductors (Goffman, 1961b; Stebbins, 1969), and if a conductor's authority is vulnerable to challenge because the reality of work does not match the musicians' view of what the situation ought to be, then the adaptive strategies whereby performers give mere surface compliance can be conceptualized as ways of maintaining both self-respect and professional integrity. These standards of role performance are expressed in role-distance behavior. In situations where musicians perceive the conductor's performance as faulty, sanctioned ways of acting and playing—a restriction of musical effort— are recognized as legitimate by the members. These behaviors are means by which musicians can take role distance and express their reactions to a situation in which they are obliged to work but which elicits little professional attachment.

Some forms of role distance can be openly observed during rehearsal: 1) in the crossword puzzles and paperbacks that pop up on players' stands, 2) in rueful head shakings and grimaces, 3) in disgusted string musicians playing with their legs crossed, 4) in musicians practicing non-related music during the silence which follows the command to stop, 5) in melodramatic accentuations of what was being asked for by the conductor, 6) in yawning, 7) in staring out into the auditorium for unusually long periods of time, and 8) in studied inattention to directives. By these behaviors, players signal to stand partners and other colleagues a disaffection from and resistance to both the conductor and his definition of the situation. These tactics are legitimate and reinforced by the members' standards and work custom. These convey sentiments about working in what is viewed as a degrading situation. These dissipate the tensions that can build up during rehearsals, relieve some of the boredom of playing well known and over rehearsed pieces, and give sub-rosa status to those players who are most adept in subtly conveying role distance. In sum, these sentiments and behaviors protect the self-conception of the musician under "intolerable" authority and sustain the collective pride of the orchestra by a covert repudiation of conductor claims.

Orchestra players also have at their disposal more overt, and merciless, techniques for "conveying disrespect" (Goffman, 1967: 89), they challenge the conductor's ear and thus his competence. Musicians test conductors, for example, by deliberately misreading notes, by playing parts correctly but up or down an octave, by avoiding and occasionally playing through retaras, and by playing soft passages loudly and vice-versa. In addition, there can be subtle contests within sections as performers compete for the quickest entrance or most precise attack on a downbeat. If one can tell something about a work group from its anecdotes, then musicians' gleeful narratives about put-ons and more open aggressions against conductors express sanctioned actions and beliefs of the orchestra culture. One story told of the ingenious tactic of strictly following the conductor's stick, a practice which, if carried to absurd lengths, undermines the sanctioned and essential leeway between the conductor's motion with the baton and collective response. Colorful anecdotes about overt challenges of conductors before colleagues and skirmishes in which players come out on top are told with relish; for at least momentarily they countermand and circumvent the attempts of some conductors to exercise total behavioral control over a group of experts.

Like the commercial dance musician who is obliged to demonstrate a studied lack of interest in performing for incompetent and inferior "squares," orchestra musicians also employ similar estimations and tactics. While the commercial player puts some ecological, and hence social distance between himself and his audience (Becker, 1963: 95–97), the orchestral musician does so by actively avoiding, in Simmel's words, ". . . the most direct and purest reciprocity which exists anywhere"— eye contact (Simmel, 1969: 358). Inattention to directives and avoidance of mutual glances are the orchestra players' counterparts of the jazzers' setting up chairs between himself and the outsider. In fact, a popular and approved anecdote tells of a principal player in a major orchestra who, when a thoroughly disliked conductor stepped on the podium, raised his stand to block any further visual interaction between them. That such gestures are seen as heroic and laudable tell us much about the culture of this work organization and its members' strategies for making and taking role distance.

These materials and the illustrative quotes from performers support the recognized necessity of highly trained professionals to have what they regard as sufficient freedom to carry out their role obligations and to implement their conceptions of coordinated work activity. The disjunctions between the evaluation of one's own highly-developed talents and chances for realization under particular conductors leads to a perceived inability to master role demands (see Seeman, 1959; Blauner, 1964; Faulkner, 1971). Inadequate and incompetent conductors who go beyond the occupationally defined zone of acceptance are like the "square" clients who are presumptuous enough to claim to direct the behaviors of commercial players. They are viewed as encroaching on a player's prerogatives.

It appears that in night clubs, on studio sound stages, or in concert halls, "maintaining freedom from control over artistic behavior," is a relevant and persistent work contingency (Becker, 1963: 102). The problematics of professional autonomy which are so prominent in the ideology and culture of the roles people are paid to perform appear at every level of the music business as well. Every line of work has its presumptuous outsiders or intruders who violate the members' conceptions of their own competence and proper use of their unique skills. By virtue of his focal position and responsibility, the conductor exercises a kind of authority and has an impact on players that is markedly different from that exerted by expert supervisors in industry and professional organizations. Nevertheless, as these descriptions of interaction between performer and conductor suggest, every calling may have its poor practitioners as well as its symbolic "squares."

Ronald C. Federico

Recruitment, Training, and Performance: The Case of Ballet

Any occupation must work within limits set by its recruitment and training systems. These provide the human resources vital to occupational stability and growth, and affect resource utilization, worker productivity, and worker satisfaction. These systems are themselves affected by societal values and institutional structures which may complement or conflict with the values and organization of the occupation. This paper will look at the recruitment and training systems in the occupation of professional ballet dancing.[1] It will relate these systems to major societal values and two occupational products, choreography and performance. Such important occupational concerns as career patterns, relationships with other occupations, and the ability to compete for societal resources are not included in this paper.

RECRUITMENT AND PERFORMANCE

Recruitment procedures are those techniques an occupation uses to involve a potential member in the training system. Such procedures may be formal or informal, depending on the degree to which there is a structured mechanism to acquaint potential professionals with the occupation. In ballet most recruitment is informal as there are few structured mechanisms for bringing potential professionals into the training system. A few formal procedures exist, most of them being in formal public educational organizations where ballet instruction is part of the curriculum, or in which lecture-demonstrations are provided. Schools exist at the grade school, high school, and university levels; examples include the High School of Performing Arts in New York City, the University of Utah's professional dance program in Salt Lake City, and the public grade schools and high schools incorporating dance in their curricula.[2] Such programs are formal structures to train professional dancers or expose general students to dance as an art and a potential occupation. These programs also maximize exposure and recruitment utility by being part of the institutionalized public educational system.

However, most recruitment programs exist in the private, profit-oriented educational and performance spheres, and do not provide systematic, institutionalized exposure.[3] The majority of such private educational programs seem to be quite selective in their recruitment since they depend on parents, peer influence, or referral through such unlikely channels as doctors who prescribe ballet lessons to help correct a variety of physical problems.[4] Table 1 compares the formal and informal recruitment networks by describing the reason the dancers studied began ballet lessons. Table 2 shows the age at which lessons were initiated, and it suggests that the informal recruitment network tends to operate considerably earlier than the formal one, especially for women (see end of paper).

There are major differences in recruitment patterns for men and women in ballet resulting from the differential use of formal and informal recruitment structures. Whereas almost the same percentage of men as women were influenced in starting to dance by the peer group, only eleven percent of the men were influenced by the family compared with fifty-four percent of the women, while forty-four percent of the men were influenced through non-family institutions compared to slightly over ten percent of the women. The effects of these differences can be seen in Table 2, which shows that eighty-five percent of the girls have begun lessons by age eleven, compared to only twenty-two percent of the boys. Given the family's early, total, and long-term socialization potential through the association of social values with physical needs (Berger and Luckmann, 1967), it becomes a powerful informal recruitment mechanism which reflects the societal belief that ballet is an activity appropriate primarily for females. Occupational choice is obviously affected since it depends on exposure, but professional competence is also affected. With ballet requiring strength and flexibility in the joints and feet, training begun at a young age is likely to produce a professional with greater technical competence than one who begins his training later. The body is more flexible at the younger age and there is more time to develop the necessary strength and stamina.[5] Greater competence increases the probability of occupational success, an important reward for members of the occupation.[6]

Early entry into the training system also enables a pre-professional to enter the profession soon enough and for a long enough period to experience strong professional socialization.[7] Ballet has many rigorous requirements, such as exhausting physical work, long and erratic work hours, isolation from non-dancers, and low pay.[8] These occupational characteristics are defined as acceptable by professional norms. The occupational socialization process supports such norms, and also helps to counteract negative societal evaluation of them. Yet even with strong socialization, Table 3 indicates that ballet dancers leave the profession early. It shows that only nineteen respondents were thirty years or over, suggesting that the occupational loses most of its members before they attain occupational maturity.[9]

The inverse relationships between socialization and occupational longevity are shown in Table 3. Women tend to enter the occupation younger than men, thereby receiving stronger occupational socialization and more extensive technical training. Yet it is the men who are more heavily represented in the upper age groups in this sample. Explanations for these data are tentative, but several can be suggested. One is that the societal definitions of the woman's role places female dancers in increasing role conflict. The major commitment required by ballet's rigorous use of a trained body makes it an occupation that is practically impossible to pursue on a part-time basis. Therefore, it is work that is most feasible before the woman marries. After marriage the demands of married life intrude on career aspirations. By then the female dancer has been in the ballet world for many years, has experienced the frustrations of a demanding and competitive profession, and has felt a diminution in societal approval when her participation in ballet moves from avocation to career. All of these factors generate discrepancies with values learned in previous socialization, and apparently the occupational structure cannot offer adequate rewards.

Men face societal norms which tend to denigrate the male role in artistic and female dominated occupations.[10] However, men typically do not experience the conflict between family and work that women do, so the transition from dance as an avocation to a vocation is more socially acceptable. The fact that men enter the occupational system later than women may also minimize the early development of boredom and frustration. It seems that the major pressures against professional male ballet dancers exist in the informal recruitment system, where men are systematically neglected, and where ballet is not presented as a viable occupational alternative. If a man does enter the occupational system, weak socialization and difficulty in attaining technical competence create additional barriers to professional commitment. Once the commitment is made, however, it receives some societal support as a meaningful work commitment. This helps a male dancer to cope with the other problems of such an occupation (low pay, erratic hours, hard physical work, the homosexual stigma, etc.). An interesting pattern seems to emerge. Women are readily recruited in an informal recruitment system, but then experience role conflict when approaching occupational maturity. The recruitment of men is weak, but those who are recruited can move into a career orientation more easily than women. More women than men are recruited overall, but the sex imbalance is related to age.

There are several effects of the sex imbalance that tend to result from the informal recruitment system. This sex imbalance affects: 1) types of roles which can be performed; [11] 2) choreographic styles and artistic performing opportunities; [12] 3) the public image of the occupation; 4) the self-image of the members of the occupation; [13] and 5) interaction patterns between occupation members. With female dominance in ballet, the socialization structure tends to focus on behavior appropriate to women. Men are a minority group, so their occupational and personal needs are not often given special consideration. The resulting homogeneity can be functional to the extent that it encourages men and women to interact easily as equals. This is helped by the occupational minimization of sexual attractiveness inherent in an activity where bodies are in close contact according to set, objective rules. However, the women also seem to minimize the appropriateness of ballet men as sex partners because of this occupational distance and personal proximity. They also seem to adopt the societal image of male ballet dancers as potential homosexuals. One dancer summarized the problem the female dancer faces in considering stigmatized male dancers as appropriate sex partners by saying, "I could never be sure." [14]

As noted when discussing Table 3, an occupation with only thirteen percent of its members over age thirty clearly loses the majority of its members in their most mature period. This places the burden of principal and solo roles on the young: Table 4 indicates that fourteen of the principals and fifty-two of the soloists were under thirty. This use of the young in major occupational positions directly influences 1) types of ballets performed, and 2) the quality of performance. In dance, youth has the great advantage of strength and suppleness but the disadvantage of artistic immaturity. In addition it affects performances indirectly through the loss of experienced artists who can coach younger dancers, influence management planning and provide mature talents to be used by a choreographer.

Given the physical and socialization benefits of early occupational entry, we have seen that the recruitment of women is likely to be more successful. However, although data are lacking, the late occupational recruitment of the men may have latent advantages for them. Any occupational socialization establishes certain value and behavior patterns, implying a certain narrowing of horizons. Art occupations value creativity. Perhaps the breadth of male experiences before occupational socialization results in greater creativity. Most major choreographers are men, while women tend to be performers and to a lesser extent teachers and administrators. Choreography involves the creation of dances, while performing is the somewhat less creative task of interpreting choreography. Teaching and administration require even less creative skills. On the other hand, choreography does not require great facility in performing. Therefore, it seems that choreography provides an outlet for the late-entering male's somewhat lower physical facility and more diversified life experiences (i.e., weaker occupational socialization). Performing, teaching, and administration are more direct results of the female dancer's earlier occupational entry and stronger socialization. It is interesting to compare ballet with modern dance. In the latter, both male and female dancers seem to enter the art relatively late in their lives,[15] and there is much more major choreography done by women than is the case in ballet. Although clearly speculative at this point, it does seem that the nature of occupational socialization, its duration, and its place in the growth cycle of the individual are important in the development of a professional ballet dancer.

TRAINING AND PERFORMANCE

The occupational training system is comprised of formal and informal occupational structures which socialize recruits into the professional subculture. When there are cohesive, clearly defined means to train recruits in such a way that they can meet professional certification standards, formal entry into the profession is facilitated. There are several problems in the training system in ballet which create an informal structure very loosely connected to actual professional entry and participation.

Certification procedures do not exist. This makes it difficult for training structures to develop pre-professional curricula. Consequently, a highly competitive, informal career entry system is created that is based on random opportunity.[16] Without certification procedures, the schools training dancers offer quite divergent training which potential dancers find difficult to evaluate. This requires a commitment on the part of the recruit to a given training ideology in order to assure oneself that one's training pattern is logical. However, there is no concrete evidence to show that one training system is better than the others.[17] The recruit is therefore exposed to a training system offering him: 1) little systematized instruction, 2) little personal protection in assuring him competent training, and 3) little security in knowing that his training will ultimately lead him into a professional position. This is the case even in schools directly associated with companies, perhaps the most formal of the training systems.[18] Problems are even greater in the other schools. The development of university level training may help this situation to the extent that such graduates are certified for teaching positions in public schools or universities, but it does not help those hoping for performing careers.

The training problem is further accentuated by severe competition resulting from an oversupply of recruits.[19] The lack of a formal recruitment system allows anyone to enter the training network. At the other end, societal demand severely restricts resources for professional dance performances. This greatly limits the number of companies and dancers able to be supported in the profession.[20] The oversupply for scarce positions combines with the ambiguity created by the lack of professional certification to result in severe competition in the field. This competition results in two practices affecting the occupational products of performing and choreography: politics, and a belief in the importance of "being in the right place at the right time."

Politics refer to a wide variety of informal interpersonal bargains between aspiring pre-professionals and teachers or directors in the aspirants' attempts to obtain a professional position. The recruit has little security in his training. He has to commit himself to a particular style with no assurance it will facilitate his success. His training does not lead to formal certification, and he is faced with many competitors in substantially the same position. Under such circumstances, any "break" or advantage is to be sought, and politics is one way to obtain such an advantage. Such politicking runs the gamut from dispensing sexual favors to being willing to do extra work or even returning part of one's pay check.[21] "Being in the right place at the right time" highlights the capricious nature of such an informal system. Another way to obtain an advantage is to be willing and able to do a needed task on very short notice. This can occur when a dancer becomes ill, when dancer-director conflicts develop, or because of carefully calculated plans to discredit another dancer for one's own potential benefit.[22] Both politics and "being in the right place at the right time" well illustrate the opportunities for random factors to operate in an informal occupational structure.

Ballet's informal training system has several weaknesses in addition to those already mentioned. It utilizes scarce resources poorly to the extent that: 1) teachers must try to teach whomever enrolls, 2) talented students unknowingly enroll in incompetent schools, and 3) potential talent is overlooked by teachers caught up with having to teach too many students. Competent dancers may be ignored because of their unwillingness to bargain, while directors can obtain excessive personal and artistic power. The training diversity may create chaos rather than achieving artistic diversity. The result is a system which encourages personal frustration by emphasizing chance factors, and which jeopardizes its own resource base.[23]

The flow of professionals through the informal recruitment and training structures existing in ballet has the result of placing a great deal of responsibility on the individual. From early in the recruitment and training processes, the dancer must make decisions about his technical training, his artistic development, and his career strategy. This allows the individual dancer substantial autonomy in planning his career pattern, and permits him to try to become the type of artist which he respects. On the other hand, such autonomy lacks security. The individual has few assurances that his decisions will make him a marketable product or a competent performer. Given that artistic creativity is not easily codified, such lack of security is probably inherent in most artistic occupations. However, the structure of ballet as an occupation tends to accentuate the dancer's insecurity.

The common reliance on luck or intrigue as a means of professional advancement is one response to the insecurity generated. Such a pattern relinquishes the dancer's personal autonomy in favor of blind luck or manipulation of or by others. The group nature of ballet requires that the dancer subjugate himself to the needs of the total production, itself a restraint on personal and artistic autonomy. However, when insecurity encourages a dance student or a dance professional to blindly put his faith in a teacher, coach, or director, he has further relinquished autonomy. It is somewhat ironic that the professional structure encourages autonomy from the earliest recruitment experiences, since the loose professional structure and overcrowded conditions encourage the voluntary relinquishing of potential autonomy for some measure of occupational security. Between the demands of working cooperatively in a group, and finding a career in a very uncertain professional structure, the average ballet dancer is a performing artist with little professional autonomy.

CONCLUSION

Since choreography and performances are important parts of the occupational product in ballet, these should be closely related to major structural features of the occupation. Two major structural parts of any occupation are the recruitment and training systems, which bring potential members into the occupation and provide the necessary socialization. Such systems will vary in the complexity and formality of their structure, and the degree to which they are tied to other parts of the occupational structure. This paper has suggested that ballet as an occupation has informal recruitment and training procedures which are poorly integrated with performing needs. These structural characteristics create competition resulting from uncontrolled entry into the training system and ambiguous criteria for professional certification. Competition and ambiguous critieria encourage politics, whereby dancers are rewarded for non-dance related abilities. The informal recruitment system recruits differentially between the sexes, and is dysfunctional in that much of the occupational socialization which occurs never results in occupational productivity.

The flexibility that leads to relatively poor occupational resource utilization can also have functional consequences. Compared with the typical state-supported rigidly structured European ballet system,[24] the American structure permits a wider recruitment effort, varied teaching philosophies, and greater opportunities for dancers with unusual physical and/or emotional characteristics. This is reflected in a distinctive body of choreography, and a more or less distinctive American type of dancer. On the other hand, the problems such a system creates for the occupation's survival in a competitive artistic and non-artistic environment, and for the individual's gratification within the occupational system, may ultimately outweigh the advantages of the system. With government support of the arts increasingly suggested as necessary, the choice of the more preferable occupational structure will soon have to be made.

TABLE 1

REASON FOR BEGINNING BALLET LESSONS BY SEX *

	Parental Influence		Peer Influence		Own Desire		After Seeing Dance		Other Institutional Exposure**	
	N	%	N	%	N	%	N	%	N	%
Males (N = 54)	6	(11.1)	8	(14.8)	8	(14.8)	8	(14.8)	24	(44.4)
Females (N = 92)	50	(54.4)	13	(14.1)	13	(14.1)	6	(6.5)	10	(10.9)
Total (N = 146)	56	(39.0)	21	(14.4)	21	(14.4)	14	(9.6)	34	(22.6)

* Shown is the respondent's first mentioned reason for beginning ballet lessons.
** The major components of this category are as follows:
  For girls: at a doctor's suggestion to help solve a medical problem, e.g., underweight.
  For boys: motivation by a school teacher or athletic coach in the course of a school extracurricular activity.

TABLE 2

ENTRY INTO THE FIELD:
AGE RESPONDENTS BEGAN BALLET LESSONS BY SEX *

	Under 6		6 through 10		11 through 16		17 through 20		21 and over	
	N	%	N	%	N	%	N	%	N	%
Males (N = 54)	0	(0)	12	(22.2)	17	(31.5)	22	(40.7)	3	(5.6)
Females (N = 92)	26	(28.3)	55	(59.8)	10	(10.9)	1	(1.1)	0	(0)
Total (N = 146)	26	(17.8)	67	(45.9)	27	(18.5)	23	(15.7)	3	(2.1)

* Lessons in other dance forms or participation in athletic activities may have begun earlier.

TABLE 3

AGE DISTRIBUTION BY SEX

	Less than 19		19 through 22		23 through 29		30 and over	
	N	%	N	%	N	%	N	%
Male (N = 54)	0	(0)	18	(33.3)	24	(44.4)	12	(22.2)
Female (N = 92)	16	(17.4)	43	(46.7)	26	(28.3)	7	(7.6)
Total (N = 146)	16	(11.0)	61	(41.8)	50	(34.2)	19	(13.0)

TABLE 4

AGE AND COMPANY POSITION

	Principal		Soloist		Corps		Total	
	N	%	N	%	N	%	N	%
Less than 19	0	(0.0)	5	(31.3)	11	(68.8)	16	(11.0)
19 through 22	5	(8.2)	22	(36.1)	34	(55.7)	61	(41.8)
23 through 29	9	(18.0)	25	(50.0)	16	(32.0)	50	(34.2)
30 and over	11	(57.9)	5	(26.3)	3	(15.8)	19	(13.0)
Total	25	(17.1)	57	(39.0)	64	(43.8)	146	(100.0)

NOTES

[1] This paper is based on the author's dissertation from which the data presented here are taken (Federico, 1968). The data were obtained from a sample of 146 dancers employed in the ten professional ballet companies existing in the United States in 1966–1967, plus one pre-professional company for comparative purposes. A combination open and closed ended questionnaire was personally administered to each respondent during the period August 1966 to April 1967. The interviews ranged in length from thirty to ninety minutes, depending on the respondent's detail in answering the open ended questions. The sample was not a random one, being selected on the basis of availability and my own attempt to get a moderately representative group by sex and company position. Only four dancers approached for an interview refused. Although there are obvious limitations to this type of sample, the resistance to scientific study among the dancers and administrators made it almost impossible to be more systematic.

[2] In Washington, D. C. and surrounding suburban schools, for example, groups such as the National Ballet, Regional Ballet Company of Washington, D. C., and Quindo's Ballet for Young People present periodic performances and lecture-demonstrations. A new group, Workshops for Careers in the Performing Arts, is working in cooperation with the public schools and local art groups to allow interested students to test their interest in artistic careers.

[3] Dance in the mass media, such as television, or in more popular arts, such as film, probably comes closest to being part of a systematic, institutionalized exposure network. Attendance at professional dance performances is both small and selective (Baumol and Bowen, 1966).

[4] Data on this point are very weak. The only data available to my knowledge are in Table 1 of this paper (and the dissertation from which the data are taken), and Ryser, 1964.

[5] The rule of thumb is that it takes ten years to make a ballet dancer. Since eighteen to twenty seems to be the most preferred age to enter a company, training should start at ages eight to ten.

[6] Competence is difficult to define in an art since any art involves technical mastery as well as artistic expression. The technical aspects of the art are more easily evaluated and, in most cases, more easily acquired. Occupational rewards may follow from either type of competence, but are most easily obtained for technical expertise. Ideally, one would be rewarded for the use of technical skills to attain artistic expression. The distinctions between technique and artistry in dance are nicely expressed in Bruhn, 1968.

[7] The importance of occupational socialization in the development of an occupational subculture has been frequently noted. A classic is Cottrell, 1940. Of particular relevance to art occupations is Becker, 1963, and Wilson, 1958. The Ryser article cited earlier, and Kolenda and Enos, 1970, focus on dance as a subculture maintained by occupational socialization.

[8] The dance literature is full of such evidence. Two particularly good examples are Mara, 1959, Bland and Peto, 1963.

[9] My data only include dancers currently employed in professional companies; data pertinent to the question of when and why one leaves are lacking. Several of my respondents mentioned that physical injury, difficulty finding a job, lack of progress in the occupation, conflict with other dance personnel, and/or working conditions as being significant factors in dancers leaving the occupation. Further ideas may be found in Joel, 1963.

[10] The problems of male roles and societal definitions of female dominated occupations are commonly discussed in the occupations literature (Slocum, 1966). The special difficulties of the male role in ballet are discussed at some length in the ballet literature. An excellent recent compilation of male dancers talking about the problems they face may be found in Youskevitch, 1969.

[11] The majority of ballets have many female roles and fewer male roles. Many pre-professional companies have such a problem recruiting any men at all that they have ballets in their repertoire which require no men.

[12] Ballet technique is somewhat differentiated for men and women. For example, only women dance on points (in toe shoes).

[13] Several dancers interviewed in the dissertation study expressed strong self-doubts as dancers and people. These dancers found it difficult to justify their occupations to non-dancers, especially their families, and the men particularly resented implications by non-dancers that male ballet dancers are homosexual.

[14] The fact that the instability of the occupation makes a "normal" family life very difficult compounds male-female relationship problems in ballet. See Babette Coffey, 1969.

[15] See Ryser, 1964, for pertinent modern dance data.

[16] Positions in companies are obtained in auditions in which the applicants are asked to dance for the company directors. The applicants may be told to dance given sequences of steps, or may be allowed to do a dance of their choice. In either case, the selection criteria are not made explicit before the dancing is executed, and the reasons for the selection of the chosen dancers afterwards are similarly not explicated.

[17] There are several codified training systems, such as the Royal Academy, Cecchetti, and National Academy syllabi. However, many well known, successful teachers do not teach any of these syllabi specifically. There is no empirical evidence that dancers trained in a given syllabus, or in a more individual curriculum, will be more successful in obtaining a job. Obtaining such evidence would be greatly complicated by the fact that many dancers have been trained in several curricula.

[18] Company schools are often simply profit-making ventures to help meet the costs of running the company. Under some special circumstances one's chances of getting into a company may be increased by studying in a company school, but on the whole the company schools bear little relationship to the procedures through which dancers get hired by the company.

19 As one writer in the field has said, ". . . ballet dancers are knee deep in toe shoes on Seventh Avenue at 56th Street!" (Woody, 1952). Also see de Mille, 1960.

20 The recent growth of governmental support for the arts may expand these limits, but it is doubtful that the opportunity will be sufficient for the dancer supply in the foreseeable future.

21 Each of these practices was encountered during my research.

22 Two classic accounts of politics and making sure one is in the right place at the right time are Nijinsky, 1934, and de Mille, 1960.

23 Trained pre-professionals who never enter the profession could be important as an audience and part of the recruitment structure. Such potential is rarely purposefully developed. My data show that dancers are not generally anxious for their children to be professional dancers, and that many dancers were influenced by mothers who had wanted to study dance and had not been allowed to do so, rather than by mothers who had studied dance.

24 Systematic data on state supported systems are not available. However, some of the characteristics of such systems can be gleaned from such works as Erik Bruhn, 1968, and Nureyev, 1963.

Harold Charnofsky

Ballplayers, Occupational Image and the Maximization of Profit

One of the first occupational "norms" I learned as a rookie minor leaguer fresh off a college campus came in the form of a stern warning by my manager. He admonished me to avoid the "three W's: women, whiskey, and weight." Although he did not spell out the reasons for these taboos, I thought I knew: I had to keep in top shape so I could contribute to the team's success. I soon discovered, however, that something else was more important to the management, a less tangible thing than wins and losses, but equally critical in terms of box office. It was "image." I must do nothing to sully the public image of the sport and the player.

Years after my brief, undistinguished, but enjoyable career as a minor leaguer, I returned to baseball as a sociologist. I found that image still viewed as the *sine qua non* of success: for the player, because his self-esteem depends upon it, and for both player and management because it is the critical difference between profit and loss. Image is box-office; it sells tickets and pays salaries.

As a sociologist rather than a ball player, I could view the role and its subtle constraints somewhat dispassionately, even critically. I realized that the American public is sensitized to think of professional baseball as a model of democracy because, the myth goes, it stresses sportsmanship, fair play, and the virtues of following the rules. Yet the reverse is in fact true. Professional baseball is anything but democratic; the manager is a complete dictator, and so is the umpire. All decisions are final, even when they are wrong. And many ballplayers relish breaking the rules while avoiding discovery. They throw spitballs, which are illegal;

they throw at batters who hit too many homers, which is illegal (and dangerous); they pretend to be hit by pitches which in fact have bounced off their bat handle; they get into fights with other players because their team is losing.

Despite these discrepancies between public image and actual behavior, the fact remains that such images are rigorously and systematically maintained. And herein lies the central purpose of this paper. In the pages that follow, I will try to describe some of the many restraints which the highly structured and bureaucratic social world of professional baseball places on the men who work in it. In the process of trying to understand the degree of control that exists over the behavior of major league professional ballplayers both in and out of the actual work environment, perhaps it will become clear that the occupation carefully screens and selects its members on the basis of psychological and ideological as well as athletic criteria.[1] After all, management could not really afford to employ anyone who did not believe in all the virtues the fans are asked to endorse, e.g., male superiority, the unadulterated joys of head-to-head competition, the importance of winning (". . . at all costs," the unspoken but understood dictum), etc.

The data in this paper are part of a much larger study (Charnofsky, 1969) conducted during 1965–1968. That work combined standard survey techniques with face-to-face interviews and intuition derived from my own experiences in the occupation.

I knew it would be difficult (and expensive) to try to gather information on all five hundred major leaguers and the thousands of minor leaguers scattered all over the country. It would also be a problem getting the players I did reach to respond to the kind of sociological digging I felt was necessary if the study was to go beyond mere sports reporting. Celebrities are cautious about discussing matters they consider to be private. A large portion of their lives is open to public scrutiny already, and they justifiably become resentful of intrusions that promise nothing for them or their career. I realized that if candor were to be obtained, anonymity had to be assured.

The complicated process of gaining access to the players was begun with a series of letters to the general managers of six major league teams, three from the American League and three from the National League.[2] I happened to be personally acquainted with these six general managers and felt reasonably certain that most of them would agree to the study. I also knew that the need for a representative sample of subjects would be met regardless of which teams were finally used, because every major league ball club has many players who have been "bought" and "sold" a number of times. Thus any given team is a microcosm of the total population of major leaguers. The letters explained the nature and purpose of the study and requested permission to interview the performers in one city, which all six teams were scheduled to visit. Conveniently, both the National and American League entries in that city shared a common home stadium. I wanted to avoid travel expenses, but also saw an advantage in becoming thoroughly familiar with the layout and rules of a single ball park.

Five of the six clubs agreed to the study.[3] Lack of contacts on other clubs, plus limitations of time and expense prevented me from expanding my sample. Interviews were conducted during the baseball season of 1965; I caught the players wherever I could—in hotel lobbies, on buses, in the dressing room, occasionally on the playing field, or over a sandwich and beer. At the same time, rather elaborate questionnaires were handed out to one hundred forty players; seventy-three of these were completed and returned.[4] To add a further dimension to my chances of understanding these men and their occupational role, I held a marathon tape-recorded talk session in my home during the winter of 1966 involving six well-known and outspoken major leaguers. Each man had completed at least one year of college which of course by no means insured perspicacity; but the players proved to be articulate and unreserved, and their commentary was frank and lively. The players were asked questions, both during the interviews and in writing, which probed broadly into political, religious, and sexual beliefs and behavior, family and social class origins, leisure time preferences and activities, education, attitudes toward gambling and drinking, views about Viet Nam, race relations, and their own occupation—with its high risks, brief tenure, and opportunity for fame and fortune.

Because the central purpose of this paper is to describe the effects of social structure and role expectations on the behavior of ballplayers both in and out of the formal occupational role setting, it is apparent that only selected portions of the collected data are of interest here.

In the highly structured occupational setting of professional baseball, generations of role incumbents, heavily influenced by management and their interest in maximization of profit, have prepared and then passed on to newly entering members a multitude of "acceptable" patterns of behavior for almost every conceivable situation.[5] The following discussion examines some of these restraints and the options they allow.

There are numerous examples of behavioral limitations imposed on ballplayers because of the nature of their work. Curfews prevail for many major league clubs, usually requiring that the players be in their hotel rooms within two or three hours after the game ends. A particularly zealous manager may even make bed checks to see if players are following the rules. Restrictions on types and degree of physical exercise during the day preceding a night game are common, with activities such as swimming, sun-bathing, and occasionally golf forbidden, or at least curtailed. Drinking *before* games is unacceptable behavior. Although a few beers, after the game is characteristic because it helps a man unwind, keeps his weight up, etc.

In their well-know study of the professional boxer, Weinberg and Arond (1952) report that boxers come to regard their hands as precious commodities, learn to watch their diets, and make certain they get adequate rest and sleep. Ballplayers similarly develop protective habits toward their throwing arms, their legs, their eyes in particular, and their general health. In fact, the player salary contract contains a clause which requires permission from the management before the athlete can take part in organized and/or potentially dangerous sports activities during the off-season. Only a few years ago Jim Lonborg of the Boston Red Sox broke his leg in a skiing accident and has never performed up to his previous level of skill. The Red Sox management was more than a little disturbed.

Other kinds of limitations, less obvious to the layman but nonetheless restrictive, impose upon the player a daily schedule which succeeds in making life inflexible both during the season, and to a lesser extent, the off-season. Many players stated during interviews that a typical game day carries with it so many occupational-related necessities that leisure activities become rather well-defined and limited. These necessities differ, of course, between a "home" day and a "road" day, but both are pervaded by common theme of keeping mentally and physically sharp for the game. Here is a capsule description of a typical day for a ballplayer.

At home the married player might rise at 11:00 A.M., eat a hearty brunch, play with his children or work around the house, or simply lounge in front of television. He reads the sports sections of the daily papers (all of them) with special attention to the box scores and critical comments by sportswriters. In general he does little that might tire his eyes or body. Some light nourishment might be taken at 4:00 P.M., and by 5:00 P.M. he must leave for the ballpark. After the game, he might go out with his wife to eat, or he might go home. He probably will not go to sleep for two or three hours while he tries to "unwind."

The single player might do the same during the day, but after the game he often has a date, or has a few drinks with other players or friends. Occasionally this daily routine will be broken by a golf game or some other form of activity, with the accompanying rationalization that instead of being tiring it is "relaxing," and gets the mind off baseball for awhile. As I noted earlier, from time to time managers feel obliged to place restrictions on activities that may tire out the players.

A typical day on the road is a bit different. After mid-morning brunch, the player may stroll around the downtown area, shoot a few games of pool, take in a movie (probably a Western),[6] or stay in his hotel room and watch television or play cards. But chances are, if he does none of these other things, he will sit in the hotel lobby. Lobbysitting is one of the classic pastimes of major league baseball players. Its popularity is all but inexplicable, yet undeniable. as one team official remarked to me with more than a little consternation:

> I can't figure these ballplayers out. They come to Washington, D. C. several times each season, and do you think they care about seeing the Washington Monument, the Lincoln Memorial, the White House? No! All they care about is sitting in the lobby of the hotel and reading the *Sporting News*. Why, once I even arranged a tour of the White House which included the likelihood of shaking hands with the President! Was I embarrassed when only two players and the batboy signed up to go. I had to *recruit*, actually go out and *plead* with several members of the team to make the tour so the ball club could save face.[7]

Part of the explanation for the reluctance of ballplayers to get involved in planned activity during the day of a night game rests with their obsession to perform at peak capacity. All else pales to insignificance before "the GAME." Anything which could cause the player to be tired, distracted, or even guilty for having spent an enjoyable afternoon thinking about something else, may be shunned in favor of familiar behavior patterns such as lobbysitting. Enigmatically, however, these same players might go to a movie, watch television, play golf, or just wander through the shops of the downtown section, all of which could tire them or strain their eyes more than a casual tour of the White House. Like all of us, ball players are creatures of habit. And as Gmelch (1971) has pointed out, superstition plays a large part in their reluctance to try anything new or different. What has served them well in the past is often repeated until the charm is broken; then a new ritual is pursued.

On the road, a typical post-game routine might include dinner at a late-serving bistro, perhaps a beer or two, conversation (maybe a post-mortem on the evening's activities), or a game of cards, and the late-late show or one of the talk shows on television. The single player might follow the same routine, or he might have a date for dinner and drinks.

Thus the days and nights of major league baseball players are rigidly circumscribed with rules, both formal and informal. On the field, behavior is even more precisely prescribed. Only a few examples are possible among the hundreds of subtle do's and don't's for these public performers. One taboo prohibits fraternization with players on opposing teams in public. Stiff fines may be' imposed (by umpires who are obliged to enforce the regulation) when violations occur. Apparently the baseball hierarchy is concerned that familiarity between opponents might somehow undermine an image the public has of unadulterated competition which is, after all, the "authorized" definition of the situation and the one calculated to maximize fan interest.

The fact is, major league baseball, and all professional (and most amateur) sports, *are* models of competition. These must be if society hopes to perpetuate its dominant value system. The nation's chief executive has repeatedly singled out athletes as exemplars of the American ethic of achievement through hard work and individual effort. The spirit of competition through sports has been hailed as one of the vital forces typifying "the American way." The ever increasing popularity of all kinds of sports in this country attests to the breadth of their influence, both actual and potential. Here is what one sportswriter says about the pervasiveness of sports in America:

> Sport permeates any number of levels of contemporary society, and it touches upon and even deeply influences such disparate elements as status, race relations, business life, automotive design, clothing styles, the concept of the hero, language, and ethical values. For better or worse, it gives form and substance to much in American life. . . . The New York Times . . . devotes more daily space to sport than it does to art, books, education, television, and the theater combined (Boyle, 1963: 3–4).

Most professional (and some amateur) sports, however, systematically exclude women from any meaningful participation. This too typifies "the American way;" one needn't be an activist for women's liberation to be sensitive to the exclusionary and sexist nature of major league baseball, football, basketball, etc. I refer not exclusively nor specifically to athletic participation, but also to jobs in management, broadcasting, sportswriting, and the like. No section of any daily newspaper is more sexist in its orientation than the male-dominated sports section.

Most professional sports also systematically exclude most blacks, Latin Americans, and other minorities from important leadership or front office positions (Edwards, 1969); this too typifies "the American way." No black player has ever managed a major league team, and few blacks and Latins serve on coaching staffs. In addition, white, black or brown players rarely spend leisure time with each other, and almost never room together on the road (Charnofsky, 1968). The "public" clamors about sports being color blind, but in private a double standard exists which is an all too familiar pattern and analogous to what happens throughout America's institutions. A white scout actually told me "confidentially" that he was looking for a white outfielder because his club had too many Negro outfielders and white fans might begin to lose a sense of identification with the ball club.

Another strong ethic in major league baseball requires that players treat fans and the paying public with courtesy. This is sometimes difficult to do, especially when a particularly obnoxious and inebriated .patron is shouting obscenities and other insults at a tense player during a dramatic moment in the game. But ballplayers have developed a way of coping with this situation. Because they are expected to respond to all such criticism, even the kind directed at them from opposing players, with a mask of impassivity, they become adept at what Erving Goffman (1959) has called "the art of impression management." Rather than act "out of character," the players perform their roles according to expectations in the "front region." However, when they are off-stage, so to speak, their anger and frustration occasionally pour forth, and often the target of their fury is the adult fan. Interviews with players reveal that many of them (perhaps most, but some do not feel free to reveal their feelings for fear of violating the occupational ethic), view adult fans in much the same way Howard S. Becker (1963) reports that jazz musicians perceive non-musicians. In plain words, adult fans are "squares," people who lack understanding of the sport of baseball or the men who play it. They are seen as naive, uninformed and fickle.

In response to the question, "What is your honest opinion of the average fan?" fourteen players gave favorable replies while twenty-two gave negative replies and twenty-nine were more or less neutral. When asked to give their opinion of the fan's knowledge of baseball, only a small number of players were able to state that the public understands or appreciates baseball, while the majority were highly critical.

Other occupational norms which relate to on-the-field behavior can be mentioned briefly. Ballplayers must not make umpires appear foolish before the public. "Don't show me up, you bastard!" is the tight-lipped epithet hissed at the over-zealous athlete bent on making the umpire regret his call. Most umpires don't mind a complaint over a call; it lends color to the game. But they object to prolonged debate, especially when a player tries to mimic their gestures comically or demean them before a partisan crowd that could become ugly if provoked. Players are frefuently ejected from games for such behavior and fines are levied by the league office, the amount depending upon the umpire's report and recommendation.

Ballplayers must not make opposing players appear inept or unprofessional in a one-side game. For example, if your team is ten runs ahead it is considered unethical to bunt for a hit. The defensive team is not expecting it, and besides, both teams already tacitly recognize the helpless position the trailing team is in. They simply want to get through the game without unnecessary embarrassment or injury. This norm is not strictly observed during the World Series or other championship type games.

Ballplayers must never subject opposing players to the risk of injury unless such a risk might have an effect on the outcome of the game. For example, the second baseman never fakes a tag on a stealing baserunner if the batter has just fouled the pitch. Such behavior might cause the runner to slide and hurt an ankle, leg, or arm. On the other hand, it is perfectly legitimate to fake a tag and trick the runner into sliding if this will prevent him from moving up an extra base.

I have mentioned only a few of the dozens, perhaps hundreds, of role prescriptions for the major league ballplayer while he is at work. Many of them, including most of the examples noted, have to do with public image. Incidentally, although there is not space to report on it fully here, the ballplayers I interviewed all had extremely positive self-images. In response to a series of questions about how they saw themselves, most players liked themselves and labeled themselves as "good guys," "friendly," and "kind."

Now let us turn to the effects of occupational structure and process on ballplayers away from the focused work situation. Because of their odd working hours compared with employees in most other occupations, and because of constant travel demands, ballplayers do not carry out their roles as citizens the way typical Americans might. For example, major leaguers vote less frequently than Americans as a whole. Table 1, at the end of this article, shows that only forty-five percent of the eligible voters sampled actually cast ballots during the 1964 presidential elections.

This may be compared with a national vote that in the past has averaged approximately sixty percent of all eligible voters (Key, 1958: 625; Lipset, 1963: 185).[8] Many players are playing "winter ball" at election time, which would take them out of the country and necessitate the use of an absentee ballot. Most people do not take advantage of the absentee ballot process. In addition, the major leaguer is faced with the likelihood of changing not only the house he lives in but the city as well, several times in his career. Trades, shifts of franchises, or simply the opportunity to make some money elsewhere during the offseason all interfere with residential stability. These prevent the player from becoming attached to or even acquainted with a community, city, or state and their attendant political and social issues. Thus the major leaguer as a political man tends to play the role of bystander. Perhaps his occupation consumes so much of his time and saps so much of his emotional energy that he is unable to become an involved and active political participant.[9]

Ballplayers attend church less frequently than the typical citizen. Among the players in the sample I studied, only twenty percent attended church once a week or more; more significantly, only thirty-six percent of the Catholics and only thirteen percent of the Protestants in the sample claimed weekly church attendance. These figures may be compared with data gathered by Gerhard Lenski (1961: 49) for the city of Detroit, which reveal that between seventy-four percent and eighty-two percent of the Catholics and between twenty-three percent and thirty-eight percent of the Protestants claimed weekly church attendance. It should be pointed out, however, that major leaguers are not necessarily less religious, nor do fewer of them believe in God, than non-ballplayers. They simply have less opportunity to attend church services. They are often on the road on a Sunday during the season, and Saturday night games followed by Sunday afternoon games leave little time for precious sleep.

Even if ballplayers themselves seem to lack involvement in religious orthodoxy, the institution of baseball is thoroughly infused with its ritual and symbolism. Baseball folklore is filled with anecdotes about the efficacy of prayer. Retiring stars can be counted on to evoke God's name while strongly hinting at His influence in any success which may have been achieved. Most baseball banquets are preceded by an invocation from a man of the cloth. All of this, too, is part of "the American way." No one perceives any inconsistency between showing faith in a loving, forgiving, and gentle Christian God and then going onto the playing field to compete aggressively, sometimes angrily and even brutally. Similarly, in the society as a whole many citizens are Christian in spirit and behavior on Sunday morning only.

For a final example of occupational norms restricting behavior away from the work setting, let us take a look at sexual practices of major leaguers. It would have been extremely awkward to have asked a formal question about the degree to which ballplayers are promiscuous or unfaithful to their wives while they are traveling about the country. However, during the tape-recorded session I did pursue this topic quite frankly. After a considerable amount of nervous joking and a few abortive attempts to change the subject, several players candidly admitted that "some cheating" went on among married players. However, they felt that married ballplayers in general were no more promiscuous than typically healthy American males in other highly mobile occupations. As for single players, that was different. The "chase" was their other passion; next to baseball itself (and in some cases, ahead of baseball!), it consumed a large measure of their energies and interest.

Tales of sexual prowess and accomplishment are, by the way, a regular part of clubhouse conversation, but the people who are allowed to hear these stories are carefully screened. Other players, trainers, clubhouse men, and selected members of the front office staff are acceptable, and occasionally some of the working press listen in. But it is clearly understood, although never, stated, that *this* topic is not for public consumption. Once again, the importance of image becomes apparent. Ballplayers are too important as marketable commodities for management to allow the tarnishing of their reputations as public heroes; thus the all-American athlete must also appear to be the all-American husband, or if single, a model of restraint and moral purity. The ballplayers themselves, significantly, strive rigorously to maintain this definition of the situation, because of their vested career interest, and ultimately because their private sexual life is their own business. As a consequence of this sexual ethic, sportswriters (who also have careers to worry about) never do columns on the sexual habits of major leaguers, although many are aware of exactly what is taking place.[10] It is interesting to note, therefore, that baseball's occupational norms extend their controls well beyond the players themselves, influencing people in a number of closely allied fields of work.

Now, a legitimate question to ask at this point might be: what happens to the ballplayer who deviates from formally and informally approved patterns of behavior? Breaches in prescribed conduct often result in harsh negative sanctions by the occupational establishment. Noted baseball author and former big league pitcher Jim Brosnan (1960, 1962) was unable to find a team which wanted his services after he had written and published two rather well-received books not entirely complimentary to the sport. More recently, ex-Yankee and later, Houston, pitcher Jim Bouton (1970) caused an uproar from fellow players, executives, and sportswriters because his book, *Ball Four* (1970), revealed too many details about the "back regions" of baseball life. Ironically, that very audience which baseball officialdom wishes to bedazzle with images of a virtuous and uncorruptable hero found Bouton's voyeuristic journey fascinating and made his book a best seller.

The business of baseball is both sexist and racist and not the model of democracy and sportsmanship it claims to be. It is, however, a suitable example of the American ethic of competition. Major league baseball is a job for hard-working professionals who happen to like their work. They recognize and enjoy the hero-status showered upon them by the public; the players themselves generally agree wholeheartedly with the images and myths they are hired to project yet in a world dangerously and tragically torn by conflict, professional sports unfortunately practice and teach more of the same. There has emerged in recent years a cultural revolution aimed at many of America's long-sacred and uncriticized traditions and institutions. So baseball, the business, might look to itself to see if it serves the people by helping to make this country a better place in which to live, or if, instead, it serves the interests of a handful of self-seeking moguls intent only on maximizing their profits.

TABLE 1

PLAYER'S 1964 VOTING BEHAVIOR
BY POLITICAL AFFILIATION

Political Party Affiliation	Number Who Voted	
Republican	5	
Democrat	14	
Closer to Republican	2	
Closer to Democrat	2	
Neither, do not know, or no answer	4	
Totals Voting	27	(45.8%)
Eligible Voters	59	(100%)

NOTES

[1] Two psychologists, Bruce C. Ogilvie and Thomas A. Tutko (1971), recently reported on the results of their eight-year study of fifteen thousand athletes. They found nothing to support the traditional idea that sports builds character. Indeed, whatever helped successful athletes survive intense competition was probably already part of their personality when they began participation. They conclude that a "ruthless" selection process . . . occurs at all levels of sport."

[2] I chose major leaguers because they had "succeeded" in their occupation whereas minor leaguers were still apprentices. My main concern was with the heroes of sport who garnered so much publicity and acclaim. If I were to study ballplayers again, however, I would include minor leaguers for sev-

eral sociological reasons not the least of which would be the matter of occupational recruitment patterns.

3 They agreed, I was later informed, precisely because each general manager I contacted knew me personally. I suspect that the social scientist without an inside contact might have difficulty gaining access to major league teams.

4 This total represented approximately fifteen percent of all major league players active at the time.

5 When William I. Thomas (1931: 41–50) introduced the concept of "Definition of the Situation," he referred to a process of examination and deliberation which precedes all self-determined acts of behavior. However, he recognized that no individual is totally free to develop his own patterns of action uninfluenced by others. For example: ". . . the child [or 'individual'] is always born [or 'enters'] into a group of people among whom all the general types of situations which may arise have already been defined and corresponding rules of conduct developed, and where he has not the slightest chance of making his definitions and following his wishes without interference."

6 Ballplayers have a fascination for Western movies. Twenty-five players in my sample of seventy-three listed Westerns among their favorites compared with eighteen who named comedies, fifteen who cited suspense, spy, murder or mystery films, and ten who preferred musicals.

7 This story was related to me during an interview in the offices of one of the major league clubs during the summer of 1965.

8 These national figures include women voters, who tend to vote less frequently than men, a fact which further emphasizes the difference between ballplayers and others.

9 In recent years, several retired ballplayers have run for political office, and one or two have won. Examples include Bobby Thompson who hit the historic homerun for the New York Giants which defeated the Brooklyn Dodgers in the 1951 National League playoff: elected to a city council seat in Somerset County, New Jersey, November, 1967; and ex-major league pitcher Bob Friend: elected controller for Allegheny County (Pittsburgh), November, 1967.

10 When ex-major league Jim Boulton disclosed some of the sexual practices of his former mates in his book *Ball Four* (1970), he was soundly condemned by baseball scribes who, I suggest, thought they perceived a threat to their meal ticket.

Clifton D. Bryant

"Lease Hounds":
The Petroleum Landman

This paper is an analysis of the occupation of petroleum landman using a sociological frame of reference. More specifically, it examines the organization of the occupation, its internal structure, and the mechanisms by which recruiting is effected, socialization is accomplished, and control is established and enforced. Additionally, the relationship of occupational members to each other and to their clientele, as well as the overall influence of membership in the occupation itself are explored.[1] This analysis will not attempt to test specific hypotheses. Rather proceeding on the basis of several broad assumptions, this description will provide some insights concerning a relatively unique occupational system.

Petroleum landwork consists of ascertaining the availability of land open for oil exploration in a given area, determining the legitimacy of the title claim of the alleged owner of the land or minerals, securing a conveyance of said land or minerals for oil exploration, and expediting the removal of any hindrances, legal or otherwise, to such oil exploration. Persons who possess the title of petroleum landman may either be salaried employees of petroleum corporations or self-employed individuals who perform the same work on a fee or commission basis.

This occupation was originally selected for study on the basis of several considerations. First, accessibility of data was a prime factor. This author was a petroleum landman at one time and the experiences gained while a member of the occupation (including friends, associates, and father, who has been an independent landman for many years) provided valuable information. Because of these contacts, it was possible to act as a participant observer in situations within the petroleum industry and to gain considerable information concerning the occupation from observations and interviews, both formal and informal over a period of approximately five years. In addition, quantitative data from a national survey of petroleum landmen were obtained. A second factor in selection of this occupation was the petroleum industry background. The petroleum industry is little more than one hundred years old, and yet ranks in size and importance with many older industries. In the process of attaining this size and importance, the petroleum industry has had to compress its growth in terms of the development of various types of work institutions and occupational specialties. Thus it was possible to examine the total development of occupational institutions within the framework of an industry that is relatively isolated from other industries in terms of its integrated nature and its short history.

Finally, the occupation of petroleum landman possesses several unique properties. There is considerable in-group feeling and camaraderie among the members, thus permitting a better view of occupational norms and control. This occupation, as well as other occupations within the industry, has many subcultural characteristics. As a result it provides an excellent opportunity for the examination of the process of occupational socialization. In addition, the duties which are involved in the occupation have increasingly required more specialized training for members. Need for more specialized skill is reflected in the changing composition of the occupational labor force. Although the present composition of the occupational membership reflects diverse educational backgrounds, a high degree of occupational value consensus among the landmen seems apparent. This is suggestive of an effective socialization process and presents a unique opportunity for the study of occupational value and attitude development.

THE HISTORY OF PETROLEUM

Petroleum has been utilized by man in one form or another perhaps as early as 6,000 B.C. Among its major uses have been those of preservant, cosmetic, medicine, waterproofing agent and weapon; in more recent times, fuel, lubricant, illuminant, and road surface.

The evidence suggests that petroleum was relatively abundant in ancient and medieval times, being obtained primarily from natural oil and gas seepages in many parts of Europe and Asia. The Chinese, drilling for salt, often encountered oil and gas, and in some instances built bamboo "pipelines" to transport the gas. In the seventeenth and eighteenth centuries, deliberate attempts to obtain petroleum in seep pits were being made in Europe. Petroleum was present in the New World and was utilized by the various Indian tribes. The early settlers also used petroleum, finding it excellent for medicinal purposes. Petroleum was frequently encountered when drilling for salt, and by the mid-nineteenth century, at least one company was enjoying unusual success at selling petroleum by the bottle as an all purpose medicine.

When it became evident that petroleum would be useful as an illuminant, some interest was evoked in the deliberate exploration for petroleum itself. In 1859, one "Colonel" E. L. Drake discovered oil outside of Titusville, Pennsylvania, at a depth of sixty-nine and a half feet. In spite of a production of only some eight to ten barrels a day, the well was a milestone, since it demonstrated that petroleum could be found and extracted by drilling for it. Shortly thereafter, a petroleum "rush" resulted, as the commercial possibilities of petroleum expanded. Pennsylvania became the center of the emerging American petroleum industry. Other petroleum discoveries were made in California, and shortly after the turn of the century, the Spindletop well in Beaumont, Texas, was brought in with the enormous production of one hundred thousand barrels per day. Some thirty years after the discovery of the Beaumont field, the East Texas field was discovered with fantastic petroleum reserves. In the meanwhile, petroleum discoveries were made in many other states. The United States became an oil producer of world importance, and the petroleum industry grew into a giant aided by the fuel demands of automobiles and industrial machines.

Although the history of petroleum is long, it was not until its fuel and illuminant potentialities could be utilized by society that a deliberate and systematic approach to its discovery became necessary. The Drake well demonstrated the feasibility of exploring for petroleum. Thus while petroleum is old the petroleum industry is relatively new. This has meant that new and unusual work specialties have emerged within the span of a few years. Petroleum landwork is one such of these specialties.

THE OCCUPATIONAL HISTORY OF PETROLEUM LANDWORK

After the Drake well discovery, it became apparent that a whole set of new work skills would be required to find and produce petroleum if the growing demand were to be met. One situation partially unique in this country is the private ownership of sub-surface minerals, as opposed to many other areas of the world where title to the sub-surface minerals, and even in some cases, the land itself, is vested in the sovereign or ruler. Added to this have been the numerous changes in title ownership of land and minerals. These result from a mobile population, the absence of entail and primogeniture laws and laws permitting land and minerals to be conveyed separately. The complexity of land and mineral ownership made the simple acquisition of the right to explore for petroleum a task beyond the competence of many persons. The situation was further complicated as leasing and drilling arrangements became progressively involved with the "law of capture" and the "Doctrine of Correlative Rights."

Lacking persons with specialized training to meet these needs, the new oil industry turned to occupations which possessed some of the necessary skills—attorneys, real estate dealers and commodity buyers. Various kinds of agents did land work, as well as the adventurers who were attracted by the boom times. In the early years of the petroleum industry, landmen tended often to be self-employed middle-men who bought and sold oil leases as a speculation. In many instances the oil driller simply acquired his own leases. The larger petroleum companies began to require permanent representation in the discovery areas. They required men who could observe the progress of a well being drilled, and if oil shows resulted, the companies could take leases in the surrounding area. Thus, the larger companies began to employ full-time landmen for this purpose, while the smaller companies utilized the services of independent landmen in much the same capacity. As competition increased, the companies needed to keep abreast of the drilling activities of their competitors. The landman then became a combination scout and landman; he gathered information on competitors' oil exploration and acted to take leases if the competition brought production or indications of petroleum.

As the nature of lease acquisition and lease management became more complex, both in terms of legality and human relations, the landman of necessity had to become a "jack of all trades." The extent to which landmen perceived this requirement is humorously illustrated by an ad inserted in a petroleum trade paper some years back by a lease broker of the "old school." [2]

I AM QUALIFIED AS A LEASE BROKER.
I HAVE THE FOLLOWING PROCLIVITIES
TO MAKE A SUCCESSFUL BROKER.

You have to have vision and ambition, be an after-dinner speaker, and before and after dinner guzzler, night owl, work all day and half the night, drive two hundred miles and appear fresh the next day; entertain bankers, farmers, cattlemen, pet widows without becoming too amorous, inhale dust, drive thru snow and sleet and work hard all summer without perspiring or acquiring BO—

Must be a man's man, a lady's man, model husband, fatherly father, a good provider, Plutocrat, Democrat, Republican, Dixiecrat, New Dealer, gin dealer, politician, engineer, mechanic, babysitter, diaper changer, and notary public—

Must be a buying genius, full of misinformation, land scout, and carpenter, visit clients in hospitals, jails, honky-tonks, flop houses, and boudoirs and always be able to step off a couple of thousand miles on ten minutes notice; must have endurance, wide range of telephone numbers, acquaintances from Cape Cod to the Pecos, own a good car, belong to everything from the Swedish Business Men's Pool, Poker and Marching Society to the Petroleum Club—

Must be a hotshot, liar, Rhumba dancer, pitch player, diplomat, financier, capitalist, lawyer, abstractor, and be an authority on dogs, dice, horses, and have peak information on blondes, brunettes, and red heads; must know geology, doodlebugging, and be able to mix drinks with everything from Vodka to corn squeezings—

Maybe the old worn out goat is right—Maybe I'll take up picketing or turtle trapping—Wonder why someone doesn't burst out with a hot oil play up in the cool mountains for the summer?

The former jack of all trades, however, had to give way to the specialization required as a result of technological change, and the increasing cost of leases and oil exploration. The petroleum landman of recent years has become more of a specialist, because he is the product of a specialized educational background. The petroleum companies themselves have, in some cases, had their landmen pursue a specialized career within the company. Although the petroleum landman has had to become a specialist, nevertheless in the course of his work he has had to play a variety of roles. In this respect he tends to resemble somewhat the traditional professional who offers an unstandardized product requiring a high degree of specialized competence.

THE WORK COMPLEX

Petroleum companies can be divided into the majors, the minors, and the independents. The majors are large, integrated corporate concerns engaged in the exploration, production, refining and processing of petroleum, and the refining, processing, production and marketing of petroleum products. The minors, for the most part, differ in the size of corporate assets, and smaller range of activities. The independent petroleum company is often owner operated or managed and in some cases is engaged in only a few phases of the total process, exploration and production, for example. In addition to the petroleum companies proper, the petroleum industry is also made up of ancillary firms which provide goods and services to the petroleum companies in every phase of the total production process.

The petroleum companies are usually broken down into several sub-units charged with the responsibility of one or more phases of the total production process. These sub-units, with the ancillary firms and individuals, make up sub-industrial complexes revolving around one of the specific functions, such as exploration, production or refining. Occupational interdependence tends to be within the functional area, rather than within the entire industry. As landwork is part of exploration and production, it is this sub-complex that is of particular interest. Within many petroleum companies the exploration and production departments often make up a group, and there is usually considerable decentralization of the activities of this group into geographical units. The smallest of these units is the *district,* usually comprising a part of a state or an entire state. The next larger geographical unit is the *division,* comprising several states or parts of states. Sometimes there are larger units than the division, often of a regional nature.

Included in the activities carried on in the exploration and production departments are geological work, scouting, land and leasing, as well as drilling and producing. The district exploration and production office is often divided into an exploration unit and a production unit. The exploration unit is made up of the geological section, the scouting section and the land and leasing section. The production unit is made up of the drilling section and the rental section. The landman usually works out of the district exploration and production office.

THE WORK STRUCTURE

In the district office, the geological section will make recommendations concerning likely areas for oil exploration and will prepare detailed maps and specifications of the selected exploration areas. The scouting section will gather and furnish information concerning the progress of all drilling wells, any oil and gas strikes, and any geological or leasing activities in the area.

Based on data from the geological and scouting sections, it is the task of the land and leasing section to acquire the right to explore and drill for oil on the prospective lands. This right generally takes the form of an oil and gas lease on the land. Upon acquisition of this right on a particular tract of land, arrangements for the actual drilling are made by personnel in the drilling section. If, and when the wells produce, the oil royalty payments are made by the rental section.

The petroleum landman, in accomplishing his task of acquiring oil leases, may do so on either a sporadic or systematic basis. Sporadic leasing is the acquisition of isolated leasing as a speculative venture, or as a hedge against production in the area. Where numerous small land remnants are leased to complete an acquisition program, it is known as "clean-up" work. Opposed to sporadic leasing is the systematic leasing plan which may fall into one of five categories. In the *checkerboard* system, relatively uniform sized leases are acquired in an alternating or skip pattern over a large favorable area. In the *block* system, a solid group of leases in a particular area of land is sought. Another system involves the leasing of *offset acreage* against a test well which entails the obtaining of leases on small tracts of land strategically located, adjoining to, or in close proximity to land where a well is being drilled or is scheduled to be drilled. In the *lease spread* system, blocks of leases around a test well are broken up into groups of smaller tracts (spreads), which are then graded in price according to their closeness to the test well and conveyed to various oil companies or individuals. Still another system is the *unit plan,* in which a petroleum company attempts to get the various landowners in an area to participate in a type of joint ownership of any oil and gas produced; they will then receive an interest in any production in direct proportion to the amount of acreage they own.

In acquiring the right to explore for oil and gas, the landmen frequently relies on a type of legal instrument known as a Producers 88 Oil and Gas Lease Form. Although lease instruments may vary somewhat in form from one part of the country to another, most will contain a number of generally similar provisions on leasing conditions and arrangements. Included in the instrument will be the name of the lessor and lessee, amount paid for the lease, date of the agreement, terms of the lease, description of the land, interest owned by the lessor, royalty to be paid by lessee, name of bank in which rentals are to be deposited, as well as a statement of some of the responsibilities of lessee in regard to drilling operations and responsibilities of lessor in regard to defense of title. The lease agreement is signed by all parties, notarized and recorded in the office of the appropriate country or parish official.

The duties of the petroleum landman include more than acquiring the right to explore and drill for oil. Before he can negotiate a lease, he must determine the actual owner of the minerals he seeks to lease. He may go out "on the ground" and seek information from the persons living on the land itself, or he may turn to the official records of land and mineral conveyances. In some cases, the land title records are arranged and indexed by a system known as the *Sectional Index.* Under this system, land transactions are broken down and classified by particular land sections under the rectangular system of townships and ranges. In other cases, land title conveyances are arranged and classified by

means of a *Direct and Reverse Index*. Under this system, land transactions are indexed in two ways: from the earliest transaction to the
most current by name of most recent owner. Once the landman determines the owner of the mineral land he wishes to lease, he must then
physically locate the owner. This in itself may involve some detective
work. The located owner may turn out to be a minor, a legally insane
person, or someone else unable to enter into a lease agreement. If the
mineral owner may legally convey his holdings, however, it is the landman's further task to persuade the owner to enter into the lease agreement with his employer or principal and also to negotiate the specific
arrangements. Normally the landman has the following three main
considerations to negotiate: 1) the amount of bonus money per acre to
pay, 2) the length of the lease, and 3) the amount of yearly rentals to
be paid. Occasionally the mineral owner may demand more than the
customary one-eighth royalty to lease his land, and this eventuality constitutes a fourth issue to negotiate.

After the lease has been signed, an attorney will examine the title of
the leased land or minerals and render a title opinion, setting forth
the problems to be corrected before having a sound title. Often this
becomes the task of the landman who plays the role of historian and
detective.

After drilling operations begin, the landman will often handle claims
for damages incurred by the well operations. He acts as liaison man
between the mineral owner and his company; he also handles well drilling contracts, prepares lease activity reports, and contracts lease buying
orders out to independent landmen. The majority of landmen are permanent full-time employees of oil companies. As such, they carry out
all of the tasks previously described, as well as others. In addition, there
are large numbers of independent landmen who are employed by petroleum companies and independent producers on a commission or day
basis for limited periods. The independent is utilized by petroleum
companies as a means of preserving anonymity in their lease acquisition
programs, as supplemental personnel during periods of peak leasing
activity and in situations where there is only occasional need of landwork. Some independents are specialists in certain phases of landwork.
Many landmen begin as company men and later become independents.
Their company employment affords them a means of acquiring landwork
skills difficult to acquire otherwise.

ECONOMIC COMPLEX

The company landman is usually paid a monthly salary, plus various
fringe benefits, including medical, hospitalization, life insurance, retire-

ment, social security benefits, profit sharing, stock purchase plans and savings plans. A few companies even permit their landmen to purchase personal royalty under leases they acquire for the company. The independent landman, on the other hand, is employed temporarily as an agent by oil companies or individuals on a commission or daily basis. On a daily basis he will usually receive from thirty-five to seventy-five dollars per day and expenses, plus mileage. Working for a commission, known as a "buying order" or "ticket" basis, usually provides one dollar per acre for all leases acquired for principals. Occasionally in buying royalty and leases, the independent landman will receive an interest rather than money. Independents are generally free to acquire leases and royalties as speculations or investments.

THE OCCUPATIONAL CULTURE

Occupations, occupational complexes and industries, tend to develop a set of beliefs, a distinctive language,[3] and customs which become traditional. The petroleum industry, with its occupational system, lacks the long history of some other occupational complexes such as medicine, law, or the military. Yet it has, in a short time period, developed an occupational culture rich in tradition which has served in some measure to influence the ideology of today's petroleum occupations.[4]

The early days of the oil business in this country were characterized by boom, excitement and risks—economic and personal. Oil exploration was dangerous; it was expensive, and it involved a gamble since scientific searching for oil was relatively new, and unknown. But the rewards were great and it was this fact that drew men from many walks of life into this new industry. The early pioneer in the oil industry was beset by many difficulties. In this search for the pot of gold, he found it necessary to rely upon himself and to trust his intuition, for there was little else to rely on. The early oilman came to place much value on hunches, luck, his five senses, and a "practical" utilitarian outlook.

In this period of great booms, speculations and gambles, it might have been expected that conditions and circumstances would have fostered widespread dishonesty. Certainly the opportunities were there and the oil industry, like other industries, had its share of crooks and "shady dealers." These were not the genuine oilmen, however. The true oil pioneer might outsmart and outtrade his competitor, but he would not swindle him. Fair dealings and trust were necessary between colleagues and between employee and employer if the emerging oil business was to grow and to flourish. As a result of this need, a kind of pioneer business morality developed among oilmen and the first commandment was to "live up to your word." Only a fraction of the individuals in the oil business labored in their own behalf. The majority worked as employees of a company or another individual. Only a fraction of the individuals in the oil business became rich. Occupational culture in the early days of the petroleum industry, then, was such that the early oilmen had to develop traits of self-reliance, ingenuity, gambling, and "rugged individualism." The nature of the business arrangements necessitated a dependence on oral contracts and verbal commitments. As a result, honesty and trust were valued attributes in members of the petroleum occupation.

Most of the conditions of the early industry changed due to advances in science and technology. The oilmen had to keep pace by becoming better educated, more scientific in his approach to oil exploration, and more specialized in his work. Many of the old characteristics lingered on, however, and continued to be highly valued. Together with pride in the growth and advances of the oil industry, there continues to be pride in the early traditions. From the very earliest days of oil pioneering in Pennsylvania, the men who faced the difficulties and challenge of exploration and production have felt an occupational kinship toward one another, much in the same way as seafaring men or railroaders, or airplane pilots. The oil business was different from other businesses requiring a different language, environment, and set of skills. The search for oil led to isolation in some cases and high geographical mobility in others. A sense of camaraderie emerged which was in later years to draw men of many occupational specialties, but all within the oil business, into a solidified collectivity known to them as the "oil fraternity." The outsider often did not understand or fully appreciate the difficulties or attractions of oil exploration, and thus could not share the identification with the industry. Common and often shared experiences developed a "consciousness of kind" which has persisted through time. Just as the oil industry created the technical innovations and skills it required, it also created its own kind of individual to work in its occupational ranks.

OCCUPATIONAL ROLES AND SOCIALIZATION

Early landmen originated to meet the needs of the business, although some came from other occupations outside the petroleum industry. Once in the oil business in any capacity, an individual was in a position to acquaint himself with the nature and mechanics of the business. He was also able to acquire skills that would be useful in almost any other oil occupation. This apparently became the occupational pattern. The use of "feeding occupations" has been institutionalized by some oil companies which have required their landmen to work as oil scouts for a period of time before being permitted to do landwork, unless they had previous experience as a landman. In some cases, the new landman would work with an older more experienced company man, acquiring skills through observation and participation in the work. Other firms often send their new inexperienced landmen out with an independent man to "learn the trade." More recently in some cases there is a regular on-the-job training program similar to those found in many other industries where the neophyte landman has an opportunity to work at a number of tasks in several different departments of the company. Also, more companies are requiring a law degree. Landmen also acquire many of their skills informally from other landmen outside of their own firms, such as abstractors, lawyers, court house clerks, and even notary publics as well as scouts, drillers etc. Landmen often come into contact "in the field" and the neophyte can often learn many of the "tricks of the trade" from the senior men they meet.

The teaching and learning situation in landwork makes it possible for the neophyte to become exposed to the occupation's folkways and mores while he develops his skills; being in contact with his colleagues also perhaps fosters a stronger sense of identity with the occupation. Under present conditions, the occupation is able to control both entrance and learning to a large degree.

The early landman was a generalist and jack of all trades, but in recent years he has increasingly become a specialist. In spite of this trend, the status of landman still involves a number of occupational roles. These can be grouped into three general categories: human relations roles which equip him to deal with clientele, technical roles which assist him in performing his part of the oil exploration process, and information sharing roles which relate him symbiotically to his fellow landmen.

THE OCCUPATIONAL CONTROL SYSTEM

The occupational norms in landwork primarily concern themselves with protecting confidential information, protecting the occupational image, preventing uncontrolled competition, and loyalty to company or principal. Several types of sanctions are available to enforce the occupational norms, including ostracizing the deviant from social activities, withholding assistance, information, and referrals, as well as direct sabotage of his work. Landwork is highly competitive, but members of the occupation can make it even more so for any member. Landmen may, on occasion, sanction an errant occupational member by spreading the word around concerning his lease buying activities when they obtain information on it. They may also refuse to cooperate with him or even "bust his block"; that is, buy leases in an area on which he was trying to obtain a solid block of leases, and thus sabotage his work. Landmen are quite sensitive to the "quack" or "shady character" who might harm the occupational or industrial image, and are particularly prone to employ sanctions to drive such a person out of the business.

THE CLIENTELE

The relationship between practitioner and client is subject to wide variation. At first consideration, it would appear that the occasion of a landman taking a lease on the land or minerals of a given individual would be a joyous occasion. For an oil and gas lease, the landowner will receive bonus money, rental payments and royalty, should oil be discovered on his land. It would seem that this opportunity would represent extreme good fortune to the landowner. To illustrate this ideal reception, consider the remarks of Harvey O'Connor (1955) who in taking the part of the landowner, says:

> So far as you are concerned, the whole thing is quite accidental. You didn't put the oil there, you didn't discover it there, and neither will you take it out. You will merely sign a document, sometimes a Lease 88, and manna will fall from the heavens. (1955: 57)

Landmen, however, encounter all kinds and types of people, including a great many who do not welcome the chance to lease their land, or at least not under the conventional arrangement. Many of the landowners will, of course, live on the land and farm or ranch. The landman with his rational business proposition sometimes encounters irrational folklore, superstition, and rural community subcultures with norms and values that run counter to those of his own. Additionally, the typical rural landowner is not very knowledgeable or sophisticated about the mechanics of leasing or oil economics. There are those individuals who are concerned that oil will be discovered on their land, and the resultant derricks, storage tanks, and other apparatus will disturb their farming activities. Some landowners are irrationally convinced that there are petroleum deposits under their property and demand an exorbitant and thus impossible price. Many landowners are apprehensive about leasing, for fear a neighbor may hold out and later receive a higher price; thus he would "lose face" for having accepted a less attractive deal. Some landowners, as members of large families, feel compelled to act as a family unit, each waiting for the other's decision delaying the land-man. Not to be overlooked are those landowners who must await a sign from the Almighty or some supernatural source. One particular land-owner from personal experience comes to mind, who leased all of her land except a small parcel, for an exceptionally good price. She wanted to think and pray about the remaining parcel of land. On contacting her a short while later, she informed us that the Lord had subsequently advised her to lease, but only at three times the bonus price, for a three-year period instead of five years, and she was to retain a one-sixteenth overriding royalty in addition to her regular one-eighth royalty. The Lord was apparently pretty well versed on the oil business.

Many rural landowners have a suspicion of all lawyers and landmen. There is a traditional agrarian fear of being cheated in the process of entering into any legal agreement. There are landowners who in all sincerity, mistakenly believe that they own the full mineral rights to their lands. Others know better but let the landmen discover it for themselves, then act surprised, if not resentful. More than one land-owner has demanded payment for full mineral rights, even while admitting that he originally acquired only one-half the mineral rights. If one landman gives in and pays the full amount in order to take a desirable lease, it is quite likely the landowner will continue to demand the same compensation for all subsequent releasing. Of course, not all land or mineral owners display these traits. Most, perhaps, are rational and reasonable people with which to deal. Some act in the other direction, by offering to lease their land at a low price. Then to obtain more money, they offer to sell their royalty or even their house and land as well.

The landman must overcome all of these suspicions and hostilities and learn to cope with the seemingly irrational arguments of some land-owners. He must also come to recognize the normative structure of the rural community and appreciate the landowner's fear of "losing face." To accomplish this, the landman must at all times be honest in his propositions, his arguments, and his agreements; he must be sincere not only for his own benefit, but also for the sake of all landmen who will come into the same area to lease.

Once the lease is in effect, the landowner may still develop hostilities toward the oil company that holds his lease and the landman who took it, especially if a well is drilled and it turns out dry. The landowner may well have other opinions about the well. As Charlies Wilkins (1959) describes it:

> He becomes especially interested in the little rainbows of oil on the slush pit made by tool joint grease. He does not ask about this because any fool can see it is oil.

One fine day he starts down for his daily well check and sees the derrick being dismantled. No one tells him whether a well has been made or not, and he may not know the difference between a plugging job or setting pipe. If the odds run true to form, he has a dry hole, but he will talk this over with neighbors and they always come up with the idea that the lease situation just was not right or the oil company just did not want to bring the well in at this time. He is a little put out with the producer, and as time goes on he becomes bitter about the whole thing. (1959: 13)

In the face of this possibility the landman must originally establish a rapport based on mutual trust with the landowner, and keep the land-owner informed every step of the way. In many cases, landmen have formed friendships with particular landowners that lasted for life. Some landowners have refused to lease land to anyone else but some favored landman friend, or refused to lease without seeking his advice.

Just as the oil business has changed, and the oilman has changed, so too has the landowner changed. Today's landowner is far more sophis-ticated about oil, and as a result makes for a more rational, though not necessarily less challenging clientele for the landman. A past president of the American Association of Petroleum Landmen put it:

Today's landman is a highly specialized and knowledgeable individual, having to deal with land and mineral owners who know just about as much concerning the oil and gas business as the landman knows (Bixler, 1962: 18).

THE CAREER OF THE PETROLEUM LANDMAN

Little headway could be made in gaining an understanding of the rela-tionship of man to his work without examining the ways an individual comes to pursue a given specialty in the division of labor. Data obtained from the previously mentioned national survey of petroleum landmen afford a composite overview of the characteristic career of the land-man (Bryant, 1964).

SOCIAL SELECTION

Petroleum landmen tend to come from small and medium-size towns in one of the Western Central States particularly the West South Central States. These states have the highest crude oil production which may well be a factor in the initial social selection process of the occupation.

The fathers of petroleum landmen have a relatively high educational level, with high school graduation as a median education; more than one-half were self-employed and a little over one-fourth of the landmen's fathers had been employed in the oil business. Petroleum landmen themselves are well educated, having a median educational level of four years of college. A significant number have had some graduate or professional work. Approximately one-half of the landmen have had some degree of legal training, a smaller number had law degrees. Landmen are predominantly white Protestant, young, married males. The picture which emerges then is that of middle-to-upper-middle class, managerial, professional or proprietorial social backgrounds, and geographical origins in mid-continent small and medium-sized towns. The social and background characteristics of the landman group suggest the presence of several mechanisms of social selection. Among these is a socio-economic background which financially permitted, and no doubt encouraged, the college and professional training necessary for a career at the technical, managerial or professional level. Geographical location and propinquity to job opportunities, as well as family contact in the oil business, perhaps help account for the pursuance of this career in the petroleum industry.

THE OCCUPATIONAL COLLEAGUE GROUP AND THE WORK GROUP

Petroleum landmen as a rule have an extremely close identification with other members of their occupation and with their co-workers in the exploration segment of the oil industry as well. They refer to this occupational community as the "oil fraternity." This group camaraderie and solidarity appear to derive from several sources. Oilmen share a collective pride in the colorful and lusty history of their industry and its "glamour." They also share a strong in-group orientation toward "outsiders" whom they view as unknowledgeable about and unsympathetic to the oil industry. Accordingly, they try to maintain appropriate social distance between themselves and those not in the oil industry. The heavy travel demands of oil work, the fact that petroleum offices and activities are often physically segregated from the mainstream of commercial life, and the relatively frequent geographical moves required of petroleum company personnel all tend to increase the social distance with non-oil people.

There are additionally a number of formal mechanisms for facilitating informal interaction among colleagues and co-workers. These include local landmen's associations, and uptown social clubs known as petroleum clubs for men in the oil business only. The American Association of Petroleum Landmen with its annual convention, auxiliary clubs and organizations for the wives, reinforce the group cohesion. The landman and his family who move to a new community can immediately join the petroleum social life via the activities, parties, and meetings sponsored by these organizations. Landmen and their wives seem to restrict voluntarily their informal interaction in large measure to other persons in the petroleum industry in terms of lunching, coffee breaks, visiting, hobby association activities, and family entertainment. They often live in a neighborhood with other members of the petroleum industry and in many instances count as their closest friends persons who are also members of the petroleum industry.

THE TREND TOWARD PROFESSIONALIZATION

The status of "professional" is a highly valued one in our society. In recent years a number of occupational groups have made claims on this status—e.g., chiropractors, life insurance agents, and funeral directors. On the basis of traditional criteria for characterizing a profession, the claims of some of these groups may not be altogether warranted. Petroleum landmen may be justified in anticipating the acquisition of professional status soon. Edward Gross (1958: 77–82) mentions six criteria of professionalization: the unstandardized product, degree of personality involvement, wide knowledge of a specialized technique, sense of obligation to one's art, sense of identity with one's colleagues, and importance to the welfare of society.

Landwork would appear to meet several of these criteria. A significant number of law graduates are already present in the occupational ranks of landwork. There is evidence that the percentage of such persons may be increasing. In addition, several universities have introduced Petroleum Land Management curriculum as undergraduate "professional" progams. Recruitment of the graduate may well be a factor in landwork achieving professional status. In summary, it might be said that while landwork does not yet meet the traditional criteria for professional status, it nevertheless has many of the "makings"; if the occupational membership persist in their efforts, landwork will continue to progress in this direction.

Landmen would like to achieve professional status and are making strong efforts in this direction. Landwork apparently is highly satisfying to its members and they find the occupational career rewarding. Also the way of life in the oil business is a meaningful experience. This satisfaction has been eloquently expressed by one landman who said:

> If I had my life to live over and had a chance to choose any field I desired, I would be a professional landman, for I know of no field that affords a man greater opportunity for a respectable, honorable and rewarding life, nor a

greater vehicle for service to the public—and the very fact that you represent a successful company marks you with the public as a successful man. (Kelley, 1957: 12).

THE FUTURE OF PETROLEUM LANDWORK

The use of petroleum as a fuel and general energy source will probably continue for many years because other types of energy such as atomic and solar have certain limitations which will not be overcome in the foreseeable future. In addition, the expanding use of petrochemicals to produce fertilizers, drugs, plastics, and even food, offers an unlimited growth potential for the oil industry. Thus as long as there is private ownership of minerals, there will be a need for landwork.

Several additional factors make the future of landwork seem even brighter. Oil exploration is expanding over a wider geographical area, and in all probability will continue. This means that larger areas each year will be actively explored for oil, thus requiring landwork. Oil leases are tending towards shorter durations because the mineral owner does not wish to keep his minerals tied up for too long a period for only one bonus payment, and because the oil companies are avoiding excessive acreage under lease at one time to save on rental payments. This means a more rapid turnover of leases, and more need for landwork. Another positive factor in the future of landwork is that with each generation, land titles are becoming more fractionalized and complex. When a land or mineral owner dies, his holdings are divided among his heirs, thereby breaking it up into smaller interests. In addition, more persons are buying mineral interests, and more landowners are separating the minerals from their land and selling all or part of them. As land titles become more complex and land and mineral owners become more scattered, there will be an increased need for landwork. Time and technology appear to be the two best friends of landwork.

NOTES

[1] This dissertation was based on interviews, observations and personal experiences as well as on quantitative data obtained from a national survey of landmen conducted in 1960 by the author. Approximately 1,500 members of the American Association of Petroleum Landmen completed questionnaires as part of this study. For a detailed discussion of the study, see Bryant, Clifton D.: 1964. Since that time several other individuals have undertaken

small survey studies of the landman occupation and in several instances have used the same instrument that we originally used. In these instances, the persons conducting these studies have supplied me with their findings, which has made it possible to keep my data updated. These persons include Carol A. Fowler, who conducted a small survey of landmen in 1968 as part of her course requirements at the University of Colgary, Canada; and Mr. John E. Norman, an executive landman with Continental Oil Company, who conducted a somewhat larger survey of petroleum landmen in 1968, as part of a Master's thesis requirement. In both instances these persons adopted my questionnaire for use in their respective surveys.

[2] A. Hawkins, "I am Qualified as a Lease Broker." This ad is apparently a variation of a short essay that was originally used by Dana H. Kelsey, once vice-president of Sinclair Oil and Gas Company, and now deceased.

[3] For some detailed discussions of petroleum jargon, see Pond, Frederick R., "Language of the California Oil Fields," and Boone, Lalia Phipps, "Patterns of Innovation in the Language of the Oil Fields."

[4] For some comprehensive accounts of petroleum history in America, see Williamson, Harold F. and Arnold R. Daum, *The American Petroleum Industry;* also Hildegarde, Nelson, *The Great Oildorado;* and Tait, Samuel W., Jr., *The Wildcatters.*

Bonnie and Vern Bullough

The Causes and Consequences of the Differentiation of the Nursing Role

Perhaps the most obvious structural characteristic of the health occupations in general and nursing in particular is the complexity of the structure of these occupations. In a recent report of health manpower published by the United States Public Health Service, (1970a: 8–10) there were thirty-three major categories of health workers listed and these categories were further divided to yield a total of seventy-four occupational roles. In the actual work setting, these occupational roles are further divided by administrative hierarchies and skill specialties until even with a program guide it is sometimes difficult to sort out the players.

Nursing and nursing related services comprise the largest category with nearly half of the 3.7 million health workers classified. Only thirty-seven percent of this group, however, are actually registered nurses, the occupation most people think of when they hear the term "nurse." Nursing care is also given by licensed practical nurses, who comprise nineteen percent of the total nursing manpower, and by hospital aides, orderlies and home health aides who make up forty-four percent of the nursing group (United States Public Health Service: 9). These workers are prepared for their jobs in a variety of settings and for varying lengths of time. Since aides (who are usually female) and orderlies (who are male) are not licensed, the quality and quantity of their educational experience is usually determined by their employers. They may be given short pre-employment courses or trained on the job. The other health workers, by law, are usually better trained. Courses for licensed practical nurses usually last one year while registered nurses may come out of two-year Junior College Associate of Arts programs, three-year hospital nursing schools, or four year baccalaureate programs.

HISTORICAL BACKGROUND

While it is true that some type of nursing care was given to the sick even in ancient times, the development of nursing as an occupational role is more recent and the nurse as a trained practitioner developed only in the last century. The present complex division of labor is even more recent, having developed only in the last twenty-five years. Nurse training programs were started in this country in the period after the civil war. While the school which was endowed and set up under the sponsorship of Florence Nightingale was used as a model, American nursing schools were from the beginning underfinanced. Unfortunately, it was found that dedicated student nurses were a cheaper source of hospital labor than the earlier untrained workers who gave nursing care. As a result, throughout the last part of the nineteenth and early part of the twentieth century, most of the hospital nursing was done by unpaid students. Graduate nurses were employed primarily as private duty nurses caring for only one patient at a time. Nurses were not unaware of the exploitive characteristics of this system and most worked to improve educational standards, particularly as the depression of the early 1930's created severe unemployment among their ranks. Eventually they were able to get some of the least adequate schools closed, to cut the on-duty time of students to approximately forty hours a week, and to increase the amount of classroom time for student nurses (Bullough, Vern and Bonnie Bullough, 1969).

As it happened, however, these educational reforms coincided with several other trends and events which increased the needs for nurses so that within a decade the problem of an oversupply of nurses was converted to one of an acute shortage. The demand for nurses to work in base hospitals and overseas during World War II created what was thought to be a temporary shortage, but after the war nurses were still needed for the long-term rehabilitation of the men in veterans hospitals. Hospitals were becoming much more important institutions as the advances in scientific medicine demanded complex diagnostic treatment facilities for procedures which could not be carried out in a home or an office. In this same period, the growth of pre-paid hospital insurance enabled more people to buy these services offered in these institutions. The federal government also aided the growth of the hospital as a major health services institution by supplying building funds under the Hill

Burton Act and by the further financial boost supplied by Medicare.

During World War II the gap in nursing services had been "temporarily" filled by volunteer aides who were trained by the Red Cross and the Office of Civilian Defense. At first these aides were allowed to perform only those tasks which were not directly related to patient care; they ran errands, cleaned equipment and carried food to patients. Eventually however, the shortage of help forced nurses to turn over some of the less complicated aspects of patient care to the aides. Their entry into the hospital was the beginning of the nursing team as a replacement for the nurse since they were able to demonstrate that much of the work performed by the nurse could safely be delegated to less expensive workers. The temporary move became permanent and what had been one occupational role quickly broke up into the present rather complex system.

Hospital management endorsed the idea of using workers with less training whenever it was possible. They were in effect seeking a replacement for the unpaid student nurses, and while they were never again able to find such a bargain in help the utilization of auxiliary nursing personnel kept labor costs down. Moreover, registered nurses were not unwilling to give up some of the routine work they had been performing. In fact, the American Nurses' Association sponsored a series of studies and reports which recommended that the nursing role be broken up. The most influential of these was one done by Esther Lucile Brown (1948) who surveyed the work nurses were doing in various settings and recommended the development of a "non-professional trained nurse" who would carry out the routine procedures and leave the registered nurse more time to concentrate on complex procedures, preventive medicine and administration. Following this recommendation schools to train practical nurses in one year programs proliferated rapidly. By 1952 thirty-nine states had established licensing regulations for practical nurses (or vocational nurses as they are called in two states) and the other states soon followed (Roberts, 1961: 514).

Not all of the role differentiation among nurses was as well planned as the move for practical nurses appeared to be. Some of it is also a consequence of an educational system that is in transition. As nursing education became more adequate it became more expensive. Hospitals found that operating nursing schools was no longer a profitable enterprise. It was in fact an expense which many hospitals found unbearable so they closed the doors of their schools. Thirty years ago there were approximately 1200 hospital schools; there are now about 700 and the current rate at which they are closing is about twenty per year (American Nurses' Association, 1960: 81; 1969: 81–120). The void left by the closure of the hospital schools is being filled by the development of the baccalaureate and Associate of Arts programs. Although baccalaureate education for nurses dates back to 1909 when the University of Minnesota started a college affiliated nursing program, it has been slow developing so that at the present time only about twenty percent of the registered nurses graduate with a bachelor's degree. The Associate of Arts program which has grown up in the last twenty-five years has developed more rapidly until approximately twenty-one percent of the graduating nurses finish in two years. Although the largest group of graduates (fifty-nine percent) are still from hospital schools, the two types of collegiate programs show gains each year (National League of Nursing, 1970: 52–57).

Higher degree programs for nurses have also expanded rapidly in recent years, partly because they have been heavily financed by the federal government. In 1955 there were 526 master's degrees granted in nursing; by 1969 that number had tripled with 1766 degrees being granted (Dineen, 1969: 22–26). The yearly output of nurses with doctorates is more difficult to measure since most of the degrees are in fields other than nursing, but since the nurses with doctorates quickly gravitate to university teaching or research positions they do not compete with the other levels of nurses for the patient care role (American Nurses Foundation, 1971: 177–180).

Although none of these educational levels translate exactly into different work roles they do complicate the stratification pattern because people with different amounts of training tend to bring different expectations about their role with them. In the hospital the three types of registered nurses all start as bedside nurses with little differentiation in the tasks they perform. All of them are eligible to become team leaders and are expected to supervise other registered nurses, practical nurses, aides and orderlies. However, the nurse with the baccalaureate degree is likely to move up faster in the administrative hierarchy or to leave the hospital for work in community health agencies where she may be allowed to better use her broader behavioral science background. The new influx of nurses with master's degrees further complicates the picture. Although many of them become administrators, some master's degree nurses are trained as clinical specialists and they are trying to find employment as skilled bedside practitioners. Relatively few hospitals have hired these specialists or when they have hired them they have given them administrative or teaching duties in addition to their patient care responsibilities.

THE CONSEQUENCES OF THE DIVISION OF LABOR

One of the consequences of the development of the nursing team has been to fragment and depersonalize nursing care. What was once the job of one nurse is now broken down into many roles. It is not unusual for a hospitalized patient to have contact with as many as thirty health workers in one day. He ordinarily sees a registered nurse only when he is acutely ill, when he needs a medication, or when he has a complex procedure performed. Some medications and routine procedures are given by the practical nurses while aides and orderlies carry out other procedures. Since each of the nursing teams works only an eight hour shift the patient is faced with a new group three times a day. Moreover he is also faced with an army of other medical and para-medical workers who visit his bedside or transport him around the hospital for consultations, tests, specialized procedures and to gather specimens from him. Seldom do any of these workers stay with him long enough for him to even learn their names, let alone feel relaxed enough to ask them any of the many questions which plague him. Moreover this fragmentation of nursing care comes at a time when physicians are in shorter supply in relation to demand than ever before so they can hardly take on more responsibility for personalizing care.

Nurses are not unaware of the highly fragmented nature of patient care. Many of them decry the fact that the role of the registered nurse, and increasingly that of the practical nurse as well, has changed to that of coordinator and administrator. The nursing literature is full of exhortations to the nurse to come back to the bedside to retain the essence of nursing (Bullough and Bullough, 1966: 95–158). The master's degree clinical specialist was developed to try to lessen some of the depersonalization of patient care by bringing the highly skilled nurse back to a primary care role (Bullough and Bullough, 1971: 1–82). Still the number of aides continues to increase much faster than any other category of nursing workers and stratification of nursing remains a problem. As the diagnostic and treatment procedures multiply, specialized workers tend to develop to carry out highly technical roles, and the trend towards fragmentation of care continues to grow.

Another consequence of the role differentiation which has occurred in nursing has been to depress nursing salaries, thus making nursing a less attractive occupation. Whether or not this is a good or bad consequence depends on your point of view since higher salaries for nurses would lead to increased medical costs. A Bureau of Labor survey done in 1946 revealed that the average nurse's salary of $2100 a year was lower than that of most teachers and social workers while nurses worked longer hours, more night shifts, more split shifts and received fewer fringe benefits than any other comparable group of female workers (United States Department of Labor: Bureau of Labor Statistics, 1947). At this point in time the roles of the nursing aide and licensed practical nurse developed. Customarily the practical nurse is paid three-fourths the salary of a registered nurse with the aides receiving even less so that salaries for the non-registered nurses were for many years often below the federal minimum wage level. This was possible because nurses, as well as hospital workers in general were originally excluded from the provisions of the law. During the next twenty years, while the cost of living doubled, the average salary for a registered nurse went up to approximately $5200 a year. In effect some gains were made but they were not enough to make nursing a really attractive occupation, particularly when new and better paying fields were opening up for women (American Nurses' Association, 1967: 137).

Unfortunately the American Nurses' Association had in 1946 made a no strike pledge in the unsophisticated hope that moral persuasion would be a strong enough incentive to motivate employers to raise nurses' salaries. Since hospitals were exempted from any obligation to participate in collective bargaining by the 1947 Taft-Hartley Labor Act, that hope proved even more unrealistic than might have been predicted. While it is a commonly held viewpoint that there was a shortage of nurses during this period, that shortage failed to push up salaries much beyond the increases in the cost of living. The lack of militance on the part of nurses coupled with the stratification of nursing made it possible for nursing positions to be filled by untrained aides, so that none of the usual consequences of a shortage followed. This failure of nursing salaries to increase has led the economist, Eli Ginzberg, to argue that there was and is no shortage of nurses; he holds that in a free market economy such a shortage would not last for more than twenty years (Ginzberg and Ostow 1969). Though his argument has merit, he fails to consider the traditional passivity that most women in the past have shown towards improving their own condition. Finally in 1966 the no strike pledge was abandoned by the California and New York nurses associations and was nationally repealed by the American Nurses' Association in 1968. Since that time there have been significant improvements in the salaries paid nurses, but the expandable aide population remains an economic reality controlling increases for both registered and practical nurses (Bullough, 1971).

Still the educational reforms that have taken place in nursing would have been much more difficult without the development of the nurses' aide and practical nurse. When higher standards started to make nursing education more expensive, many hospitals were willing to give up their schools and even to lobby for the establishment of nursing schools in educational institutions because they could replace student nurses with a less expensive source of labor. Even when nurses aides came under the federal minimum wage law in 1962, the cost of maintaining a nursing school seemed too high for many administrators, and they were willing to turn to paid workers to replace their students.

A fourth and final consequence of past moves to stratify nursing and other health occupations has been to set up a pattern of further role differentiation. It seems that complex organizations learn patterns of behavior just as people do, with the result that new problems tend to be solved in the same way that old problems were solved. There is now a growing public feeling of discontent with the present health care delivery system. Some of this feeling comes from the growing evidence that the United States is falling behind in the statistics which describe the well being of a nation such as maternal and infant mortality rates and life expectancy figures. For example, in 1950 United States had an infant mortality rate of 29.2 per 1000 live births which ranked us in sixth place in the world (Shapiro, Schlesinger, Nesbitt, Jr., 1968: 119). While that rate has continued to decline the reductions have not been as great as those of other industrialized countries. The latest available figures give us an infant mortality rate of 22.1, but there are at least fifteen other countries with lower infant mortality rates starting with Sweden whose rate is 12:9 (United Nations, Statisticial Office, 1969: 99–100). Poverty and a lack of medical care for the poor seem to be the chief causes of the higher American mortality rates as can be seen when diifferential rates within the American population are examined. For example the mortality rate for non-white infants is double that of white infants and the non-white maternal mortality rate is triple the white rate (United States Department of Health, Education and Welfare, 1967: 17).

Because of these inequities and the growing public awareness of them, reform of the health care delivery system seems imminent. However, one of the real barriers to any expansion of the system to cover more of the population with an adequate level of care is the acute shortage of physicians. It is not an actual decrease in physicians that is causing the shortage, but rather the revolutionary changes which have taken place in medicine which make it more complex and time consuming. The ratio of physicians to population remained constant at 149 per 100,000 persons from 1950 to 1963 but it increased slightly in 1967 to 157 (United States Public Health Service, 1970a). That increase, however, has been insufficient to meet the current levels of demand for care. Unlike the nursing shortage the doctor shortage has resulted in sharply rising incomes, particularly during the last decade. This probably indicates not only a more severe shortage, but also that physicians were able to exercise more power over the institutions.

While suggestions have been made for revising the medical curriculum to shorten the training time and medical schools have been urged to increase their enrollment (Carnegie Commission on Higher Education, 1970), these measures do not seem sufficient to solve the problem. It seems likely that the major solution to the problem of a shortage of physicians will come from greater use of non-physicians to perform medical tasks. In effect the present role of the physician will be differentiated into at least two component roles and another level of worker will develop. Although non-nurse physicians' assistants are being trained at Duke University and in six Medex programs (which admit discharged independent duty-corpsmen) it now seems that the major source of the new middle medical workers will be from nursing, partly because there are simply more nurses available than independent duty corpsmen. There are now at least twenty-three programs to train pediatric nurse practitioners in operation with another forty or so in some stage of development.[1] There are also similar programs opening up to train nurses in maternal, geriatric, psychiatric and family practice.

Using the experience of nursing as a model it is possible to speculate about the possible consequences for medicine of this new move towards role differentiation. It seems likely that more physicians will be pushed into supervisory and coordinating roles as well as the highly technical medical jobs, while nurse practitioners and ex-corpsmen trained as physicians' assistants take on some of the responsibility for primary care of patients. Undoubtedly this move away from direct patient care will cause some discontent among physicians just as it has among nurses. Another possible consequence of stratification may be that reform of medical education may be facilitated. If the new paid medical workers could relieve residents and interns of some of their responsibilities for service, the heavy work week and the long years spent by these trainees could be re-evaluated in terms of educational objectives and perhaps be shortened and made more functional. And finally, it seems reasonable to predict that if these new workers are utilized to the extent that the problem of shortage is solved the relative incomes of physicians will fall. Supporting such a possibility are two other related trends. More physicians are becoming salaried workers rather than individual entrepreneurs so they have less independent power. Also the women's liberation movement is causing female para-medical workers, including nurses, to demand a larger share of the health care dollar. It will be interesting to watch the coming developments in the next decade.

NOTE

[1] National Center for Health Services Research and Development, "Health Manpower: An R. & D. Approach," *Focus* No. 5, Summer, 1970, pp. 7–9. These courses are developing so fast that it is difficult to keep an accurate count. See also Priscilla M. Andrews and Alfred Yankauer "The Pediatric Nurse Practitioner, The Growth of the Concept," *American Journal of Nursing* 71 (March, 1971): 504–506. They located 42 nurse practitioner courses in a telephone survey.

Bud B. Khleif

Professionalization of Psychiatric Residents*

This paper examines the training career of a group of thirty psychiatric residents and the three-year process during which they are transformed from medical physicians to psychiatric ones. The data consist of interviews and field notes. The paper is centered on the viewpoints of the residents themselves. It is concerned with issues of autonomy and constraint in the resident's work.

The training setting is that of a short-term, intensive treatment hospital that has three functions: training, treatment, and research. Among the training staff, there is tension between those who define themselves as Freudian, psychoanalytic, or "dynamically oriented" and those who are committed to social psychiatry. In the first year of training, the resident is exposed to social psychiatrists; in the second, to Freudian ones; and the third, to those whose specialty is neuropsychiatry and psychosomatic medicine. Because nurses run the wards and the resident regards them as having inferior status, there is a conflict throughout training. The resident especially resents the nurses because they, together with the promoters of social psychiatry in the hospital, the clinical director and his staff, form a solid coalition against him. They are a clique that controls his work.

In this connection, Merton's concept of the "role-set" can be useful

* Data for this paper were gathered in the course of the author's work as a sociologist in the research department of a mental health foundation. The author is indebted to Charles B. Wilkinson and Richard L. Pentecost for helpful suggestions in the initial stage of the paper.

for examining the social structure of the hospital. For each institutional status, such as that of psychiatric resident, there is a set of groups that determine the relationship feeding into and out of the status, a structure of competing power, a "role-set" complementing the particular status (Merton, 1957a). The hospital can thus be seen as an intricate web of role sets, all partially intertwined and partially integrated. In the three years of training, the problem of the resident is to figure out the balance of power in his role set and to interpret its expectations, to safeguard his autonomy by insulating himself from one part of his role-set and disregarding another.

Professionalization, as adult socialization, depends upon structure and culture, that is, an authority and belief system. The trainer's status and values are presumed to be inherently superior; those of the trainee, inferior. In this regard, professional training is "ceremonious fighting" (Waller, 1961: 10–11, 109). It is but a clash between the trainee's quest for autonomy and the trainer's for compliance; a clash fraught with painful experiences as Hughes and others have emphasized (Hughes, 1959; Mechanic, 1962b; Towle, 1964; Selby and Woods, 1966). From the medical student's point of view, for example, medical training is but a series of stressful situations and regimentations that seem to be necessary for a physician's identity formation (Walter, 1965). From the law student's point of view, his training is but a progression from firm to loose institutional demands and from prescribed to elective courses (Ricarde, 1965). The first year business administration student often sees his training completely devoid of personal freedom; one likens his school to a boot camp (Ullyot, 1965). In such training situations, the trainee's peer group, as several observers have emphasized, is of crucial importance in stress reduction, morale building, and identity transformation (Evan, 1963; Coles, 1966; Geer et al., 1968). Obviously, life is with people. The trainee needs an enclave to interpret crises for him, a group of peers that form Gemeinschaft within his training Gesellschaft to share his triumphs and setbacks.

George Herbert Mead's (1934) theory of the self provides us with a clue as to how the individual is turned into a new person, how his frame of reference is altered. Meanings, as Mead points out, are not inherent in acts or objects, but are imputed to them in the course of the person's interaction with others and the consensus he senses is shared by others (Blumer, 1966). A person perceives and defines himself as he believes others perceive and define him (Mead, 1934: 135–178). The person "must rely on others to complete the picture of him of which he is allowed to paint only certain parts" (Goffman, 1956: 493). In other words, the trainers define for the trainee what is desirable or undesirable; his behavior is ratified through the labels and interpretations they use; his progress rests on their definitions.

Psychiatric training, like all intense *resocialization* situations, is a process in which the psychiatric resident learns a new set of concepts to redefine illness and health at the same time that his allegiance to organic medicine is being systematically attacked. This is similar to religious conversion and to the process of acculturation into drugs, whereby a non-user becomes a marijuana or LSD user (Becker, 1963: 41–58; 1970: 307–327). As formulated by Becker, this process consists of the following stages: stereotype breaking and suppression of old concepts; provision of new concepts as a stable set of categories to be constantly used for interpretation; redefinition of the situation to point out errors, heresies, subtleties, methods of defense against outsiders, and inherent pleasures; reassurance, encouragement, and the urging of the trainee to become a connoisseur of the new ideology and experiences. These phenomena represent an attempt at making the trainee into a new person. He is confronted with them simultaneously rather than serially. By viewing these as foci of socialization, one purpose of this paper is to clarify in some detail how the psychiatric resident progresses from a novice to a connoisseur.

THE FIRST-YEAR PROGRAM

First-year residents are trained through treatment teams (composed of resident, psychologist, nurse, social worker, and staff psychiatrist), supervisory conferences, clinics, and reading seminars. The tight weekly schedule of the first-year resident consists of the following: (1) Admission team, two hours; (2) screening clinic supervision, one hour; (3) treatment team, eight hours; (4) individual supervision, one hour; (5) case-presentation conference, two hours every other week; (6) seminar on interviewing techniques, two hours every other week; (7) patient discharge interview, one hour; (8) after-care clinic, two hours; (9) neurology conference, two hours; (10) reading seminar, two hours; (11) visiting speakers program, one hour; (12) joint-conference with the staff of the Department of Neurology and Department of Psychiatry at a neighboring teaching hospital, one hour every two weeks; and (13) on-call duty, *every third night*. The first year resident works one weekend and is off two weekends.

What are the initial reactions of first year residents to their training schedule? During the first two weeks at the hospital, residents are eager to work and to learn. By the end of the first month, however, they start complaining about being overburdened with work—it is a heavy schedule of conferences and duties that they cannot escape. Residents resent doing physicals for the psychologists' as well as their own patients. At the after-care clinic, first-year residents see eighty to one hundred patients per night, which gives each resident eight to eighteen patients. Residents feel rushed because of their load of patients. Indeed, all throughout their first year, residents complain that they have no time for leisure, for any outside activities beyond the hospital. Especially in relation to the on-call duty every third night, first-year residents feel they are taken advantage of. They resent the second-year residents who are on call only once a month, and third-year residents who are freed from any on-call duty. Throughout the first year, there are emotional flare-ups between the first and second year residents. In the beginning of the year, first-year residents cooperate among themselves in such matters as doing physicals for one another's patients or occasionally taking an on-call duty for one another. But by the middle of the year, such cooperation ceases and tension within the group and aggression against second-year residents and others become noticeable.

Introduction of first-year residents to psychiatric terminology means that they are asked to discard their old occupational lenses for diagnosis and disease and to acquire new ones. They are required to view what used to be familiar occupational events in a new way to adopt new explanations. The initial reaction of first-year residents to psychiatric terminology is to make fun of such terminology: "Have you ever seen an ego walking down the street?"; "so the patient has an ulcer because he's obsessive-compulsive—I never knew that!"; "communication, communication—so mental illness is due to 'interactive events' in the life of the patient!"; and so forth. Residents complain of the rigorous supervision they receive and that "organicity" in the new liturgy of diagnoses is to be somewhat regarded as a dirty word! They resent the belittling of old familiar medical diagnoses and the reduction of explanation to "dependency needs" and the "Oedipal conflict." Some of the residents, former general practitioners, who do not comply with the deliberate use of the new terminology in discussion of cases and who find it futile to "buck" their individual supervisor drop out at the end of the first year. Residents trained in internal medicine or pathology and regarding themselves as medically superior to the general practitioners among the first-year group, experience even more pressure from their supervisors and feel that their supervisors are out to stamp out all explanations except the psychiatric. In bouts of aggression within the group itself and between it and the staff and rest of the residents, first-year residents, however, begin to use the new psychiatric terminology to diagnose themselves and others; the terminology becomes a part of their world-view.

The feeling of being overburdened with duties and of being required to renounce familiar medical explanations in favor of new ones are but secondary issues to the main issue around which the first year resident's experience is organized—that of status reduction. From a full fledged professional—a physician—the resident becomes a student, a novice. The first stage of status reduction is that of "culture shock," a confrontation that forces the resident to re-examine himself, his values, and the major emphases of his old occupation. He is forced to see what he is not, as a step towards seeing what he might wish to become. He undergoes an identity crisis. He is marginal to the new group. He is a stranger in limbo between occupational groups. The resident is forced into making sense out of the new occupational experience, into making choices on a new basis, into expanded awareness. From being shocked, the resident becomes enlightened—enlightened as to want to join the new group of healers, seek a different specialty, or go back to general practice.

All socialization situations seem to require that the initiate who is to undergo attitude change be placed at the bottom or near the bottom of the social hierarchy. Necessarily, a status and power differentiation is maintained between trainers and trainees. The trainee is considered a supplicant awaiting social, cultural, or professional salvation. This is true, for example, in the family, monastery, school, mental hospital, prison, and the army. Psychologists might say that this provides the trainee with "identificatory learning" or an "achievement motivation," an incentive to climb a particular ladder of success. Dornbusch, in his study of the military academy, suggests that the "assignment of low status . . . *requires that there be a loss of identity in terms of pre-existing statuses . . .* The role of the cadet must supersede other roles the individual has been accustomed to play" (1955: 317, emphasis added). Goffman discusses this loss of previous identity as a process of role-dispossession, of severance from earlier attachments, and of enforced deference, deface-ment, and mortification (1961a: 14–35). The literature on monastic train-ing abounds with references to the obedience, reverence, and mortifica-tion demanded of low status novitiates towards their religious superiors (St. Benedict, 1948; Sister Mary Francis, 1956). What differentiates intense professionalization from its mild variety (e.g., that of school teachers and librarians) is the presence of clear-cut rites of passage, of ordeals for induction. In essence, intense professionalization is but a cycle of crises and conceptual hurdles, a symbolic-death-and-rebirth progression, an irrevocable crossing of membership thresholds between groups (Khleif, 1971).

It can be said—to borrow a psychiatric term—that the physician comes to psychiatric training with a "presenting" professional culture, that of general medicine. Unless he is thoroughly decontaminated at the outset of his training, his psychiatric trainers regard him as remaining "fixated" at the organic level of medicine and exhibiting "regression" symptoms and "counter transference" to organicity. It can thus be argued that a training period's purpose is not so much to teach skills and facts as to ensure that the trainee becomes one of the in-group, i.e., becomes committed to its values and ways of doing things. In essence, professional training is but an initiation into a fraternity, a commitment to an ideology (Hughes, 1958: 116–130; Jaco, 1958: 288–350; Seeman and Evans, 1962a; Berger, 1964: 211–241; Hughes, 1970: 178–179).

In their study of psychiatric training, Masserman *et al.* (1949: 362–369) speak of the psychiatric residents' "morass of bewilderment" and their "futile flounderings in misunderstood psychoanalytic theory and misapplied analytic therapy." The authors, themselves trainers, state that "often enough our most difficult initial task is to clear away the misinformation and prejudices in the minds of our residents." In Goffman's terms, the "stripping of the self" is a prelude to an acquisition of a new identity; the new identity is seen as a "rebirth" (Goffman, 1961a: 66–70, 161–169). *It is thus important that there be no competing definitions: "Organicity Is Out!"* Hence, early in his psychiatric training, the resident begins to feel as though he was beginning an internship without having gone through medical school (Sharaf and Levinson, 1964: 139).

The harshest encounter in the first-year resident's experience is that of the treatment team—composed of the resident, a staff psychiatrist, a nurse, a psychologist, and a social worker; a team that meets for four mornings every week. The reactions of the first year residents to the team members could be depicted as follows:

(a) Learning that all team members, regardless of status, are to be regarded as equally important. "You learn a new philosophy: The doctor alone did not take care of the patient; every person on the team was as important as the doctor, the social worker as important as the supervisor (staff psychiatrist). The group was supposed to function as a unit, but we had a powerful leader and, without him, the group did not function at all—it disintegrated as soon as he stepped out of the room."

(b) Conflict of roles between the resident and the psychologist. "The resident is the patient's liaison with the team, but the psychologist had his own patients. The resident did all the medical work for the psychologist. When the patient met the resident and the psychologist together, he was confused because he thought the resident was his doctor, not the psychologist—because the resident had given him a physical exam. Later the patient learned to look at the psychologist as his doctor, as the person to work with."

(c) Resident has to compete with nurses for status—persons he had learned to consider of low status; he feels they block his access to patients. "The doctor is the representative of the hospital to the patient; here it is an entirely different approach. When learning medicine—it is like the army—the resident would be responsible for the care of the patient, the nurses would be responsible to the resident, and the resident to the staff supervisor. Here, the resident has no say except as one vote on the team . . . In the hazy role of the resident, responsibility is demanded of him for the care of the patient, but the wherewithall, the armament, is not supplied. That is what I mean by a 'bind'; the resident cannot use his judgment except through mediation by the team."

On two occasions at least, one of the first-year residents tried to counteract a decision by the nurses but was "put in his place." The first incident involved a teenage girl who had been told to go bowling with the rest of the patients on the ward during day-time. The girl's dress had holes in it and she was sensitive about it and did not want to accompany the rest of the patients. The attendant, as instructed by the nurse, tried to haul the girl into the elevator, but the resident ordered him to let her go back to the ward. The reaction of the clinical director and his assistant (who were also treatment team chairmen) to this incident was to tell the resident that his action was "interference with the nursing command" and that "no matter how bad the decision of the nursing personnel was, the thing should not be handled on the spot by the resident, but should be later discussed in team meeting." The second incident involves patients who one Sunday were told by the nurses to go to church. One of the patients did not want to go and complained to the resident, who made arrangements for her to stay. As a result of the two incidents, the nurses planned to teach the resident a lesson. During a psychodrama practice session, the assistant director of nurses took the part of the alter ego for the ward nurse whose decision the resident had overruled and humiliated the resident in front of the group. First-year residents quickly learned to fear what Garfinkel (1956) has called "successful degradation ceremonies." It should be added that all along in the reading seminar, the resident is not only introduced to social psychiatry as dogma but also to emphasis on the status equality of all members of the treatment team, especially the nurses. He begins to realize that he can disregard this emphasis at his own peril.

Since the American Board of Psychiatry and Neurology requires that the resident has experience with chronic hospitalized patients, the first-year resident is assigned for three months to a state hospital in another town. He comes back to his home hospital for half a day every week to see patients at the screening clinic and attend the night-time seminar, the reading seminar on social psychiatry. At the state hospital, the resident confronts a discrepancy between the "total push" approach of the state hospital with its electric shock and reliance on drugs (that are taboos in his training), and the social psychiatry approach he had learned at his home hospital. Hence the importance of the reading seminar as a socializing situation, of the resident's return to home-base for clarification of issues (e.g., arguments pro and contra shock therapy) and for enlargement of perspective on social psychiatry—that is, for guidance as well as prevention of occupational "regression" or heresy!

In addition to the ideological discrepancy between the social psychiatric component in the resident's training and what he sees done at the state hospital, the resident experiences a discrepancy in his status, that is, in the way he is given responsibility for making decisions at both places. At the state hospital, the resident has a doctor's, not a student's status. He is in charge of a ward and directions are given by him. The "therapeutic plan" is solely determined by him. The training sojourn at the state hospital, among other things, enables the resident to examine his ocupational situation and to decide whether to "stick it out" and finish his training or move on to another specialty.

In addition to assignment at the state hospital, first-year residents are also assigned in rotation to spend around three months at the day hospital division of their home hospital. Here, the social atmosphere is more congenial and informal; nurses wear street clothes; the patients are more tractable; and everybody tries to maintain a sort of school or family spirit. First-year residents at this juncture in their training feel they are given more freedom and responsibility—their identity as *doctors* is enhanced.

THE SECOND-YEAR PROGRAM

During the second year, psychiatric training consists entirely of out-patient assignments. The weekly schedule of the second-year residents consists of the following: (1) Screening clinic, three hours; supervision, one hour; (2) individual therapy, eight to ten hours; supervision, two hours; (3) one family therapy case, one hour; supervision, one hour every other week; (4) two group therapy sessions, two hours; supervision, one and a half hours; (5) continuous case seminar, two hours;

(6) therapy conference, two hours; (7) reading seminar, one and a half hours; (8) group therapy seminar, one and a half hours; (9) visiting speakers program, one hour; (10) administrative staff meeting, one hour; (11) joint conference with the staff of the Department of Neurology and Department of Psychiatry at a neighboring teaching hospital, one hour every two weeks; and (12) on-call duty, one night a month.

In comparison with the first-year, the second-year resident feels more at ease with the institution—he has survived the first year's ordeal and knows the ground rules of the "joint." He has accepted that nurses run the wards and does not interfere with their authority. He finds he has more responsibility and status:

> "(The clinical director, his assistant,) and the nurses determined the social structure of the hospital; residents didn't have much of a hand in it—they worked in it, under it. Last year, you didn't get the perception of it, of what was happening on the ward. This year, I have a better grasp of what's happening in Inpatient. This year, the resident has more authority; he is a planner of group therapy, but he is not a planner of the social organization of the ward—that is strongly held by the administrative people."

The second-year resident also discovers that his first year experience on the team was not without value, that he has picked up some of the team leader's supervisory techniques, especially as applied to nurses. Other reactions of the second-year residents to their training include remarks that they have more leisure and more time to spend with their families in the second year, and they feel more relaxed: "Things that used to infuriate me about the psychology department are not that important this year. You know, you order a blood test or medication, but they think 'order' is a command or a punitive demand. Psychologists who have 'grown up' in state hospitals don't like psychiatrists!" Another second-year resident, in summing up his experience, said, "I feel better this year; I can deal with the patients directly."

In the second year of training, one of the noticeable phenomena among residents is that of the "true believer." Second-year residents appear to be more serious about their studies and try to come to grips with the psychoanalytic literature. They hardly joke about psychoanalytic terminology, contrary to what they used to do occasionally as first-year residents. In contrast with the first year, which is heavily laden with social psychiatry, the second year is devoted to psychoanalytic literature and the trainers are mostly "analytically oriented." Freud becomes a demigod for second-year residents and they can quote him chapter and verse.

THIRD-YEAR PROGRAM

The requirements for the third year of training are more flexible. The schedule of the third-year residents is basically organized in six-month blocks rather than weekly or monthly. It consists of the following activities: (1) Individual therapy: at least two patients carried over from the second year, plus an hour for supervision per week; (2) six months of neurology and consultation service at a neighboring general hospital, divided into two blocks, three months each; (3) six months full-time at the Department of Child Psychiatry; and (4) three months reading seminar devoted to psychosomatic medicine, four months child psychiatry, and three months of thought in psychiatry and medical psychology.

Having been treated as a student during his first year of training, and as a proto-colleague during his second, the third-year resident is treated as a colleague by the staff. He himself feels he has "arrived." Those around him build up his identity as a psychiatrist. His opinion is sought by first and second-year residents. In his contact with medical residents during his consultation service at the general hospital and in his treatment of psychosomatic cases, his identity as an "M.D." is reestablished; the two components of his training, "organicity" and psychic explanation, partially severed during his first two years of training, are now rejoined. The third-year resident, having forgotten part of his general medical knowledge, re-establishes his interest in it: "I had forgotten anything beyond giving physicals and treating colds (laughter) . . . In the last three years, I had really forgotten I had an M.D. after my name. I am proud of it."

The third-year residents have no on-call duties. They have more leisure—"This year I have time I can call my own." Some of the residents begin their own analysis with one of the analysts in town, the three hundred hours of psychotherapy recommended as a professioinal requirement for therapists. Freud ceases to be a demigod for residents in the third year of their training; they have discovered Harry Stack Sullivan and psychosomatic medicine and become eclectic. They can even joke about the way they were so intensely wrapped up in psychodynamic thinking in their second year. As one third-year resident remarked, "I thought I would indulge myself before going into analysis, so I bought this Austin-Healey. I would like to follow the 'pleasure principle' before I get to the 'reality principle'!"

Some of the residents go into further training in psychoanalytic therapy after they finish their three years of training at the hospital. Others are tapped for positions as staff psychiatrist in the adult or the child guidance divisions of the hospital—a gesture of esteem after the torture of the first year.

CONCLUSION

Professional training is a blend of both coercive and permissive practices. Training can be described as an obstacle course or an endurance test, a "career" in the sense of a race course, a maze into which the trainee is thrust (Hughes, 1963: 1–2). Goffman has described the mental hospital as a total institution for the patient (1961a: 1–124): It can be said that it is also a total institution for the first year psychiatric resident (the neophyte), a semi-total one for the second-year resident (the proto-colleague), and an open one for the third-year resident (the colleague).

Occupational commitment can be considered a series of side bets and of glimpses and attainment of "scores" or rewards (Becker, 1960: 32–40; Geer, 1968: 221–234). Obviously not all residents react to the training situation with its inherent fighting and struggle in the same manner. As their situation unfolds from coercion to freedom, they can be said to go through three stages of orientation:

(a) *From the organic to the astrological,* that is, from emphasis on laboratory tests and X-rays to an emphasis on complexes and needs.

(b) *From the astrological to the Calvinistic,* that is the stage of the "true believer," to his belief in conceptual predestination: "In the beginning was psychoanalysis, and psychoanalysis was made into Freud!" The resident at this stage is a walking library and a ready source for checking printed information.

(c) *From the Calvinistic to the Unitarian,* that is when the resident discovers other prophets besides Freud, e.g., Harry Stack Sullivan, and begins to entertain contrary opinions and to take pride in knowing general medicine in addition to psychiatry. As one third-year resident put it, "In the last three years, I had really forgotten I had an M.D. after my name; I am proud of it."

Each of the aforementioned stages generally coincides with a year of training. However, a few residents go through the three stages even in their first year. The first year, and the first stage associated with it, seems to be crucial; from one sixth to one third of the residents drop out at the end of the first year, returning to general medicine or taking up a different residency in another hospital. Those who survive the first year seem to have a lot at stake; they have made their side bets and can glimpse the finish line.

Obviously, graduates of a professional training program cannot be considered uniform units; they assimilate its ideology in different degrees. Seeley hypothesizes that among psychiatric practitioners, the following types may be found: "Those who thought they could practice by mother wit and in the light of nature; those who thought they could practice by merely adding knowledge about psychodynamic theory and consulting room practice; and those who thought that all that had to be considered was their own once-and-for-all analysis" (Vidich *et al.*, 1964: 160). Follow-up studies relating psychiatric training to practice are needed. One wonders, for example, to what extent, in actual practice, different psychiatrists adapt differently to the "vocabulary of ill motives" in which they had been trained, as Mills has termed it, and to "motive mongering" vis-à-vis clients (Mills, 1940: 904–913; 1943: 165–180).

Professional training, especially psychiatric training, highlights the fact that what is essential about man, perhaps, is that he is a symbol-maker, symbol-manipulator and symbol-consumer. He mystifies and demystifies, mythologizes and demythologizes, in a never ending circle. Fiction is important for his everyday life; he treats abstractions *as if* they were concrete (Vaihinger, 1912). It seems that, regardless of his pretensions to enlightenment, man continues, as Dostoevski has said, to be moved by "myth, miracle and authority," two of which at least, seems to be essential to professionalization.

Analysis

Occupational Control

Two main areas in which the occupation can control its autonomy are in the tasks performed and the way the occupation is organized. In this section, both types of control are examined. Certain occupations have more or less autonomy at both the role and group levels according to the nature of the tasks performed. The obvious example is the mass production worker who has little control over his work because the tasks are defined by the organization. Only through sabotage and work slow-down can a worker on the line have any control at the role level. At the group level, the organization of the occupation itself becomes important. Unions can and often do work for greater control over the work situation for their members though this is not necessarily their main function. However, no matter how powerful and strong a union is, the tasks performed are important mechanisms of work control. In this section, the work tasks of the various occupations will be the major unit of analysis. Several of the occupations, the psychiatric resident and the ballet dancer in particular, are presented such that organization of the work at the group level is the most important variable for the way autonomy is limited. Both of these tasks, dancing and the practice of psychiatry, under certain defined circumstances can be very autonomous. However, at the recruitment and training stage the organization of the occupation helps to define limits on this freedom.

Our main thesis is that for all occupations each of the controls (societal and cultural, organizational, occupational and client control) interact in various degrees. The result of this interaction is greater or lesser autonomy for an occupational group and for occupational roles. This has been demonstrated in the sections on societal and organizational control. The work task is often neglected by sociologists who put more emphasis on outside controls such as status, prestige and organizational context. On the other hand, those interested in job satisfaction, the professional status of an occupation, and alienation have considered the task, possibly even over-emphasizing the task, in relationship to other forms of control. Part of our purpose, therefore, is to put the task in perspective with the other concepts.

THE SALESWOMAN

The tasks of the saleswoman are to: 1) sell merchandise to a customer; 2) keep the merchandise in order; and 3) perform related jobs such as taking inventory of stock. The act of selling and serving customers is the most important. The more a saleswoman sells, the more she is rewarded both with financial success and status. The main emphasis in Melville Dalton's paper on saleswomen is the phenomenon of ratebusting. A number of investigators have studied ratebusting in industrial settings (see Dalton's paper). Ratebusting is possible only when the worker is rewarded on a piece basis. The term suggests that one worker is turning out more pieces of work than others doing the same task. For saleswomen, ratebusting is rewarded by success, power and autonomy. While there may be some negative social sanctions, such as resentment and unpopularity with co-workers, the rewards are financial and social as well. (For instance, the saleswoman in Dalton's study who made the most sales had the highest income because income was determined by the number and amount of sales.)

In addition, the ratebuster had more free time away from the job, and more autonomy over job-related decisions. She was free to decide where to stand in order to able to be the first to receive customers and was granted the freedom to decide whether merchandise should be put aside for special customers. Also, she was allowed to put merchandise aside for future sale when it would be reduced in price. In that sales situation the task encouraged ratebusting and gave the ratebuster a superior position over her colleagues. Ratebusting then becomes earned autonomy. Essentially, the task of selling, because of the direct interaction with the client, cannot be supervised closely. Decisions concerning who one serves and does not serve, and whether one does the housekeeping chores can be, and are, closely supervised and controlled. The saleswomen in the situation described by Dalton is not autonomous at the group level, but at the role level certain sales personnel seem to have earned this autonomy by manipulating the situation in their favor.

THE WIREMAN

John Brewer's paper provides an example of how the task contributes to occupational autonomy. Skills needed for different aspects of the work required in construction has led to informal specialization of one group of construction workers. The wiremen are electrical construction workers who perform a specialized task that is not officially recognized within the light and power company in which they work. These men have become specialists in the technique of wiring small, intricate circuits. While this is not their only work, when extensive wiring of this type is to be done, a wireman is assigned to the job. The interviews Brewer did with wiremen reveal that a major attraction of the role is the greater control over their work and work relationships which wiring gives them. Because of their specialization, wiremen are rarely asked to do much other work, especially the heavier and dirty work. The wireman could work independently of the crew leader who would simply provide him the necessary circuit diagrams. This autonomy at the role level illustrates how informal norms can operate in a formal structure and are dependent on that structure.

The autonomy enjoyed by the wiremen is not a form of particularism. When men who are specialized as wiremen do other tasks for the construction team they are treated as others doing similar tasks. Performing the services of wireman, the role itself, gives the wireman special privileges (in the form of exemption from unpleasant work and more autonomy) but as people they did not get special recommendations for bonuses and promotion. In other words, the rewards were attached to the work role and not to other benefits which seemed to be judged on different criteria.

A possible reason for this is that wiremen are not an occupational group in the formal sense. Brewer is talking about a case of informal specialization. Although there is agreement that the regular and exclusive work performed by wiremen entitles them to certain rights because of their special skills, these rights do not extend into the formal sphere. Thus wiremen, because they are not a formally organized work group, do not have control over certain aspects of work. In order to get special privileges at the group level, it might be necessary to be organized and to have the title officially recognized. Thus wiremen have autonomy at the role level but are not an occupational group at the organizational level.

Norma Shosid emphasizes the unscheduled encounter between the client and librarian. Hers is one of the few papers in this volume which considers the actual interaction between the client and the worker. Shosid points out problems in trying to please clients and how many factors affect the encounter. While the librarian would like to be in control of the interaction, structural conditions make the encounter between the librarian and the client both variable and problematic. The client has considerable control because he defines the subject to be investigated by the librarian. Even though the client seeks advice, there is no way to know if the advice is followed. Possibly the client may be better informed in the subject area than the librarian. Thus the reference encounter is extremely unpredictable.

In the case of the librarian the nature of the task is more important than the organization of the occupation or actual work setting. Some librarians are in specialized fields and have knowledge and skills that may be unfamiliar to the layman. An example of this would be the scientific librarian or one who is familiar with information retrieval by the use of computers. However, even the special librarian is dealing with a client who has knowledge in his area specialty. For those who work with the general public, Shosid's examples are most fitting. In daily contact with people of all kinds, the public librarian is unable to select his clientele and must deal with a variety of requests. In this respect, the work of the librarian is much like the cab driver or the saleswoman. The tasks to be performed become an important consideration which influences work. Regardless of how well organized librarians are as a group, informal control at the role level is with the client.

At the group level, librarians are comparable to other occupational groups Etzioni (1969) calls semi-professionals. The librarian must work in some organizational setting. The body of knowledge associated with the occupation is not limited to the occupational group. In fact, many scholars in specific fields are more knowledgeable about bibliographic sources than the librarian. Group autonomy is regulated primarily by the organizational setting and the social context of the work. At the role level, the client is powerful. Structural division of the occupation into various groups, the relationship of the occupation to technology, and other issues have not been explored in this paper. In the sociology of work, these are important. Since Shosid is drawing on her personal experiences as a librarian, her paper has methodological limitations. While one cannot generalize from her findings, she does provide useful insights into what happens in the real world of the public librarian.

THE MUSICIAN

Robert Faulkner provides another example of the point made in the previous section. Musicians in an orchestra do not have autonomy at the group level. Faulkner agrees that the performer can have little control over major decisions concerning his work. In the symphony orchestra he studied, musicians had to play under a number of guest conductors. The conductor decides what music is to be played and how the music is to be played. Faulkner does note that at the role level limited autonomy is possible because of the interdependence of the orchestra leader on the player. Here autonomy is defined as non-compliance which is an informal process operating at the role level. The industrial worker who sabotages production, the bureaucrat who does not carry out company policy as well as the baseball player who throws spitballs provide other examples of how control as non-compliance can be exercised at the role level. These examples empirically demonstrate that role autonomy is a different dimension from group autonomy. At the role level, such autonomy is always tied to the way the task is performed. It can become institutionalized in varied forms of activity.

While musicians may recognize the authority of conductors to choose music, they consider conductors to be interfering when they claim expertise in the prescription of performance style or on solo work. Lore and custom define the extent of legitimate authority over a range of role behaviors. Compliance then, according to Faulkner, becomes problematic. Musicians do not automatically give the conductor the right to direct the total performance. Within a work situation where authority does come from above and where the flow of communication is from the podium downward, there still exists the opportunity for non-compliance and for decision-making at the role level by the individual players. Non-compliance or compliance, therefore, is not only dependent on the organization of the tasks themselves, but also how musicians define the situation. An issue not studied by Faulkner is how far a musician can go before non-compliance is negatively sanctioned.

Faulkner's paper is important since he demonstrates that the system of authority is more than a pattern of static roles and statuses. He sees the orchestra as a network of interacting human beings. This is a necessary perspective when one considers autonomy in all occupations. The orchestra, the baseball team, and the ballet troupe all appear to be controlled from above with little authority or autonomy left to the people playing or dancing. However, in each of these highly skilled occupations, because managers, orchestra leaders and ballet masters, are dependent on the skill of their performers, some autonomy must be granted at the role level. The task demands that autonomy at the group level be limited for team success. But in order to do creative and skilled tasks, some autonomy must be institutionalized at the role level. Autonomy as non-compliance becomes part of the occupational culture and is expected behavior under certain circumstances.

THE BALLET DANCER

Ronald Federico provides another example of how the structure of the occupation can affect the degree of autonomy an occupational group holds. He suggests that ballet (in the United States) does not meet performing needs because of its informal recruiting and training procedures. Differential recruitment favoring women and lack of clearly defined training opportunities does not often result in actual performance by the dancer. It encourages political intrigue where dancers are rewarded for skills other than dancing.

Federico suggests that in any ballet troupe, regardless of the way the occupation is structured, the nature of the dance itself requires the dancer to subjugate himself to the needs of the total production. This is a strain on both personal and artistic autonomy. We have noted earlier that the same situation exists by necessity for the baseball player and the orchestra musician. The unique experiences of the American ballet dancer is tied to the way the occupation is structured. It is not only the demands of working in a group which requires cooperation but also the problems of finding a career in a very uncertain occupational structure which gives the American ballet dancer so little autonomy. The situation is one where early training encourages autonomy because selection is almost a choice situation. This is replaced by the constrictions of a structure which definitely discourages autonomous participation when the career choice is made.

THE BASEBALL PLAYER

The baseball player has limited control over his work and personal life. Charnofsky provides an example of how occupational tasks limit autonomy over work and non-work activities. Occupational influence over non-occupational aspects of a person's life is not being explored in our analysis although several authors have addressed this question in a peripheral way (see Peters, Bernard and Epstein for example). Charnofsky makes this a major emphasis. The tasks performed by a baseball player, by necessity, must limit his personal freedom. Other occupational groups where physical skill and condition are important attributes probably have similar limitations. Such occupations provide excellent examples of why the professional model of occupational stratification is of limited use. For example, the baseball player receives payment for performing tasks which are highly specialized, and which can be performed by only a few skilled people in the society. In order to become a baseball player there is a relatively long socialization process which for most players starts in childhood. The occupational group has community recognition with relatively high prestige and status (although this prestige is attached usually to the team rather than the occupation). Players are committed to the game. One might say that the baseball player is performing a public service by providing entertainment and pleasure. Given these characteristics, it might be expected that baseball players would have autonomy at the group level.

The reality is that baseball players control little of their work at group level and almost none at the role level. At the group level the baseball players are organized professionally. Their organization was powerful enough to sustain a strike for several weeks in the spring of 1972 resulting in the postponement of the opening of the season. By striking the players gained some added benefits but control over schedules, trades of personnel, and number of games to be played in a season still remains with the owners.

At the role level some players have more control than others because of their popularity which is often related to their skill. This is another example of earned autonomy. For most players, decisions are made by the managers, coaches and umpires. As mentioned earlier, in any group where the occupational task is performed primarily in concert with others, autonomy is limited regardless of the degree of skill and knowledge required. This may explain why the model of a professional occupation has so little relevance to team players, musicians in orchestras, and others who perform tasks as part of a group effort.

THE LANDMAN

The landman is an unusual occupation. Petroleum landwork consists of ascertaining the availability of land open for oil exploration in a given area. In order to acquire the land for drilling the landman must determine the legitimacy of the title claim of the alleged owner. (See Bryant for further details.) The duties, however, include more than simply acquiring rights to explore and drill. Finding the actual owner of the land is often very complex because of the laws in the United States concerning ownership. The need for men to do these tasks in the United States results from a mobile population, the absence of entail and primogeniture laws, and laws permitting land and minerals to be conveyed separately.

Because of the complexity of land and mineral ownership, a specialized occupational group was required to carry out the tasks of acquisition of rights. The landman provides an example of an occupation which has autonomy by definition. The occupation developed because the tasks were too complex to be handled by the uninformed. Oil company managers and freelance speculators do not have knowledge of how to acquire land. Thus the task itself has to be autonomous, free from control, simply because the skills and knowledge possessed are not easily acquired. These are specialized and unknown to the general population.

The landman provides an example of autonomy at the role level which can lead to the emergence of group autonomy. Bryant calls this professionalization of the occupation as do so many others. As Moore (1970) notes it is group autonomy which is an important characteristic of the professional occupation. Bryant has provided an example of the process of a group obtaining the necessary autonomy. This paper shows how autonomy is tied to special knowledge and tasks, and how the organization in which landmen work adapts and encourages certain kinds of occupational specialties. Because of the dependence of the organization on the special skills of the landman, autonomy is possible even when the worker must perform tasks with organizational support.

NURSING

The tasks of the nurse are both complex and differentiated. As Bonnie and Vern Bullough show, not only can a nurse perform a number of different tasks but there are a number of different kinds of nurses, each with a specialized occupation. Basically the nurse is concerned with various aspects of patient care and record keeping. In the article by Bullough and Bullough the word autonomy does not appear. They are interested in the tasks nurses perform which contribute to their status and position. This is a common concern of many who are interested in the work force and occupations in general. Throughout this literature the assumption is made that the most skilled and knowledgeable occupations enjoy the most autonomy. Our evidence is somewhat mixed on this point. However, the registered nurse specialist who concentrates on complex procedures, preventive medicine and administrative tasks is probably more independent and more autonomous than the non-specialized registered nurse. Independent tasks, according to the Bulloughs, seem to lead to more status and higher financial rewards. They explore how the nursing role became differentiated and stratified, giving some nurses more independence than others.

An important point in this paper is that the tasks for the different kinds of nurses which have been developed since the end of World War II have been defined by the nursing occupation itself. The nursing organization with societal support from various institutions has developed a number of different nursing roles each of which is stratified according to tasks performed. The consequences of the redefinition has had ramifications in the kind of medical care available and in the occupational identity of the nurses themselves. Many of the changes in the nurses' roles were the outcome of direct action by the nurses through organization. Another major emphasis in this paper is that the structure of medical occupations and medical care is presently changing once more: a new nursing role is developing, the nurse practitioner, who will take on some responsibility for primary care of patients. If this should occur, both the nursing organization and the nurse practitioner at the role level, should have more autonomy over task related decisions. As Bullough and Bullough say, "it will be interesting to watch coming developments in the next decade."

THE PSYCHIATRIC RESIDENT

The primary purpose of this paper is to describe the socialization of the psychiatric resident, that is, how he is trained for this role. The focus here is on learning the tasks. The purpose of the residency program is to take a group of physicians, already socialized to one set of medical standards and inculcate a new and often opposite orientation to patient care. In the process of being socialized the resident's autonomy varies from little control of the work situation in the first year to increased freedom in the third year. Bud Khlief (quoting Hughes) notes that training can be described as an obstacle course or an endurance test. During the first year autonomy is almost totally limited—the physician-resident must take orders from others he considers subordinate to him. During the second year autonomy is less limited. By the third year the resident is more autonomous and is treated by others as a medical colleague. The process of socialization might be described as earned autonomy. However, it is different from the earned autonomy of the saleswoman and others described in this section. Residents earn autonomy by internalizing the standards and skills set by the occupational group. By suffering through the residency program the trainee becomes a colleague. Autonomy so earned is compliance rather than non-compliance. This is different from the orchestra musician. Also autonomy is granted to all physicians who complete the residency program. It is not a special privilege granted to a deviant few as is the case with the ratebuster saleswoman.

Khlief describes the processes of assimilation and commitment to occupational norms as the ideals of an occupation. He points out that becoming "professionalized" may be different for different individuals, but each resident must go through the program. Residents may proceed to the desired goal at different rates and may perceive the process differently. Autonomy at the role level is acquired by an acceptance of the occupational standards. One occupational standard (among many others) that is accepted by all who finish the program is that the training is legitimate. This does not mean that all residents are equally committed, but it does mean that the occupation has control of basic standards.

4

THE CLIENT

Introduction

Client Context

Autonomy and client-control are closely related. Autonomy is seen as important to occupational groups and role performance by many of the authors in this volume. Hall-Engel and Vollmer consider this as being the most powerful of all occupational characteristics. These papers suggest that autonomy depends on occupational control over members of an occupational group. When the client or the organization specify and evaluate performance, the occupational group loses autonomy and power. The difference between the two papers is essentially that according to Hall and Engel occupational control is a necessity for occupations to become professional, whereas Vollmer suggests the general public rather than an interest group will benefit from client-control. These two papers are presented as a general framework for consideration of ongoing problems and as a background for a discussion of issues in client control. Client evaluation and control are discussed in detail in our concluding chapter.

AUTONOMY AND EXPERTISE: THREATS AND BARRIERS TO OCCUPATIONAL AUTONOMY

Richard H. Hall
Gloria V. Engel

A great deal of attention has been paid to occupational autonomy in recent years. More and more occupations have developed expertise or knowledge which is specialized (esoteric to the non-specialist). This has led to increased power in the work situation. The judgement of the expert becomes an important component of the decision making process for the organization and the society as a whole. In this paper we will examine threats to the autonomy of the established professions. In addition we will look at the barriers to autonomy experienced by occupasions seeking full professional status.

THE IMPORTANCE OF AUTONOMY

Goode (1960b) suggests that autonomy is the key variable differentiating professions from non-professions. If an occupation cannot exercise autonomy, it essentially has limited power and is subject to control from clients, employing organizations, other occupations and professions, the government, and so on.

Moore (1970:16) states that autonomy is the final point on a scale of professionalism which he develops. It is the "ultimate value for self-identified members of an occupational category. . . ." According to Moore, this pinnacle of autonomy is reached because of specialization through knowledge which is not available to the laity.

In the same vein, Hall (1969:81) states: "In a very real sense, autonomy can be considered the key element of professionalization, since the knowledge base, community sanction, and colleague control of behavior are all elements of autonomy. If these factors are present in a work environment that does not allow the exercise of autonomy, then an individual or group cannot utilize their professional abilities."

There is a strong convergence on the point that autonomy is *a*, if not *the* major consideration in whether or not an occupation can be called a profession. It is our purpose here to move beyond the closure achieved by theoretical agreement and indicate what this means for the occupations and individuals involved as they seek to gain or retain autonomy during a period of rapid social change.

Before looking at some of the important changes, an obvious, but often ignored point must be made. Ritzer (1970) has made the point that professionalism must be considered on two levels—the individual and the collective or occupational. The same point holds for autonomy. We must think of variations in degree of autonomy among various occupations and among the individuals within an occupation. Thus, social workers are undoubtedly less autonomous than physicians as a group, but undoubtedly some members of these near professional groups are more autonomous than some physicians.

At both the collective and individual levels, autonomy is closely related to, indeed is a component of, the more general process of power. Autonomy is power granted to someone or some group because of their presumed *expertise* and the absence of the ability on the part of the laity to gain such expertise. In discussing power in this way we are using the conceptual framework of French and Raven (1968) in which they distinguish among the various bases of power. Professionals certainly can and do have other power bases, such as referent or reward, but the primary one remains the expertise.

To the idea of expertise must be added the fact that what the professional is expert in must be important to the society around him.

We are interested in barriers and threats to autonomy. If the view of autonomy as a form of power is accepted, then we must look more carefully at this idea before turning to barriers and threats to autonomy and their consequences. Power is a relationship between two or more parties in which one party is able to have the other one do something he otherwise would not do (Dahl, 1957) or, in Weber's terms, the possibility of imposing one's will upon the behavior of other persons (Weber, 1967:323). Another component of power is the fact that it involves mutual dependency (Emerson, 1962). The power holder is dependent upon the power recipient's conformity for the attainment of his own goals and aspirations, while the power recipient is dependent on the power holder for rewards as the avoidance of punishment. In the case of professionals this can be easily seen in the professional-client relationship. The client behaves as the professional desires because of the power of the professional over him. He *needs* the expertise for his own good. At the same time the professional is dependent upon the client's behavior for his own extrinsic and intrinsic rewards from the situation, even his own survival.

THREATS TO AUTONOMY

The most commonly noted threat to professional autonomy is the employing organization which is often viewed as some ogre about to devour the sacred professional virgin. The issues in the professional-organizational relationship have been well documented (Kornhauser, 1962; Marcson, 1960; Scott, 1965; Hall, 1969). Most of these issues reduce to threats to professional autonomy in terms of evaluation of the professional, decision making on goals, the use to be made of professional judgments, and so on. Since the professional in many organizations does not have clients *per se*, the recipient of his services is the organization. The organization is also his employer so that he is in the ambiguous position of trying to tell his own employer what to do.

Recent studies of the professional-organizational relationship have moved beyond the assumption of conflict for the professional into a closer examination of what happens to both the organization and the professional in such situations. Since it is quite clear that more and more professionals will be employees of organizations over time, it is useful to look at this relationship rather carefully. The pattern that seems to be emerging is that organizations can adjust to the presence of professionals by altering their structures to accommodate some of the needs for autonomy on the part of the professionals. Some mechanisms here are altered supervisory practices with more freedom of research choice and encouragement of a professional climate (Miller, 1967). The sections of organizations which employ professionals tend to be less bureaucratic than the balance of the organization (Hall, 1969). This does not mean that the organization permits professionals to do just what they want, but that organizations alter conditions to optimize the presence of the professionals. A situation in which there appears to be a greater potentiality for professional-organizational conflict is in the so-called heteronomous professional organization (Scott, 1965) in which ultimate organizational control is in the hands of a controlling board outside the organization and the occupations involved do not enjoy full professional status. Coincidentally or not, the occupations in these settings—teaching, social work, and librarianship—are those which are heavily staffed by women, a factor which may also contribute threats to autonomy (Simpson and Simpson, 1969). In these settings the typical finding is that the professional does not feel that he has as much control over what he does as he would like to have.

The organization can be viewed as a mechanism for guiding the behavior of individuals. Individual professional autonomy is an alternative. When the professional alternative is taken, it is assumed that the individual will guide his behavior on the basis of his learned professional standards and that this will operate for the benefit of clients and/or the employing organization. The craftsman can be viewed in the same perspective. Since we have seen that organizations do tend to give their professionals more autonomy than most other personnel, the threat to autonomy from the organization has probably been overstressed in the literature. This is undoubtedly due to a preoccupation with an image of the professional as solo practitioner. The professional-organizational relationship can now be viewed as one of reciprocity in terms of autonomy.

There is a situation in which the professional's autonomy in the organization can be viewed as being subject to a new sort of threat. As organizations employ more professionals of different types and more and more occupations acquire expertise and thus approach professional status, organizations are going to be increasingly faced with the problem of coordinating the tasks which their professionals are performing. While there is an implicit coordination of professional tasks in the wider society, this becomes an explicit need when the organization is confronted by diverse opinions and findings from its scientists, engineers, accountants, lawyers, personnel experts, public relations experts, advertising experts, computer experts, etc. It would appear that in such instances the autonomy of the professionals in the organization may in fact be threatened. The threat comes from the organization, through one process or another, deciding on some hierarchy among the various occupational groups in terms of which group's opinion carries the most weight under what circumstances. In this case it is not really a matter of an organizational threat to autonomy, but in an abstract sense the profession's and professional's ability to convince the organization of the ultimate correctness of its position. In the real world, of course, the role of power and politics is probably much more central. In this case, whatever the decision making basis happens to be, the selection of one type of professional advice over another is a reduction of autonomy or at least a serious threat to the loser.

Thus the organization will increasingly present the professional with a situation in which the traditional view of autonomy—that of the solo practitioner making decisions on behalf of his client's welfare on the basis of his expertise—is no longer viable. This does not mean that this is in any way the most useful way to view autonomy. Rather, if we view autonomy for the profession and the professional as something which is closely linked to a condition of power over the relevant decisions affecting the occupation and occupational roles, then the organizational setting is one in which there *may be* threats to autonomy from the organization and other professions within the organization. This is not a necessary condition, however. The organizational threat to autonomy is not a given and it is not reasonable to view the relationship through a solo-practitioner model only.

BARRIERS TO AUTONOMY

Returning now to the professions found in the heteronomous setting, we now can look at some barriers to professional autonomy. Here we find a barrier to the very heart of the autonomy concept. Among many of the near professions typically found in the heteronomous setting—particularly teaching, social work, and librarianship—the knowledge base of autonomy is under constant question from the public, clients, and parents of clients. There appears to be a sort of "anyone can do it" attitude toward these near professions and professionals. It is most easily seen in the case of teaching, in which many parents undoubtedly think that they could teach their own children, and probably others, as well as the classroom teachers. This is particularly the case at the lower grades where the knowledge specialization is slight. The same sort of attitude seems to operate for social work and librarianship.

Part of this is a form of public relations problem, but the more central issue seems to be that the knowledge base of the professions is in question. None, in fact, have much of a theoretical base which requires a long learning period and is difficult for the layman to grasp. The many horror stories about the training of teachers and the frequent diversity of backgrounds of social workers and librarians (at least previous to graduate training) suggests the absence of a coherent body of knowledge for these professions. It seems evident that the requirement of advanced degrees has not helped the whole situation a great deal thus far. In essence these professions have not demonstrated to their significant others that they have a sufficient knowledge base to be granted a great deal of autonomy.

Knowledge, or the perceived lack thereof, can be a barrier to autonomy in another way. As research in a wide variety of areas continues, new specialties can develop which threaten existing professions. For example, the clergy is seriously threatened by alternative occupations which can provide counseling of one kind or another. In academic professions the rise and fall of specialties is quite evident. New combinations of scientific fields, because of new theoretical developments, are relatively commonplace, placing several established disciplines in some jeopardy. The development of new knowledge in the past has led to the demise of other professions.

SOCIAL CHANGE AND AUTONOMY

Within an organization and in the wider society the relationships between professions must be viewed not only from the standpoint of knowledge, which implicitly assumes that truth will out, but also from the political-economic perspective. The great amount of political and economic infighting in an organization and the appeals for public support indicate the importance of this dimension. Such overt and covert conflict situations are clear threats to professional autonomy. It would appear that a decline in political and economic support for a profession would eventually lead to its decline, although this is an area which has received little attention.

Part of the contemporary political-economic situation surrounding many near professions is the issue of unionization. Many view the unionization of near professions as a severe threat to their autonomy, particularly at the individual level. Collective bargaining is seen as a technique whereby the individual is submerged to the needs of the total occupation. In many ways this seems to be more rhetoric than fact. Unions of the near professions actually are seeking increased autonomy in the political-economic sphere. Much of the unionization effort, of course, is aimed at occupations which are weakly organized as it is. Engineers, teachers, some college professors, and nurses are already rather vulnerable groups in terms of their autonomy. Unionization would hardly seem to be a threat to the existing low level of occupational autonomy. Except for the emotional connotation given to the term unionization, the movement toward unions really appears to be a simple substitution of one organizational title for another. The question remains open as to whether or not individual autonomy, in terms of the use of individual merit as a criterion for promotion and salary increases, will be threatened by unionization.

The final threat to autonomy to be discussed is that coming from the recipients of many professional's services—the clients. (The emergence of the paraprofessional can also be viewed as a threat from a different direction, but there is too little information presently available to permit a coherent discussion of this phenomenon.)

We can see organization, protest, and revolt among welfare recipients, medical clients, students, and some legal clients. This is a real threat to autonomy as we have been discussing it, since the clients are saying in effect: "You don't really know all that there is to know about treating our problems." The professional's expertise is thrown into question. Also severely questioned in many cases is his altruism in terms of the directions of his loyalty—to himself, his profession, or his clients. All oaths and wall hangings aside, the loyalty has tended to be away from the client to the other two components.

This threat to autonomy occurs in two ways. The first is the possibility that the client revolt could become so deep that the professional is excluded from providing any service at all and, in the absence of alternative clients, is essentially forced out of business. This may be what happens when college and university enrollments drop because of a belief that a college education is not as important as it once was, and faculty members are released to cut costs. Of course, the faculty members that are released may not be to blame for the change in client beliefs, but at the macro-level the adjustment is made.

The second threat to autonomy in this situation is more subtle. If the clients are successful in increasing their own decision making power about their course of treatment, legal rights, or the organization of the delivery of professional services, the professional still may be able to operate in his area of expertise, but with lessened power over the clients. Many would say this is a good thing. At any rate, the rise of client power is a distinct threat to professional autonomy.

IMPLICATIONS

We have already suggested some of the implications of the threats and barriers to autonomy. The purpose of this section is to put these threats and barriers into a perspective that allows a linkage into the literature on professions and to look more broadly at the nature of autonomy.

The first thing that can be noted is that there will be a continuing movement of professionals into organizations. This will be coupled with the continued emergence of new occupations with new expertise called for by the organizational world. Some of these occupations will achieve professional status and others will not. Professionals and near professionals will be employees of organizations. At the same time we can anticipate continued client concern with those professions and organizations which have direct contacts with a set of clients. Therefore it seems that we can anticipate that the control of a profession over its own operations will be modified. Control over admission, licensing and certification, legislation and professional practice itself will increasingly be broadened to include both organizational and client publics. This will occur in the political arena over time. The autonomy of the professions will diminish as more and more considerations are brought into the decision making process.

At the same time there will be a reciprocal effect on the organizations involved. They will undoubtedly move in a direction of debureaucratization. We can expect "looser" organizational structures as clusters of experts are brought together for problem solving and the generation of new ideas.

The second point is that when a broader perspective is taken, the professional's expertise is actually not threatened at all. In fact, as research proceeds and becomes more esoteric in many areas, the professional will increasingly become the only one who can interpret situations and make decisions about them. His power will thus increase in his area of specialization, while it diminishes in others. At the same time these occupations which are not recognized as having usable or real expertise will continue to be barred from full professional status. The profession and the professional will therefore become more limited in the areas of their autonomy as new expertise and new political-economic power is available in these other areas. This is not to suggest that all of this will occur without some major battles and that the level of expertise in all areas of life will develop simultaneously. There will continue to be vast areas of ignorance and guesswork about man's affairs and a great deal of trial and error solution-seeking.

The domain (Thompson, 1967) of the profession, like that of the organization, is a variable thing. The professions seem to be in a period when their domain is shrinking somewhat. Professional autonomy, which included more elements than just expertise (see French and Raven, 1968, for a discussion of additional bases of power), will increasingly be limited to this one area. The recipients of the profession's power, either in the form of the client or the organization, are exerting more power in return and in new areas. While this can be analyzed in fairly nice, neat terms, the nature of existing power struggles suggests that any transition such as the one suggested will not take place on the grounds of rationality and good sportsmanship. Many other elements will be introduced. If expertise and the social organization of knowledge remain important societal prerequisites (which is expected as the society becomes increasingly complex), then professional autonomy will increase in importance. It will exist, however, on a more specialized basis than our current conceptualizations and practice.

Howard M. Vollmer

Performance Evaluation: Some Social Aspects

We are constantly evaluating each person we meet. That is to say, we put people into categories. We cannot help doing this. It is the only way we can interact with other people in social situations. We need to make judgments about what social category they fall into. Then we have some idea about how to begin to relate to them. Thus if we have any social sophistication at all, we relate differently to dignified "little old ladies" than the way that we might relate to fellow members of a crowd at a football game. Until the days of the women's liberation movement, at least, men have generally been accustomed to treating women differently from men. Racial stereotypes are difficult to erase from our unconscious modes of thought and behavior. Members of the younger generation have developed new ways to categorize each other, and they relate to their peers differently from the ways they tend to relate to older persons. Certainly we act differently toward "strangers" than we do toward close friends.

All these different methods of evaluating each other constitute modes of performance evaluation. When we put people into certain categories, we expect them to behave (or perform) in certain predictable ways. Usually we attach different degrees of prestige or respect toward the different categories into which we place people, according to our own particular system of values. Moreover, many of the social categories we use in classifying people take on the characteristics of *ascribed* status, even though individuals may originally enter these categories through a process of *achieved* status.

Ralph Linton (1936) is commonly recognized as the originator of

334

the distinction between "ascribed statuses" and "achieved statuses."
He wrote that:

> *Ascribed* statuses are those which are assigned to individuals without ref-
> erence to their innate differences or abilities. They can be predicted and
> trained for from the moment of birth. The *achieved* statuses are, as a
> minimum, those requiring special qualities, although they are not neces-
> sarily limited to these. They are not assigned to individuals from birth
> but are left open to be filled through competition and individual effort.
> *The majority of the statuses in all social systems are of the ascribed type,
> and those which take care of the ordinary day-to-day business of living
> are practically always of this type.* (emphasis added)

Close examination of Linton's use of this dichotomy reveals that he
had in mind societies in which the division of labor was essentially fixed
during the lifetimes of individuals from the moment of birth. In such
societies, *sex* distinctions and *age* distinctions were the aspects of status
differentiation that were most crucial to "the ordinary day-to-day business of living." Linton identified sex and age as the major forms of
ascribed status in these societies—i.e., those forms of status that are
most predictable, that can be trained for from birth, and that are unrelated to individual differences in ability or performance.

However, since Linton's time, and especially in the past ten years,
we have become more aware of the extremely *dynamic* character of
modern technological society. Sex and age roles are not as distinct as
they were in past forms of society, and they are losing their importance
in the day-to-day aspects of living. *Occupational* distinctions become
more central indicators of status and role in advanced forms of industrialization. Occupational roles, especially in occupations that are more
highly professionalized, seem to be taking on many of the elements of
ascribed status that Linton attributed to sex and age roles in former
societies. These roles can be predicted and trained for from an early
age (if not precisely from birth) and they do not appear to be as sensitive to individual differences in ability and performance as we might
first imagine. At the same time society with advanced forms of technology requires occupational roles that *are continuously subject to performance evaluation*—i.e., that are achievement oriented in a dynamic,
continuing way throughout the lifetimes of individual occupants of these
roles. Yet the way we commonly categorize people depends more upon
our judgment as to *who they are* (that is, what group, occupational or
otherwise, that they belong to), than it does as to what they have
recently achieved as individuals.

Some might question this generalization. Have not we in America always believed that we are primarily an achievement-oriented society? In our national pastime, do we not applaud athletes for an outstanding performance on the football field, or perhaps a diva for an outstanding performance at the opera? This is true, but on closer inspection it appears that the way we evaluate individual performance does not usually break down our stereotypes of ascribed group status until we have viewed contradictory individual behavior for a long period of time. A football player is still a football player to us as long as he is on the team. We tend to overlook poor performance as long as possible. Our tendency to categorize people in terms of ascribed status can be stronger than our tendency to observe contradictory performance in individual situations.

The "American Dream"—the ideal vision of the United States—has been that anybody could follow Horatio Alger's advice and become a success by his own effort. American society has commonly been described as an achieving society from the days of De Tocqueville and other early observers until the present (De Tocqueville, 1862). At the same time, however, Myrdal and others have noted contradictory tendencies in our way of life. They have pointed out that America has never offered the same kinds of opportunities for certain categories as for others (Myrdal, 1944). Those of African heritage, American Indians, persons of oriental extraction, and members of a number of ethnic and religious minorities have not had equal opportunities to advance by their individual accomplishments at various times in American history.

Instead of being a real contradiction or dilemma in American society, the racial and ethnic discrimination that has existed can be seen as part of the general tendencies toward categorizing people in terms of ascribed status *that exist in all societies*. We could suggest the hypothesis that moving into a modern technological society does not cause people to change from a system of ascribed status to one of achieved status, but rather *to develop new categories into which people are classified in ascribed terms*. Thus the proud Jewish immigrant woman may talk about "my son, the doctor," but she is still doing what many preceding generations did in more traditional societies in Europe. She has no way of evaluating whether her son is a good doctor or not; to the mother the important thing is that he is "my son" and "a doctor." Interestingly enough, the important thing to the son's patients is also that he is a doctor. He has a diploma on his wall from medical school to prove it, and he has been a long standing member of the A.M.A. He is listed in the directory. Few, if any, of his patients will really be able to assess how effective his individual performance has been lately.

We can hypothesize further that America is not basically an achieved status society; it is an ascribed status society, but with continuously new categories of ascription. The fact that it takes considerable indi·vidual achievement to get into an ascribed category of occupational status (e.g., going through medical school or some other kind of gradu·ate professional school) should not obscure the fact that once one passes the entry exams, he is likely to have a sinecure in his particular status category. That is what obtaining an M.D. degree and passing the medical exams does for the physician; what passing the bar examination does for the attorney; what obtaining a Ph.D. does for the research scholar, and what obtaining a tenured postion does for the university professor. By achievement, these individuals have gone through the necessary rites of passage to admit them to a particular category of status that, once entered, is then treated as ascribed by others. Socio·logically, the process is essentially no different than for the youth who becomes an adult in a preliterate tribe by trial by ordeal. Once he has passed his entrance examination, no one can deprive him of his new status, except for the most serious and flagrant cause.

This procedure has some real disadvantages to it. It establishes a high degree of status security for members of an occupational in-group. At the same time it can support mediocrity and even malpractice from the standpoint of client groups—the persons in society who depend upon these occupational groups for certain kinds of specialized service. For example, it has been estimated that the "half-life" of an engineer·ing degree is about ten years on the average. In other words, about half of what an engineer has learned in a technical education is out of date ten years later. The period for obsolesence of technical knowl·edge is much shorter for rapidly changing specialty fields, such as those connected with electronics, than for the slower changing fields such as civil engineering or mechanical engineering.[1] Surveys have led to the estimate that as high as half the engineers and at least one fifth of the scientists in the United States experience technological obsolescence as a serious problem that limits their professional mobility.[2] These limits in professional mobility of engineers and other technically trained spe·cialists have become particularly evident during the last few years, when unemployment of technical manpower has increased in many areas along with cutbacks in federally sponsored defense programs. Although problems of technological obsolescence are especially evident among engineers and scientists at present, there is no reason to believe that individuals in other professional groups and technically trained occupations do not experience similar problems of keeping up to date in relevant areas of knowledge.

From the standpoint of the well being of a technological society, there is a need for periodic reassessment of the competence of persons in important occupational fields. A once-and-for-all entrance examination is not sufficient to assure continuing competence. Reliance on an ascribed status system—even with new sets of status categories—may well be insufficient to support a viable social order under conditions of significant technological change.

Yet there are two major processes in modern society that work to perpetuate ascribed status in occupational terms. These are the processes of bureaucratization and professionalization.

THE EFFECTS OF BUREAUCRATIZATION

Bureaucratic principles more or less pervade all modern large scale organizations. In their "ideal type" form, bureaucratic organizations are characterized by the following elements: (1) there is a clear-cut division of labor into job positions along functional lines; (2) there is a hierarchy of managerial positions structured into a pyramid of increasing generality of authority over subordinate positions; (3) work activities are governed by a consistently applied system of formal and informal rules generated from organizational practice (i.e., precedent); (4) impersonality characterizes the performance of job requirements— for example, an employee is hired according to the characteristics of a particular job, rather than having jobs redesigned to suit individual interests; and (5) a career progression is provided for entrants at the bottom level, moving upward through the management hierarchy as increasing experience is acquired by the individual at each managerial level.[3] Although these principles are often modified in modern organizations in practice, there still seem to be tendencies in this direction as institutions of business and government become larger and more complex. With increasing size and complexity in the division of labor, organizations tend to become more bureaucratized—i.e. to take on the "ideal type" characteristics of bureaucracy.

Performance evaluation in organizations subject to the process of bureaucratization is essentially a management responsibility. The performance of each individual is periodically evaluated by his immediate manager in terms of two major criteria, in theory at least. One criterion is the degree to which the individual is performing according to the requirements of his present position. The other is the degree to which he is capable of moving to the next higher position provided for his occupational career line in the organizational hierarchy.

In practice, however, the latter kind of evaluation is often not made as effectively as the former. It is always much easier to determine whether an individual is performing his present job well than to try to determine whether he is capable of taking on larger responsibilities. The former requires some reasonable method for work *measurement*, of both the quantity and the quality of work where possible. The latter requires both *measurement* and *prediction*, or inference with regard to future behavior. Since it is much more difficult to predict the future than to measure the present, it is often assumed that the employee who performs best at each level in an organizational heirarchy is there- "Peter principle"—the idea that each individual tends to be promoted to his particular level of incompetency. Compensation systems and promotion systems that are based mainly upon seniority or time-in-grade encourage ultimate incompetency in an entire organization.

What happens here is that individual achievement and capability is ignored in favor of what turns out to be just another form of ascribed status. Where seniority is the key to career development in more bureaucratized organizations, people are judged in terms of the length-of-service category that they happen to fall into, rather than by close examination of what they have been doing or what they can do in the future.

THE EFFECTS OF PROFESSIONALIZATION

We know that the process of professionalization affects every occupational group to some extent. Its effects are minimal in some groups and quite marked in others that are commonly known as "professions" —among physicians, attorneys and clergymen, for example. Among major elements in the ideal-type profession are the following: (1) occupational practice is based upon an underlying body of systematic theory and knowledge; (2) certification is used to assure an appropriate level of understanding of this body of theory and knowledge and expertise in related areas of practice at the time the individual enters and gains full-fledged status in the occupational group; and (3) protection of the body of knowledge and control of entry into the occupational category is undertaken by a formal association of members of the occupation.[4]

Performance evaluation in more professionalized occupational groups tends to be a once-and-for-all action at the time of entry. Those who have passed their medical examinations, or passed the bar examinations, or been duly ordained into the ministry, are considered to be fully qualified thereafter to practice their professional arts for the rest of their working careers. In terms of the old concept of "calling," they are considered to be set aside from other men. Only moral turpitude or serious violation of professional ethics are considered valid reasons for debarring or defrocking a member of a professional group.

Another important aspect of performance evaluation in professional groups is that it is characteristically done by other accepted members of the profession. Outsiders are not considered competent to judge professional expertise. Only members of the occupational fraternity are considered competent to judge other members.[5] The criteria upon which members of more professionalized groups are evaluated therefore tend to be oriented to what is valued by the occupational group, rather than what might be valued by clients whom the professionals serve. It is well known, for example, that expertise in theory or accomplishments in research—the kinds of things that are more likely to be valued in universities and professional schools—are more likely to give physicians, attorneys, or clergymen greater recognition in their own professional circles than such things as service to patients or clients. Scientists who specialize mostly in applied research activities often complain about being treated as "second-class citizens" by the more theoretically oriented scientists who usually deminate their professional associations. (Vollmer, 1969)

The patterns of performance evaluation that prevail in professional groups can become a source of conflict when professionals are employed in large bureaucratic organizations. The principle that professional performance should only be judged by professional peers can obviously conflict with the bureaucratic principle that performance should be judged by one's immediate supervisor, unless the immediate supervisor happens to be a certified member of the same professional group as the subordinate. Even here, performance evaluation becomes awkward, because it is commonly assumed that members of a professional group become peers at the time that they enter it. It is incongruous with a concept of professional equality for any one professional to be placed in a position of judging the work of another professional, especially after the professional has initially been certified as being competent anyway. Different concepts of performance evaluation can become the crux of conflict between management and professionals in bureaucratic settings.

This conflict can be resolved in various ways. One way is for individual professionals to become less professionalized in their career orientation and more committed to a bureaucratically oriented career in the organization that employs them. Another way is for organizations that employ large numbers of highly professionalized persons to become less bureaucratized in their organizational characteristics—to accommodate to professional performance criteria. This results essentially in abandonment of performance evaluation as a continuing process; the only judgment is made at the time of initial employment of a professional person, as to whether he is in fact a certified professional. This is the course that has been followed by some organizations that employ large numbers of highly professionalized scientific personnel. On the other hand, many scientists who are employed in industrial firms that are not primarily scientific in their overall orientation are more likely to accommodate themselves to bureaucratic patterns of performance evaluation and career development.

A third way to resolve professional-bureaucratic conflicts in performance evaluation is to develop a client-oriented evaluation system. No occupational group in a highly differentiated technogolical society can exist by itself. The final purpose of every occupation must be to serve all the utilitarian justification that acknowledges the interdependence of mankind in a shrinking "spaceship earth." Such a concept implies that evaluation by superiors and evaluation by professional peers must ultimately be subordinated to avaluation by the clientele who provide the basic rationale for the existence of the occupation.

CLIENT ORIENTED PERFORMANCE EVALUATION

Educational institutions, applied research organizations, and some other service organizations are beginning to experiment with client oriented performance evaluation systems. These embody some of the main characteristics of both bureaucratic and professional modes of evaluation. The essential characteristics of these new evaluation systems are as follows: (1) they involve continually updated measures of performance, usually on an annual basis; (2) criteria for performance are set jointly by professionals and managers and involve the collection of information on continuing professional competence, along with measures of the degree to which the individual has met client-oriented performance expectations that are appropriate to his employing organization; (3) the actual operation of the performance evaluation procedure is a joint activity, including a periodic conference between a professional and his manager (or a management authorized review committee) on the degree to which each is satisfied with the support and assistance that the other has given to him; and (4) the results of the evaluation are fed into a "management information system" in the employing organization whereby a continuing record is kept of (a) the progress of individual professionals in keeping up to date in their occupational fields and in moving toward various career objectives, and (b) the collective performance of various departments or divisions in meeting overall organizational goals and objectives.

The way this procedure operates can be shown by a specific example. A large independent research organization, conducting applied research projects for a variety of governmental, industrial, and other clients throughout the world, had a performance evaluation procedure that had been in operation for over twenty years. It is essentially a bureaucratically oriented procedure in which managers were asked to write open-ended comments on "how well this individual has performed with regard to previously set goals during the past year" and other general comments on his future potential, as estimated by his manager. In practice, however, this became a pro forma procedure. Little guidance was provided to managers on how to make comparable evaluations. Many professionals claimed that professionally valued accomplishments were not recognized sufficiently in the process. Specialists in the personnel office complained that managers often gave satisfactory ratings, or even glowingly outstanding ratings, to employees that they would want to dismiss from their jobs a few months later. In short, both managers and professionals were dissatisfied with the system.

Recently these mutual dissatisfactions in the face of severe economic strictures has led to an entirely new performance evaluation system being devised and installed in this research organization. Although the system has not been entirely implemented at the time of writing, the major features are as follows. A work planning and performance evaluation session is held annually between each professional employee and his immediate supervisor (annual review sessions had lapsed in many cases under the old procedure). The major criteria for performance evaluation in these sessions have been determined after a series of conferences with professionals and managers in the organization during a development period of about a year. These criteria for evaluation have been grouped under the following general headings on a form completed by the professional himself and brought to the review session: (1) a list of major assignments, projects, or tasks that the individual has completed during the past year; (2) a list of major proposals for the development of new projects that the individual has completed during the same period; (3) the individual's own evaluation of his satisfaction with the accomplishment of his own project assignments— for example, the degree to which each project was accomplished on time, within budget limitations, and to the satisfaction of the client, with explanations where any of these criteria were not achieved; (4)

a list of professional activities that the individual engaged in during the year, including seminars or courses attended, published professional papers, oral papers given at professional meetings, patent applications and patents received, professional awards or honors, and other evidence of keeping up-to-date in professional education and related activities; (5) a description of the plans of the individual to modify, change or accelerate any of his work or professional activities in the soming year; (6) a statement of how his manager might modify his own behavior or otherwise support the professional to achieve his work and career objectives in the future.

The supervisor, in turn, is asked to record his own evaluation of the accuracy and appropriateness of the information that the professional has assembled for the review session. The supervisor is also asked to answer a set of specific questions (with categorized responses) on such matters as the degree to which the individual has completed his work assignments on time, within budget, and to the client's satisfaction during the past year; how successful he has been in new research proposal writing activities; how current and up-to-date he believes that the individual is in his main technical field; how fluent he is in his ability to communicate his technical ideas to clients in writing; how articulate he is in verbal communication; how effective he is in working with others on research terms; how good he is in working with professionals from other disciplines on project tasks (a very important item in this organization); how well this person has been able to work with the supervisor making this rating and other project supervisors during the review period; how aptly suited he believes that this individual is for the position he now occupies and his estimate of his potential move into (a) technical positions or (b) managerial positions of more responsibility in the employing organization in the future. In the procedure, questions regarding reactions to work performed must be fully documented by letters from clients.

This review procedure has already been tried in several divisions of the organization. The first reaction of individual professionals and managers has been greater satisfaction with this procedure than with the previous one. The new system causes both the professional and the manager to prepare relevant information in advance and to bring it to a joint discussion in which the professional can show (and document) what he has done in appropriate detail, and can be encouraged to express his expectations and satisfactions (or dissatisfactions) with the kind of guidance and assistance that his supervisor has provided during the past year. In turn, the supervisor can review this information and make inputs himself on a number of specific items relating to the past performance and future potential of the professional being evaluated.

The important thing to recognize here is that the items being evaluated are related as such as possible to aspects of client service that are appropriate in this kind of research organization. Furthermore, this information is assembled and collected in as "objective" a manner possible, where it can be scrutinized by the individual professional and the manager for accuracy. Finally, this information will be assembled in a systematic way and recorded as part of the general management information system in this organization. As a result, it is expected that, over time, "career maps" will be available of the progress that various individuals have been making as they move through the organization. There will also emerge a means to identify common patterns of career development that will be especially useful for manpower planning by management. Management will be able to aggregate important information on strengths and weaknesses in the performance of different divisions of the organization in the management of their professional manpower resources. Thus an *individual* performance evaluation system of this kind can become an important component of *organizational* performance evaluation.

Universities have begun to develop annual performance evaluation procedures for faculty which rely in part upon student evaluations of teaching performance. These procedures characteristically apply to faculty personnel actions connected with annual reappointment of non-tenured faculty. On the other hand, tenured faculty are typically exempt from these annual student (client) review procedures. Tenured faculty status can perhaps be considered to be the ideal type example of ascribed status (after tenure is achieved) that is essentially immune to client evaluation.

What might be the broader social significance of new individual performance evaluation systems that are client-oriented? One aspect might be that they could become a major tool for overcoming conflicts between the bureaucratic requirements of large organizations and the professional requirements of occupational groups—in industrial and governmental, as well as educational and research organization. However, perhaps an even more important item of significance would be the degree to which client-oriented performance evaluation systems might be able to overcome the tendencies of both bureaucratic institutions and professional institutions to operate in terms of in-group criteria rather than general public benefit. The only way that we can be reasonably sure that the general public, rather than special interest groups, will benefit from the way we organize work activities in modern society is to avoid concentrating all the power in the hands of any one group. The pluralistic democratic solution is to develop performance evaluation procedures that will lead to an appropriate balance in the interests of various institutional forms, a balance that will be public service-oriented in its main thrust.

NOTES

[1] These estimates are based upon studies conducted by Professor Glen Strasburg of the Department of Engineering of California State College at Hayward, California, and are substantiated by similar estimates that have been made by other engineering educators.

[2] These estimates are based upon nationwide data from several sources that are reviewed and discussed in a preliminary report by the author (Vollmer: 1967).

[3] These elements of bureaucratization were first discussed systematically by Max Weber. See Gerth and Mills (1946) and Henderson and Parsons (1947).

[4] These three common elements in the process of professionalization are a synthesis of common elements described in various ways by a number of writers on the subject. See Vollmer and Mills (1966).

[5] Examples of peer group evaluations of performance among clergymen, attorneys, physicians, social workers, and other groups are given by Joseph H. Fichter and Everett C. Hughes in Vollmer and Mills (1966:145–150).

Client Control

The papers presented in this section (Hall-Engel and Vollmer) are the only two in the book which directly address the questions of client evaluation and control of occupational groups. Several of the papers (Shosid, Henslin, Epstein and Tygart) have discussed client control at the role level. At both the role level and group level the relationship between a worker and his client (customer or audience, as defined in the Overview) is complex. Little is known about the influence of client behavior on workers. Most of the papers presented stress the control exerted on the occupation from societal norms and values, from the organization where work takes place, or from the occupational group and tasks. Because most of the occupations discussed in this volume serve clients directly (housewife, lawyers, clergy, cab drivers, school teachers, nurses, saleswomen, and psychiatric residents), the interrelationship of the client to the worker should be a major concern. Yet this level of control, while mentioned briefly in several papers, is neglected as a primary emphasis by most who study occupations. There have been several in the past such as Freidson (1960) and Becker (1951) who have written on client-worker relations on the role level. Their conclusion is that at this level clients limit the autonomy of workers when the worker and client directly interact, regardless of the status of the occupation or the organizational context where work takes place. At the group level, the client can also limit occupational autonomy. More recent articles such as the one by Haug and Sussman (1969) as well as the evidence from the press and other news reports, suggest that the client is now organizing in order to be able to control and evaluate the work of several occupational groups. Parent groups are demanding community control of the schools, welfare recipients are demanding control over the social service agencies, and consumers are demanding quality control over goods. The issues involved in assessing the client's power over the worker and work are complicated and often indirect. In this section some of the issues mentioned above will be discussed in greater detail. Also, several suggestions for client research will be made. It is only through research that the relationship of the client to the worker, both at the role and group levels, can be understood.

ISSUES IN CLIENT CONTROL

Some work takes place in situations where the client and the occupational member are in direct contact (physicians, nurses, librarians, saleswomen, etc.). Workers such as musicians, ballet dancers, and baseball players perform before a live audience or an anticipated audience. Still others such as industrial workers, scientists and engineers work in organizations where the contact with the client is obscured. In all work situations, however, the client or the customer for the product is important whether the contact between them is direct or indirect. In the first two cases, the client can have some control at both the group and role levels. In the last case the client's indirect control is more likely to cover the occupational group as a whole.

In situations where contact with customers is indirect, control is mediated through the employing organization. These organizations operate under contractual guidelines, reached in agreement with the appropriate employees unions, guilds or professional-type associations. While it is the organization which decides whether the workers stay on the job, are transferred to other work, or are fired, it is the customer who exercises another kind of control. By his decision to buy or not to buy the product, the client can force the organization to re-evaluate its policies, goals and resources. Also, the customer or client can force the occupational association to re-evaluate policy. Thus the client can be a powerful force at the group level though he influences role relationships only indirectly.

The customer's decision against buying may be due to obvious reasons such as lack of financial means, lack of need for the product and poor or unappealing quality of the product. Other more complex reasons may be operating as well. Industries dependent on government contracts or on general affluence must be concerned with more than simply making a good product which will satisfy customers. World political situations, general public opinion about the values of certain commodities and the state of technology (automation, for instance) can influence the work situation and may result in few jobs with much autonomy. Such situations can even influence whether or not an occupational group will survive. Demand for products bears an important relationship to work in general; without some demand, an occupational role cannot exist.

As more of the formerly free professionals, creative writers and artists work under bureaucratic control, the real or imaginary conflicts between such workers, the organizations and clients can be studied. Studies show that adaptation to these conflicts depends on the workers' training and their reference group orientation. (See both Loether and Miller in this volume.) Three major groups play a part: the organization hiring the workers, the clients, customers or audience, and the occupation. The studies suggest that the occupational group should exercise the most control, and that the client and organization would both benefit if the professionalized occupations were self-controlling. However, in recent years a shift in orientation can be detected in favor of client control. Ralph Nader, community action organizations and community groups have been focusing on the importance of client control. More sociologists are beginning to explore the question of whether or not clients will limit occupational autonomy by evaluating workers. (Haug and Sussman, 1969, Hall-Engel, Vollmer in this volume).

The question of whether the client should have more control over services and products has been confused with the question of whether the client does have control. In this volume Hall and Engel discuss the conditions which have made the client more powerful and the organization and occupational group less powerful in defining work roles. If they are right about changing societal conditions affecting occupations, then it is clear that autonomy depends on more than technical knowledge or organizational context. This is not a new idea as others have demonstrated. The power of an occupational group in the political and economic spheres is very important. (Moore, 1970; Freidson, 1970). The contribution of the Hall and Engel paper is that autonomy is seen as a variable which depends on several characteristics and conditions; it is an ever changing commodity. For example, if an occupational group works for legal autonomy (license) for its members and obtains guild status, (see Gilb, 1966) it may be that this autonomy will be subject to change from other sources as consumer groups, social recipients, and the general public become more knowledgeable and more demanding (see Hall-Engel). On the other hand, as certain technical knowledge becomes more esoteric, autonomy will become more secure for groups having privilege to that knowledge. These opposing conditions make the problem of client evaluation and control a research question for each occupational group. It is not possible for anyone at this time to see professionalization as the final stage of progression for an occupational group. For those occupations which have obtained true professional status (possibly only lawyers, physicians and dentists) the situation is also changing as more formerly free professionals work in organizations and as clients are better informed.

Howard Vollmer in his article on client evaluation presents a complimentary approach to Hall and Engel. Hall and Engel note that others (especially the client and also the organization employing workers) do evaluate the work of those who have had autonomy in the past or would like more autonomy in the future. Vollmer is saying that there should be even greater client evaluation by those receiving the services of an occupational group. In his critique of the professional model, he notes that in the more professionalized occupations (see his paper for the definition of a profession) workers are evaluated "once-and-for-all" at the time of entry into the occupation. This may be changing as more physicians are being evaluated by patients, faculties by students, and social service workers by clients. However, most evaluation of performance is done by those inside the profession. Outsiders who obtain the services of the professional are usually considered incompetent to judge the performance of the worker. The evidence Vollmer presents is limited by the nature of his paper which is essentially a thought piece suggesting research and social action. In reality, the complexity of the relationship of the worker and his client at the role level depends on more than the achieved status of the worker. It depends also on the social context in which work is performed, what group the worker is trying to satisfy, the client's definition of the situation and the worker's mode of adaptation to the work situation. However, Vollmer believes that too much professional control (autonomy) over work may not be beneficial to the publics being served. His suggestions for change, many of which are being used by large organizations and being considered by others, would contribute to the deprofessionalization of occupational groups. According to Vollmer, occupational groups must be evaluated eventually by the clientele because the clientele provide the basic rationale for the existence of the occupation. Evaluation of performance by the client can lead to less control by the occupation and more control for the client, thus less autonomy for the worker at both the group and role levels. Hall-Engel and Vollmer are concerned with changes in the public consciousness, the growth of large bureaucracies and the increased power of certain privileged occupational groups. While these processes may seem contradictory, they are happening simultaneously.

Client control is difficult to evaluate. Most work is performed in large organizational settings where the worker has no contact with the client or where the organization mediates between the client and the worker. Even with those workers who do have day to day associations with the client (the librarian, the saleswoman, physician, the cabdriver, etc.) the kind, size and structure of the organization which hires the worker must be considered. The school teacher, who must be concerned with clients on a day to day basis, certainly adapts teaching activities to the student. The size of the school district also limits autonomy in performance of the occupational role. The three papers on teaching (Samuels, Loether, and Mennerick) demonstrate the variability in kinds of organizations, kinds of students and the conditions which make adaptation to the teaching role variable. University professors' expertise in a field may give them more autonomy and freedom than elementary school teachers on the group level. But many who have taught in universities during the last decade would probably agree that expertise is hardly enough to protect occupational autonomy. Student groups, legislative interest or interference, government support the size and kind of school, the ability of the students, and the general public acceptance of higher education are only several of the factors which influence the professor's autonomy in his teaching activities.

In this volume, the occupations which involve direct work encounters with clients were not studied in a way that make it possible for us to compare the degree of control exercised by the client. Several papers in this volume discuss briefly the influence of the client on those performing specific roles. Henslin, for instance, notes that the urban cab driver is in the situation where fear of his passenger plays a very important part in defining the work situation. While his client may not always be a stranger to him (he could have "regular fares" on a daily basis), most of his clients are. He does not know what dangers await him with each new fare; he fears threats to life and property. The cab driver must adapt to these situations. One form of adaptation is fatalism, another is avoidance. Shosid's paper on the librarian discussed in an earlier section also studies the kind of control clients can have in situations where the worker deals directly with the client.

Some of the papers show that the role of the client on both work evaluation and control of the work situation is often indirect. This may be one reason why research on the interaction between the client and the work has been neglected. Other structural factors (the size and kind of organization, the norms and values of the society in general, and political and economic situations) seem to be more important in defining work and occupational roles. *The need or demand for services can be considered one aspect of client control.* Bullough and Bullough demonstrate that the demand for nurses to work in base hospitals during World War II contributed to a shortage of nurses. This led to frequent use of less trained personnel which in turn freed highly trained nurses to perform complex procedures, and work in preventive medicine and administration. Patient care has changed as roles become differentiated with fewer registered nurses actually caring for patients. The role of the clergy provides another example of how demand for services changed the definition of the occupational role and the occupational group. Tygart presents a study on the effects of changing client power over clergymen in the Western world, especially in the United States. As clients obtained authority to judge the competence of clergymen, the clergy adapted in several ways. The conservative-fundamentalist faction sought to preserve the evangelical mission of religion; the liberal clergy sought to update their religious ideas and mission in the light of scientific changes. In either case, the clergy provides an instructive example of the deprofessionalization process of an occupation, as indicated by the laity's power to choose their pastors.

SUGGESTED RESEARCH TOPICS

In order to systematize and clarify the relationship of clients to occupational groups and roles several different types of research could be undertaken. More research is needed on the interaction between workers and clients. The papers in this volume by Dalton, Faulkner and Brewer provide methods of data collection and analysis that would be appropriate. Also, because so little is known about community and client organizations, descriptive studies about such groups should be undertaken. The social characteristics of formal and informal client groups could be surveyed. More importantly, it would be germaine to study consumerism as a social movement to determine how the power of an occupation at the group level depends on a community mandate.

The kind of research that has been undertaken primarily by those interested in advertising, marketing research and public opinion could also be incorporated by those interested in work and occupations. This would supply descriptive information which could allow the occupational group to provide better services for their clients. Such research would also provide some evidence of the actual power of the client over work, information as to how the client evaluates work performance and what kind of service the client expects. The demographic characteristics of those using the services of an occupational group are also important. This knowledge allows one to examine subtle effects operating on occupational group identification, status and attitude toward the services performed. It is important to examine workers' attitudes toward their clients. Are people working for themselves, the client, the organization, or their colleagues? What are the important reference groups which influence the work situations? Only by answering these and other research questions can the relationship of the client to the worker be made clear.

Client and customer evaluations are only one source of control. Unknown is the degree of control the client actually does have over the work situation at the group and role levels. At which level is the client capable of evaluating. In what areas does the client want evaluative power? What kinds of power, shared or absolute? At the role level, client control has always been important to workers who have direct interaction with their clients. At the group level, the evidence suggests that the client will have influence more in the future. For instance, in Fairfax County, Virginia, a high school student has been appointed as a paid member of the school board. In other areas of work and services, the clients are organizing into groups. Welfare mothers, classical music lovers, patients and other sub-groups are trying to exercise some control over the product and services rendered by workers. Client control at the occupational group level is becoming more important to many occupations. The unanswered question is how much group and role autonomy will be lost as the client's power grows?

CONCLUSIONS

This book develops a perspective for examining the social control of occupational groups and roles by investigating four sources of such control on occupations: cultural and societal, organizational, occupational, and client control. Empirical studies illustrate how these sources modify group and role autonomy separately or in combination. The political, economic, ideological and sociological importance of autonomy is described in some of the studies; others only raise the issue.

Some clarifying ideas on occupational autonomy can be made from the findings of these limited studies. Social control of occupations can be understood by considering two units of analysis: occupational groups and roles. Conditions that might enhance role autonomy do not necessarily enhance group autonomy. Furthermore, social control may shift from one source to another, i.e. from predominantly cultural and societal to organizational or client. In addition, control may be combined in several sources simultaneously. A shift from one source to another will be affected by several conditions in the larger social system: technological, economic, political and ideological conditions.

TECHNOLOGICAL, ECONOMIC, POLITICAL & IDEOLOGICAL CONDITIONS

An expanding technology, characteristic of a post industrialized society, may contribute in some occupations to changing sources of social control, e.g. from within the occupation to organizational control or even to client control. Physicians for example, need to rely on sub-specialties within the field of medicine since more technical experts are necessary to absorb and utilize increased technical knowledge. Generation of new occupations in the medical field plus the continued movement of physicians into large organizations suggests that physicians will have to share their autonomy with other medical groups and roles. Physicians' assistants and nurse specialists, while under the direct supervision of physicians in large organizations, function primarily as team members. Even though the physician is the captain of this team, the degree of specialized knowledge held by these sub-specialties upon whom the physician is increasingly dependent suggests that role autonomy will be shared with other functionaries. The process of establishing sub-specialties as a means of control within medicine is likely to be followed by other occupations. The traditional professions are often models for other occupations to follow. Physicians, at this time, have more to lose than others with less autonomy. While reduction of role autonomy may be slow to change, the combination of increased technology, the organization of medical services into large scale organizations and the development of many technical specialists within the occupation of medicine suggest that physicians' autonomy will be shared with other roles and new spheres of control defined. However, at the group level, change in the autonomy of the American Medical Association will be more gradual, generated by different conditions (perhaps economic) and from another source—that of client regulation and participation.

Technology can also provide the client with greater control over both the organization and the occupation. This is rarely discussed but Gurevitch and Elliot (1972) raise questions concerning the status of broadcasters and other media personnel when technological change brings forth the multiplication of television channels. The key question they raise is how far technological change is likely to maintain or disrupt the mass characteristics of the broadcasting media. The first expectation is that cable television, audio-visual discs and cassettes will result in a process of decentralization of the production and dissemination of media materials. They expect wide ranging impact both on the structure of media organizations and on the nature of occupations in the media. They envision the fragmentation of large media organizations into small ones, characterized by increased flexibility and temporariness on the one hand and by greater room for creativity on the other. The process of decentralization and consequent proliferation of communication outlets would create new needs for broadcast materials and would increase the number of workers in the field. The problem of projecting into the future is obvious. The number of personnel may not increase because of automation. Presently American radio stations, though large in number, are operated by few people because of automation.

Gurevitch and Elliot (1972) raise the question of these changes on the creators of content. They consider such technological changes as eventually deprofessionalizing the media occupations:

"One thing is certain, however. There will be little room for professional elitism which thrived in the situation when the broadcaster not only could presume he knew what was best for the public but was also encouraged to do so by those anxious to keep control over popular culture."

While there are problems justifying this position, the rationale is worth exploring that community television via the cable will provide the subgroups in the audience with more control and the broadcasting organizations with less control. In the United States, there has been little occupational autonomy among media personnel. Cantor (1971), Gans (1957) and Breed (1955) have noted that various occupational groups are highly committed to occupational norms that include creative control over content. However, the evidence more than suggests that the organization providing the channels for the content not only control the type of programming available but also control who works and when. The opening of new channels may provide more opportunity for occupational control because certain creators will be able to provide information and entertainment to segmented audiences with tastes close to their own. The shift from organizational to audience (client) control can result in more autonomy rather than less for the communicator. It is these information and entertainment industries which may be the prototype of the effects of technology. Certainly, they should be studied as the changes occur. The elitism noted by Gurevitch and Elliot is the result of powerful organizational structures. If such structures are in fact disestablished as they suggest, changes in occupational control will occur.

Ideologically, autonomy is important because group autonomy is a form of elitism. The guild which limits membership by setting educational and recruitment standards is elitist by definition. Practicing an occupation gives one certain rights and privileges along with obligations to do the work properly. Vollmer's paper has noted that while this may benefit the worker, it is possible the system can have detrimental effects on the client. Benefits to the guild member can be greater than simply security or income. Inherent in the guild philosophy is the sense of occupational community (see Lipset, Trow, and Coleman, 1956, Goode 1957, Bryant in this volume). Also, group action is related to ideology and guild membership. According to Krause (1971:89):

"Occupational ideologies are used by specific occupational groups to gain the support and action of target groups, such as the occupation's direct clientele (if there is one), other occupational groups with which the group deals, the government, and the general public."

Thus the kind of political action an occupation may take is greatly affected by whether the occupation is organized as a guild or as a union.

Unionization as compared with guild activity is closely associated with ideology and political action. Unionization assumes several beliefs, for instance that the tactics and symbols of organized labor will benefit members more than the elitism of the guild. Jesse Pitts (1972: 17) notes that the faculty at Oakland University went on strike because they believed that they would gain more benefits than they lost in prestige. Chances of securing a greater share of the educational dollar as well as maintaining traditional rights such as tenure and low teaching loads were greater through the unionization movement than by the more traditional organizational methods. This reflects a changing ideology, a changing form of political action, an imbalance between supply and demand of faculties, and a changing attitude to group autonomy.

Vernon Dibble (1962) and Krause (1971), see ideology as a force which gives meaning to group action. Using this definition, autonomy itself is an important ideology. The belief in occupational autonomy becomes the basis for group action. In the past this ideology contributed to the desire for and development of guild organization. Autonomy is still important politically and ideologically. The organizational form that occupational groups use may be changing because of the failure of the professional type of organization to secure control for its members; white collar unionism, a new form of organization, may be an example of such an emerging trend. This does not mean that autonomy is less valued—only that the means to gain autonomy is changing. Some occupational groups may still work for guild status; certainly that seems to be the indication given by Bryant with his example of the professionalization of the landman. Other occupations may use the tactics and organizational methods of unionism.

The studies in this book, along with other findings, indicate that autonomy as a value or ideology is not decreasing in importance. In fact, it seems that occupational autonomy is the concern of many groups in the labor force regardless of status, such as cab drivers, baseball players, and blue collar workers. For example, in a study conducted by Harold Sheppard it was found that young blue-collar workers seek jobs which allow them to be more active and autonomous (Sheppard and Herrick 1972). While the major purpose of the organizations of the groups mentioned is to secure greater financial rewards, a secondary benefit of organization is more group autonomy. Autonomy at the role level often follows from group autonomy since group support gives the worker leverage and control in the work organization. Finally, autonomy is a variable which can be examined empirically at the group and role levels of occupations.

WHY STUDY AUTONOMY?

Two major questions are discussed in the final section of this chapter. The first concerns the reasons why autonomy and control are the focus of this book. The second question is more substantive. Are occupations generally becoming more autonomous as autonomy is defined in this book, or are occupations being controlled more by the cultural and societal aspects of the work environment, the organizational setting and the client? These questions are interrelated and of great importance to those interested in the future of work and the composition of the work force. In order to discuss whether or not occupational control is becoming more or less important it is necessary to explain why this is a major emphasis.

The sociological literature on occupations shows that autonomy or occupational control has concerned researchers for some time. The discussion in the Overview indicated that autonomy is considered primarily by those who have studied the professions. Many who have been interested in mass production workers and lower status occupational groups have focused on the problems of alienation and job satisfaction. As previously stated, the problems of job satisfaction and alienation follow from the questions and assumptions which were brought up in the nineteenth century as the Western countries were becoming industrialized. Both Marx and Weber were concerned about workers' lack of control over their product in industrial and bureaucratic settings; this lack of control leads a worker to both dissatisfaction and alienation. According to their analyses, the worker becomes a tool and another machine. In contemporary American society unions are concerned with changing societal conditions in order to remove barriers of authority and compliance so that individuals have the right to determine their tasks.

On the other hand, sociologists and others have noted a counter trend among occupational groups. This trend has usually been called "professionalization." From the late nineteenth century on, arguments have developed for increasing occupational professionalism. The rationale can be summarized as follows: as the division of labor increases, occupations become more specialized, even within occupational groups (see Bullough and Bullough in this volume for an example). This is due to several structural factors such as the expansion of knowledge and increased technology. Also, certain occupational groups have worked to improve their own situation within the labor force by trying to become professionalized. Whereas the mass production worker in the past used the trade union as the organization to improve worker status, other workers organized differently. The professional association, which limits membership by setting entry and socialization standards, has an opposite philosophy from the trade union. The union's chief strength lies in its power to shut down the factory or shop by organizing all workers to join and participate. The guild or professional association has strength only when membership is limited to those the occupational group defines as desirable and competent.

As has been indicated in several of the papers, the above comparison is based on an "ideal type." Many unions are closer to guilds in their mode of operation and many guilds encourage their members to strike and organize similar to union practices. The presence of both models can be found in the same occupation. This raises the question of how occupational groups should organize to maximize their autonomy at the group and role levels. Competition among several organizations within the same occupation may be disadvantageous for the occupation as a whole. The occupation of teaching provides a good example of varying responses within the same occupation to a desire for improved status and control. The National Education Association, The American Association of University Professors (AAUP), and the American Federation of Teachers all exist to represent teaching faculties. Today, changing economic and political conditions in the larger social system present uncertainty for university faculties. The original means of organizing (AAUP—a professional association) does not appear to be adequate for economic bargaining nor for preservation of competence and standards of excellence. The American Federation of Teachers (a union type organization) represents increasing numbers of university faculties and negotiates in more and more areas. The primary benefit of the AFT organization for faculties at this time is economic. Opponents argue that continued acceptance of this form of organization on universities will result in lessened educational quality and performance. The evidence is not yet manifest as to which model of organization will enhance group and role autonomy. Since both models seem to be developing features of the other, the answer to the question of maximum group and role autonomy is empirical at this time. This book presents a perspective whereby group and role autonomy are considered for analytic purposes. Hopefully this will be useful in determining a new model which combines both the union and guild forms of organization.

The question that has been asked in the past is whether the labor force as a whole is becoming professionalized. (See Vollmer and Mills 1966, Wilensky 1964, Foote 1953, Goode 1969.) The question is really concerned with group autonomy and not professional status. Elitism and the quest for power are part of even the most egalitarian social systems. Both Wilensky (1964) and Goode (1969) believe that whether or not an occupation does obtain control makes little difference as to whether or not it is a real profession. Because the definition of a profession has caused so much inquiry, the problem brought up early by Carr—Saunders (1933), and later by Foote (1953) and others has been bogged down in a discussion which is essentially limited by semantics. The real question is whether occupational autonomy and control are possible in a society which is highly bureaucratized and where technology is constantly changing the composition and competence of the work force. However, the political structure of a society will determine to some degree whether or not group and role autonomy are valued and thus negotiable. These factors, along with a growing and educated population in American society, make the problems of occupational control and autonomy more complex than simply considering a linear progression towards professionalism. It is these factors which led us to choose autonomy as the major focus of control.

IS AUTONOMY INCREASING?

This leads to the second question of this summary, for which there is no final answer. Are occupations becoming more or less autonomous? It seems that some occupations are becoming more autonomous while others are losing their autonomy, but all are striving for autonomy. This is an ordered phenomenon within occupational groups; lower status craft occupations which have not been eliminated by automation seem to be becoming more autonomous, while several of the traditional professions are becoming less autonomous. *Because autonomy is considered a variable often associated with status, each occupational group and role needs to be empirically examined separately in relation to the control exerted on it by cultural and societal values, the organizational setting and the client. This provides a basis for comparing the social control of occupations.*

The ordering of occupations along the dimension of autonomy however, is not fruitful and will likely lead to the same types of problems as the dimension of a professional continuum. Comparing occupations according to sources of control is explanatory since changes in occupational structure and positions can be more clearly delineated. This suggests that neither status, economics nor type of work are the major emphases. More important is the work force as it is seen in the societal context. In addition, status, function, political, and economic situations can be examined by this focus.

The factor of autonomy is related to another issue—the meaning of work. While this book does not discuss the meaning of work in a post industrial society, it must be noted that autonomy in occupational groups and roles is significant only if the meaning of the work role is important. Autonomy implies that the work role and group identification in an occupation do have important significance in relation to other roles in the social system. The degree of interface between work and non-work roles is demonstrated in this book by Charnofsky where baseball players must center non-work duties and activities primarily around the work role and group affiliation. Coordination of the work and non-work roles for actresses as suggested by Peters in this volume indicates that the relationship between work and non-work is very intricate. Perhaps the primary significance of the work role is attached to the resource it provides the worker to control the non-work roles in the social system.

In recent years, the term deprofessionalization has been used to discuss the loss of control by occupational groups over role performance. The primary historical example of this is the clergy. In this volume, Tygart explains why the clergy went from a sociologically strategic occupation to one of lesser importance. The process which led to the loss of status and control by the clergy also accounts for the rise of other occupational groups. According to Tygart, the clergy probably was largely responsible for the development of the other learned professions because of the clergy's control of education. In addition, the related forces of developing industrialization, capitalism and the nation state made the need for applied knowledge more forceful. Lawyers were the first to operate outside the church because of the demands of the nation-state for civil law. At the present time, services performed by the clergy are very specialized as the dominance of religious ideas in the culture diminishes. The structural changes have resulted in limited role autonomy for clergy and limited control over the work situation. Even though control of work varies in different Protestant denominations, control is limited by the laity of the congregation in every denomination. This includes client evaluation of professional competency.

While the erosion of clerical control was gradual over several centuries, contemporary discussions of deprofessionalization often focus on new occupations which are not professions in the traditional sense. Before these emerging occupations attain autonomy, societal conditions change. What some are calling deprofessionalization is occuring before professionalization is complete. Haug and Sussman (1969) note that professional autonomy among certain groups is being eroded by client revolt. Their discussion focuses not only on the physician but also on professors, social workers and other groups which may not be considered true professions. This may be due to their marginal status or because they have always been dependent on an organizational structure to practice their occupation.

Regardless of the status of these occupations, Haug and Sussman (1969), Hall and Engel (in this volume) are among the researchers who are noting that the client is becoming more powerful by evaluating the work of the professional. Haug and Sussman state that professional expertise is being questioned by many groups. The reasons they give are closely associated with changing values and behavior in various subgroups in the population. Students are no longer willing to accept without question the word of professors and administration concerning their welfare. Also, welfare recipients question if the social workers really know about their community needs, problems and solutions. This revolt of the client is part of the larger movement toward consumerism. As the status differential between the client and professional becomes narrower or is perceived as narrower by the client, occupational autonomy is threatened. Thus groups which are striving for professionalism have, at least this time, become thwarted.

Finally, increased consumer participation in all occupations will lead to some clarity on which areas the client is able to enter a meaningful judgement of role and group activities. The issue of accountability in occupations is not new. In fact, it is implicit in the lay usage of the terminology, "a professional performance." This generally suggests objectivity, high standards and accountability, and an approach to a task rather than the identification of a task with a "profession." Freidson, (1970) indicates that the laity define profession in an *evaluative* perspective and that social scientists emphasize a *descriptive* perspective. He further argues that the laity will continue to use "profession" evaluatively to determine the worth of an occupational performance irrespective of a theory of professions. Thus what appears to be new is the question of the *means* all occupations use to implement accountability to clients, to organizations, or to the larger society. What kinds of power does the occupation seek, shared or absolute; and what are the political, technical and economic implications of the occupational control? The answers to these questions will provide knowledge for a beginning theoretical synthesis on the social control of occupations.

Biographical Sketches of Contributors

Jessie Bernard, Ph.D. 1935—Washington University. Research Scholar Honoris Causa at Pennsylvania State University. With Lida Thompson, *Sociology: Nurses and Their Patients in a Modern Society*, 8th ed. (C. V. Mosley Co., 1970); *Women and the Public Interest* (Aldine-Atherton, 1971); *The Future of Marriage* (World, 1972); numerous other publications.

John D. Brewer, Ph.D. 1968—University of Chicago. Chairman and Associate Professor, Trinity College, Hartford, Connecticut. "Organizational Patterns of Supervision: a Study of Debureaucratization of Authority Relations in Two Business Organizations," article in *The Sociology of Organizations*, Oscar Grusky and George A. Miller (Free Press, 1970).

Clifton D. Bryant, Ph.D. 1964—Louisiana State University. Professor and Head, Department of Sociology, Virginia Polytechnic Institute, Virginia. Editor of *Sociological Symposium;* the *Social Dimensions of Work* (Prentice-Hall, 1971); *Introductory Sociology: Selected Readings for the College Scene* (Rand-McNally, 1971).

Bonnie Bullough, Ph.D. 1968—University of California, Los Angeles. Assistant Professor School of Nursing, University of California at Los Angeles. With Vern Bullough *The Emergence of Modern Nursing* (MacMillan, 1969); with Vern Bullough *New Directions for Nurses* (Springer, 1971); *Social-Psychological Barriers to Housing Desegregation* (University of California Housing, Los Angeles and Berkeley, 1969); numerous other publications.

Vern L. Bullough—Professor of History, San Fernando Valley State College. (For publications see Bonnie Bullough)

Muriel G. Cantor, Ph.D. 1969—University of California, Los Angeles. Associate Professor, American University, Washington, D.C. *The Hollywood Television Producer* (Basic Books, Fall 1971). Contributor to Volume I; *Media Content and Control*—a section of the Technical Report to the Surgeon General's Scientific Advisory Committee on Television and Social Behavior, 1971.

Harold Charnofsky, Ph.D. 1968—University of Southern California, Los Angeles. Associate Professor, California State College, Dominquez Hills, California.

Melville Dalton, Ph.D. 1949—University of Chicago. Emeritus Professor, Department of Sociology, Institute of Industrial Relations, University of California, Los Angeles. "Cooperative Evasions to Support Labor-Management Contracts," in *Human Behavior*, Arnold Rose ed. 1962. *Men Who Manage* (Wiley, 1959); "Preconceptions and Methods in Men Who Manage" in *Sociologists at Work* (Basic Books, 1964); "Reorganization and Accommodation: A Case In Industry," in *Institutions and the Person*, edited by Howard Becker (New York: 1968, Aldine Publishing Co.); numerous other publications.

Gloria V. Engel, Ph.D. 1968—University of California at Los Angeles. Assistant Professor, Department of Community Medicine and Public Health, University of Southern California School of Medicine. "Bureaucracy and Autonomy" *Journal of Health and Social Behavior*, Vol. 10. March 1969.

Cynthia Fuchs Epstein, Ph.D. 1968—Columbia University. Associate Professor, Queens College, CUNY, and Senior Research Associate, Bureau of Applied Social Research, Columbia University. *Women's Place* (University of California Press, 1969); *The Woman Lawyer* (University of Chicago, 1971); *The Other Half*, edited with W. J. Goode (Prentice-Hall, 1971); numerous other publications.

Robert R. Faulkner, Ph.D. 1968—University of California, Los Angeles. Assistant Professor, University of Massachusetts, Amherst, Massachusetts. *Hollywood Studio Musicians* (Aldine, 1971).

Ronald C. Federico, Ph.D. 1968—Northwestern University, Associate Professor, Department of Sociology, University of North Carolina, Greensboro, North Carolina.

Richard H. Hall, Ph.D. 1961—Ohio State University. Professor, Department of Sociology, University of Minnesota. *Occupations and the Social Structure* (Prentice-Hall, 1969); *Organizations: Structure & Process* (Prentice-Hall, 1972); numerous other publications.

James M. Henslin, Ph.D., 1967—Washington University. Associate Professor, University of Illinois, Edwardsville. *Studies in the Sociology of Sex* (Appleton-Century-Crafts, 1971); *Down to Earth Sociology* (The Free Press, 1972).

Bud B. Khleif, Ph.D. 1957—Johns Hopkins University. Associate Professor, University of New Hampshire. *The Schooling Careers Military Dependents: A Sociocultural Study* (U.S. Office of Education, 1971).

Joseph Lengermann, Ph.D. 1969—Cornell University. Associate Professor, University of Maryland, College Park, Maryland.

Herman J. Loether, Ph.D. 1955—University of Washington. Professor of Sociology, California State College, Dominquez Hills. *Problems of Aging* (Dickenson Publishing Company, 1967); "The Meaning of Work and Adjustment to Retirement," in Arthur B. Shostak and William Comberg (eds.), *Blue Collar World: Studies of the American Worker*, 1965.

Lewis A. Mennerick, Ph.D. 1971—Northwestern University. Assistant Professor, University of Kansas, Lawrence, Kansas.

George A. Miller, Ph.D. 1966—University of Washington, Seattle. Associate Professor, University of British Columbia, Vancouver, Canada. *The Sociology of Organizations* with Oscar Grusky (The Free Press, 1970); numerous articles.

Anne K. Peters, Ph.D. 1971—University of California, Los Angeles. Assistant Professor, California State College, Dominquez Hills.

Joanna J. Samuels, Ed.D. 1966—University of California at Los Angeles. Assistant Professor, School of Dentistry, University of Minnesota. "Impingements on Teacher Autonomy," *Urban Education*, Vol. 5, No. 2, July 1970.

Phyllis Langton Stewart, Ph.D. 1968—University of California, Los Angeles. Assistant Professor, Department of Sociology, George Washington University. "Adaptations of Scientists in Five Organizations: A Comparative Analyses," (two volume monograph with Howard M. Vollmer, Stanford Research Institute, May 1964).

Norma J. Shosid, Ph.D. Candidate, University of California at Los Angeles. Vanderbilt University, Tennessee. "Freud, Frug, and Feedback," *Special Libraries*, October 1966.

Clarence E. Tygart, Ph.D. 1969—University of California, Los Angeles. Associate Professor, California State College, Fullerton. Articles in *American Journal of Sociology, Pacific Sociological Review* and *Sociological Analysis*.

Howard M. Vollmer, Ph.D. 1959—University of California, Berkeley. Senior Sociologist, Bechtel Corporation, San Francisco, California. *Professionalization* with Donald Mills (Prentice-Hall, 1966); numerous other publications.

References and Selected Bibliography

Abel, Bruce.
   1963   "The firms what do they want?" Harvard Law Record. 37
          (December 12):1ff.
American Nurses' Association.
   1960   Facts About Nursing: A Statistical Summary. New York:
          American Nurses' Association.
   1967   Facts About Nursing. New York: American Nurses' Associa-
          tion.
   1969   Facts About Nursing. New York: American Nurses' Associa-
          tion.
American Nurses' Foundation.
   1971   "1971 supplement to the 1969 directory of nurses with earned
          doctorate degree." Nursing Research 20 (March-April):177–
          180.
Anderson, Jack.
   1971   "Pension benefits for housework." Washington Post (Novem-
          ber 7).
Anderson, Nels.
   1964   Dimensions of Work: The Sociology of a Work Culture. New
          York: David McKay Co., Inc.
Andrews, Priscilla M. and Alfred Yankauer.
   1971   "The pediatric nurse practitioner, the growth of the concept."
          American Journal of Nursing 71 (March):504–506.
Anonymous.
   1886   The Old Farmer's Almanack. Number 94.
Bailyn, Bernard.
   1960   Education in the Forming of American Society. Chapel Hill:
          University of North Carolina Press.
Banton, Michael.
   1965   Roles: An Introduction to the Study of Social Relations. New
          York: Basic Books Publishers.
Barber, Bernard.

1963   "Some problems in the sociology of the professions." Daedalus 92 (Fall):669–688.

Barnard, Chester.
1938   The Functions of the Executive. Cambridge, Massachusetts: Harvard University Press.

Bauer, Raymond.
1958   "Communicator and the Audience." Conflict Resolution 2 (March):66–76.

Baumol, William and William Bowen.
1966   Performing Arts: The Economic Dilemma. New York: Twentieth Century Fund.

Becker, Howard S.
1951   "The professional dance musician and his audience." American Journal of Sociology 57 (September):136–144.
1952   "Social class variations in the teacher-pupil relationship." Journal of Educational Sociology 25 (April):451–465.
1960   "Notes on the concept of commitment." American Journal of Sociology 66 (July):32–40.
1963   Outsiders: Studies in the Sociology of Deviance. New York: The Free Press.
1970   Sociological Work: Method and Substance. Chicago: Aldine.

Becker, Howard S. and James Carper.
1956   "The elements of identification with an occupation." American Sociological Review 21 (June):341–348.

Becker, Howard S. and Anselm S. Strauss.
1956   "Careers, personality, and adult socialization." American Journal of Sociology 62 (Nov.):253–263.

Berger, Peter L.
1964   The Human Shape of Work. New York: MacMillan Co.

Berger, Peter L. and Thomas Luckmann.
1967   The Social Construction of Reality. Garden City: Doubleday-Anchor.

Bernard, Jessie.
1942   American Family Behavior. New York: Harper.
1971a   "Changing lifestyles: one role, two roles, shared roles." Issues in Industrial Society 2 (January):21–28.
1971b   Women and the Public Interest: An Essay on Policy and Protest. Chicago: Aldine-Atherton.
1972   The Future of Marriage. New York: World Publishing Co.

Bixler, George.
1962   "AAPL president in casper." The Landman 6 (February):18.

Bland, Alexander and Michael Peto.
   1963   The Dancer's World. New York: Reynal.
Blau, Peter M.
   1955   The Dynamics of Bureaucracy. Chicago: University of Chicago Press.
   1956   Bureaucracy in Modern Society. New York: Random House.
   1964   Exchange and Power in Social Life. New York: Wiley.
Blau, Peter M. and W. Richard Scott.
   1962   Formal Organizations. San Francisco: Chandler.
Blau, Peter M. and Richard A. Schoenherr.
   1971   The Structure of Organizations. New York: Basic Books.
Blauner, Robert.
   1964   Alienation and Freedom. Chicago: University of Chicago Press.
Blumer, Herbert.
   1966   "Sociological implications of the thought of George Herbert Mead." American Journal of Sociology 71 (March): 535–548.
   1969   Symbolic Interactionism: Perspective and Method. Englewood Cliffs, New Jersey: Prentice-Hall.
Boone, Lalia Phipps.
   1949   "Patterns of innovation in the langauge of the oil fields." American Speech 24 (February):31–37.
Bottomore, T. B. (ed.).
   1963   Karl Marx: Early Writings. New York: McGraw-Hill (1964 ed.).
Boulding, Kenneth E.
   1955   Economic Analysis. New York: Harper.
Bouton, Jim.
   1970   Ball Four. New York: Dell Publishing Co.
Boyle, Robert H.
   1963   Sport—Mirror of American Life. Boston: Little, Brown and Co.
Breed, Warren.
   1955   "Social control in the newsroom: a functional analysis." Social Forces 33 (May):326–335.
Brewer, John.
   1970   "Organizational patterns of supervision: a study of debureaucratization in two business organizations." Pp. 341–347 in Oscar Grusky and George A. Miller (eds.), The Sociology of Organizations: Basic Studies. New York: The Free Press.
   1971   "Flow of communications, expect qualifications, and organiza-

tional authority structures." American Sociological Review 36 (June):475–484.

Brosnan, Jim.
1960 The Long Season. New York: Harper and Brothers.
1962 The Pennant Race. New York: Harper and Brothers.

Brown, Esther Lucille.
1948 Nursing for the Future. New York: Russell Sage Foundation.

Bruhn, Erik.
1968 "Beyond technique." Dance Perspectives 36 (Winter).

Bruyn, Severyn T.
1966 The Human Perspective in Sociology: The Methodology of Participant Observation. Englewood Cliffs, N. J.: Prentice-Hall.

Bryant, Clifton D.
1964 "The petroleum landman: a sociological analysis of an occupation." Unpublished Ph.D. dissertation. Baton Rouge: Louisiana State University.

Bullough, Bonnie.
1971 "The new militancy in nursing." Nursing Forum 3:273–288.

Bullough, Bonnie and Vern L. Bullough (eds.).
1966 Issues in Nursing. New York: Springer.
1971 New Directions for Nurses. New York: Springer.

Bullough, Vern L. and Bonnie Bullough.
1969 The Emergence of Modern Nursing. New York: Macmillan, Second edition.

Burck, Gilbert.
1971 "Famine years for the arms makers." Fortune 83 (May):162–167, 242, 244, 247–8.

Callahan, Raymond E.
1962 Education and the Cult of Efficiency. Chicago: University of Chicago Press.

Cantor, Muriel G.
1971 The Hollywood TV Producer: His Work and His Audience. New York: Basic Books.

Caplow, Theodore.
1954 The Sociology of Work. Minneapolis: University of Minnesota Press.

Caplow, Theodore and Reece J. McGee.
1958 The Academic Marketplace. New York: Basic Books, Inc.

Carlin, Jerome.
1966 Lawyers' Ethics: A Survey of the New York City Bar. New York: Russell Sage Foundation.

Carnegie Commission on Higher Education.
   1970   Higher Education and the Nation's Health Policies for Dental and Medical Education. New York: McGraw-Hill.
Carr-Saunders, Alexander M. and Paul Alexander Wilson.
   1933   The Professions. Oxford: The Claredon Press.
Charnofsky, Harold.
   1968   "The major league professional baseball player: self-conception versus the popular image." International Review of Sport Sociology 3:39–55.
   1969   "The major league professional baseball player." Unpublished Ph.D. dissertation. Los Angeles: University of Southern California.
Charters, Werrett W., Jr.
   1956   "Survival in the teaching profession: criterion for selecting teacher trainees." Journal of Teacher Education, 7 (September):253–255.
   1964   Teacher Perceptions of Administrative Behavior. St. Louis, Mo.: Washington University.
Clark, Burton R.
   1962   Educating the Expert Society. San Francisco: Chandler.
Coffey, Babette.
   1969   "Toni Lander and Bruce Marks on and off stage." Dance Magazine 43 (August):34–39.
Cohen, Percy S.
   1968   Modern Social Theory. New York: Basic Books.
Cole, Jonathan R.
   1971   "American men and women of science," paper presented at the meetings of the American Sociological Association, Denver, Colorado (September 1).
Coles, Robert.
   1966   "A psychiatrist joins 'the movement'." Transaction 3 (January-February):27–29.
Cordtz, Dan.
   1970   "The withering aircraft industry." Fortune 82 (September):114–117, 199–201.
   1971   "Bringing the laboratory down to earth." Fortune 83 (January):106–108, 119–120.
Corwin, Ronald G.
   1963   The Development of an Instrument for Examining Staff Conflicts in the Public Schools, CRP No. 1934. Columbus: Ohio State University.
Costner, Herbert L.

1965 "Criteria for measures of association." American Sociological Review 30 (June):341–353.

Cottrell, William.
1940 The Railroader. Stanford: Stanford University Press.

Crozier, Michel.
1964 The Bureaucratic Phenomenon. Chicago: The University of Chicago Press.

Dahl, Robert.
1957 "The concept of power." Behavioral Science 2 (July):201–215.

Dalton, Melville.
1948 "The industrial ratebuster: a characterization." Applied Anthropology (Winter):5–18.
1959 Men Who Manage. New York: Wiley.
1964 "Preconceptions and methods in Men Who Manage." Pp. 50–95 in Phillip E. Hammond (ed.), Sociologists at Work, New York: Basic Books.

Davis, James A.
1964 Great Aspirations. Chicago: Aldine Publishing Co.

Davis, Kingsley and Wilbert Moore.
1945 "Some principles of stratification." American Sociological Review 10 (April):242–249.

DeMille, Agnes.
1960 To a Young Dancer. Boston: Little, Brown & Co.

Dermerath, Nicholas J. III, Richard W. Stephens and R. Robb Taylor.
1967 Power, Presidents, and Professors. New York: Basic Books, Inc.

Demerath, Nicholas J. III and Phillip E. Hammond.
1969 Religion in Social Context. New York: Random House.

De Tocqueville, Alex (trans. by Henry Reeve and ed. by Francis Bowen).
1862 Democracy in America. Cambridge, Massachusetts: Sever and Frances.

Dewey, John.
1958 Art as Experience. New York: Capricorn Books.

Dexter, Lewis A.
1970 Elite and Specialized Interviewing. Evanston: Northwestern University Press.

Dibble, Vernon.
1962 "Occupations and Ideologies." American Journal of Sociology 68 (September):229–241.

Dineen, Mary A.

1969   "Current trends in collegiate nursing education." Nursing Out-
        look 17 (August):22–26.
Dornbusch, Sanford M.
1955   "The military academy as an assimilating institution." Social
        forces 33 (May):316–321.
Dubin, Robert.
1958   The World of Work. Englewood Cliffs, New Jersey: Prentice-
        Hall, Inc.
Durkheim, Emile.
1964   The Division of Labor in Society (Papered). New York: The
        Free Press of Glencoe.
Edmunds, Anne C.
1971   "Railroad tracks and alphabet soup." College and Research
        Libraries 32 (July):269–270.
Edwards, Alba M.
1943   Comparative Occupational Statistics for the United States
        1870–1940. Washington, D. C.: United States Government
        Printing Office.
Edwards, Harry.
1969   The Revolt of the Black Athlete. New York: The Free Press.
Emerson, Richard M.
1962   "Power-dependence relations." American Sociological Review
        27 (February):31–41.
Engel, Gloria V.
1968   "The effect of bureaucracy on the professional autonomy of
        the physician." Unpublished Ph.D. dissertation. Los Angeles:
        University of California.
1970   "Professional autonomy and bureaucratic organization." Ad-
        ministrative Science Quarterly 15 (March):12–21.
Epstein, Cynthia F.
1968   "Women and professional careers: The case of the woman
        lawyer." Unpublished Ph.D. dissertation. New York: Colum-
        bia University.
1970a   "Encountering the male establishment: Sex limits on women's
        careers in the professions." American Journal of Sociology 75
        (May):965–982.
1970b   Woman's Place: Options and Limits in Professional Careers.
        Berkeley: University of California Press.
1971   "Law partners and marital partners: strains and solutions in
        the dual-career family enterprise." Human Relations 24 (De-
        cember):549–564.
Etzioni, Amitai.

1964   The Moon-Doggle: Domestic and International Implications of the Space Race. New York: Doubleday and Company.

1969   The Semi-Professions and Their Organizations. New York: Free Press.

Evan, William M.

1963   "Peer group interaction and organizational socialization: A study of employee turnover." American Sociological Review 28 (June):436–440.

Fanning, D. M.

1967   "Families in flats." British Medical Journal 4 (November): 382–386.

Faulkner, Robert.

1971   Hollywood Studio Musicians: Their Work and Careers in the Recording Industries. Chicago: Aldine-Atherton.

Federico, Ronald.

1968   "Ballet as an occupation." Unpublished Ph.D. dissertation. Evanston: Northwestern University.

Feld, Sheila.

1963   "Feelings of Adjustment," Pp. 331–352 in W. Lois Wladis Hoffman and F. Ivan Nye (ed.). The Employed Mother in America. Chicago: Rand McNally.

Fern, Fanny.

1870   Ginger-Snaps.

Foote, Nelson N.

1953   "The professionalization of labor in Detroit." The American Journal of Sociology 58 (January):371–380.

Form, William H. and Gregory P. Stone.

1957   "Urbanism, anomymity and status symbolism." American Journal of Sociology 62 (March):504–514.

Form, William.

1968   "Occupations and Careers." Pp. 245–253, in David L. Sills (ed.), International Encyclopedia of the Social Sciences Vol. eleven. New York: Free Press and MacMillan.

Freidson. Eliot.

1960   "Client control and medical practice." American Journal of Sociology 65 (January):374–382.

1961   Patient's view of Medical Practice—A Study of Subscribers to a Prepaid Medical Plan in the Bronx. New York: Russell Sage Foundation.

1970   Professional Dominance: The Social Structure of Medical Care. New York: Atherton Press.

Friedan, Betty.

1963   The Feminine Mystique. New York: Norton.

Friedman, George
1961   The Anatomy of Work. New York: The Free Press.
French, John R. P. and Bertram Raven.
1968   "The bases of social power." Pp. 359–369 in Dorwin Cartwright and Alvin Zander (eds.), Group Dynamics. New York: Harper and Row.
Gans, Herbert J.
1957   "The creator-audience relationship in the mass media." Pp. 315–324 in Bernard Rosenberg and David Manning White (ed.), Mass Culture. New York: Free Press.
Gardner, Burleigh Bradford.
1945   Human Relations in Industry. Chicago: Richards A. Irwin, Inc.
Garfinkel, Harold.
1956   "Conditions of successful degradation ceremonies." American Journal of Sociology 61 (March):412–425.
1967   Studies in Ethnomethodology. Englewood Cliffs, N.J.: Prentice-Hall.
Geer, Blanche.
1968   "Occupational commitment and the teaching profession." Pp. 221–234 in Howard S. Becker, Blanche Geer, David Riesman, and Robert S. Weiss (eds.) Institutions and the Person. Chicago: Aldine.
Geer, Blanche, Jack Haas, Charles ViVona, Stephen J. Miller, Clyde Woods, and Howard S. Becker.
1968   "Learning the ropes: situational learning in four occupational training programs." Pp. 209–230 in Irwin Deutscher and Elizabeth J. Thompson (eds.), Among the People: Encounters with the Poor. New York: Basic Books.
Gilb, Corrine L.
1966   Hidden Hierarchies: The Professions and Government. New York: Harper and Row Publishers.
Gilman, Charlotte P.
1968   "Economic basis of the woman question," Pp. 331–352 in Aileen S. Kraditor (ed.), Up from the Pedestal. Chicago Quadrangle.
Gilman, Glenn.
1962   "An inquiry into the nature and use of authority," Pp. 105–142 in Mason Haire (ed.), Foundations for Research on Human Behavior: Organization Theory in Industrial Practice. New York: John Wiley.
Ginzberg, Eli and Miriam Ostow.
1969   Men, Money and Medicine. New York: Columbia University Press.

Glaser, Barney G.
   1963   "The local-cosmopolitan scientist." American Journal of So-
          ciology 69 (November):249–260.
Glaser, Barney G. and Anselm L. Strauss.
   1964   "Awareness contexts and social interaction." American Socio-
          logical Review 29 (October):669–679.
Glock, Charles Y., Benjamin R. Ringer and Earl R. Babbie.
   1967   To Comfort and To Challenge: A Dilemma of the Contem-
          porary Church. Berkeley: University of California Press.
Glock, Charles Y. and Rodney Stark.
   1968   Patterns of Religious Commitment. Berkeley: University of
          California Press.
Gmelch, George.
   1971   "Baseball magic." Transaction 8 (June): 39–41, 54.
Goffman, Erving.
   1951   "Symbols of class status." British Journal of Sociology 2 (De-
          cember):294–304.
   1956   "The nature of deference and demeanor." American Anthro-
          pologist 58 (June):473–502.
   1959   The Presentation of Self in Everyday Life. New York: An-
          chor Books.
   1961a Asylums. New York: Anchor Books.
   1961b Encounters. Indianapolis, Ind.: Bobbs-Merrill.
   1963   Stigma: Notes on the Management of Spoiled Identity. Engle-
          wood Cliffs, New Jersey: Prentice-Hall, Inc.
   1967   Interaction Ritual. New York: Doubleday and Company.
Goldner, Fred H., and R. R. Ritti.
   1967   "Professionalization as career immobility." American Journal
          of Sociology 72 (March):489–502.
Goode, William J.
   1957   "Community within a community: the professions." American
          Sociological Review 22 (April):194–200.
   1960a "A theory of role strain." American Sociological Review 25
          (August):483–496.
   1960b "Encroachment, charlatanism and the emerging professions:
          psychology, sociology and medicine." American Sociological
          Review 25 (December):902–914.
   1962   "The librarian: from occupation to profession?" Pp. 8–22 in
          Philip H. Ennis and Howard W. Winger (eds.) Seven Ques-
          tions about the Profession of Librarianship. Chicago: Univer-
          sity of Chicago Press.
   1969   "The theoretical limits of professionalization," Pp. 226–314

in Amitai Etzioni (ed.), The Semi-Professions and Their Organization. New York: The Free Press.

Gordon, C. Wayne.
1955   "The role of the teacher in the social structure of the high school." Unpublished paper. Los Angeles: University of California.

Gouldner, Alvin W.
1957–58   "Cosmopolitans and locals; toward an analysis of latent social roles." Administrative Science Quarterly 2 (December): 281–306, and 2 (March):444–480.
1959   "Reciprocity and autonomy in functional theory." Pp. 254–260 in Llewllyn Gross (ed.), Symposium on Sociological Theory. New York: Harper and Row.

Gouldner, Alvin W. and Helen P. Gouldner.
1963   Modern Sociology: An Introduction to the study of Human Interaction. New York: Harcourt, Brace and World, Inc.

Greenwood, Ernest.
1957   "Attributes of a profession." Social Work 2 (July):45–55.

Griffen, Verna E.
1958   Employment Possibilities for Women in Legal Work. United States Department of Labor. Washington, D. C.: United States Government Printing Office.

Gronseth, Erik.
1970   "The dysfunctionality of the husband provider role in industrialized societies." Presented to the Seventh World Congress of Sociology, Varna, Bulgaria.

Gross, Edward.
1958   Work and Society. New York: Thomas Y. Crowell Co.
1964   "Industrial relations," Pp. 619–679 in Robert E. L. Faris (ed.) Handbook of Modern Sociology. Chicago: Rand McNally and Company.
1968   "Universities as organizations: a research approach." American Sociological Review 33 (August):518–544.

Grusky, Oscar and George A. Miller.
1970   The Sociology of Organization: Basic Studies. New York: The Free Press.

Gurevitch, Michael and Philip Elliot.
1972   "New communications technologies and their consequences for the future of media professions" paper presented at the International Symposium on communication at Annenberg School of Communication: University of Pennsylvania: March 23–25.

Gustafson, James M.
1965 "The clergy in the United States," Pp. 70–90 in Kenneth S. Lynn (ed.), The Professions in America. Boston: Houghton Mifflin Co.

Gwinup, Thomas.
1971 "The reference course: theory, method and motivation." Journal of Education for Librarianship 2 (Winter):231–242.

Hadden, Jeffrey K.
1969 The Gathering Storm in the Churches. Garden City, New York: Doubleday.

Hagstrom, Warren O.
1965 The Scientific Community. New York: Basic Books.

Hall, Oswald.
1946 "The informal organization of the medical profession." Canadian Journal of Economics and Political Science 22 (February):30–44.
1948 "Stages of a medical career." American Journal of Sociology 53 (September):326–336.

Hall, Richard H.
1962 "Intra-organizational structural variation: application of the bureaucratic model." Administrative Science Quarterly 7 (December):295–308.
1967 "Some organizational considerations in the professional organizational relationship." Administrative Science Quarterly 12 (December):461–478.
1968 "Professionalization and bureaucratization." American Sociological Review 33 (February):92–104.
1969 Occupations and the Social Structure. Englewood Cliffs, New Jersey: Prentice-Hall.
1972 Organizations. Englewood Cliffs, New Jersey: Prentice-Hall.

Hammond, Phillip E.
1966 The Campus Clergyman. New York: Basic Books, Inc.

Harmon, L. R.
1965 "High school ability patterns: a backward look from the doctorate." Scientific Manpower Report #66 Washington, D. C.: National Research Council.

Haug, Marie and Marvin B. Sussman.
1969 "Professional autonomy and the revolt of the client." Social Problems 17 (Fall):153–160.

Hawkins, A.
1952 "I am qualified as a lease broker." Mississippi Oil Review (July 29):3.

Hawley, Mary B.
    1970   "Reference statistics." Reference Quarterly 10 (Winter):143–147.
Henslin, James H.
    1967   "The cab driver: an interactional analysis of an occupational culture." Unpublished Ph.D. dissertation, St. Louis, Mo.: Washington University.
    1971   "Sex and cabbies." Pp. 193–223 in James M. Henslin (ed.) Studies in the Sociology of Sex, New York: Appleton-Century-Crofts.
    1972a   "Studying deviance in four settings: research experiences with cabbies, suicides, drug users, and abortionees." Pp. 35–70 in Jack D. Douglas (ed.), Research on Deviance. New York: Random House, Inc.
    1972b   "What makes for trust?" Pp. 20–32 in James M. Henslin (ed.), Down to Earth Sociology: Introductory Readings. New York: The Free Press.
Hieber, Caroline E.
    1966   "An analysis of questions and answers in libraries." Unpublished M.S. Thesis. Bethlehem, Pennsylvania: Lehigh University.
Hildegarde, Nelson.
    1959   The Great Oildorado. New York: Random House.
Holter, Harriet.
    1970   Sex Roles and Social Structure. Oslo: Universitetsforlaget.
Homans, George C.
    1961   Social Behavior: Its Elementary Forms. New York: Harcourt, Brace and World.
Hopkins, Charles H.
    1940   The Rise of the Social Gospel in America Protestantism. New Haven: Yale University Press.
Hughes, Everett C.
    1958   Men and Their Work. Glencoe, Illinois: Free Press.
    1959a   "Stress and strain in professional education." Harvard Educational Review 29 (Fall):319–329.
    1959b   "The study of occupations." Pp. 442–458 in Robert K. Merton, Leonard Broom, and L. J. Cottrell Jr. (eds.), Sociology Today: Problems and Prospects. New York: Harper and Row.
    1962   "Education for a profession." Pp. 38–115 in Philip H. Ennis and Howard W. Winger (eds.), Seven Questions about the Profession of Librarianship. Chicago: University of Chicago Press.

1963 "Careers." Paper read at the center for research in careers, Harvard Graduate School of Education, Cambridge, Mass.

1970 "Institutions." Pp. 123–185 in A. M. Lee (ed.), Principles of Sociology. New York: Barnes and Noble.

1971 The Sociological Eye. Chicago: Aldine-Atherton.

Hurtwood, Lady Allen of.

1968 Planning for Play. Cambridge, Massachusetts: MIT Press.

Husén, Torsten.

1967 International Study of Achievement in Mathematics; Volume II. New York: John Wiley.

Hutchins, Margaret.

1944 Introduction to Reference Work. Chicago: American Library Association.

Ichheiser, Gustav.

1970 Appearances and Realities. San Francisco: Jossey-Bass, Inc.

Israel, Joachim.

1971 Alienation: From Marx to Modern Sociology. Boston: Allyn and Bacon, Inc.

Jaco, E. Gartley (ed.).

1958 Patients, Physicians, and Illness. New York: Free Press, Macmillan.

Jaffe, Abram J. and Charles D. Stewart.

1951 Manpower Resources and Utilization, Principles of Working Force Analysis. New York: John Wiley and Sons, Inc.

Jaques, Elliot.

1956 Measurement of Responsibility. London: Tavistock.

Jeffries, Vincent and H. Edward Ransford.

1969 "Interracial social contact and middle-class white reactions to the Watts riot." Social Problems 16 (Winter):312–324.

Joel, Lydia.

1963 "Dance is an adolescent passion." Dance Magazine 37 (October):26–27.

Johnson, Benton.

1966 "Theology and party preference among Protestant clergymen." American Sociological Review 31 (April):200–208.

1967 "Theology and the position of pastors on public issues." American Sociological Review 32 (June):433–442.

Kaplan, Norman.

1965 "Professional scientists in industry: an essay review." Social Problems 13 (Summer):88–97.

Katz, Fred E.

1958 "Occupational contact networks." Social Forces 37 (October): 52–55.

Kelley, Frank H.
1957 "It pays to be a fair trader, says Magnolia's star landman Frank Kelley." The Landman 2 (November):12.

Key, V. O., Jr.
1958 Politics, Parties, and Pressure Groups. Fourth edition. New York: Crowell.

Khleif, Bud B.
1971 "Modes of professionalization." Unpublished paper.

Kohn, Melvin L.
1969 Class and Conformity: A Study in Values. Homewood, Ill.: The Dorsey Press.

Kolenda, Pauline and Sandra Forsyth Enos.
1970 "Conflict, cooperation and group cohesion in the ballet company," Pp. 221–255 in Milton C. Albrecht, James H. Barnett & Mason Griff. The Sociology of Art and Literature. New York: Praeger.

Kornhauser, William (in collaboration with Warren O. Hagstrom).
1962 Scientists in Industry: Conflict and Accommodation. Berkeley and Los Angeles: University of California Press.

Kozol, Jonathan.
1968 Death at an Early Age. New York: Bantam Books.

Krause, Elliot.
1971 The Sociology of Occupations. Boston: Little Brown and Company.

Kreitlow, Burton W.
1962 Long-Term Study of Educational Effectiveness of Newly Formed Centralized School Districts in Rural Areas. Madison: University of Wisconsin.

Kucera, Daniel J.
1963 "Women unwanted." Harvard Law Record 37 (December 12):1ff.

Labovitz, Sanford.
1967 "Some observations on measurements and statistics." Social Forces 56 (December):151–160.
1970 "The assignment of numbers to rank order categories." American Sociological Review 35 (June):515–524.

La Porte, Todd.
1965 "Conditions of strain and accommodation in industrial research organizations." Administrative Science Quarterly 10 (June):21–38.

Lazarsfeld, Paul F. and Wagner Thielens, Jr.
1958 The Academic Mind. Glencoe, Illinois: The Free Press.

Lebold, William L., Robert Perrucci and Warren Howland.

1966 "The engineer in industry and government." Journal of Engineering Education 56 (March):237–273.

Lengermann, Joseph J.
1969 "The professional autonomy of professionals in bureaucratic organizations: a study of certified public accountants." Unpublished Ph.D. dissertation. Ithaca, New York: Cornell University.
1971 "Supposed and actual differences in professional autonomy among CPAs as related to type of work organization and size of firm." The Accounting Review 46 (October):665–675.

Lenski, Gerhard.
1961 The Religious Factor. New York: Anchor Books.

Lieberman, Myron.
1956 Education as a Profession. Englewood Cliffs, New Jersey: Prentice-Hall.

Linton, Ralph.
1936 The Study of Man. New York: Appleton-Century-Croft.

Lipset, Seymour M.
1963 Political Man: The Social Bases of Politics. New York: Anchor Books.

Lipset, Seymour M., Martin A. Trow and James S. Coleman.
1956 Union Democracy. Garden City, New York: Doubleday.

Lockmiller, David A.
1969 Scholars on Parade. New York: Macmillan Company.

Lombard, George F.
1955 Behavior in a Selling Group. Boston: Harvard University, Graduate School of Business Administration.

Loomba, R. P.
1967 A Study of the Re-Employment and Unemployment Experience of Scientists and Engineers Laid Off from 62 Aerospace and Electronics Firms in the San Francisco Bay Area during 1963–65. San Jose, California: Center for Interdisciplinary Studies, San Jose State College.

Lopata, Helena.
1971 Occupation Housework. New York, Oxford University Press.

Lortie, Dan C.
1969 "The balance of control over autonomy in elementary school teaching." Pp. 1–53 in Amitai Etzioni (ed.), The Semi-Professions and Their Organizations, New York: Free Press.

Lynd, Robert S. and Helen M. Lynd.
1929 Middletown, A Study in Contemporary American Culture. New York: Harcourt, Brace.

Lynn, Kenneth S.
   1965   The Professions in America. Boston: Houghton Mifflin.
Malinowski, Bronislaw.
   1950   Argonauts of the Western Pacific. New York: E. P. Dutton
          and Company, Inc.
Mann, Michael.
   1970   "The social cohesion of liberal democracy." American Socio-
          logical Review 35 (June):423–439.
Mara, Thalia.
   1959   So You Want To Be A Ballet Dancer. New York: Pitman.
March, James G. and Herbert H. Simon.
   1963   Organizations. New York: John Wiley.
Marcson, Simon.
   1960   The Scientist in American Industry. New York: Harper.
Marx, Gary T.
   1967   Protest and Prejudice: A Study of Belief in the Black Com-
          munity. New York: Harper and Row.
Mason, Ward S., Robert J. Dressel, and Robert K. Bain.
   1959   "Sex role and the career orientation of beginning teachers."
          Harvard Educational Review 29 (Fall):370–383.
Masserman, Jules H., Arthur O. Hecker, Joseph Pessing, and Bert E.
Booth.
   1949   "Philosophy and methodology in the training of 500 psychi-
          atric residents." American Journal of Psychiatry 106 (Novem-
          ber):362–369.
McColvin, Lionel R., and Eric R. McColvin.
   1947   Library Stock and Assistance to Readers: a Text Book. Lon-
          don: Grafton.
McHugh, Peter.
   1966   "Structured uncertainty and its resolution: the case of the
          professional actor." Unpublished paper.
McKinley, Donald.
   1964   Social Class & Family Life. New York: The Free Press.
Mead, George H.
   1934   Mind, Self and Society. Chicago: University of Chicago Press.
Mechanic, David.
   1962a "Sources of power of lower participants in complex organiza-
          tions." Administrative Science Quarterly 7 (December):349–
          364.
   1962b Students Under Stress. New York: Free Press.
Mennerick, Lewis A.
   1971a "The county jail school: problems in the teacher-student rela-

tionship." The Kansas Journal of Sociology 1 (Spring):17–35.

1971b "The impact of external environment on a county jail school." Unpublished Ph.D. dissertation, Evanston, Illinois. Northwestern University.

1972 "External control of recruits: the county jail school." American Behavioral Scientist 16 (September/October): 75–84.

undated "The county jail school: custody-security or a constraint." Unpublished paper.

Merton, Robert K.

1957a "The role set: problems in sociological theory." British Journal of Sociology 8 (June):106–120.

1957b Social Theory and Social Structure. Glencoe: The Free Press.

Merton, Robert K. and Elinor Barber.

1963 "Social ambivalence." Pp. 91–120 in Edward Tiryakian (ed.). Theory, Values and Sociocultural Change. New York: The Free Press.

Miller, George A.

1967 "Professional in bureaucracy: alienation among industrial scientists and engineers." American Sociological Review 32 (October):755–768.

1971 "Some aspects of satisfactory and unsatisfactory work conditions among aerospace scientists and engineers." Unpublished manuscript.

Miller, George A. and L. Wesley Wager.

1971 "Adult socialization, organizational structure, and role orientations." Administrative Science Quarterly 16 (June):151–163.

Miller, Jeffrey.

1972 Cabbies fight Van Aresdale-Employer axis." New Politics (January):55–60.

Miller, Stephan J.

1964 "The social base of sales behavior." Social Problems 12 (Summer):15–24.

Mills, C. Wright.

1940 "Situated action and vocabularies of motive." American Sociological Review 5 (December):904–913.

1943 "The professional ideology of social pathologists." American Journal of Sociology 49 (September):165–180.

1951 White Collar. New York: Oxford University Press.

Montagna, Paul D.

1968 "Professionalization and bureaucratization in large professional organizations." American Journal of Sociology 74 (July):138–145.

Mooney, Joseph D.
   1969   "An analysis of unemployment among professional engineers and scientists." Industrial and Labor Relations Review 19 (July):517–528.
Moore, David G. and Richard Renck.
   1955   "The professional employee in industry." Journal of Business 28 (June):58–66.
Moore, Wilbert E. (in collaboration with Gerald W. Rosenbloom).
   1970   The Profession: Roles and Rules. New York: Russell Sage Foundation.
Morris, Richard T. and Raymond J. Murphy.
   1959   "The situs dimension in occupational structure." American Sociological Review 24 (April):231–239.
Myrdal, Gunnar (with the assistance of Richard Sterner and Arnold Rose).
   1944   An American Dilemma. New York: Harper.
Naegele, Kaspar D. and Elaine C. Stolar.
   1960   "The librarian of the northwest." Pp. 51–137 in Morton Knoll (ed.) Libraries and Librarians of the Pacific Northwest. Seattle: University of Washington Press.
National Center for Health Services Research and Development.
   1970   "Health manpower: an R. and D. approach." Focus 5 (Summer):7–9.
National League of Nursing.
   1970   "Educational preparation for nursing—1969." Nursing Outlook 18 (September): 52–57.
Niebuhr, Helmut R. and Daniel D. Williams.
   1956   The Ministry in Historical Perspective. New York: Harper and Row.
Nijinsky, Romola.
   1934   Nijinsky. New York: Grosset and Dunlop.
Nureyev, Rudolf.
   1963   Nureyev. New York: Dutton.
O'Connor, Harvey.
   1955   The Empire of Oil. New York: Monthly Review Press.
Ogilvie, Bruce C. and Thomas A. Tutko.
   1971   "Sport: if you want to build character, try something else." Psychology Today 5 (October):60–63.
Olson, Mancur, Jr.
   1968   "Economics, sociology, and the best of all possible worlds." The Public Interest 12 (Summer):96–118.
O'Neil, W. A.

1968 "Paul Robert's Rules of Order: the misuse of linguistics in the classroom." Urban Review 2 (June).

Orth, Charles D.
1965 "The optimum climate for industrial research." Pp. 194–210 in Norman Kaplan (ed.), Science and Society. Chicago: Rand McNally.

Park, Robert E. and Ernest W. Burgess (eds.)
1969 Introduction to the Science of Sociology. Chicago: University of Chicago Press, Third Edition.

Parker, Ralph H.
1962 "Points of entry to librarianship," Pp. 46–57 in Philip H. Ennis and Howard W. Winger (eds.), Seven Questions about the Profession of Librarianship. Chicago: University of Chicago Press.

Parsons, Talcott.
1939 "The professions and social structure." Social Forces 17 (May):457–467.
1959 "The social structure of the family." Pp. 241–274 in Ruth Ashen (ed.), The Family: Its Function and Destiny. New York: Harper.
1968 "Professions." Pp. 536–547 in David L. Sills (ed.), International Encyclopedia of the Social Sciences. Vol. 12. New York: Free Press and MacMillan.

Pavalko, Ronald M.
1971 Sociology of Occupations and Professions. Itasca, Illinois: Peacock Publishers, Inc.

Perkins, James A.
1966 The University in Transition. Princeton: Princeton University Press.

Perrucci, Robert and Joel E. Gerstl (ed.)
1969 The Engineers and the Social System. New York: John Wiley and Sons, Inc.

Peters, Anne K.
1971 "Acting and aspiring actresses in Hollywood: a sociological analysis." Unpublished Ph.D. dissertation. Los Angeles: University of California.

Pitts, Jesse R.
1972 "Strike at Oakland University." Change Magazine (February):16–19.

Pond, Frederick R.
1932 "Language of the California oil fields." American Speech 7 (April):261–272.

Quinley, Harold E.
1970 "The Protestant clergy and the war in Vietnam." Public Opinion Quarterly 34 (Spring):43–52.

Ricarde, A. L.
1965 "Law school: much work and little play." Harvard Crimson (October 14).

Riegel, John W.
1958 Intangible Rewards for Engineers and Scientists. Ann Arbor: University of Michigan Press.

Riesman, David.
1950 The Lonely Crowd. New Haven: Yale University Press.
1955 "Thoughts on teachers and schools." Anchor Review 1. New York: Doubleday.
1964 "Introduction to 'Academic Women'," in Academic Women by Jessie Bernard. University Park: Pennsylvania State University.

Ritti, Richard.
1968 "Work goals of scientists and engineers." Industrial Relations 7 (February):118–131.

Ritzer, George.
1970 "Professionalism: An ignored dimension." Unpublished paper presented at the American Sociological Association annual meeting. Washington, D. C.

Roach, Jack L., Llewelyn Gross and Orville R. Gursslin.
1969 Social Stratification in the United States. Englewood Cliffs, New Jersey: Prentice-Hall, Inc.

Roberts, Mary M.
1961 American Nursing: History and Interpretation. New York: MacMillan.

Roethlisberger, F. J. and W. J. Dickson.
1939 Management and the Worker. Cambridge: Harvard University Press.

Robinson, John R., Robert Athanasiou, and Kendra B. Head.
1969 Measures of Occupational Attitudes and Occupational Characteristics. Survey Research Center. Ann Arbor: Institute for Social Research.

Rose, Arnold.
1945 "A research note on experimentation in interviewing." American Journal of Sociology 51 (September):143–144.

Rose, Sanford.
1970 "Marking the turn to a peacetime economy." Fortune 82 (September):110–113.

Rossi, Peter H.
  1962   "Discussion." Pp. 82–83 in Philip H. Ennis and Howard W. Winger (eds.), Seven Questions about the Profession of Librarianship. Chicago: University of Chicago Press.
Ryser, Carol P.
  1964   "The student dancer." Pp. 95–121 in Robert N. Wilson (ed.), The Arts in Society. Englewood Cliffs, New Jersey: Prentice-Hall.
Saint Benedict.
  1948   St. Benedict's rule for Monasteries. Translated by L. J. Doyle. Collegeville, Minnesota: Liturgical Press.
Saltz, Arthur.
  1944   "Occupation: theory and history." Pp. 424–435 in Edwin R. A. Seligman (ed.), Encyclopedia of the Social Sciences, Vol. eleven. New York: The MacMillan Co., Publishers.
Samuels, Joanna J.
  1966   "Bureaucratization of school districts and teacher autonomy." Unpublished Ph.D. dissertation. Los Angeles: University of California.
Sayles, Leonard R.
  1958   Behavior of Industrial Work Groups. New York: Wiley.
Scheff, Thomas J.
  1968   "Negotiating reality: notes on power in the assessment of responsibility." Social Problems 16 (Summer):3–17.
Schein, Edgar H. and J. Steven Ott.
  1962   "The legitimacy of organizational influence." American Journal of Sociology 67 (May):682–689.
Schulder, Diane B.
  1970   "Does the law oppress women?" Pp. 139–157 in Robin Morgan (ed.), Sisterhood is Powerful. New York: Random House.
Schutz, Alfred.
  1962   Collected Papers I: The Problem of Social Reality. The Hague: Martinus Nijhoff.
  1964   Collected Papers II: Studies in Social Theory. The Hague: Martinus Nijhoff.
  1966   Collected Papers III: Studies in Phenomenological Philosophy. The Hague: Martinus Nijhoff.
  1967   The Phenomenology of the Social World. Evanston, Illinois: The Northwestern University Press.
Scott, W. Richard.
  1964   "Theory of organizations," pp. 485–529 in Robert E. L. Faris (ed.), Handbook of Modern Sociology. Chicago: Rand McNally and Company.

Scott, W. Richard.
  1965 "Reactions to supervision in a heteronomous professional or-
        ganization." Administrative Science Quarterly 10 (June):
        65–81.
Scoutten, E. F.
  1962 "Application at the Maytag Company." Pp. 76–87 in Mason
        Haire (ed.), Organization Theory in Industrial Practice. New
        York: John Wiley.
Seeman, Melvin.
  1959 "On the meaning of alienation." American Sociological Re-
        view 24 (December):783–791.
Seeman, Melvin and John W. Evans.
  1962a "Alienation on learning in a hospital setting." American Soci-
        ological Review 27 (December):772–782.
  1962b "Apprenticeship and attitude change." American Journal of
        Sociology 67 (January):365–378.
Seidman, Joel.
  1969 "Engineering unionism." Pp. 219–245 in Robert Perrucci and
        Joel E. Gerstl (eds.), The Engineers and the Social System.
        New York: John Wiley and Sons, Inc.
Selby, H. A. and C. M. Woods.
  1966 "Foreign students at a high pressure university." Sociology of
        Education 39 (Spring):138–154.
Sexten, Patricia C.
  1967 The American School: A Sociological Analysis. Englewood
        Cliffs, New Jersey: Prentice-Hall.
Shapiro, Sam, Edward R. Schlesinger and Robert E. L. Nesbitt, Jr.
  1968 Infant, Prenatal, Maternal and Childhood Mortality in the
        United States. Cambridge, Massachusetts: Harvard Univer-
        sity Press.
Sharaf, Myron R. and Daniel L. Levinson.
  1964 "The quest for omnipotence in professional training: the case
        of the psychiatric resident." Psychiatry 27 (May):135–149.
Sharp, Lawrence J., and F. Ivan Nye.
  1963 "Maternal Mental Health." Pp. 309–319 in W. Lois Wladis
        Hoffman and F. Ivan Nye, The Employed Mother in America.
        Chicago: Rand McNally.
Shepherd, Clovis R.
  1961 "Orientations of scientists and engineers." Pacific Sociological
        Review 4 (Fall):79–83.
Sheppard, Harold and Neal Q. Herrick.
  1972 Where Have All the Robots Gone? Worker Dissatisfaction In
        The Seventies. New York: The Free Press.

Shosid, Norma J.
1966 "Freud, frug and feedback." Special Libraries 57 (October): 561–563.
1970 "No visible effect? Librarianship as a profession in process." Unpublished paper.
Simmel, George.
1950 The Sociology of George Simmel, trans. and edited by Kurt Wolf. Glencoe, Ill.: The Free Press.
1969 "Sociology of the senses: visual interaction." Pp. 356–361 in Park and Burgess (ed.), Introduction to the Science of Sociology, Chicago: University of Chicago Press, Third Edition.
Simon, Herbert A.
1944 "Decision-making and administrative organization." Public Administration Review 4 (Winter):16–30.
1965 Administrative Behavior. New York: The Free Press.
Simpson, Richard L. and Ida H. Simpson.
1969 "Woman and bureaucracy in the service professions." Pp. 196–265 in Amitai Etzioni (ed.), The Semi-Professions and Their Organization. New York: The Free Press.
Sinclair, Dorothy.
1971 "To merge or not to merge." Reference Quarterly 10 (Spring): 197–200.
Sister Mary Francis.
1956 A Right to be Merry. New York: Sheed and Ward.
Sizer, Theodore R.
1965 "Reform movement or panacea." Saturday Review (June 19): 52–54.
Slater, Philip E.
1970 "What hath Spock wrought?—freed children, chained moms." Washington Post (March 1).
Slocum, Walter L.
1966 Occupational Careers: A Sociological Perspective. Chicago: Aldine Publishing Company.
Smigel, Erwin O., Joseph Monane, Robert B. Wood and Barbara R. Nye.
1963 "Occupational sociology: a reexamination." Sociology and Social Research 47 (July):472–477.
Solomon, David N.
1968 "Sociological perspectives on occupations." Pp. 3–13 in Howard S. Becker, Blanche Geer, David Riesman and Robert S. Weiss (ed.), Institutions and the Person. Chicago: Aldine.

Soo, Chong.
  1969 "The monetary value of a housewife." American Journal of Economics and Sociology 28 (July):271–284.
Sorenson, James E.
  1967 "Professional and bureaucratic organization in the public accounting firm." The Accounting Review 42 (October):553–565.
Stannard, D. L.
  1971 "White cabdrivers and black fares." Transaction 8 (Nov.–Dec.):44–46, 68.
Stebbins, Robert.
  1969 "Role distance, role distance behavior and jazz musicians." British Journal of Sociology 20 (December):406–415.
Stewart, Phyllis L.
  1968 "Organizational change in an advanced research and development laboratory: a study of attrition." Unpublished doctoral dissertation. Los Angeles: University of California.
Sussman, Marvin B.
  1965 Sociology and Rehabilitation. Washington, D. C.: American Sociological Association.
Tait, Samuel W., Jr.
  1946 The Wildcatters. Princeton: Princeton University Press.
Taxi Union News
  1967 January, March, April.
Taylor, Lee.
  1968 Occupational Sociology. New York: Oxford University Press.
Terman, Lewis M. and Catherine C. Miles.
  1936 Sex and Personality: Studies in Masculinity and Femininity. New York: McGraw Hill.
Terrien, Francis W. and Donald C. Mills.
  1955 "The effect of changing size upon the internal structure of organizations." American Sociological Review 20 (February):11–13.
Thomas, William I.
  1931 The Unadjusted Girl. Boston: Little, Brown & Co.
Thomas, W. I. and Florian Znaniecki.
  1918–1920 The Polish Peasant in Europe and America. Chicago: University of Chicago Press.
Thompson, James D.
  1967 Organizations in Action. New York: McGraw Hill.
Titmuss, Richard M.

1971   The Gift Relationship: from Human Blood to Social Policy. New York: Pantheon.

Toeffler, Alvin
1970   Future Shock. New York: Bantam.

Towle, Charlotte.
1964   The Learner in Education for the Professions. Chicago: University of Chicago Press.

Tumin, Melvin.
1953   "Some principles of stratification: a critical analysis." American Sociological Review 18 (August):387–394.

Turner, Ralph H.
1962   "Role taking: process versus conformity." Pp. 22–40 in Arnold Rose (ed.), Human Behavior and Social Processes. Boston: Houghton Mifflin.
1964   "Some aspects of women's ambitions." American Journal of Sociology 70 (November):271–285.
1968   "Role sociological aspects." Pp. 552–557 in David L. Sills (ed.), International Encyclopedia of the Social Sciences. Vol. 13. New York: MacMillan.

Tygart, Clarence E.
1969   "A study of clergymen: work, ideas, and politics." Unpublished Ph.D. dissertation. Los Angeles: University of California.
1970   "Theology and political preferences among pastors: a replication." Paper presented at Pacific Sociological Association. Los Angeles, California.

Ullyot, J. R.
1965   B-school: pragmatism and professionalism." Harvard Crimson (October 19).

United Nations: Statistical Office.
1969   Statistical Yearbook. New York: United Nations Publishing Service.

United States Arms Control and Disarmament Agency.
1965   A Case Study of the Effects of the Dyna-Soar Contract Cancellation Upon Employees of the Boeing Company in Seattle, Washington. Washington, D. C.: Government Printing Office.

United States Bureau of the Census, Statistical Abstract of the United States.
1960   Washington, D. C.: Government Printing Office.
1970   Washington, D. C.: Government Printing Office.

United States Department of Health, Education and Welfare.

1967 Human Investment Programs: Delivery of Health Services for the Poor. Washington, D. C.: Government Printing Office.

United States Department of Labor: Bureau of Employment and Security.

1965 Dictionary of Occupational Titles. Washington, D. C.: Government Printing Office.

1966 Occupations in the Field of Library Science. Washington, D. C.: Government Printing Office.

United States Department of Labor: Bureau of Labor Statistics.

1947 The Economic Status of Registered Professional Nurses, 1946–47. Bulletin Number 931. Washington, D. C.: Government Printing Office.

1970a Ph.D. Scientists and Engineers in Private Industry 1968–80. Washington, D. C.: Government Printing Office.

1970b Scientific and Technical Personnel in Industry, 1967. Washington, D. C.: Government Printing Office.

United States Department of Labor: Women's Bureau.

1969 1969 Handbook on Women Workers. Washington, D. C.: Government Printing Office.

United States Public Health Service: National Center for Health Statistics.

1970a Health Resources Statistics, 1969: Health Manpower and Facilities. Washington, D. C.: Government Printing Office.

1970b Selected Symptoms of Psychological Distress. (August 4) Washington, D. C.: Government Printing Office.

Vaihinger, Hans.

1912 Fir Philodophie der Als Ob (The Philosophy of the As If). Tübingen: Tübingen University.

Veblen, Thorstein.

1953 The Theory of the Leisure Class: An Economic Study of Institutions. New York: New American Library. (First Published in 1899.)

Vidich, Arthur J., Joseph Bensman and Maurice R. Stein.

1964 Reflections on Community Studies. New York: Wiley.

Vollmer, Howard M.

1967 "Organizational design: an exploratory study." R & D Studies Series. Menlo Park, California: Stanford Research Institute.

1969 "Toward a sociology of applied science." The American Sociologist 4 (August):244–248.

Vollmer, Howard M. and Donald L. Mills (eds.)

1966 Professionalization. Englewood Cliffs, N. J.: Prentice-Hall.

Vollmer, Howard M., Todd La Porte, William Pedersen, and Phyllis
L. Stewart.
1964 "Adaptations of scientists in five organizations." Systems Analysis Program. Vol. II (May). Menlo Park, California: Stanford Research Institute.

Waller, Willard.
1961 The Sociology of Teaching. New York: Russell and Russell.

Walter, Edwin.
1965 "Med school: hard grind for future Harvard M.D.'s." Harvard Crimson (October 15).

Wax, Murray L., Rosalie H. Wax, and Robert V. Dumont, Jr.
1964 Formal Education In An American Indian Community. Monograph No. 1. Society for the Study of Social Problems, Supplement to Social Problems II (Spring).

Wayland, S. R.
1962 "The teacher as decision-maker." Pp. 46–51 in A. Harry Passow
(ed.), Curriculum Crossroads. New York: Bureau of Publications, Teachers College, Columbia University.
1964 "Structural features of American education as basic factors in
innovation." Pp. 587–613 in Matthew B. Miles (ed.), Innovation in Education. New York: Bureau of Publications,
Teachers College, Columbia University.

Weber, Max.
1924 "Schwankungen der industriellen arbeitsleistung." Pp. 61–
225 in Paul Siebeck (ed.), Gesammelte Aufsatze Zur Sociologie and Sozialpolitik. Tübingen: Verlag von J. C. B.
1946 From Max Weber: Essays in Sociology. (Hans H. Gerth and
C. Wright Mills, eds.), New York: Oxford University Press.
1947 The Theory of Social and Economic Organization. New York:
Oxford University Press.
1949 The Methodology of the Social Sciences. (Edward Shils and
Henry A. Finch, eds.), New York: The Free Press of Glencoe.
1964 The Theory of Social and Economic Organization. Paperback
edition. (Translated by A. M. Henderson and Talcott Parsons.), New York: The Free Press.
1967 On Law and Economy and Society. New York: Simon and
Schuster.

Weinberg, S. Kirson and Henry Arond.
1952 "The occupational culture of the boxer." American Journal
of Sociology 58 (March):460–469.

Weyer, James I.

1930   Reference Work: A Textbook for Students of Library Work and Librarians. Chicago: American Library Association.

Who's Who of American Women.
1958–59   Chicago: A. N. Marquis Company.

Whyte, William Foote.
1948   Human Relations in the Restaurant Industry. New York: McGraw-Hill.
1955   Street Corner Society: The Social Structure of an Italian Slum. Enlarged Edition. Chicago: University of Chicago Press.

Wilensky, Harold L.
1956   Intellectuals in Labor Unions. Glencoe, Ill.: Illinois Press.
1964   "The professionalization of everyone?" American Journal of Sociology 70 (September):137–158.

Wilkins, Charlie S.
1959   "But he doesn't forget." The Landman 4 (September):13.

Williamson, Harold F. and Arnold R. Daum.
1959   The American Petroleum Industry. Evanston: Northwestern University Press.

Wilson, Logan.
1964   The Academic Man. New York: Octagon Books, Inc.

Wilson, Robert N.
1958   Man Made Plain. Cleveland: Howard Allen.

Wittrock, M. C.
1965   "Changing the contingencies operating on the teacher." Presented to the convention of the American Research Association.

Woodring, Paul.
1965   "Breaking up the big systems." Saturday Review (July 17): 51–52.

Woody, Regina.
1952   Young Dancer's Career Book. New York: Dutton.

Youskevitch, Igor.
1969   "The Male Image." Dancer Perspectives 40 (Winter).

Zadrozny, John.
1959   Dictionary of Social Science. Washington, D. C.: Public Affairs Press.

Zald, Mayer.
1971   Occupations and Organizations in American Society. The Organization Dominated Man. Chicago: Markham Publishing Company.

Index of Authors

Index of Subjects